ON THE FINAL DRAMA

Nothing about this production is ordinary. This is a miracle play full of surprises. Jesus is the playwright. He gave John the vision and told him to write it down. The script is preserved for us in the last book of the Bible.

As the playwright, the Lord decides on the time. He viewed events from the one single vantage point and looked forward and backward from that day. He used two stages, heavenly and earthly, and cast both himself and John as actors. He called in angels as supporting cast.

We look through John's eyes to see what he saw. At times, he is caught up to Heaven and we hear his voice speaking from there. In other places, he speaks from Earth.

Through John's, miraculous experiences, we are given a view of Heaven never seen before. We not only find out what it looks like but exactly where it is located . . .

We are privileged to be told what lies ahead of us just before it begins to take place in reality. There are very few times when we can be sure of what events are on the track ahead. This is one of those rare times . . .

From *Revelations 2000*

Other Avon Books by
M. J. Agee

THE END OF THE AGE
HEAVEN FOUND

REVELATIONS 2000

2000

M. J. AGEE

AVON BOOKS ◆ NEW YORK

**Dedicated to
my wonderful husband Ed, without
whose support this book would not
have gotten finished before the
Rapture, and to our children,
Carol and Dave**

AVON BOOKS
A division of
The Hearst Corporation
1350 Avenue of the Americas
New York, New York 10019

Copyright © 1997 by Marilyn J. Agee
Published by arrangement with Archer Press
Visit our website at http://www.AvonBooks.com
Library of Congress Catalog Card Number: 96-37032
ISBN: 0-380-73085-5

First Avon Books Printing: January 1998

AVON TRADEMARK REG. U.S. PAT. OFF. AND IN OTHER COUNTRIES, MARCA
REGISTRADA, HECHO EN U.S.A.

Printed in the U.S.A.

WCD 10 9 8 7 6 5 4 3 2 1

Contents

Introduction

"The Revelation of Jesus Christ" is like a play, written, produced and directed by Christ. He cast both himself and John as actors and had John record the script. Jesus used angels as supporting cast. His angel transmitted his monologue when he gave his State of the Church message.

As the playwright, Jesus set the scene and decided what "time is at hand." It just did not happen to coincide with 96 A.D., when the apostle John recorded the script. Figuring out what "time is at hand" is the key to understanding the prophetic revelation correctly.

In the mind of the author, the time at hand is when the Rapture of the Church takes place. This is when he reveals himself as the "Lord God Almighty, which was (at the First Advent), and is (at the Rapture), and is to come (at the Second Advent)." From the vantage point of the Rapture, he looks both backward and forward to describe the players and present the action.

His skeleton outline seems to have started out with Introduction by John, Preview of the Rapture, State of the Church, the Rapture, the Tribulation, etc.

As soon as John introduces the play, we are immediately treated to a quick preview of the Rapture. On the first day of the week (i.e., Rapture Sunday), John hears Jesus' "voice, as of a trumpet," becomes "in the Spirit," and is caught up to Heaven where he sees the glorified Lord still holding the stars that represent the church's star performers in his hand. Not only did Jesus just snatch them up, but he is surrounded by overcomers—the Bride of Christ.

He then tells John, "Write the things which thou hast seen (the state of the churches), and the things which are (at the Rapture), and the things which shall be hereafter (Tribulation, Second Coming, etc., 'things which must shortly come to pass')." John begins to write about the churches as Jesus transmits his monologue. In its seven parts, Christ presents himself as John saw him in the preview of the Rapture, such as he "who walketh in the midst of the seven golden candlesticks."

After describing the state of the church, Jesus causes John to act out the Rapture. The same trumpet voice John heard in the Preview says, "Come up hither, and I will shew thee things which must be hereafter." After John describes the heavenly scene, the play launches into the Tribulation.

Understanding that the time "which is" is the time of the Rapture not only shows that the Rapture is on Sunday, it reveals a hidden truth in Revelation 17:10. There "are seven kings; five are fallen, and **one is**, and the other is not yet come." The king that "is" holds office at the time of the Rapture, not when John recorded the script. The one that "is" and the one that has not yet come are the sixth and seventh, the Beast and False Prophet of the end times. The first king was Nimrod at the Tower of Babel, the mother of false religion. The empires represented are Babylon I (Nimrod), Babylon II (Nebuchadnezzar), Media-Persia, Greece, Rome, Ecclesiastic Rome, and Babylon III (on the Euphrates).

Three "new" things have often been misunderstood, new Heaven, new Earth, and New Jerusalem. Do the new Heaven and Earth appear during the Millennium or after it? Is New Jerusalem a triangle or cube, or is it a heavenly body, an orbiting sphere of equal length, breadth and height?

These things, plus others not commonly understood, are explained in "Revelations 2000." Even the location of God's Heaven is revealed. However, the major breakthrough is, in my mind, the identification of exactly what "time is at hand" in the third verse and in Revelation 22:10. It colors everything between them.

I have used direct quotations from Scripture rather than my own words whenever possible. God's word can speak to hearts when my words can't. If God said it, you can believe it. It's the only rock-hard absolute truth we have.

The Lord said in Jeremiah 33:3, "Call unto me, and I will answer thee, and shew thee great and mighty things, which thou knowest not." I called, and he answered. Truly, "Known unto God are all his works from the beginning of the world" (Acts 15:18). All clues are already in Scripture. Jesus said, "I have foretold you all things" in Mark 13:23.

Bible references are from the King James Version unless indicated otherwise. Margin references are from the Scofield Bible. Italics in Scripture may be in plain type. The beginning of quotations from the Bible are not capitalized unless capitalized in the original. The bold emphasis is mine.

I pray that God will open your understanding now as never before, for the Rapture is near. In Jesus name, Amen.

M.J. Agee

The Vantage Point

Revelation 1

As we begin to read the apostle John's vision of things to come, it is as if great theater doors have just swung open on oiled hinges so we can slip in and settle into plush seats to listen to John read a play—the most momentous play ever written. Different from any other, it is spellbinding.

> Title: "The Revelation of Jesus Christ"
> Author, Producer, and Director: Jesus Christ
> Scenes: Earth and Heaven
> Time: When the Rapture is at hand
> Main actors: Jesus and John
> Supporting cast: Angels
> Narrator: John
> Method of transmitting the script: A vision
>   Sent and signified by His angel to John

Nothing about this production is ordinary. This is a miracle play full of surprises. Jesus is the playwright. He gave John the vision and told him to write it down. The script is preserved for us in the last book in the Bible.

As the playwright, the Lord decided on the time. He viewed events from one single vantage point and looked forward and backward from that day. He used two stages, heavenly and earthly, and cast both himself and John as actors. He called in angels as supporting cast.

We look through John's eyes to see what he saw. At times, he is caught up to Heaven and we hear his voice speaking from there. In other places, he speaks from Earth.

Through John's miraculous experiences, we are given a view of Heaven never seen before. We not only find out what it looks like but exactly where it is located.

We also find out what will happen after Jesus comes to take his Bride to Heaven. He tells us precisely what we will see and hear right after we are transported to His Place in the Pre-Tribulation Rapture.

In John's vision of this play, it is almost as if certain scenes are photographed with a movie camera with a telescopic zoom lens that can penetrate the mists of time. Far off things can be brought up close for a good look at the details. Only the Lord could direct this type of work accurately. Most of the scenes have register marks to show us where they fit in his overall Plan of the Ages if we will but look for them. Every detail is preplanned and well thought out.

Feeling the hush descending, we focus our thoughts for this drama is not only entertaining, but prophetic. Some of the things depicted can happen to us personally. Almost all will take place during the lifetime of this terminal generation now living on the edge of destruction of civilization as we know it. Afterward, it will take the return of Christ to bring true peace and to restore the world and make it habitable again, as he did in Genesis.

We are privileged to be told what lies ahead of us just before it begins to take place in reality. There are very few times in this life that we can be sure of what events are on the track ahead. This is one of those rare times. The mathematics are given to measure time during the Tribulation.

This could be our last shot at trying to understand the coming end-time events. The Rapture is very near, when Christ will come, meet his Bride in the air, and take the believers who are spiritually clad in white wedding garments to be with him where he is—in Heaven.

We need the information contained in this play to be able to make wise choices, for we are living in "the time of the end." Expect great things, for we live at the very time when "knowledge shall be increased,"[1] as was revealed to the prophet Daniel.

This knowledge is not only of secular and scientific things, but includes knowledge of the deeper meaning of

Scripture. Understanding of Bible prophecy is to be increased, as we will find out in this elaborate production that Jesus has planned for our entertainment and edification.

In this play, there are actors, dialogue, costume changes, scene changes, and graphic symbols with striking imaginative power. At various times, inanimate things, such as thunder or the altar, are personified and given voices of intelligible speech. It is all very dramatic, interesting, informative.

The title of the play is inviting, The Revelation of Jesus Christ. It draws you with its hint of wonderful secrets waiting to be revealed, both of Jesus Christ and of prophecy, and it fulfills the promise, exceeding all expectations.

THE REVELATION OF JESUS CHRIST

The title is a key to the whole play

Jesus Christ will actually be revealed when he is seen and heard at the Rapture. The word translated Revelation, *Apocalypse* in Greek, means appearing or coming. First Corinthians 1:7 makes this clear. Paul mentioned "waiting for the coming (*apokalupsin*) of our Lord Jesus Christ." This is the appearing or coming of Jesus Christ, and he will first appear when he comes to get his Bride at the Rapture.

John recorded "The Revelation of Jesus Christ" in 96 A.D., when the church was 66 years old. At that time, he was given a preview of the Rapture first and then told later what will follow it. This has an application to us today. We can now preview the Rapture just before it happens and know what will follow it. We can already see the event-strewn pathway that leads right into the terrible Tribulation. There should be no doubt that the Rapture is near.

All is to be revealed ahead of time. Amos 3:7 says,

> the Lord GOD will do nothing, but he revealeth his secret unto his servants the prophets.

The apostle Peter was talking about the Rapture, when Christ comes for the church, when he said,

> Wherefore gird up the loins of your mind, be sober, and hope to the end for the grace that is to be brought unto you at **the revelation of Jesus Christ.**[2]

The script of this play is our Lord Jesus Christ's last written word to us. From the day that John recorded the final Amen, God's written word has been forever finished.

This is the Lord's grand finale, the most magnificent scenario of the whole show. It is perfect. Nothing can be added or subtracted. We can only interpret what is already there. Near the end of the last chapter, Jesus warns,

> If any man shall add unto these things, God shall add unto him the plagues that are written in this book: And if any man shall take away from the words of the book of this prophecy, God shall take away his part out of the book of life, and out of the holy city, and *from* the things which are written in this book.

Revelation was penned in 96 A.D., before the turn of the century in 101. In 1996. I thought, "We too are near the turn of the century, and 'things happened unto them (Israel) for examples, and they are written for our admonition, upon whom the ends of the ages are come.'[3] " I knew that the Rapture would soon be "at hand."

Jesus told Peter, "If I will that he (John, the beloved apostle) tarry till I come (i.e., at the Rapture), what is that to thee? follow thou me."[4] John lived until Jesus came to him in this vision—when the Rapture is "at hand." When John recorded what the Lord gave him in this play, he was the last apostle alive. John represented the church when she is white haired, but still living. When he was caught up to Heaven, it represented the Rapture of the **beloved** Bride of Christ.

Ever since John wrote this in 96 A.D., we have had the rest of the scriptures to help us understand what the Lord was saying to us, yet The Revelation contained more mysteries to be solved than had ever been recognized in the past. As we listen to John, we will learn marvelous new things.

The story line grabs our interest because we know it will come true, most of it in our days. The import of the portrayed events is stupendous. They will change the world as we know it. Like clay under the seal, the face of the planet will be altered. The lineup of nations will be modified. The chain of command will be different.

Revelation is masterfully multi-faceted. Not only a drama, it is Scripture's master key that unlocks the meaning of many obscure Old Testament prophecies.

It is an outline of the end times intended to be fleshed out with details gleaned from the Old and New Testaments. This outline helps us arrange those obscure "here a little, and there a little"[5] prophecies in the correct chronological order. As we assemble the clues, new pictures will flash out at us.

All clues necessary for interpretation are contained in Scripture. In Mark 13:23, Jesus emphatically said,

> But take ye heed: behold, **I have foretold you all things**.

The prophetic picture is fragmented and contains many symbols, but it is complete when the puzzle is pieced together. As we listen to the script of this play, the Lord helps us put the scattered pieces into the greater picture in our minds so that a new wave of understanding can sweep over us. For me, goose bumps accompany each wave.

The Lord teaches us many things by examples, types, or similitudes. Hosea 12:10 in the literal Concordant Version is so easy to understand, I prefer using it. The word "likenesses" is so descriptive. The Lord says,

> I will speak by the prophets, And I will increase the vision, And by the hand of the prophets **I will use likenesses**.

Right away, in the very first book of Scripture ever committed to writing, the Lord told us, in Job 11:6, that

the secrets of wisdom...are double (duplicate copies) **to that which is.**

Some future events are almost carbon copies of past events. By the master's design, this history does repeat itself. The history of Israel dramatized many things to come. When we finally grasp this, we can understand why certain things were included in the scripture record. All the clues to put the prophetic puzzle together are in the Bible.

A thumbnail sketch

First in the order of major coming events is the Rapture of the church saints, the Bride of Christ. Our Lord will descend from his heavenly home and hover over the face of the Earth as the Holy Spirit hovered over the face of the waters in Genesis 1:2. Just as the breath of God in that day caused many molecules of water to be transformed into clouds of mist that floated upward into the air, Jesus Christ will draw clouds of transformed Spirit-filled believers to himself. If they are filled with the breath of God, they will float up to meet him in the clouds like helium-filled balloons.

If you are in this special group, you will be transported to Heaven, a real place which will be revealed to us as we listen to the play, so you won't have to go through the terrible times ahead on this planet. You will assemble on the heavenly Mount Zion[6] and in they holy New Jerusalem.[7]

In John 14:2-4 (New King James) Jesus said,

> In my Father's house (*oikia*, inhabited edifice, i.e., in Heaven[8]) are many mansions (*monai*, residences)...I go to prepare a place for you...I will come again, and receive you unto myself; that where I am, there ye may be also. And **where I go ye know**, and the way you know.

Compare the last part of this with the Phillips translation:

> I am coming again to welcome you into **my own home**, so that you may be where I am.

You know where I am going and you
know the road I am going to take.

"You **know** where I am going" is an astonishing
statement. Heaven is Christ's home, and we already "know"
where it is. Its name and appearance from Earth are familiar
to us. Glowing with inner light, it is the prettiest thing in our
solar system. It is a well-known site that was recognized by
man at least as far back as the Babylonian Empire. Visible to
the Babylonians without a telescope, it is certainly not out of
the realm of our understanding in these days since our
Voyager I and II space probes photographed it. The script of
this play contains clues that point to Heaven's exact location.

After the Rapture, there seems to be a hiatus of exactly four years, according to Jewish inclusive reckoning,
before the seven-year Tribulation will begin. We would
count them as three years because we do not count the first
year as number one as the Jews do. I think the four years
will start and end on Pentecost, also called the Feast of
Weeks. Jesus mentioned these four years in the parable of
the barren fig tree. Luke 13:6-9 says,

> He spake also this parable: A certain man
> (Jesus) had a fig tree (Israel[9]) planted in his
> vineyard; and he came (at the Rapture) and
> sought fruit thereon, and found none. Then
> said he unto the dresser of his vineyard, Be-
> hold, these **three years** (the year of the
> Rapture plus two years after the Rapture) I
> come seeking fruit on this fig tree, and find
> none: cut it down; why cumbereth it the
> ground? And he answering said unto him,
> Lord, let it alone **this year also** (the fourth
> year), till I shall dig about it, and dung it: And
> if it bear fruit, well: and if not, then after that
> thou shalt cut it down.

The cutting down is the Tribulation, also called the
Seventieth Week of Daniel because it is the last week of
years of the 490-year prophecy recorded in Daniel 9:24-27.

Revelation is built around the number seven. We find seven letters, seven churches, seven stars, seven angels, seven candlesticks, seven spirits, seven lamps, seven eyes, seven seals, seven trumpets, seven vials, seven heads, seven horns, seven thunders, seven mountains, seven kings, and seven groups that are called blessed.

During this time of the terrible sevens, Satan will bring such escalating evil on the world that judgment must fall. On the 2,300th day,[10] the Tribulation must suddenly be cut short or no flesh would be saved.[11] Mankind would be wiped out in exactly the same way that dinosaurs, saber-toothed tigers, and mammoths were exterminated in ancient times. On that 2,300th day, events will be dealt out fast, both in Heaven and on Earth. No other day is like it—ever.

As Lot was taken by the hand in the morning, led out of Sodom, and told to escape to the mountain before the fire fell, Christ will draw the cloud of Tribulation saints out of here in Rapture II just before the fire falls at noon.[12] Truly, they will be saved so as by fire that day, which is the Feast of Trumpets. In that day the scripture will be proved true, that "THERE is therefore now no condemnation to them which are in Christ Jesus."[13]

The 1,000-year Day of the Lord called the Millennium, will begin the day the shortened Tribulation ends in a catastrophic blinding flash that knocks this planet upside down. Isaiah 24:1 says that

> the LORD maketh the earth empty, and maketh it waste, and turneth it upside down.

A binary asteroid will split apart and collide with Earth. The two main impact blasts will cause firestorms and out-of-control seas to sweep over the land. People will scramble for the hills. As in the days of Lot, this fire fall is an Act of God, a natural catastrophe of such severity that it will be a vexation just to understand the report of the consequences that follow. Isaiah 28:15-19 in the NIV says,

> You boast, 'We have entered into a covenant with death (the False Prophet), with the grave

(Hell, i.e., Satan) we have made an agreement. **When an overwhelming scourge sweeps by**, it cannot touch us, for we have made a lie our refuge and falsehood our hiding place.' So this is what the Sovereign LORD says...hail will sweep away your refuge, the lie, and **water will overflow your hiding place**. Your covenant with death will be annulled; your agreement with the grave (Satan) will not stand. When the overwhelming scourge (tsunami) sweeps by, you (who did not escape in either Rapture) will be beaten down by it. As often as it comes it will carry you away; morning after morning, by day and by night, it will sweep through. **The understanding of this message will bring sheer terror**.

Satan is behind the lie that the overwhelming scourge cannot touch us, just as he was when the serpent said unto Eve, "Ye shall not surely die."[14] Eve died, and the unregenerate will die by this scourge after this age ends.

Right after its termination, the terror will be so great that men will appear as though they are about to give birth. Jeremiah 30:6 says,

wherefore do I see every man with his hands on his loins, as a woman in travail, and all faces are turned into paleness? Alas! (woe) for **that day is great, so that none is like it**: it is even the time of Jacob's trouble, but he shall be saved out of it (in Rapture II and in the birth of the remnant that will live on into the Millennium).

Hearts will fail from fear. We don't want to be on Earth at that time. We MUST leave here in the Raptures. The alternative is just too terrible to consider.

After Earth sustains oblique hits by a binary asteroid that breaks "asunder," Israel must bury the dead to cleanse the land, then Christ will return in the Millennium as King of kings and Lord of lords to heal and restore. In those days, they will say, "This land that was desolate is become like the garden of Eden; and the...ruined cities...are inhabited."[15]

After the complete seven-year period ends, the Judgment of the Nations will take place, followed by Armageddon, the last battle ever fought. When it is over, Satan will be chained and lasting world peace will blossom.

The real scene is already set. Rapture I, the next event on the prophetic calendar, is almost upon us. At that time, Christ will come escort his Bride to his home.

Some of us will barely be able to listen to the entire play before the Rapture whisks us away to a high balcony seat in the third heaven[16] for a second viewing of the end of the age in real time. Then, we will see the actual events taking place on Earth from a safe distance, from Paradise, "the secret place (*cether*, hiding place) of the most High."

It will remind us of hits Jupiter took when a string of 21 pieces of the Comet Shoemaker-Levy 9 began to strike it on July 16, 1994. The Orange County Register ran an article on the 18th, "Comet puts on a show." It said,

> Only 18 hours after the first pieces of rock and ice struck, astronomers at the Space Telescope Science Institute in Baltimore were trying to understand why they had seen such an impressive show.

The Bible can show them why. A similar event is going to take place on Earth when this age ends and the Millennium begins. It helps us understand that such a collision is possible and the terrific energy it would release. God teaches by similitudes or likenesses. He gave us a sign.

When Jesus spoke of the heavenly Paradise, he also revealed what we have to do to get there: believe in him. Please believe in him, what have you got to lose? You have everything to gain and nothing to lose. Jesus said,

> For God so loved the world, that he gave his only begotten Son, that whosoever (put your

name here) believeth in him should not perish, but have everlasting life.[17]

LET not your heart be troubled: ye believe in God, believe also in me.[18]

The Psalms show that we will be in Heaven when the catastrophe takes place at the end of the shortened Tribulation. Psalm 91:1,8 says, "He that dwelleth in the secret place of the most High shall abide under the shadow of the Almighty," and then reassuringly adds,

Only with thine eyes shalt thou behold and see the reward of the wicked.

The pace of the play we are about to listen to is quick. It starts with astonishingly rapid action, and events sweep on toward "the consummation" spoken of by Daniel. From the Rapture of the church saints to the Second Coming of Christ is only about ten years. The last seven of those years are the Tribulation.

On Nisan 1, the first day of the Jewish Regnal Year, the long awaited kingdom of our Lord Jesus Christ will become a reality on Earth. True peace will soon soothe the remnant left on this tortured planet as they struggle to recover from a blow big enough to knock the nonsense out of the few survivors left.

In the theater of our minds

We imagine the magnificent scenery of the six-by-ten-mile barren rocky island of Patmos, where John is in exile about fifty miles from Ephesus. The cliff where John is forced to chip off granite and carry it to the dock is seen. The granite is used to build foundations and pave roads in Domitian's Roman Empire.

The white craggy shore line and the azure waters of that portion of the Aegean known as the Icarian Sea can be seen. Behind Patmos is a sky-blue curtain with some wispy white clouds slowly undulating in a whisper-soft breeze. Several sea birds wheel in a never ending search for food.

Our set reminds me of Isaiah 40:22 in the Concordant Version: "Who is stretching out as a thin gauze the heavens, And bagging them out as a tent to dwell in?"

Before the opening curtain is drawn aside, the wrinkled, sun-tanned, silver-haired John, the last apostle alive, takes his stand in Patmos. His hands and feet are callused from his hard, exhausting work in the quarry. About 90 years old, he represents the church when it is old and white-haired—in our days.

Since white represents the righteousness of saints, and nothing that defiles can enter heaven, The apostle is wearing a white robe. I imagine him with a sheepskin scroll in his hand, similar to a Dead-Sea Scroll found in the Qumran cave, and an ink horn, in which pens and ink are stored, strapped to his side. An expectant hush falls as the curtain in front parts. John turns toward us and this elaborate production begins.

THE REVELATION OF JESUS CHRIST

The time: when the Rapture is at hand

John announces the title of the play

After announcing the title, John gives credit to the author, tells why it was written, and adds details about the unusual way the script was transmitted to him. He will narrate this play for us. Listen as he begins to speak in a deep resonant voice. He starts off with the title of the play.

THE Revelation of Jesus Christ, which God gave unto him, to shew unto his servants things which must **shortly** come to pass; and he sent and signified *it* by his angel unto his servant John: Who bare record of the word of God, and of the testimony of Jesus Christ, and of all things that he saw.[19]

The "testimony of Jesus is the spirit of prophecy."[20] This prophetic play was written to reveal who Christ actually is and to show us things that will "shortly come to pass" **in our days.**

The time is at hand

The very first verse of Revelation tosses us a stimulating challenge. Do not pass over it in haste. Stop and try to figure this out. We are to be shown things which must **shortly** come to pass. How can that be when this was written in 96 A.D. and most of these things are still future in our days?

The Bible was expressly written for us upon whom the ends of the ages have come,[21] and in our frame of reference, 1,900 years is not a short time. It is more than 25 lifetimes.

As John continues delivering the Lord's words, he promises us a blessing for hearing and restates our problem:

> Blessed *is* he that readeth, and they that **hear** the words of this prophecy, and keep (Greek, *terountes*, hold fast, observe) those things which are written therein: for **the time *is* at hand.**[22]

How can the time be at hand? Many explain that the Greek *eggus* not only means at hand, but near. However, by now, we can see that these things were not actually very near, and *eggus* definitely means at hand for it is from *en* and *guion*, hand.[23] Yet, the Scriptures cannot lie. It is up to us to figure out what time is at hand.

> When we solve this problem, we will remove a great stumbling block and uncover a long-hidden secret.

An easy way to put this book of Revelation in its proper perspective is to look at it as a play, and listen attentively to the reading of the script. In a play, the playwright sets the scene and chooses the time. In Revelation, before the curtain is drawn, the setting is on Earth in the latter days

21

of this age. The time is just before the Rapture takes place. From that vantage point, and actually from ours today also, the time is **at hand**.

It should be easy for us to project ourselves into this scene, for in our days, in 1996 A.D., as it symbolically was in 96 A.D., the Rapture is due soon, but hopefully not too soon for us to repent of our sins and be filled with the Holy Spirit. He is our transporter. The Greek *pneuma,* translated Spirit, means a breath or blast of air. This is the breath of God. More than a transfer ticket, the Holy Spirit is the means by which we will be floated up from Earth and whisked to heaven.

It actually will happen very quickly. When the disciples had rowed out about twenty-five to thirty furlongs into the Sea of Galilee, Jesus came to them walking on the sea. "Then they willingly received him into the ship: and **immediately** the ship was at the land whither they went."[24] We who willingly receive him will meet Christ in the air, and then we may appear "immediately" at the assembly point in Heaven, for "with God all things are possible."[25]

When we repent and confess our sins, we are as pure virgins clothed with white wedding garments and filled with the oil of the Holy Spirit. Although Revelation does not tell us what time of day the Rapture will take place, the parable of the ten virgins suggests "midnight"[26] as one possibility. Jesus said to "Watch...for ye know not when the master of the house cometh, at even, or at midnight, or at the cock-crowing, or in the morning."[27] Notice that he did not say that we do not know the day.

To God, we must shine as beckoning lights in the darkness when we are to be picked up. None whose lamp is going out will be taken. To the foolish virgins, he will sternly say, "I know you not."[28]

There will be no crashing the wedding party. Matthew 22:12-14 explains what could happen if anyone tried:

> Friend (Tribulation saints are friends of the Bride), how camest thou in hither not having a wedding garment? And he was speechless (Laodiceans do not realize they are blind and

naked). Then said the king to the servants,
Bind him hand and foot, and take him away,
and cast him into outer darkness; there shall
be weeping and gnashing of teeth. For many
are called, but few are chosen.

The Tribulation saints are not part of the Bride of
Christ. They are invited to the Marriage Supper of the Lamb
as friends of the Bride. The Old Testament saints are the
friends of the Bridegroom.

I used to think the Rapture would be so secret that no
one would see it take place. We would just vanish. That is
not quite right. Psalm 40:1-3 indicates otherwise. It says,

> I WAITED patiently (as the Philadelphians
> do[29]) for the LORD; and he inclined (leaned
> down) unto me, and heard my cry. **He
> brought me up** also out of an horrible pit
> (as acted out by Jeremiah[30]), out of the miry
> clay (i.e., out of the body made from 'the
> dust of the ground'[31]), and set my feet upon a
> rock (Heaven), and established my goings
> (the Rapture). And he hath put a new song
> (sung after the Rapture[32]) in my mouth, even
> praise unto our God: **many shall see it**
> (the Rapture), **and fear, and shall trust
> in the LORD**.

John, scribe, narrator, and actor in this play, stands
firmly on the rocky Earth as he introduces The Revelation of
Jesus Christ, but as soon as the cue "the time is at hand" is
out of his mouth, he quickly disappears from Patmos and
reappears above the undulating curtain of the sky. He has
just gone through a great door onto the heavenly stage. On
the other side is heavenly "Zion, the perfection of beauty."[33]

Snap! That quick, he acted out the Rapture just as he
does when he hears "Come up hither" in chapter 4, verse 1.
In 4:1, he speaks from Heaven immediately after the Rapture. Here, he does the same thing; his next words are spoken from Heaven. This is like a preview of what will take

place in 4:1. We get a foretaste of things to come. Our wonderful playwright gives us this preview shot for several reasons. One is to prepare us so we will recognize the Rapture later when it happens just as quickly.

This happened so quickly that I need to go back and reread what John said just before the snap. He said,

> Blessed *is* he that readeth, and they that hear the words of this prophecy, and keep (hold fast, observe) those things which are written therein: for **the time *is* at hand.**[34]

The next thing John knows, he is in Heaven. It was years before I realized that the time indicated here was that close at hand. The Rapture is at hand—only moments away.

Transported, John speaks from Heaven

He identifies himself to the churches on Earth and delivers a salutation before Christ begins to speak. John's dialogue from the heavenly stage opens with these lines:

> JOHN to the seven churches which are in Asia (which means mud, i.e., in bodies of clay on Earth): Grace *be* unto you, and peace, from him (God) which **is** (at the Rapture), and which was (at the First Advent), and which is to come (at the Second Advent); and from the seven Spirits which are before his throne; And from Jesus Christ, *who is* the faithful witness, *and* the first begotten (firstborn[35]) of the dead, and the prince of the kings of the earth. Unto him (Christ) that loved us, and washed us from our sins in his own blood, And **hath made** (past tense) us kings and priests (at the Rapture that he just played out) unto God (Jesus Christ) and his Father; to him (one person, our Lord Jesus Christ, who said, 'I and my Father are one'[36]) *be* glory and dominion for ever and ever. Amen. Behold, he cometh with clouds; and every

eye shall (in the future) see him (at the Second Advent), and they *also* which pierced him: and all kindreds of the earth shall wail because of him. Even so, Amen.[37]

Christ is the firstborn from the dead. First Corinthians 15:23 says, "Christ the firstfruits; afterward they that are Christ's at his coming."

A trumpet voice speaks from Heaven

With no more introduction than that, the majestic Lord Jesus Christ speaks with a voice like a trumpet because it is a feast day, when the trumpet is sounded. This is the revelation, when Christ reveals who he really is.

He does not start out, "Ladies and gentlemen," or pussyfoot around. Right away, he smacks us with his credentials and establishes his authority. He is THE ALMIGHTY. His forceful words strike our ears, register in our brains, and raise up our hair with awesome effect.

> **I am** Alpha and Omega, the beginning and the ending, saith the Lord, which **is** (at the Rapture), and which was (at the First Advent), and which is to come (at the Second Advent), **the Almighty.**[38]

Wow! Alpha and Omega are the first and last letters in the Greek alphabet. This indicates that Christ is both the first and the last, both Yahweh (or Jehovah, according to the system of transliteration used) of the Old Testament and Jesus Christ of the New Testament.

Isaiah told us this long ago in the Old Testament, if only we had believed it. Isaiah 44:6 says, "Thus saith the LORD (Yahweh) the King of Israel, and his redeemer (Christ) the LORD (Yahweh) of hosts; **I am the first, and I am the last**; and beside me there is no God." Verses 16 and 17 continue the theme: "Come ye near unto me, hear ye this; I have not spoken in secret from the beginning; from the time that it was, there am I: and now the Lord GOD (1), and his Spirit (2), hath sent **me** (3). Thus saith the LORD

(Yahweh), **thy Redeemer**, the Holy One of Israel; **I am the LORD** (Yahweh) **thy God.**" The Almighty always was the one who dealt with mankind.

"Hearken unto me, O Jacob and Israel, my called," he thunders in Isaiah 48:12,13; "**I am he; I am the first, I also am the last.** Mine hand also hath laid the foundation of the earth, and my right hand hath spanned the heavens: when I call unto them, they stand up together."

He is both Yahweh[39] (from the Hebrew YHWH, which means He is, He was, and He will come) and Yahwehshua (which means Yahweh is Saviour), which in the shortened form is Yahshua or Y'shua (Iesous in Greek, Jesus in English). He is the Messiah, Jesus Christ (Yeshua Mashiach to the Messianic Jews), both Lord and Saviour. He is, and always was, The Almighty. Acts 2:36 says,

> Therefore let all the house of Israel know assuredly, that God hath made that same **Jesus**, whom ye have crucified, **both Lord and Christ.**

This doctrine is not new; it is just clarified here. This is the same truth taught in II Corinthians 5:18,19. There, Paul spoke of "God, who hath reconciled us to himself by Jesus Christ" and went on to state very clearly that "God was in Christ, reconciling the world unto **himself.**"

Jesus taught this doctrine while on Earth. In John 14:9,11, he told "Philip...he that hath seen me hath seen the Father...Believe me that **I am in the Father, and the Father in me.**" He is of one substance, or essential nature with the Father. This is important, for Jesus said,

> Ye neither know me, nor my Father: if ye had known me, ye should have known my Father also....**I am from above** (from Heaven)... I am not of this world. I said therefore unto you, that ye shall die in your sins: for **if ye believe not that I am he, ye shall die in your sins**...They understood not that he spake to them of **the Father...I am he.**[40]

This is of paramount importance. We need to get this straight. The Lord Jesus Christ is the only one of his kind, the God-man, the Word who was with God in the beginning, who was God, and who was made flesh so he could become our Saviour.[41] This is what Hebrews 10:5 means when Jesus says, "a body hast thou prepared me." He has two complete natures, both God and man.

If this is not all entirely clear to us now, it will be immediately after the Rapture takes place. At that time, we will see him as he is. In the meantime, we can pray for the Lord to increase our understanding. He does, step by step, as soon as we are ready for it.

Isaiah 9:6 helps us comprehend the two natures of one person, our Lord **and** Saviour Jesus Christ.

> For unto us a child is born (his humanity, the nature he inherited from his mother), unto us a son is given (his deity, the nature he inherited from his Father) and the government shall be upon his shoulder: and **his name shall be called** Wonderful, Counsellor, **The mighty God, The everlasting Father,** The Prince of Peace.

Jesus Christ is the Almighty, the "everlasting Father". "The first man (the first Adam) is of the earth, earthy: the second man (the second Adam) **is the Lord from** heaven."[42] Like the first Adam, Jesus Christ was a creature of a different kind. Truly, "God was in Christ, reconciling the world unto himself" (II Corinthians 5:19).

The word Revelation is *apokalupsis* in the Greek. It has several meanings: disclosure, appearing, coming, uncovering, unveiling, and revealing. All are appropriate. The Revelation of Jesus Christ lifts the veil and reveals exactly who Jesus Christ is in his person and in his offices. He is priest, king, judge, "The mighty God, The everlasting Father, The Prince of Peace." You can trust it and believe it. Scripture says it. It is the absolute diamond-hard truth.

Psalms 50:1-6 speaks of Yahweh doing the very things that other scriptures indicate that Jesus Christ will do:

The mighty God, even the LORD (*YHWH*, Yahweh), hath spoken, and called the earth from the rising of the sun unto the going down thereof. Out of Zion (the heavenly one), the perfection of beauty (Paradise), God hath shined. Our God shall come (Yahweh in Jesus Christ at the Second Advent), and shall not keep silence: a fire shall devour before him (the catastrophe), and it shall be very tempestuous round about him. He shall call to the heavens from above (to gather those who were taken to Heaven in the first Rapture), and to the earth (to bring the Tribulation Saints to Heaven in Rapture II), that he may judge his people (at the Judgment Seat of Christ). Gather my saints together unto me; those that have made a covenant with me by sacrifice (Jesus Christ's was the perfect sacrifice, and it applies to all who believe in him). And the heavens shall declare his righteousness: for God is judge himself.

God, the judge, is Jesus Christ, the Son of God, for "the Father judgeth no man, but hath committed all judgment unto the Son."[43] This is fair to us, for he knows exactly what it is like to live as a human being.

The Revelation of Jesus Christ embraces three of Christ's future appearances, at both Raptures and at the Second Advent. At the first Rapture, righteous believers will rise up to meet him in the air. He will transport them to heaven so they do not have to go through the coming shortened 2,300-day[44] Tribulation. On day 2,300, he will appear (the Sign of the Son of Man[45]) and pluck the Tribulation saints unscathed out of their fiery furnace. Their clothing will not even smell of smoke. At the Second Advent, he will touch down on the Mount of Olives,[46] the same place from which he ascended.[47]

Since our Lord Jesus Christ is the Almighty, his divine nature knows everything, even when he is coming. Job

24:1 says that "**times are not hidden from the Almighty**." They cannot be. He planned everything before he did anything. When Jesus said, "But of that day and hour knoweth no **man**, no, not the angels of heaven, but my Father only,"[48] he spoke as **man**, but the Father in him knew. He had two natures. He could speak as man, or he could speak as God. He did not want people of those days to know when he was coming. That information was reserved for us, as the Rapture and end of this age draw near.

John's explanation of the previous action

In our play, because the Rapture happened so quickly, almost as soon as the curtain opened, John now explains the action that has just taken place so we will not fail to recognize it and become disoriented. In verses 9 and 10, he says,

> I John, who also am your brother, and companion in tribulation, and in the kingdom and patience of Jesus Christ, **was** (before the Rapture) in the isle that is called Patmos (which means mortal), for the word of God, and for the testimony of Jesus Christ. I was (margin: **became**) **in the Spirit** on the Lord's day (Sunday[49]), and heard behind me a great voice, as of a trumpet.

Instead of "became in the Spirit," the New English Bible has, "I was caught up by the Spirit." This is the same trumpet voice he hears as chapter four begins. The passage in 4:1 has been recognized as depicting the Rapture. It says,

> a door was opened in heaven: and **the first voice which I heard** *was* as it were of a trumpet talking with me; which said, **Come up hither**, and I will shew thee things which must be hereafter. **And immediately** I was (margin: became) in the spirit (or as in the New English Bible, '**I was caught up by the Spirit**.'): and, behold, a throne was set in heaven, and *one* sat on the throne.

When the trumpet voice shouts, "Come up hither," the Rapture will happen quickly—snap! There will be no time for foolish virgins to go buy oil. Those that try will come back and find the door closed, as the Laodiceans do.[50]

Both the shout of the Lord and a trumpet are mentioned in Paul's account of the Rapture in I Thessalonians 4:13-18 (New Scofield Bible):

> For if we believe that Jesus died and rose again, even so them also which sleep in Jesus will God bring with him. For this we say unto you by the word of the Lord, that we which are alive and remain unto the coming of the Lord (at the Rapture) shall not precede them who are asleep. For the Lord himself shall descend from heaven with a shout, with the voice of the archangel, and with the **trump** of God: and the dead in Christ shall rise first: Then we who are alive and remain shall be caught up together with them in the clouds, to meet the Lord in the air: and so shall we ever be with the Lord.

The apostle Paul made it very clear that all those who believe in Jesus Christ

> should live soberly, righteously, and godly, in this present world; Looking for that blessed hope (the Rapture), and the glorious appearing of **the great God and our Saviour Jesus Christ** (one person, both God and our Saviour Jesus Christ); Who gave himself for us, that he might redeem us from all iniquity, and purify unto himself a peculiar (special, being beyond the usual) people, **zealous of good works**[51] (the Laodiceans are not zealous[52]).

In the early days, people saw through a glass darkly, but now that the scriptures are complete, we can see him as if face to face. In our play, he is about to visually appear to John in the heavenly New Jerusalem right after the Rapture.

Believers are to be snatched away when the trumpet sounds. This is significant. The trumpet sounded on Pentecost at Mount Sinai, and on every feast. When the morning service began at the Temple, the door was opened at the sound of a trumpet. This door to Heaven opens at the sound of a trumpet, probably on Pentecost. That is when Moses went up Mount Sinai and received the ten commandments.

We are to escape from all the terrible troubles coming upon the earth during the Tribulation and be transported to Heaven, a definite place that Jesus has prepared for us.[53] When Jesus indicated that he came down from Heaven, he meant that he was from a real place. When he was taken up to Heaven to prepare a place for us, it was to a real place. When we are taken to his home, we will be taken to a real place. Heaven has a recognizable address.

Remember, "the secrets of wisdom...are double (duplicate copies) to that which is."[54] Israelite history contains many types of things to come. Her capitol city represents a heavenly one. There are two Jerusalems and two Mount Zions (Zion from Hebrew, or Sion from Greek), one on Earth and the other in Heaven. Hebrews 12:22-24 addresses us right after the Rapture. It shows that we are going up to another Jerusalem, in the heavenly Sion. Sion may indicate the Father's throne, New Jerusalem Christ's throne.

> But ye are come unto mount Sion, **and** unto the city of the living God, the heavenly Jerusalem, and to an innumerable company of angels, To the general assembly and **church of the firstborn**, which are written in heaven, and to God the Judge of all, and to the spirits of just men made perfect. And to Jesus the mediator of the new covenant.

As John was caught up by the Spirit on the Lord's day, believers will be born into heaven during the night or early morning and will attend services at the church of the Firstborn in heaven at the proper time, on Sunday morning.

Jesus, the head of the body of Christ, the church, emerged from the rock-hewn tomb on Sunday, went to Paradise,[55] and took the souls waiting in the womb of the Earth to heaven. It would be quite in character for God, who loves to provide us with examples, types, similitudes, and likenesses, and who thinks, plans, and works logically, to see that the rest of the body of Christ is born, or expelled, from mother Earth on Sunday.

In Heaven, Jesus speaks to John
In Revelation 1:11, John tells us what the voice like a trumpet says to him after he acts out the Rapture.

> Saying, I am Alpha and Omega, the first (Yahweh) and the last (Jesus Christ): and, What thou seest, write in a book, and send *it* unto the seven churches which are in Asia (mud, symbol of the Earth or these bodies of clay); unto Ephesus, and unto Smyrna, and unto Pergamos, and unto Thyatira, and unto Sardis, and unto Philadelphia, and unto Laodicea.

The Lord speaks from behind John, so John naturally twists around to face the speaker. As he turns, he sees what we will see after the Rapture, except that the real things will replace their symbols. Just imagine all of the Bride of Christ standing there with him, turning around and suddenly seeing our Lord Jesus Christ in all his radiant glory. That sight will be breathtaking.

First, John heard a voice, then saw a form. So will we. Next, John describes what has just taken place:

Christ in the midst of seven candlesticks
John sees Christ in the midst of symbols that represent the raptured church.

> And I turned to see the voice that spake with me. And being turned, I saw seven golden candlesticks; And in the midst of the seven

candlesticks *one* like unto the Son of man (Jesus Christ), clothed with a garment down to the foot, and girt about the paps (or 'girded across His breast' as in the NASB) with a golden girdle. His head and *his* hairs were white like wool, as white as snow; and his eyes *were* as a flame of fire; And his feet like unto fine brass, as if they burned in a furnace; and his voice as the sound of many waters. And he had in his right hand seven stars: and out of his mouth went a sharp twoedged sword: and his countenance *was* as the sun shineth in his strength.[56]

This is our great Lord shining in his splendid majesty. To God, believers indwelt by the Holy Spirit "shine as lights in the world,"[57] some even like stars, but Christ is the Sun of righteousness who will arise with healing in his wings.[58] On the mount of transfiguration, Peter, James, and John got to see a preview of Christ's glory. At that time, his face shone like the sun, and his raiment was as white as the light.[59]

Christ is the brightness of God's glory. Hebrews 1:1-3 helps us understand. It says,

GOD, who at sundry times and in divers manners spake in time past unto the fathers by the prophets, Hath in these last days spoken unto us by his Son (literally, in Son), whom he hath appointed heir of all things, by whom also he made the worlds; Who being the brightness of his glory, and **the express image of his person**, and upholding all things by the word of his power, when he had by himself purged our sins, sat down on the right hand of the Majesty on high.

In our play, we first see him wearing his long priestly robe, a vestment that suggests the truth, honor, and dignity that befits his role at this moment. His hair is white like wool. This ties in to Daniel 7:9, where the Ancient of days is seen with hair like pure wool.

His voice, like the sound of many waters, ties in with Ezekiel 1:24, where the voice of the Almighty, the voice of speech, is like the noise of great waters. These and the golden girdle across his chest are symbols of Christ's deity that almost shout the great news. He is The great high priest, "The mighty God, The everlasting Father, and The Prince of Peace."[60]

The girdle was a symbol of authority in the ancient world. The working man wore a short loose-fitting tunic and no girdle.

In Scripture, when one thing is described as being "like" or "as" something else, it is figurative language. For example, Christ's eyes are not literal fire. They are "as a flame of fire," symbolic of the intensity of his power to know all, see everything, do anything, and judge righteously. The New American Bible says, "his eyes blazed like fire."

We might say his eyes shot fire, showing his indignation over those things that were not right within the churches. It ties in with his feet looking like brass, a symbol of judgment throughout Scripture. At this time, he is judging the church to choose his Bride. She must be as a virgin wearing a white robe (pure, with no unconfessed sin).

When Ezekiel saw him, he exclaimed, "From his waist upwards I saw what might have been brass glowing like fire in a furnace; and from his waist downwards I saw what looked like fire. Radiance encircled him."[61]

When we see him at the Rapture, he is not wearing a crown. Therefore, Coronation Day has not yet arrived. Here, he is the Son of Man who is judge of the churches.[62]

Somewhere, Scripture shows us what its symbols represent. It interprets itself. A good example is found in verse 20. Listen as Christ explains what the stars and candlesticks stand for. We want to be part of this group.

> The mystery of the seven stars which thou sawest in my right hand, and the seven golden candlesticks. The seven stars are the an-

gels of the seven churches; and the seven candlesticks which thou sawest are the seven churches.

Luke said that the children of the resurrection can't die any more, for they are "equal unto the angels."[63] Therefore, these angels must be members of the church that have just been raptured. They seem to be the choice leaders that are part of the Bride of Christ, special people, active in the Lord's work, leaders that minister to the church, messengers that take God's message to the people.

After the Rapture, the seven candlesticks that represent all the churches are seen around Christ, but these leaders in his hand are the outstandingly talented stars, the top performers, the apostles, the John Wyclifs, the Martin Luthers, the Billy Grahams. They are still in his hand because he has just snatched them up at the Rapture. Since seven means complete, the seven stars represent the entire group.

Out of Jesus Christ's mouth went a sharp two-edged sword. This is the Word of God, called the "sword of the Spirit" in Ephesians 6:17. According to Hebrews 4:12, it is "sharper than any two-edged sword."

It is necessary at the Rapture because there are some unrepentant ones who will be cut off from the group. These are the foolish virgins whose flickering lights are going out for lack of the oil of the Holy Spirit.[64] He does not want any of our light to become shadow. He wants us glowing bright and strong through and through.

In the message to the church in Pergamos, "where Satan's seat is," we find the strong warning, "Repent: or else I will come unto thee quickly (at the Rapture), and will fight against them (the Nicolaitanes) with the sword of my mouth."[65] The Nicolaitanes are those who divide believers, who are actually all priests,[66] into priests and laity.

Church leaders are meant to be the Lord's servants and feed his lambs. Luke 12:45,46 shows that if a faithful and wise steward does not give the church their portion of

meat in due season (when the Lord's coming is near[67]), but says in his heart, "My lord delayeth his coming: and shall begin to beat the men-servants and maidens, and to eat and drink, and to be drunken; The lord of that servant (a believer) will come in a day when he looketh not for him, and at an hour when he is not aware, and will cut him in sunder (the Jerusalem Bible has, 'cut him off'), and will **appoint him his portion with the unbelievers**.

What is this "meat" that is to be given in "due season"? Some information or understanding is to be given the church when Christ's coming is near that was not given to the infant church. No new scriptures can be given. The existing ones can not be added to. All the clues are in the Bible already. In Mark 13:23, Jesus said, "But take ye heed: behold, **I have foretold you all things.**"

We need to read our Bibles very carefully now. Everything we need to know is there somewhere. The only new things are current events. They tie in with the Bible and open our eyes to new truths. Our Lord Jesus Christ hid the necessary clues in the existing scriptures. We only need to find them and understand what they really say to this generation.

This is most important today, for there are leaders who say that we cannot know when Christ will return, it may be a long way off, it doesn't matter, just be ready any time, but are the individuals who listen to them prepared? Those who hear these people do not feel the urgency of being ready RIGHT NOW, it could happen at any time, and it has been like this ever since Jesus ascended.

I know of one man who has written several books and puts out a newsletter. He says that Jesus will probably not return until 2028, forty years after 1988. Those who hear this and believe it could be standing on dangerous ground, thinking that they have plenty of time to shape up. They can be caught at an hour when they are not alert.

Even though Christ walked among them, the Pharisees were not aware. They were the blind leading the blind. They should have been able to figure out the time of Messiah's first coming from Daniel 9:24-26, but they did not.

The things that happened to Israel are examples of what will happen in our days. First Corinthians 10:11,12 is clear.

> Now all these things happened unto them for ensamples: and they are written for our admonition, upon whom the ends of the world (ages) are come. Wherefore let him that thinketh he standeth take heed lest he fall.

We need to prepare ourselves RIGHT NOW. It is already urgent. The Rapture is very near. We must be wearing the white wedding garment, which is the righteousnesses of saints, when he appears. There will be no time to prepare ourselves after we see him. The Rapture will happen quickly. It is too late to prepare for the lightning after the thunder crashes. In Luke 12;1,2,56, Jesus warned,

> Beware ye of the leaven of the Pharisees, which is hypocrisy. For **there is nothing covered, that shall not be revealed; neither hid, that shall not be known**....Ye hypocrites (Pharisees), ye can discern the face of the sky and of the earth; but how is it that ye do not discern this **time**?

We have many Pharisees today. Like their first century counterparts, they cannot, will not, and do not want to even try to discern this time. Along with others, on this subject they are "Ever learning, and never able to come to the knowledge of the truth."[68]

I believe that the timing of the end time events is the church's portion of meat to be understood and taught in due season, when the church is old and gray headed, as John was in 96 A.D. and as the church is today.

> For every one that useth milk is unskilful in the word of righteousness: for he is a babe. But **strong meat belongeth to them that are of full age** (just before the Rapture).[69]

All the information we need to figure out the timing of end-time events is in Scripture. Since we are living in the time of the end, those receiving this meat today can be aware of when to expect Christ. We are supposed to be looking for his appearing when he comes for us at the Rapture.[70]

Israel is back in the land and the Sign of the End of the Age has already appeared. Israel has already grown leaves fulfilling the fig tree parable of Matthew 24:32-34. The terminal generation has already been born. (See *Exit: 2007, The Secret of Secrets Revealed.*[71])

John acts out resurrection

In our play, John is overwhelmed when he sees Christ, as were Ezekiel,[72] Daniel,[73] and Paul.[74] Jesus lays his right hand on him to show that John is one of the stars. John says,

> And when I saw him, I fell at his feet **as dead.** And he laid his right hand upon me, saying unto me, Fear not; I am the first and the last: I *am* he that liveth, and was dead; and, behold, I am alive for evermore. Amen; and have the keys of hell and of death.[75]

Instructions to the scribe

After simulating the resurrection of the dead that is part of the Rapture, as he brings John out of his swoon, Christ gives John the directions for writing the rest of the script. Both Jesus and John are in heaven right after the Rapture has taken place. Only now, in verse 19, does Christ say,

> Write the things which thou hast seen, and the things which **are** (NOW, at the Rapture), and the things which shall be hereafter.

The usual interpretation is that the things past are the Patmos vision, the things present are the churches, and the things future are the events after the Rapture. Influenced by well known scholars, I steadfastly held on to that interpretation for too many years. However, it is a bit skewed.

The beloved apostle was actually writing from the beginning of the vision. Verse three mentioned keeping "those things which are written." John was told in verse 11, "What thou seest, write in a book." He followed those instructions and immediately wrote of the things he saw in heaven at the time of the Rapture.

After recording that scene, he is again told to write. In verse 19, there are three parts to these instructions.

The first is to write the things he had seen, and the very next thing he writes is the message to the church of Ephesus. Following the Lord's instructions to the letter, he immediately begins to write about the churches that he had seen just before he was exiled to the island of Patmos.

I believe that the "things which thou hast seen" concern the seven churches that were literally contemporary with John. Eusebius of Caesarea, called the Father of Church History, said that John spent his final years in Ephesus.[76]

The "things which are" consist of the Rapture and the first view of the heavenly scene. The "things which shall be hereafter" are the events that follow the Rapture, such as the throne scene in heaven, the Tribulation on Earth, the second coming of Christ, Armageddon, and the Millennium.

When we understand that John was on Earth as this play began and was suddenly transported to be with the Lord in heaven, we can easily see that the Rapture is the only coming event that would bring that about. When he was told to write about the things that are, the most natural thing for him to do was to write about the Rapture, because he had just been caused to act it out and was standing with the Lord in heaven at the time. The Rapture fits the facts.

The Rapture is at hand

Jesus presented this play as if it was written on the very day the Rapture takes place. He stood at that point in time and looked both backward and forward to describe events of the past and future. His vantage point is the Rapture. Everything is viewed from this perspective. The Rapture is that pinnacle he stands on to view everything else.

This is an important issue. If we can grasp the fact that all of Revelation is written as if the Rapture was at hand, we can understand it so much better. As the title of this play tried to tell us, this is The Revelation of Jesus Christ, and he will be revealed to us at the Rapture.

Christ comes quickly at the Rapture. This is why it happened so lightning fast as our play began. It was because it was so totally unexpected that it took us by surprise. We had no chance to prepare for it. Neither will the foolish virgins or the Laodiceans. Our only chance is to prepare ahead of time. The wise virgins are ready.

In this play, Christ declares several times that he will come quickly. In Revelation 2:5, he tells the church of Ephesus, which means relax, that they have left their first love. He tells them to "repent" and then adds, **"or else I will come unto thee quickly,** and will remove thy candlestick out of his place." The whole candlestick can be taken out of His Place and be left to go through the Tribulation.

In Revelation 2:16, he says to the church of Pergamos, which means thoroughly married (i.e., to the world), "Repent; **or else I will come unto thee quickly,** and will fight against them (the Nicolaitanes) with the sword of my mouth." Those who separate the clergy from the laity can be cut off and appointed their portion with the unbelievers.

In contrast to these, in 3:11, Jesus tells the church of Philadelphia, which means brotherly love, "Behold, I come **quickly:** hold that fast which thou hast, that no man take thy crown." In all of these, he is talking about the Rapture when he says he comes quickly. At the second Advent, every eye will see him coming. That could take longer.

As Christ signs off in the last chapter of Revelation, he mentions coming quickly three times. They all obviously represent the Rapture, which is the next prophesied event.

These sayings *are* faithful and true: and the Lord God of the holy prophets sent his angel to shew unto his servants the things which must shortly be done. Behold, **I come quickly:** blessed *is* he that keepeth the sayings of the prophecy of this book.[77]

This ties directly in with the beginning of chapter one; the first verse mentions "things which must shortly come to pass." The last chapter calls them "the things which must shortly be done" and adds, "Behold, I come quickly," referring to the Rapture. Verses 12-14 say,

> And, behold, **I come quickly**; and my reward *is* with me, to give every man according as his work shall be. I am Alpha and Omega, the beginning and the end, the first (Yahweh) and the last (Jesus Christ). Blessed *are* they that do his commandments, that they may have right to the tree of life, and may enter in through the gates into the city (in heaven).

The Alpha and Omega, the beginning and the end, also tie in with chapter one. "He which testifieth these things saith, Surely **I come quickly**" in verse 20.

THE VANTAGE POINT FROM WHICH REVELATION IS TO BE VIEWED IS WHEN THE RAPTURE IS AT HAND

From beginning to end, the vantage point from which all events in this play are to be viewed is that particular Sunday when the Rapture is at hand. Things either happen before the Rapture, at the time of the Rapture, or after the Rapture. John is told to write the things he saw just before it happens, "the things which are" at the time of the Rapture, and things that will follow during the Tribulation.

This interpretation reveals a secret—that the Rapture will take place on Sunday. That would be the best possible day for resurrection because Christ arose on Sunday, the Lord's Day. When John said that he became in the Spirit "on the Lord's day," he immediately heard Christ's voice like a trumpet talking with him just as we will hear Christ right after the Rapture transports us to the assembly area in Heaven.

Luke 17:22-26 shows that the Rapture is "one of the days of the Son of man." It is not the only one. The Rapture is the Son's day, that Sunday when we will see Christ's face shining "as the sun shineth in his strength."[78]

The Secret of the Stairs

I believe the Rapture will be at hand on a Sunday in the springtime. Solomon, the son of David, the wisest of men, is a type of Christ, the Son of David.[79] In the Song of Solomon 2:8-14, we are given some excellent clues to show when the Rapture will take place. This is my favorite passage of Scripture. It is a beautiful picture to focus on when you need cheering up. It reminds me of Jacob's ladder.

The Secret of the Stairs

The voice of my beloved! (Christ) behold, he cometh leaping upon the mountains, skipping upon the hills...My beloved spake, and said unto me, Rise up, my love, my fair one, and come away. For, lo, the winter is past, the rain is over and gone; The flowers appear on the earth; the time of the singing of birds is come, and the voice of the turtle is heard in our land; The fig tree putteth forth her green figs, and the vines with the tender grape give a good smell. Arise, my love, my fair one, and come away. O my dove, that art in the clefts of the rock (Christ), in the secret *places* of the stairs.

The word "places" is not in the original. It was supplied by the translators. This is the secret of the stairs. It is the Rapture being acted out. In Revelation 4:1, Christ says, "Come up hither." In the Song of Solomon he says, "Rise up, my love, my fair one, (the Bride of Christ) and come away (the Rapture). For, lo, the winter is past (it is spring), the rain is over and gone." The latter rain of the Jewish Nisan[80] (our March/April) is over.

"The flowers appear on the Earth (it is May, when April showers bring May flowers); the time of the singing of birds is come (spring, when we will sing "a new song" as we migrate and fly up to heaven[81]), and **the voice** of the turtle (*tor*, turtle dove, a migratory bird that returns suddenly in the spring and is a symbol of the Spirit of Christ;[82]) is heard in our land" (i.e., the voice that says, "Rise up.")

"The fig tree (Israel[83]) putteth forth her green figs (the fruit of Israel is not yet ripe when the Rapture takes place), and the vines with the tender grape give a good smell (it is the time of the firstripe grapes, the same time of the year that the Israelites spied out their promised land in the Jewish month of Sivan,[84] the month of the Feast of Pentecost). **Arise,** my love, my fair one and **come away** (the Rapture). O my dove (one sealed with the Spirit of God until the day of Redemption), that art in the clefts of the rock (in Christ, for "that Rock was Christ"[85]), in the secret of the stairs."

Like Jacob's ladder, the top of the stairs reaches to heaven, angels ascend and descend on it and the Lord stands above it. At the Rapture, we will go up these symbolic stairs and through a great door in heaven to stand before our Lord.

God has given us exciting time clues. It is not dreary winter, or even autumn, when the Feast of Trumpets is celebrated, but beautiful spring, and after the latter rain, every sprig is coming to life with lush foliage. Spring is appropriate for it is a time of resurrection, not only of growing things, but Christ was resurrected in the spring, and some of the Body of Christ are to be resurrected at the Rapture. The green figs enable us to place the Rapture between the end of the latter rain (the Jewish Nisan, our March/April) and the end of May or early June, when the early figs ripen.

The Lord's timing is perfect. Beautiful spring puts us in the mood to fly as soon as we hear the voice saying, "Come up hither." We will be transported to the third heaven to visit our habitation[86] while the Tribulation takes place.

Did you notice that in Song of Solomon, the Lord "cometh leaping upon the mountains, skipping upon the hills"? Think of Jacob's ladder. It had steps reaching to Heaven. There are stepping stones on the way to the "third heaven" Paul told us about in II Corinthians 12:1-3:

I will come to visions and **revelation of the Lord**. I knew a man in Christ above

43

fourteen years ago, (whether in the body, I cannot tell; or whether out of the body, I cannot tell: God knoweth;) such an one **caught up to the third heaven**...he was caught up into paradise.

This man also played out the Rapture, when the Lord will be revealed. He was caught up to the third heaven, showing that there are at least three heavens, and Paradise is on the third one. The other two here are like stepping stones along the way. Remember this, we will see how important it is as the play progresses.

Pentecost, the Jewish Sivan 6, falls in the narrow time slot described in the Song of Solomon, and a trumpet will be blown that day as it is on each of the Jewish feasts. I believe that when the rains are over in Israel and the migratory birds have returned, when the green figs, firstripe grapes and May flowers appear, that this trump will sound and we will be caught up to heaven on Pentecost Sunday. On that day, the firstborn sons were to be brought into the house of God at the same time the firstfruits of the ground were to be brought into the house of the Lord.[87]

In Revelation 4:1, at the Rapture, the Lord speaks with the voice of a trumpet, saying, "Come up hither." Exodus 19:13 says, "when the trumpet soundeth long, they shall come up to the mount." The first trump was on Pentecost.

The clincher seems to be in the line, "The...voice of the turtle (turtle dove) (i.e., the Holy Spirit) is heard in our land (Israel)." The Holy Spirit descended on the church on Sivan 6, Pentecost Sunday in 30 A.D. Jesus ascended on the 40th day after his resurrection, but the Holy Spirit descended on Pentecost, the 50th day, to demonstrate something special. Think of what Job 11:5,6 says,

> **THE SECRETS OF WISDOM...THEY ARE DOUBLE TO THAT WHICH IS!**

That verse has helped me find many secrets hidden in the pages of Scripture. Don't ever forget that the Lord teaches by using types, similitudes, examples, or likenesses

44

that are like carbon copies of past events. Scripture's history of the Israelites is chock full of them.

The secret revealed by the day of the Holy Spirit's descent could become fulfilled prophecy very soon. Pentecost means fifty. Fifty years from when Israel became a nation in 1948 is 1998. If the coming of the Holy Spirit on Pentecost was a type of Christ coming for his Bride, the Rapture could take place on Pentecost Sunday, May 31, 1998, the very **last time** Pentecost will fall on Sunday before the Lord returns. It is the **only time** Pentecost falls on Sunday within the remainder of the 40-year generation since the Sign of the End of the Age, the Six-Day War of 1967. We won't have to wait long to find out. Personally, I expect the Rapture to take place on Pentecost, May 31, 1998.

Whether on that day or on some other day, the Rapture is soon. We stand at the same place that John did when Jesus Christ gave him his messages for the seven churches in 96 A.D. The Rapture is at hand.

The Rapture is to be a day of assembly, and *panegurei* means a public festal assembly. It looks possible that the Pentecostal period begins and ends on the Feast of Pentecost in the first Jubilee since Israel was reborn as a nation.

If the Rapture is to take place at night, as suggested by the parable of the ten virgins, this resurrection of the dead in Christ will be similar to the resurrection of Christ himself. He arose in the night. By dawn on Sunday morning, the tomb was empty.

Jesus is the head of the Body of Christ. Believers are the body. Since the head arose in the night, it would be very fitting for more of the body to arise in the night. I want to be ready at 6:00 P.M. Saturday, for that is when the Jewish Sunday begins. Our Lord Jesus Christ commanded us to

> **Watch** ye therefore: for ye know not when the master of the house cometh, at even, or at midnight, or at the cockcrowing, or in the morning (please take heed; he did not mention that we do not know the day): Lest coming suddenly he find you sleeping. And what I say unto you I say unto all, **Watch**.[88]

Chapter 1, The Vantage Point

In "Pentecost a Type of the Rapture," Gary Steadman said Ruth lay at the feet of Boaz, her kinsman redeemer, on Pentecost. Boaz found her at midnight but married her later. Like the Jews who stay up all night on Pentecost, I want to stay up on Pentecost in 1998, starting when it begins in Jerusalem. In "Legends of the Jews," H. L. Ginzberg said Enoch was raptured on Pentecost. Others say he was born on Sivan 6 too, good signs that both the birth and Rapture of the Church will be on Sivan 6, Pentecost.

We are not to watch for the Antichrist, but for the real Messiah to appear. Christ will come before the Tribulation begins. The wicked one cannot be revealed until the Bride of Christ is gone. We are the salt that keeps the leaven from rising. Second Thessalonians 2:6-9 in the New Scofield Reference Bible says,

> And now ye know what restraineth (the Holy Spirit restrains him) that he might be revealed in his time. For the mystery of iniquity doth already work; only he (the Holy Spirit) who now hindereth will continue to hinder until he be taken out of the way (when he takes the saints to Heaven in the Rapture). And then shall that wicked one be revealed, whom the Lord shall consume with the spirit of his mouth, and shall destroy with the brightness of his coming, Even him whose coming is after the working of Satan with all power and signs and lying wonders.

We must make ourselves worthy of the prize to be able to go to Heaven in the first Rapture. Overcomers are promised to eat of the Tree of Life, not to be hurt of the second death, to eat of the hidden manna, to be given the morning star, to not have their names blotted out of the Book of Life, to be pillars in the temple of God, and to sit with Christ in his throne. Salvation is a free gift, but we can run the race and win the prize of being in this privileged group that will be taken to Heaven in Rapture I. Only this group will be counted as a member of the Bride of Christ. Please be ready.

[1] Daniel 12:4
[2] I Peter 1:13
[3] I Corinthians 10:11
[4] John 21:21
[5] Isaiah 28:13
[6] Hebrews 12:22-34
[7] Revelation 3:12
[8] Thayer's Lexicon, p. 439
[9] Hosea 9:10; Joel 1:6,7; Ezekiel 36:8
[10] Matthew 24:21,22; Daniel 8:14
[11] Matthew 24:22
[12] Amos 8:9,10
[13] Romans 8:1
[14] Genesis 3:4
[15] Ezekiel 37:35
[16] II Corinthians 12:2-4
[17] John 3:16
[18] John 14:1
[19] Revelation 1:1,2
[20] Revelation 19:10
[21] I Corinthians 10:11, NASB
[22] Revelation 1:3
[23] Thayer's Lexicon, p. 164
[24] John 6:21
[25] Matthew 19:26
[26] Matthew 25:6
[27] Mark 13:35
[28] Matthew 25:1-12
[29] Revelation 3:10
[30] Jeremiah 38:13
[31] Genesis 2:7
[32] Revelation 5:9
[33] Psalms 50:2
[34] Revelation 1:3
[35] NRSV
[36] John 10:30
[37] Revelation 1:4-6
[38] Revelation 1:8
[39] Or Jehovah
[40] John 8:19-28
[41] John 1:1,14
[42] I Corinthians 15:47
[43] John 5:22
[44] Daniel 8:14

[45] Matthew 24:30
[46] Zechariah 14:4
[47] Acts 1:11,12
[48] Matthew 24:36
[49] Acts 20:7; I Corinthians 16:2
[50] Revelation 3:20
[51] Titus 2:12-14
[52] Revelation 3:19
[53] John 14:2
[54] Job 11:6
[55] Luke 23:43
[56] Revelation 1:12-16
[57] Philippians 2:15
[58] Malachi 4:2
[59] Matthew 17:2
[60] Isaiah 9:6
[61] Ezekiel 1:27, NEB
[62] John 5:22
[63] Luke 12:35,36
[64] Matthew 25:1-13
[65] Revelation 2:16
[66] I Peter 2:5
[67] Deuteronomy 11:14; Psalm 145:15
[68] II Timothy 3:7
[69] Hebrews 5:13,14
[70] Revelation 3:3
[71] Archer Press, 8641 Sugar Gum Rd., Riverside, CA 92508
[72] Ezekiel 1:28
[73] Daniel 10:9
[74] Acts 22:7
[75] Revelation 1:17
[76] Unger's Bible Dictionary, p. 316
[77] Revelation 22:6,7
[78] Revelation 1:16
[79] Matthew 15:22
[80] In Israel, the former rain starts in Tishri, the latter rain in Nisan
[81] Revelation 5:9
[82] Romans 8:9
[83] Hosea 9:10; Joel 1:6,7; Ezekiel 36:8
[84] Numbers 13:20, Unger. *op cit*, p. 164
[85] I Corinthians 10:4
[86] Job 5:24
[87] Nehemiah 10:35,36
[88] Mark 13:35-37

2

Torchbearer's Wake-Up Call

Revelation 2 and 3

𝔄 gold prospector half his life, now turned painter, came to my house to tell me how much he liked my first book. He said he died twice, at two different times—and went to hell.

Both times, doctors revived him after his heart attacks and he was given another chance. Few are so lucky.

He has now accepted Christ as his own personal Saviour, and although not much of a reader in the past, has read his Bible all the way through except some of the book of Judges. He told me, "You can't believe how terrible it is to be in a dark place without God."

Like the apostle Paul, his unusual experience turned him around. It was his wake-up call. He now talks about Christ and the Bible to those who will listen. He knows how important it is.

I think of him as I listen to our play, "The Revelation of Jesus Christ," and hear these words repeat like a chorus near the end of each message to the seven churches:

> He that hath an ear, let him hear what the
> Spirit saith unto the churches.[1]

The Lord is good at loading his vehicles with extras. Man could never have packed so much information into such a small book as the Bible. There seems to be no end to what we can learn. This alone proves divine inspiration. It is only possible for one who knows the end from the beginning.

In these messages to the seven churches, we can detect different layers of meaning. They are all examples of various members of the church on Earth just before the Rapture takes place. At the same time, they present the only panoramic view of the entire church age given in Scripture. The early fulfillment helps us identify these groups today.

In each of the first five messages, the Lord digs into the past and gives us a glimpse of one segment of church history, then stretches it up to the present time, just before the Rapture. The sequence of the segments fits the history of the church exactly.

Like a waterfall, there is overflow from one phase to another. Once an evil is introduced, the dye it produces colors the water all the way down. There are still those on Earth who are in young churches that have left their first love, who are persecuted for their faith, who hold the doctrines of Balaam and the Nicolaitanes, who are under the Papacy, and who are in state churches or denominations formed during the days of the Reformation.

Most of the over comers of the first five churches are already DEAD. They are the dead in Christ, those who sleep in Jesus who will come with Christ when he comes for us at the Rapture. Yet, all five groups have living members today. We can be sure of this because the descriptions of Christ are extracted from our view of him at the Rapture. There are also other statements that apply to the time when the Rapture is at hand or to the Tribulation that follows the Rapture of the church.

The church of Ephesus hears "repent, and do the first works; or else I will come unto thee quickly, and will remove thy candlestick out of **his place** (Heaven)." Christ comes quickly at the Rapture and transfers the candlesticks to His Place. Our light must be shining brightly, or our candlestick will be removed from Heaven. Matthew 5:16 says,

> Let your light so shine before men, **that they may see your good works**, and glorify your Father which is in heaven.

The message to Smyrna is not as clear cut. She hears that "the devil shall cast *some* of you into prison, that ye may be tried; and ye shall have tribulation ten days: be thou faithful unto death, and I will give thee a crown of life." Crowns are given at the Rapture, and the trial that follows is the Tribulation, when the devil indwells the False Prophet and persecutes the saints.

Some will "have tribulation ten days." This is a type of the ten year period on the Jewish calendar (nine on ours) from the Rapture of the church Saints in 5758 to the Rapture of the Tribulation Saints in 5768, on the last day of the 2,300-day Shortened Tribulation.[2] That day is also the Feast of Trumpets, the Jewish New Year, and the first 24-hour day of the 1,000-year Day of the Lord called the Millennium.

The church in Pergamos, hears "Repent; or else I will come unto thee quickly, and will fight against them with the sword of my mouth." Christ comes quickly at the Rapture, and we saw a sharp two-edged sword coming out of his mouth at the time of the Rapture.

After some time to repent, Thyatira hears,

> I will cast her into a bed, and them that commit adultery (join) with her into great tribulation...as many as have not this doctrine, and which have not known the depths of Satan, as they speak...hold fast **till I come.** And he that overcometh, and keepeth my works unto the end, to him will I give power over the nations:[3]

This coming is the Rapture. The Great Tribulation is the last part of the Shortened Tribulation, when Satan inhabits the Israeli False Prophet. The end refers to the consummation of this age at the end of the Great Tribulation.

The message to Sardis reveals that if we do watch, we will know when Jesus will come at the Rapture. He said,

> **If therefore thou shalt not watch,** I will come on thee as a thief, and **thou shalt not know what hour I will come** upon thee.[4]

If we watch, he will not come on us as a thief, and we will know when he will come. Some of these over comers are ALIVE at the Rapture. They are either **watching, and know** what hour he will come upon them, **or not watching, and will not know** what hour he will come.

Christ mentions some things in these five messages that obviously stretch past the Rapture. They are examples of things to come during the seven-year Tribulation. There will be new churches and another time of persecution. Satan will have his own men on his throne during those years. The first beast of Revelation thirteen will rule during the first half. The False Prophet will rule during the last part, the Great Tribulation. Those that commit adultery (join) with "Jezebel," the harlot,[5] are to be cast into the Great Tribulation. Death will strike the harlot church's children. This death is both literal and symbolic. Revelation 6:8 says,

> And I looked, and behold a pale horse: and his name that sat on him was **Death** (the False Prophet), and Hell (Satan) followed with him.[6] And power was given unto them over the fourth part of the earth, to kill with sword, and with hunger, and with **death**, and with the beasts of the earth:

The Tribulation saints are those who have "defiled their garments."[7] When they appear in heaven, they will have "washed their robes, and made them white in the blood of the Lamb.[8] They are purified during the ten Jewish years between the Raptures. Revelation 7:14-16 describes them:

> These are they which came out of great tribulation (i.e., the last part), and have washed their robes, and made them white in the blood of the Lamb. Therefore are they before the throne of God, and serve him day and night in his temple: and he that sitteth on the throne shall dwell among them. They shall hunger no more, neither thirst any more; neither shall the sun light on them, nor any heat.

In the last two messages Jesus sends to our churches of today, he does not touch on church history at all. He addresses individuals within the entire splintered church on Earth. All church groups are represented. These are mainly the believers who are still ALIVE when the Rapture is at hand. They have the chance to be translated to heaven without having to die. Christians of this last generation,[9] are among them.

These living Christians are of two types, those who display clear evidence of being filled with the Holy Spirit—brotherly love—and those who are indifferent, neither cold nor hot. The church in Philadelphia represents the former, the church of the Laodiceans the latter. The wise virgins represent the Philadelphians. They are clad in the white wedding garments. The foolish virgins[10] are the Laodiceans. They do not have on white wedding garments and do not even realize that they are not worthy to be chosen as the Bride of Christ because their light is not bright.

In Luke 11:33 in the Phillips translation, Jesus warns,

> No one takes a lamp and puts it in a cupboard or under a bucket, but on a lampstand, so that those who come in can see the light. The lamp of your body is your eye. When your eye is sound, your whole body is full of light, but when your eye is evil your whole body is full of darkness. So **be very careful that your light never becomes darkness** (the Laodiceans are 'blind'[11]). For if your whole body is full of light, with no part of it **in shadow**, it will all be radiant—it will be like having a bright lamp to give you light.

We must not let our light diminish and become shadow if we want to be chosen as the Bride of Christ. Remember, the Bride always wears white. She shines like the stars.

The methods Satan has used to combat the church are clearly seen in these messages. However, in spite of every thing he has been able to do, over comers emerge from all seven phases. All believers from the past, the present, and even the future Tribulation, will stand with the Lord in heaven at the consummation of this age. Those who go to heaven in the Rapture before the Tribulation, are the church saints. Those who go just before the seven trumpet judgments hit on the Feast of Trumpets that kicks off the Millennium are the Tribulation saints.

As our play began, John was quickly transported to heaven in the Rapture, a long missed point. He was privileged to be able to view Christ in his glory. Then Jesus told him to "Write the things which thou hast seen (the state of the churches), and the things which are (the Rapture), and the things which shall be hereafter."[12]

Before he can begin to write, the scene changes abruptly. We have a flashback so John can record things he has seen in the past.

Instant replay of the Preview

What we have already seen turns out to be a preview of where this Act is taking us. In case the Rapture happened too fast for us to be sure it took place, it will be acted out again, almost like instant replay. The preview also should help us recognize the Rapture when it happens at the end of these seven messages. It will happen quickly, as before. As lightning flashes unexpectedly, the Rapture will take place for any believer in a single stroke of time. The wise virgins will be transported to heaven, the foolish ones left behind. Be forewarned. Stay alert or you can miss it again.

Suddenly, John is back on the island of Patmos. The curtain of the sky is closed behind him. The Rapture is again at hand.[13] Jesus is no longer visible, but we have seen the preview so we know how he looks when the Rapture takes place. We have a better chance this time to recognize the Rapture. In the preview, the Lord looked much the same as when Daniel saw him just before Gabriel made him understand what would happen in the latter days. Daniel said,

> I lifted up mine eyes, and looked, and behold
> a certain man clothed in linen, whose loins

were girded with fine gold of Uphaz: His body also was like the beryl, and his face as the appearance of lightning, and his eyes as lamps of fire, and his arms and his feet like in colour to polished brass, and the voice of his words like the voice of a multitude.[14]

Brass is a symbol of judgment. He is judging the church, to choose his Bride from among the entire professing church. Bride and Bridegroom must love each other.

He is stationed on the other side of a closed door beyond the soft blue of the atmospheric curtain. The door, a symbol of the Rapture, will open in Revelation 3:8. A description of what happens after it opens is in Revelation 4:1.

"THE THINGS WHICH THOU HAST SEEN"

In our mind's eye, we see the white-robed John sit on a rock, unroll his sheepskin scroll, and position his pen to write the things that he has seen on Earth. We are taken back to just before the Rapture snaps us up. Jesus is going to show us how the church looks to him at that time.

THE LORD'S MONOLOGUE: PART 1

Message to Ephesus
In the viewfinder: those who have left their first love
Here the Lord launches into his monologue. It is addressed to the churches just before the Rapture, and there are seven sections because seven means complete. We stand at this point in time right now and should take these warnings to heart. His script is found in Revelation two and three.

UNTO the angel of the church of Ephesus write; These things saith he that holdeth (present tense) the seven stars in his right hand, who walketh (right now) in the midst of the seven golden candlesticks;[15]

The preview of the Rapture and our view of Christ at that time was presented so we would accept his authority because he is the Almighty, also so we would understand that all seven messages to the churches apply to the churches of today. We have already seen him in heaven in the midst of the seven golden candlesticks with the seven stars in his right hand at the time of the Rapture. The repetition of sections of this description of him in the messages to the churches drums it into us that the Rapture is at hand.

The word Ephesus means desirable one, relax, let go. The city, about halfway between Jerusalem and Rome, has been thought to have been Paul's home for two years and John's for 30. John probably wrote his Gospel and three Epistles there. Its Temple of Artemis was one of the Seven Wonders of Antiquity. The church of Ephesus appropriately represents the young first-century church. That was the apostolic era, and John was the last apostle alive. However, it applies to us today also.

Right after the Holy Spirit descended on Pentecost in 30 A.D., the church was desirable as a bride because of it's exuberant young love of Christ. It was joyous, enthusiastic and Spirit filled. But, by 96 A.D., the members had already begun to relax and let go of their first love. Listen as Jesus continues his monologue:

> I know thy works, and thy labour, and thy patience, and how thou canst not bear them which are evil: and thou hast tried them which say they are apostles, and are not, and hast found them liars (or false): And hast borne, and hast patience, and for my name's sake hast laboured, and hast not fainted. Nevertheless I have (right now) *somewhat* against thee, because thou hast left thy first love (*agapen*).[16]

Patience is important. It is mentioned here twice, and again in both the fourth and sixth messages. The Greek word used, *hupomonen*, means a patient, steadfast waiting. This kind of patience will be well rewarded at the Rapture.

Those early false apostles were forerunners of the great liars to come, the as yet unrecognized Beast[17] and False Prophet. The final False Prophet will be the *pseudo-prophetes*, a pretend foreteller, who will end up as Satan's robotic body during the last half of the Tribulation—the Great Tribulation. His thoughts and actions will be totally controlled by Satan. His words will be Satan's words.[18]

Apostles are not mentioned again in these messages, thus reinforcing the conclusion that Ephesus represents the apostolic church. They obey Romans 16:17, which says to "mark them who cause divisions and offenses contrary to the doctrine which ye have learned; and avoid them."

The hot-blooded early love of these Ephesians has cooled. They have yielded up some of their first love. Sin has quenched the Spirit to some extent. First Corinthians 13:2,3 shows that even though we do great things, we must have God's love, *agape*.

> And if I have the gift of prophecy, and know all mysteries and all knowledge; and if I have all faith, so as to remove mountains, but do not have love, I am nothing. And if I give all my possessions to feed the poor, and if I deliver my body to be burned, but do not have love, it profits me nothing.[19]

One of the characteristics of the essence of God is love. We have his love in us if we are filled with his Holy Spirit. It is the fruit of the Spirit.[20] First John 4:13-17 says,

> Hereby know we that we dwell in him, and he in us, because he hath given us of his Spirit. And we have seen and do testify that the Father sent the Son to be the Saviour of the world. Whosoever shall confess that Jesus is the Son of God, God dwelleth in him, and he in God. And we have known and believed the love that God hath to us. God is love (*agape*); and he that dwelleth in love (*agape*) dwelleth in God, and God in him.

First Thessalonians 5:19 says, "Quench not the Spirit." Sin quenches the Spirit. Therefore God's love is suppressed and the level recedes. The sinner's light becomes shadow.

The Ephesians left their first love. The word translated "left" is *aphekas* in the Greek, which means to yield up, emit. Some of the Spirit has been emitted.

This ties in with the meanings of Ephesus: "relax" and "let go." The Ephesians are no longer filled with the Holy Spirit. To be filled, as they were when they first believed, they have to confess their sins. This is why Christ tells them to repent.

> Remember therefore from whence thou art fallen, and **repent,** and do the first works; **or else** I will come unto thee quickly (at the Rapture), and will remove thy candlestick out of **his place** (Heaven), except thou repent.[21]

Repentance causes confession of our sins to God. Confession brings forgiveness. Forgiveness allows the Holy Spirit, called a fountain of living water, to well up within us and fill us with God's love. Jesus said, "He that believeth on me, as the scripture hath said, out of his belly shall flow rivers of living waters."[22]

"If we confess our sins," according to 1 John 1:9, "he is faithful and just to forgive us our sins, and to cleanse us from all unrighteousness." Forgiveness makes it possible for us to be filled with the Holy Spirit for it gets rid of the barrier sin places between us and our Holy God. If we are filled with his Holy Spirit, we have *agape* love.

We can be sure that this message carries forward to the present day, because Jesus says to repent "or else I will come unto thee quickly." He comes quickly at the Rapture. Ephesus also prefigures similar young churches in our days. We must take this message to heart. It is intended for today.

Christ continues his message to the Ephesians:

> But this thou hast, that thou hatest the deeds of the Nicolaitanes, which I also hate.[23]

The word Nicolaitanes means people conquerors, from *nikao*, to conquer, and *laos*, the people. It is symbolic of the ascendancy of the hierarchical clergy. It will culminate in the rule of the Satanic False Prophet.

Certain men declared themselves to be above and to have power over the people. Instead of being servants of the congregations, following the example set by Jesus, they became supreme rulers who could dictate to the people below. Believers were divided into priests and laity.

Although it is clear that there are to be leaders in each assembly—bishops, deacons, elders—the Bible calls all believers priests. First Peter 2:5 shows that even those of the dispersion are priests. Peter addresses them when he says, "Ye also, as lively stones, are built up a spiritual house, an holy priesthood, to offer up spiritual sacrifices, acceptable to God by Jesus Christ."

The titles Rabbi, Father, and Master are forbidden. Matthew 23:8,9 is explicit. Jesus said,

> But be not ye called Rabbi: for one is your Master, even Christ; and all ye are brethren. And **call no man your father** upon the earth: for one is your Father, which is in heaven. Neither be ye called masters: for one is your Master, even Christ. But he that is greatest among you shall be your servant. And **whosoever shall exalt himself shall be abased**; and he that shall humble himself shall be exalted.

Nick, especially Old Nick, means the Devil, Satan.[24] The Devil is behind the Nicolaitane cancer growing within the church. One of the meanings of the verb nick is to catch off guard, to trick, cheat, defraud, and this is precisely his intent. If we are not careful, he will trick us by catching us off guard.

This cancer will grow until the Devil places his own Satan-possessed man on the throne, not only over the whole church left on Earth during the Tribulation, but over all people, tongues, and nations. He will be both high priest (top religious leader) and king (top political leader) of the world, usurping offices and titles that rightfully belong to Christ. Look out! This is where this New World Order so often mentioned in the news recently is headed.

Promise to over comers

Jesus concludes his message to Ephesus with these words:

> He that hath an ear, let him hear what the Spirit saith unto the churches; To him that overcometh (right now) will I give to eat of the tree of life, which is in the midst of the paradise of God (the heavenly one).[25]

It is vital that we take heed of what the Spirit says to the churches now that the Rapture is at hand, so we will hear his "Come up hither." He will give the tree of life, which imparts immortal life, to those who are caught away to Paradise, in the third heaven.[26]

How can we be over comers? First, we must believe that Jesus is the Son of God and be filled with the Holy Spirit. Second, every time we sin, we can pray, confess our sin to God, and ask forgiveness. This way, we keep in fellowship and are wearing white wedding garments.

The Sovereign of the universe decided that belief in Christ was the way to be saved before man was ever created. It is an immutable law. There is no other way in spite of what the many counterfeit religions Satan has perpetrated have to say. It is not enough to be on the path, seeking.

The Old Testament saints believed in him as Yahweh. We believe in him as Yeshua, or Jesus, which means Yahweh is Saviour.

First John 5:5 asks, "Who is he that overcometh the world, but he that believeth that Jesus is the Son of God?" Christianity is the only true religion and Jesus, the Son of God, the only true Saviour. Acts 4:12 shuts out anyone else, declaring: "**Neither is there salvation in any other: for there is none other name under heaven given among men, whereby we must be saved.**" If you believe that it doesn't matter which religion you choose, you believe a lie.

THE LORD'S MONOLOGUE: PART 2

Message to Smyrna
In the viewfinder: the persecuted church

Smyrna means myrrh or bitterness, which is connected with death and resurrection. Myrrh has to be crushed and beaten small to give forth its fragrance.

Used for embalming the dead, it foreshadowed his death when the wise men gave it to the babe in the manger. Those wise men recognized their signs. They actually were wise. They understood who he was, the time of his coming, what he came to do, and that they should bring him expensive gifts. In our days also, "the wise shall understand,"[27] but as then, they will be in the minority. We also have many Pharisees who do not recognize the signs and few wise men who do.

Irenaeus said that John appointed Polycarp bishop of Smyrna. This was the church under persecution. During this phase, the ancient Roman Empire tried to eradicate the faith of Christ from the Earth. The church was crushed and beaten small. The more she was beaten, the more fragrant her testimony. Martyrs met the lions and the burnings at the stake with brave words, praising God, singing psalms, and quoting Scripture.

Significant threatening words, beginning with tribulation, echo menacingly through this message. Tribulation— poverty—suffer—prison—death—all reverberate in our ears. Not one word of rebuke is given this brave church that is willing to defend their faith at the risk of their lives. All who are martyrs for their faith are given white robes.[28] During the Tribulation, martyrs will be beheaded.[29]

The full application of the message extends to the end of this age. During the Great Tribulation, the World Empire will again try to eradicate the faith of Christ from the Earth. People will again have to defend their faith at the risk of their lives. In Revelation 6:9, we see "under the altar the souls of them that were slain for the word of God, and for the testimony which they held." There is no condemnation for the persecuted saints of the Tribulation. They wear white.[30]

As the Lord continues his monologue, he speaks to Smyrna and identifies himself as the first and the last:

> And unto the angel of the church in Smyrna write; These things saith the first [Yahweh] and the last [Jesus Christ], which was dead, and is alive [just as Christ said in the preview, showing that this is when the Rapture is at hand]; I know thy works, and tribulation, and poverty, (but thou art rich) and *I know* the blasphemy of them which say they are Jews, and are not, but *are* the synagogue of Satan.[31]

Why anyone would say they are Jews when they are not, I cannot understand. However, we have those today who claim that the British are the ten lost tribes of Israel. The Lord has seen to it that the Jews have retained their physical identity wherever they are. They are easy to pick out in a crowd. Do the British people have Jewish features?

Jesus' warning should cause anyone to take a long careful look at any such claim. My grandmother, born in London, came over here from Stratford-on-Avon when she was sixteen and married a man whose parents came here from Willenhall, England in 1840. Locksmiths in England, they became farmers here. They were staunch Methodists, as were my parents. (Me—I'm Methodist-become-Baptist.) My dad was straitlaced British through and through. He had light sandy-brown hair and had the same type of distinctive appearance as the Duke of Windsor. Dad wouldn't have dared claim to be of the ten lost tribes of Israel; neither would I.

Jesus continues:

> Fear none of those things which thou shalt suffer: behold, the devil shall cast *some* of you (the ones left behind at the Rapture) into prison, that ye may be tried; and ye (Tribulation saints) shall have tribulation ten days (time periods, i.e., ten times, or ten

years): be thou faithful unto death, and I will
give thee a crown of life.[32]

During the years between 96 A.D., when John
recorded The Revelation, and 313 A.D., there were ten re-
curring waves of deadly brutality under Roman Emperors
plus some relatively minor ones. The first persecution began
during the reign of Domitian in 96. They built in intensity
during the reigns of Trajan, Hadrian, Antonius Pius, Marcus
Aurelius, Severus, Decius, Valerian, and Aurelian. The
worst came last. It raged during the **ten years** from the
three edicts of Diocletian in 303 to Constantine's Edict of
Milan in 313.

These ten years prefigure things to come in the ten-
year period, on the Jewish calendar, between the two Raptures. There will certainly be martyrs.[33]

Domitian, who was ruling the Roman Empire in 96
A.D., called himself "Lord and God" and had some forty
thousand Christians killed. The apostle John himself was
exiled to the isle of Patmos during his rule.

Under cruel Trajan, **Simeon,** bishop of Jerusalem,
half-brother of Jesus Christ, was crucified when
120 years old. Ignatius, bishop of Antioch, was also killed.

The most barbarous and cruel of all the persecutions,
was under Marcus Aurelius. Thousands of Christians died,
Justin Martyr among them. Bodies were stacked in piles in
the streets.

Septimius Servius forbade the spread of both Christianity and Judaism. Leonidas, whose son was Origen, the
theologian, was killed.

Emperor Decius tried to exterminate Christianity per-
manently. There were more martyrs at that time than in any
previous persecution.

Valerian was even worse. He tried to undermine
Christianity by inflicting the death penalty on the leaders of
the church.

The tenth persecution, started in 303 under Diocletian
and lasting **ten years**, was the worst one of all. He was
determined to abolish even the name Christian. He issued
edicts saying that all Christian churches were to be razed,

Bibles were to be burned, and Christians were to be deprived of civil rights and required to sacrifice to the pagan gods on pain of death. This will repeat in the Tribulation.

During those early years of the church, Christians were fed to lions, crucified, covered with tar and set on fire, boiled in oil, and burned at the stake, as was Polycarp, a disciple of the apostle John, about 156 A.D. Some estimate that five million Christians were killed during those terrible times.

It is awful to think that this horror will repeat during the Great Tribulation, the last part of the seven years. Some Christians will suffer tribulation during ten revolutions of time between the Rapture of the Bride of Christ and the Rapture of the rest of the Body of Christ, the Tribulation saints.

During the rule of the False Prophet, he will try to abolish the name Christian. He and the ten kings will burn churches,[34] Bibles and Christian books. Christians will be deprived of civil rights, including banking rights, and required to bow down to another god on pain of death.

Promise to overcomers
Jesus says,

> He that hath an ear, let him hear what the Spirit saith (right now, at the time of the Rapture) unto the churches; He that overcometh shall not be hurt of the second death.[35] (The second death is in the lake of fire.[36])

THE LORD'S MONOLOGUE: PART 3

Message to Pergamos
In the viewfinder: the church under imperial favor
Pergamos was the political capital of Asia Minor. It was famous for its extensive library of 200,000 volumes. Parchment was invented there.

This is the city where the first temple had been erected long ago to worship the Emperor as a god. Pergamos became a city of temples dedicated to idol worship. Its grove was filled with statues. There was a temple dedicated to Æsculapius, the god of health, symbolized by the serpent. The caduceus, symbol of the medical profession today, was his symbol. There was a great temple dedicated to Zeus, called *Soter Theos*, the savior god, another one of Satan's counterfeits that reveals his prior knowledge. Zeus was another name for Kronos—Saturn.

The word Pergamos means elevation, tower, citadel, or thoroughly married. It represents the church after Emperor Constantine's Edict of Toleration, which granted freedom of worship. Persecution by the emperors ended at that time.

The edict was issued because Constantine, when suffering reverses, saw a vision of a huge luminous cross above the afternoon sun with the words "In this sign conquer." He decreed that the religion of the Roman Empire was Christianity. Professing himself Christian, he compelled his army to march through the river to baptize them. The eagle on the Roman standards was replaced with the cross. After his victory, Christianity was elevated to the state religion.

This seemed good, and it did put an end to the persecutions. However, there was a downside. It siphoned pagans and their customs right into the Christian church. No doubt Satan was dancing and snickering in the background, "If you can't beat 'em, join 'em."

Coming up out of the mixture, we see that the old Mystery Religion of Babylon in its many forms has donned the vestments of Christianity. It is cleverly disguised, but to informed eagle eyes, tell-tale signs blow its cover.

The Empire began to patronize the expanding church. Soon the church and state became one, and the emperor became the head of the church. This led to the head of state dictating to both church members and politicians. Does this remind you of the Beast of the end times?

Constantine called the Council of Nicea to decide the question of whether Jesus was truly God, or just the greatest being that God had brought into existence. Constantine presided sitting on a golden throne, acknowledged head of the Christian church. Yet, he bore the pagan title Pontifex Maximus, the high priest of the idolatrous Babylonian religion.

The meanings of Pergamos turned out to be prophetic. At first, Christians used pagan temples, but later, elaborate citadels and towers came to be built exclusively for the Christian church that was joined to the state.

In Noah W. Hutchings book, "Petra in History and Prophecy," he tells us that the 130-foot obelisk, symbol of the fertility cult, that Semiramis erected in Babylon to the memory of Nimrod was copied in essence and placed in front of temples in widely scattered areas of the world. One is even in front of St. Peter's Cathedral today. It was transported from the pagan temple of Heliopolis, where an inscription reads, "I, Dionysus, dedicated these phalli to Hera, my stepmother." A twin of the obelisk at St. Peter's is in front of the church at St. Sophia in Constantinople's town square. On page 79, Mr. Hutchings said,

> In temples, shrines, mosques, and churches of all religions of the world, obelisk-like spires and towers are included in construction. Many of these elongated units simply follow tradition without any realization of their meaning or relationship to the mystery religion of Babylon.[37]

Instead of patiently keeping herself as a pure virgin Bride of Christ, the church found herself thoroughly married to both pagans and the state. It was Satan's ingenious trick, a pitfall hard to avoid or to get out of.

During the Tribulation, Satan will spring a similar trap. The church and state will again become one. The head of the church will become the head of world religion and of world government. At first, the Beast of Rome will be in charge. Later, the Israeli False Prophet will rule this unholy alliance with an iron fist. The early rallying cry of the world's nations at the beginning of the Tribulation may be, "UNITED WE STAND!" but by its end, the sad truth will emerge: under the wrong leader, united we fall.

When he becomes Satan possessed and has control, he will turn on those who "have the testimony of Jesus Christ."[38] Those in Jerusalem will have to run for their lives.

> For then shall be great tribulation, such as
> was not since the beginning of the world to
> this time, no, nor ever shall be. And except
> those days should be shortened, there should
> no flesh be saved: but for the elect's sake
> those days shall be shortened.[39]

The elect of those days are the Tribulation saints who will go
to heaven at the end of the 2,300-day shortened Tribulation.

We hear Jesus begin his address to the church under
Imperial favor with these words:

> And to the angel of the church in Pergamos
> write; These things saith he which hath the
> sharp sword with two edges;[40]

The cancer first found in Ephesus has spread to Pergamos. The sharp two-edged sword that was seen coming
out of Christ's mouth in the preview will cut off those who
are not over comers. They will be left behind to go through
the Tribulation. The cancer will grow until another sword,
called the "sword of the LORD (that) shall devour from the
one end of the land even to the other end of the land" in Jeremiah 12:12, will excise it for good at the consummation of
this age.

As Jesus continues his monologue, we find out
where Satan's throne is located.

> I know they works, and where thou dwellest,
> *even* where Satan's seat (*thronos*) *is*: and
> thou holdest fast my name, and hast not de-
> nied my faith, even in those days wherein
> Antipas *was* my faithful martyr, who was
> slain among you, where Satan dwelleth.[41]

Satan's throne must be the chair of the Pontifex
Maximus, who was originally the high priest of the Mystery
Religion of Babylon. This Satanic counterfeit religion was
started at the Tower of Babel by Nimrod and his wife Semiramis. It featured Semiramis and their son, Tammuz, as ma-

donna and child. She said the light-brown-haired Tammuz was gored to death by a wild boar and then came back to life. He was worshipped both as the sun god and as Saturn.

Satan concocts some pretty good counterfeits to confuse mankind. They reveal his prior knowledge.

Jesus was Jewish. I don't think he had light brown hair as some picture him. Rembrandt pictured him with black hair, which seems a lot more reasonable. The Song of Solomon 5:10-16 describes Jesus. Verses 10 and 11 say,

> My beloved is white and ruddy, the chiefest among ten thousand. His head is as the most fine gold (symbol of deity), his locks are bushy, and black as a raven.

Idols of Semiramis alone or of Semiramis and Tammuz, as madonna and child, were used. When you see idols today, how do you know who they are actually modeled after, the true or the counterfeit?

After the languages were confused, this same goddess appeared in other countries under many other names, such as Ashtoreth, Astarte, and Ishtar. Easter, a spring fertility festival, was celebrated with eggs. The birthday of Tammuz was celebrated with evergreen trees on December 25 during the Saturnalia, the festival of Saturn. These pagan customs later became associated with and were adapted to Christianity.

Jesus was probably born September 8, B.C. 5. He was born as the "former rain"[42] on the Feast of Trumpets, which is the Jewish New Year, not on December 25. The celebration on that date came about when Rome threw pagan ceremonies and Christian doctrine into the same mixer.

The headquarters of this false religion was first moved to Pergamos then to Rome when Attalus III willed Pergamos to Rome. It is there yet.

When the dragon gives the two beasts of Revelation thirteen power during the coming Tribulation, Satan's throne will be moved from Rome to the literal city of Babylon on the Euphrates River in Iraq. The headquarters of the harlot religion will be built there on her old foundation, the Tower of Babel.[43] It is now in the desert. This is why in the Olivet discourse, Jesus said,

> For then shall be great tribulation, such as was not since the beginning of the world to this time, no, or ever shall be. And...those days shall be shortened. Then if any man shall say unto you, Lo, here is Christ, or there; believe it not. For there shall arise false Christs, and false prophets, and shall shew great signs and wonders; insomuch that, if it were possible, they shall deceive the very elect. Behold, I have told you before. Wherefore if they shall say unto you, Behold, **he is in the desert**; go not forth: behold, he is in the secret chambers; believe it not.[44]

The tabloid, "Weekly World News" of January 23, 1996, says on the cover, "IS JESUS BACK ON EARTH?" In the article by Ann Victoria, we find that 19-year-old Jacob Katzan supposedly raises the dead, changes water into wine, "heals the sick, walks on water—and swears he's none other than Jesus Christ!" Do not believe that for a minute. Satan has his counterfeits. To protect us from such, Jesus said,

> For as the lightning cometh out of the east, and shineth even unto the west: so shall also the coming of the Son of man be.[45]

The Second Advent will not be secret. Jesus will not come to the desert (i.e., Babylon) or hide away in secret chambers. He will touch down on the Mount of Olives and the mount will split into two pieces. If it has not split, Jesus has not yet arrived. The light of that day will be out of the ordinary too. Zechariah 14: 4-7 describes that scene:

> And his feet shall stand in that day upon the mount of Olives, which is before Jerusalem on the east, and the mount of Olives shall cleave in the midst thereof toward the east

and toward the west, and there shall be a very great valley; and half of the mountain shall remove toward the north, and half of it toward the south....and the LORD my God shall come, and all the saints with thee. And it shall come to pass in that day, that the light shall not be clear, nor dark: But it shall be one day which shall be known to the LORD, not day, nor night: but it shall come to pass, that at evening time it shall be light.

The beast of Revelation 13:4-10 will sit on Satan's throne during the first half of the seven-year Tribulation. After his accident, the Satan-possessed False Prophet will sit on it until Babylon, already rebuilt by Saddam Hussein in the Iraqi desert, is swept off the face of the Earth by the Lord's broom of destruction, the asteroid.[46] It is interesting to find that the ancient Chinese called a comet a broom star.

In his monologue, Jesus mentioned Antipas, which means against all. This man must have been a follower of Athanasius, deacon of the Alexandrian church, called the father of Orthodoxy. This was the period when Athanasius argued against the Arians to vindicate the deity of Christ. The emperor Theodosius told him that the world was all against him. To this Athanasius replied, "Then I am against all the world." He prefigured those who must take a stand against the world during the Tribulation.

The cry of "Athanasius against all." rang on for over 100 years. Torch light parades through the streets shouted it out. It was continued at the Council of Nicea in 325 A.D., which was presided over by Emperor Constantine, and the Council at Constantinople in 381.

These councils upheld the full deity of Christ. In the Nicene Creed, he is "true God from true God, begotten not made, **of one substance (*homoousios*) with the Father,**" God and man in one person. They held fast his name and did not deny the faith.

Constantine did the church a great service when he ordered Eusebius, who was the bishop of Rome, to have 50 copies of the Scriptures prepared for use in the churches.

Continuing his message, Christ warns the church of Pergamos about a stumbling block:

> But I have a few things against thee, because thou hast there them that hold the doctrine of Balaam, who taught Balac to cast a stumblingblock before the children of Israel, to eat things sacrificed unto idols, and to commit fornication.[47]

Balaamism is compromise with the world. The name Balaam means destroyers of the people. Balac (or Balak), king of Moab, hired Balaam to curse Israel. On the way to the Israelite camp, the angel of the Lord appeared to block the way. Balaam's ass balked three times and finally fell down. Exasperated, Balaam hit her three times with his staff. Finally, the Lord opened the mouth of the ass, and she said,

> Am not I thine ass, upon which thou hast ridden ever since I was thine unto this day? was I ever wont to do so unto thee? And he said, Nay. Then the LORD opened the eyes of Balaam, and he saw the angel of the LORD standing in the way, and **his sword drawn in his hand** (symbolizing the Sword of the Lord that will strike Earth at the end of this age): and he bowed down his head, and fell flat on his face. And the angel of the LORD said unto him, Wherefore hast thou smitten thine ass these three times? behold, I went out to withstand thee, because thy way is perverse (improper) before me.[48]

God made our eyes so that we cannot easily see the angels. It may have something to do with the gel in our eyeballs. The eagle has better eyesight than we do, and they have oil in their eyes. However the Lord did it, he did it for a reason. He said of the whole host of heaven, "I shewed them not to thee that thou shouldest go after them."[49]

The sword of the Lord threatened three times. This is significant. It slew the Gibeonites on Joshua's long day, it destroyed Sodom, Gomorrah, and the cities of the plain, and it will exterminate Babylon. The third time will be twice as bad as the second time, and the second time, it split the Earth all the way from Syria to Lake Victoria in Africa. Ezekiel was told,

> Seeing then that I will cut off from thee the righteous (at the two Raptures) and the wicked, therefore shall my sword go forth out of his sheath against all flesh from the south to the north: That all flesh may know that I the LORD have drawn forth my sword out of his sheath: it shall not return any more (it's a one time thing)....Thou therefore, son of man, prophesy, and smite thine hands together, and let the sword be **doubled the third time**, the sword of the slain: it is the sword of the great men that are slain...I have set the point of the sword against all their gates, that their heart may faint, and their ruins be multiplied: ah! it is made bright, it is wrapped up for the slaughter....I will also smite mine hands together, and I will cause my fury to rest: I the LORD have said it.[50]

God controlled the situation so that Balaam could only bless Israel, so Balaam taught Balac that the Israelites could still be corrupted by marriage with pagan Moabite women. This way they would pick up pagan ways. He was right. It happened.

> Israel...began to commit whoredom with the daughters of Moab....they called the people unto the sacrifices of their gods: and the people did eat, and bowed down to their gods. And Israel joined himself unto Baal-peor (meaning **lord of the hole**); and the anger of the LORD was kindled against Israel.[51]

You know who the lord of the hole is—Satan. Revelation 17:8 speaks of him as the beast that he is:

> The beast that thou sawest was (in Judas Iscariot), and is not (is not inhabiting a human body at the time of the Rapture): and **shall ascend out of the bottomless pit** (to inhabit the body of the False Prophet), and go into perdition: and they that dwell on the earth shall wonder, whose names were not written in the book of life from the foundation of the world, when they behold the beast that was, and is not, and yet is.

The church of Pergamos became addicted to idolatry by her marriage to the state. That reverence for idols that started in Pergamos overflowed and is found in a certain segment of the church in our times. By "marrying" a pagan woman, they pick up pagan ways.

The commandment concerning idols
As found in Exodus 20:3-17 in the King James Version, the ten commandments given to Moses condense into the following list. (Pay attention to number two in all three lists.)

1. Thou shalt have no other gods before me.
2. **Thou shalt not make unto thee any graven image, or any likeness of any thing...Thou shalt not bow down thyself to them, nor serve them.**
3. Thou shalt not take the name of the LORD thy God in vain.
4. Remember the sabbath....keep it holy.
5. Honour thy father and thy mother.
6. Thou shalt not kill.
7. Thou shalt not commit adultery.
8. Thou shalt not steal.
9. Thou shalt not bear false witness against thy neighbour.

10. Thou shalt not covet thy neighbour's house, thou shalt not covet thy neighbour's wife, nor his manservant, nor his maidservant, nor his ox, nor his ass, nor any thing that is thy neighbour's.

In the Catholic New Confraternity Version, the commandments condense into this similar list:

1. You shall not have other gods besides me.
2. **You shall not carve idols for yourselves in the shape of anything... you shall not bow down before them or worship them.**
3. You shall not take the name of the Lord, your God, in vain.
4. Remember to keep holy the Sabbath.
5. Honor your father and your mother.
6. You shall not kill.
7. You shall not commit adultery.
8. You shall not steal.
9. You shall not bear false witness against your neighbor.
10. You shall not covet your neighbor's house. You shall not covet your neighbor's wife, nor his male or female slave, nor his ox or ass, nor anything else that belongs to him.

Why then, does this same edition, the Saint Joseph Edition of the Holy Bible, containing the New Confraternity-Douay Old Testament and the Confraternity New Testament, published in 1963 by the Catholic Book Publishing Company of New York, list the commandments on the fly leaf as follows? (Note numbers two, nine and ten.)

1. I am the Lord Thy God; thou shalt not have strange gods before Me.
2. **Thou shalt not take the name of the Lord Thy God in vain.**

3. Remember thou keep holy the Sabbath Day.
4. Honor thy father and thy mother.
5. Thou shalt not kill.
6. Thou shalt not commit adultery.
7. Thou shalt not steal.
8. Thou shalt not bear false witness against thy neighbor.
9. Thou shalt not covet thy neighbor's wife.
10. Thou shalt not covet thy neighbor's goods.

Can you believe this? The list on the fly leaf actually disagrees with the scripture on page 78 in the same copy of the Holy Bible. **What happened to the prohibition against carving idols or bowing down before them? It was dropped and number ten was split into two commandments to make up the difference**. By what authority was this done? and why? Could it have been because of compromise with the pagan element within the church? How can they get away with this? Are people so non observant that they fail to compare the two lists?

This change in the list of the ten commandments is not a solitary occurrence. The book, *This is the Faith: Catholic Theology for Laymen*, by Francis J. Ripley, published in 1951 by the Birchley Hall Press, Billings, England, and reprinted in 1960 in the United States, is commended by Richard, Archbishop of Liverpool and bears the following:

Nihil Obstat:
J. CANONICUS MORGAN, S. T. D.,
CENSOR

Imprimatur:
RICHARDUS,
ARCHIEPISCOPUS LIVERPOLITANUS,
Liverpolii die 25a Januarii 1951

On pages 71 through 75, in chapter VIII, titled "The Commandments of God," we find the following list:

The Ten Commandments in their briefest form are as follows:

1. I am the Lord thy God. Thou shalt not have strange gods before Me.
2. **Thou shalt not take the name of the Lord thy God in vain**.
3. Remember that thou keep holy the Sabbath day.
4. Honor thy father and thy mother.
5. Thou shalt not kill.
6. Thou shalt not commit adultery.
7. Thou shalt not steal.
8. Thou shalt not bear false witness against thy neighbor.
9. Thou shalt not covet thy neighbor's wife.
10. Thou shalt not covet thy neighbor's goods

Protestants divide the First Commandment into two and join the Ninth and Tenth into one....**The First Commandment does not forbid the making of statues**. There are several examples from Scripture of the lawful use of images of angels in the Jewish Tabernacle, the Brazen Serpent, the adornments of the walls of the Temple....Statues and holy pictures teach or recall important truths or the example of holy men; they catch and fix the attention and help devotion.

How can they say that the commandment does not forbid the making of statues when the Scripture is so specific? As mentioned before, Exodus 20:1-5 in their New Confraternity version plainly states, "You shall not carve idols." The whole passage follows (emphasis mine).

I, the Lord, am your God, who brought you out of the land of Egypt, that place of slavery. You shall not have other gods besides me. **You shall not carve idols** for yourselves in the shape of anything in the sky

above or on the earth below or in the waters
beneath the earth; **you shall not bow
down before them or worship them.**

Yeast versus salt

The doctrine of Balaam, teaching that those who could not
be cursed could still be corrupted by marriage with pagan
women, is viciously effective. This leaven, joining with pagan religions, is still working today. As soon as the Rapture
transfers the church to Heaven, this kind of yeast will soon
leaven the whole lump.

Jesus said that we are the salt of the earth.[52] Do you
understand what that means?

On page four, my West Bend Automatic Bread maker instruction book says, "SALT has several functions in
making bread. It inhibits the yeast growth while strengthen-
ing the gluten structure to make the dough more elastic...
Using too little can cause the dough to overproof; using too
much can prevent dough from rising."

As long as we are present on Earth, we inhibit the
growth of evil. Therefore, the ultimate evil one, the False
Prophet, cannot be revealed until after the Rapture.[53] After it,
when the salt is gone, and the Holy Spirit has stopped hin-
dering, the leaven will work rapidly.

Since the Rapture is at hand, the Lord is seen standing in the way with a two-edged sword coming out of his
mouth. He will cut off those whose way is improper before
him. Even the salt can be cast out. Luke 14:34,35 says,

Salt is good: but if the salt (i.e., the believer)
have lost his savour, wherewith shall it be
seasoned? It is neither fit for the land, nor yet
for the dunghill; but men cast it out. **He that
hath ears to hear, let him hear.**

Immediately after the consummation of this age,
Rapture II will catch the Tribulation saints up to heaven first,
then the Sword of the Lord will strike. The remnant of the
world church which is corrupted by its marriage with pagans
will be destroyed. Judgment begins at the house of God.[54]

Doctrine of the Nicolaitanes

Continuing his message, Christ mentions another thing he hates and includes a threat:

> So hast thou also them that hold the doctrine
> of the Nicolaitanes, which thing I hate. Re-
> pent; or else I will come unto thee quickly,
> and will fight against them with the sword of
> my mouth. He that hath an ear, let him hear
> what the Spirit saith unto the churches.[55]

The deeds of the Nicolaitanes in the first message, have become the doctrine of the Nicolaitanes by the third. The cancer Satan seeded within the church is growing. A priestly cast and a reverence for idols are rising within the church. Therefore the admonition given to them is to be taken very very seriously—"Repent; or else."

Promise to overcomers

> To him that overcometh will I give to eat of
> the hidden manna, and will give him a white
> stone, and in the stone a new name written,
> which no man knoweth saving he that receiv-
> eth it.[56]

Manna is angel's food. This indicates that the overcomers will go to their heavenly promised land when the doors of heaven open at the time of the Rapture. When Israel came out of Egypt to go up to their promised land, Canaan, it was a type of the church going up to our promised land.

In the wilderness, God fed the Israelites manna from heaven, but along the way, his

> anger...came up against Israel; Because they
> believed not in God, and trusted not in his
> salvation: Though he had commanded the
> clouds from above, and opened the doors of
> heaven, And had rained down manna upon

them to eat, and had given them of the **corn of heaven**. Man did eat angels' food.[57]

Did you notice that angels' food was called "the corn of heaven?" That sounds like food grows in heaven, doesn't it? Also, when we are shown the New Jerusalem, Revelation 22:2 says, "In the midst of the street of it, and on either side of the river, was there the tree of life, which bare twelve manner of fruits, and yielded her fruit every month." Evidently Heaven has soil, water, grain and trees. Our astronomers are in for a great shock.

The white stone in the message to Pergamos was like a jury vote for acquittal in those early days. It shows that Christ is judging the churches, and only the over comers will get the white stone.

THE LORD'S MONOLOGUE: PART 4

The message to Thyatira
In the viewfinder: the church under the Papacy
As Jesus launches into the next section of his monologue, we can see that both Nicolaitanism and idolatry have grown into a cancer that cannot be healed. It has metastasized and spread. This church is full of works, service, and faith, but so indulgent of error that it has overlaid the truth, deceiving its members. Jesus says,

> And unto the angel of the church in Thyatira write; These things saith the Son of God, who hath his eyes like unto a flame of fire, and his feet *are* like fine brass (both are symbols of judgment seen in the preview of the Rapture); I know thy works, and charity, and service, and faith, and thy patience, and thy works (margin: last works to be; i.e., during the Tribulation); and the last *to be* more than the first.[58]

Eyes like fire and feet like brass judge this church. Take warning. In Scripture symbolism, a woman represents a religious group. Here, Thyatira means dominating female, feminine oppression, or continual sacrifice. Historically, it represents the Dark Ages, when the so-called mother church found itself under the thumb of the Papacy, which either began with Gregory I (590-604 A.D.) or with Boniface II in 607.

The continual sacrifice points to the mass, in which the priests declare that they offer a continual sacrifice for the sins of the living and the dead. They forget that Christ offered up the perfect sacrifice, "once for all." Hebrews 10:10-14 says that

> we are sanctified through the offering of the body of Jesus Christ **once for all**...this man, after he had offered **one sacrifice for sins for ever**, sat down on the right hand of God...For **by one offering he hath perfected for ever them that are sanctified.**

During the Dark Ages, the completeness of the finished work of Christ was not often recognized. Salvation by faith and salvation by grace were all but forgotten precepts. Legalism, works, rituals, and sacrifices of many types seem to have taken their place.

A long list of unscriptural things were added. The doctrine of purgatory was introduced.

Prayers were directed to Mary, the cup was forbidden to worshipers at communion, tradition was given equal authority with Scripture, and the apocryphal books were added to the Bible.

The scriptures were forbidden to laymen, so not many were able to read Ephesians 2:8, which plainly says,

> For by grace are ye saved through faith: and that not of yourselves: it is the gift of God: **Not of works**, lest any man should boast.

This church even looks on the mass as a continual sacrifice in which Christ is sacrificed again and again. However, Hebrews 9:12,24-26 shows that Jesus' one sacrifice obtained eternal redemption for us. It says,

> Christ is not entered into the holy places made with hands...but into heaven itself, now to appear in the presence of God for us: Nor yet that he should offer himself often, as the high priest entereth into the holy place every year with blood of others; For then must he often have suffered since the foundation of the world: but now **once** in the end of the world (*sunteleia ton aionon*, consummation of the ages) hath he appeared to put away sin by the sacrifice of himself...So Christ was **once** offered to bear the sins of many.

The word Pope means papa, father. This title is used in spite of Matthew 23:8's forbidding the calling of any man father.

At first all bishops in western Europe were called Father or Pope. About 500 A.D., Pope began to be restricted to the bishop of Rome, and it came to mean universal father, meaning the bishop over the whole church on Earth.

The legend that Peter was the first bishop of Rome is not borne out by history. The Council of Nicea (325 A.D.) mentioned the bishop of Rome only incidentally. The other later councils were not convened by the bishop of Rome nor presided over by his legates. The Synod of Chalcedon declared the patriarch of Constantinople his official equal in 451 A.D.

The fall of the western empire in 476 enabled the Roman bishops to increase their power over the provinces. They soon proclaimed themselves superior to other rulers. Between 1073 and 1303, the papacy rose to the summit of its power. The Popes became lords of the Earth.[59]

According to historical records, the papal throne has been occupied by some degraded men. Things got so bad that Gregory VII (1073-1085) tried to reform the clergy and to eliminate simony, the buying or selling of church office. He insisted on celibacy to cure the immorality of the priests.

The very apex of the Papal power was under Innocent III, (1198-1216). He instituted the Inquisition and forbade reading of the Bible in the common languages. He claimed the titles vicar (one serving as a substitute or agent) of Christ and vicar of God. He also claimed the title **supreme sovereign over the church and the world**, just as the final Antichrist will do at the end of this age.

Sixtus IV (1471-1484) issued a decree that said money would deliver souls from purgatory. Innocent VIII (1484-1492) sold church offices for money and appointed Thomas of Torquemada inquisitor general in Spain. Innocent VIII ordered so-called heretics delivered to this terrible man whose later counterpart was the despicable Heinrich Himmler in Germany.

Julius II (1503-1513) bought the office, forgave sin for money, and shocked Martin Luther when Luther visited Rome. However, Leo X (1513-1521) was Pope when Luther kicked off the Reformation. Leo X issued indulgences and considered the burning of Protestants to be a divine appointment.[60] In the list of 43 so-called heresies of Martin Luther, Leo X called it heresy when Luther said, "To burn heretics is against the will of the (Holy) Spirit."[61] Those days have rightly been called the dark ages of the church. They will be repeated at the end of this age.

We hear Jesus continuing his message to Thyatira:

> Notwithstanding I have a few things against thee, because thou sufferest that woman Jezebel, which calleth herself a prophetess, to teach and to seduce my servants to commit fornication (join with the world or with another god), and to eat things sacrificed unto idols.[62]

In the Old Testament, Queen Jezebel was a pagan, married to the wicked Jewish king Ahab, the eighth king of Israel. She was a cruel idolatrous woman who had the prophets of Jehovah killed, and caused Ahab to turn from the true God to idolatry. She supported 450 prophets of Baal, plus 400 of Astarte, and had Naboth killed to get his vineyard. Baal and Astarte were derivatives of Tammuz and Semiramis of Babel.

Jezebel's name means woe to the dunghill. She is a fitting type of the harlot church, the Mystery Religion of Babylon, when she is joined to the Jewish False Prophet indwelt by Satan. The Devil himself is "the god of this world,"[63] and "the eighth" beast of Revelation 17:11.

The harlot church of the Tribulation will also kill to get a vineyard. Revelation 17:6 says that she will be "drunken with the blood of the saints, and with the blood of the martyrs of Jesus." Hell is insatiable.

Jesus continues his message to Thyatira:

> And I gave her space to repent of her fornication (joining with another god); and she repented not. Behold, I will cast her into a bed, and them that commit adultery (join) with her into great tribulation, except they repent of their deeds.[64]

The space she has been given to repent has already stretched over more than 1,380 years, from 607 A.D to the present. Since she repented not, she is now, except for the over comers, to be left on Earth during the seven year Tribulation. The last part is called the Great Tribulation. Her judgment at the consummation of this age will be deadly.

Jesus uses strong words as he continues:

> And I will kill her children with death; and all the churches shall know that I am he which searcheth the reins and hearts: and I will give unto every one of you according to your works. But unto you I say, and unto the rest in Thyatira, as many as have not this doctrine (that they should join with another god and eat things sacrificed unto idols), and which have not known the depths (*bathe*, **mysteries**) **of Satan**, as they speak; I will put upon you none other burden. But that which ye have *already* hold fast till I come.[65]

The mysteries of Satan probably refer to the Mystery Religion of Babylon, the harlot religion of the end time, after she strips off the cloak of Christianity.

Promise to overcomers
Jesus ends his long message to Thyatira with these words:

> And he that overcometh, and keepeth my works unto the end, to him will I give power over the nations: And he shall rule them with a rod of iron; as the vessels of a potter shall they (the nations) be broken to shivers (by the asteroid): even as I received of my Father. And **I will give him the morning star**. He that hath an ear, let him hear what the Spirit saith unto the churches.[66]

In all seven church assemblies, there are over comers that will be taken to heaven in the Rapture, even in this one. They are the ones who truly believe that Jesus is the Christ and are filled with his Holy Spirit. They are to be given the morning star. This morning star is both symbolic and literal.

The "bright and morning star" that will be given to the overcomers symbolizes Christ. Revelation 22:16 says, "I Jesus have sent mine angel to testify unto you these things in the churches. I am the root (Yahweh) and the offspring of David (Jesus), and the bright and morning star." In Numbers 24:17, he is the Star that will come out of Jacob.

(The surprising literal meaning of the bright and morning star will be explored in the next two chapters.)

THE LORD'S MONOLOGUE: PART 5

The message to Sardis
In the viewfinder: the church of the Reformation
The word Sardis means a remnant or those who have escaped. It represents the church of the Renaissance (rebirth) and the Reformation. On October 31, 1517, Martin Luther tacked his 95 theses to the church door in Wittenberg, Ger-

many, and touched off the Reformation that nearly cost him his life. Once he got hold of the heart of the gospel, salvation by faith, believers split into two main groups, Protestants and Catholics.

Martin Luther was a Catholic monk who practiced all the scourgings, fastings, and other cruel practices of Penance. Once, while crawling up Pilate's Stairs, the meaning of "The just shall live by faith"[67] flashed in his mind, and there he was trying to earn salvation by works. His church had held the world in their grip by teaching that salvation was by works.

Also, ever since Pope Pascal (817-824), Indulgences had been sold for the forgiveness of sin. In Wittenberg, Tetzel said that the sin was forgiven as soon as the coin hit the bottom of the box. Martin Luther was horrified; only God can forgive sin.

Indulgences of our days

Do you think that Indulgences are a thing of the past? The New American Catholic Edition of The Holy Bible printed in 1952 by the Benziger Brothers, Inc., has the Douay Old Testament, the Psalms from a Newer Latin Version, and the Confraternity New Testament. The following quote is in the front, preceding the title page. Notice the date, 1932.

INDULGENCES

> The Faithful who spend at least a quarter of an hour in reading Holy Scripture with the great reverence due to the Word of God and after the manner of spiritual reading, may gain an indulgence of 300 days (S. C. Ind., Dec. 13, 1898; S. P. Ap., **March 22, 1932**).
> *The Raccolta)Preces et Pie Opera)*
> *No. 645.*

In the following quotes, plenary indulgence is listed. Webster's Dictionary defines plenary indulgence as "a remission of the entire temporal punishment due to sin." On page six of this Bible, we find more Indulgences listed:

INDULGENCES FOR READING
THE BIBLE

An indulgence of three years is granted to the faithful who read the Books of the Bible for at least a quarter of an hour, with the reverence due to the Divine Word and as spiritual reading.

To the faithful who piously read at least some verses of the Gospel and in addition, while kissing the Gospel Book, devoutly recite one of the following invocations: "May our sins be blotted out through the words of the Gospel" — "May the reading of the Gospel be our salvation and protection" — "May Christ, the Son of God, teach us the words of the Holy Gospel":

an indulgence of 500 days is granted;

a plenary indulgence under the usual conditions is granted to those who for a whole month daily act in the way indicated above;

a plenary indulgence is granted at the hour of death to those who often during life have performed this pious exercise, provided they have confessed and received Communion, or at least having sorrow for their sins, they invoke the most holy name of Jesus with their lips, if possible, or at least in their hearts, and humbly accept death from the hand of God as the price of sin

(Enchiridion Indulgentiarum, 694)

The reading of the Gospel is NOT our salvation, although it could lead to it. Christ is our Saviour. Belief in him is necessary. We have to be careful that "pious exercise" such as the above does not obscure that fact.

In the early days, the Roman church tried to stop those who were escaping from her clutches during the Reformation. The Massacre of St. Bartholomew's Night on August 24, 1572, when 70,000 Huguenots were put to death, showed that this "Jezebel" would kill to keep a vineyard.

The Roman church waged war on Protestants in Germany, in the Netherlands, in France, in England. Millions perished, but fire and sword could not stop them.

The Protestant churches that broke away clung tenaciously to three important principles:

> 1. Salvation by faith
> 2. Supremacy of the Scriptures
> 3. The priesthood of the believer

Johann Gutenberg had completed his printing press about 1450. The first book he printed was a Latin Bible, produced at Mainz, Germany before 1456. His Bibles helped make the scriptures accessible to more people.

The reformers could quote Scripture to back up their claims. However, most people who were entrenched in the Papal church were not allowed to read the scriptures to see if what they heard was true or not. Pope Gregory VII ordered that Latin would be the universal language of worship and excluded all reading of the Bible in the common languages. Pope Innocent III prohibited even the private possession and reading of the Bible. This will probably happen again during the Tribulation.

With this background in mind, listen as Christ continues his messages to the churches, this one is to Sardis.

And unto the angel of the church in Sardis write; These things saith he that hath the seven Spirits of God (the perfect sevenfold Holy Spirit[68]), and the seven stars (seen in Heaven in the preview of the Rapture); I know thy works, that thou hast a name that thou livest, and art dead. Be watchful, and strengthen the things which remain, that are ready to die: for I have not found thy works perfect before God. Remember therefore how thou hast received and heard, and hold fast, and repent.[69]

The works were not perfect. The cancer was operated on, but they didn't get it all. It was only checked and will grow again at the end of the age until it strikes Jezebel's children with death. The pagan practices remained in the Papal church and some were even carried over into Protestant churches.

The main reason the fires of the Reformation died out could have been because so many of those Protestant churches became state churches. In a time of economic need, they trusted the state instead of God.

Jesus warns the Protestant churches of today:

If therefore thou shalt not watch, I will come on thee as a thief, and thou shalt not know what hour I will come upon thee.[70]

The churches were to keep alert and watch for some important event to happen. If we do not watch, we will not know what hour he is coming to the churches at the Rapture. Some will be taken, others left behind. A woman represents a religious group. In Matthew 24:41-44, Jesus said,

Two women shall be grinding at the mill; the one shall be taken, and the other left. Watch therefore: for ye know not what hour **your Lord** (both are believers) doth come. But know this, that if the goodman (the leader) of the house (church) had known in what watch the thief (Christ) would come, he would have watched, and would not have suffered his house (church) to be **broken up**. Therefore be ye also ready: for **in such an hour as ye think not the Son of man cometh.**

Christ scolded the Pharisees. "O ye hypocrites," he said, "ye can discern the face of the sky; but can ye not discern the **signs of the times?**"[71] They should have known when he was coming from the prophecy in Daniel 9:24-26.

Jerusalem was destroyed because they did not discern the signs of the times. Jesus said that "they shall not leave in thee one stone upon another; **because thou knewest not the time of thy visitation."**

Will our modern religious leaders do any better? We have plenty of modern-day Pharisees who think that we cannot know when Christ will return and do not even examine the clues given in the Bible. They pay no attention to Mark 13:23, where Jesus said, "But take ye heed: behold, **I have foretold you all things."**

However, what if we do watch? Turn it around and see. If we do watch, he will not come on us as a thief, and **thou shalt know** what hour he will come upon thee. He told us to watch for a good reason.

What were we watching for? That event was the Six-Day War of 1967. That war between Israel and Egypt, plus other Arab states, was the Sign of the End of the Age because it fulfilled the fig tree parable in Matthew 24:32-34.

When the disciples asked Jesus when these things would be and what would be the sign of his coming and the end of the age, Jesus answered their question with the parable in Matthew 24:32-34:

> Now learn a parable of the fig tree (Israel[72]); When his branch (modern Israel) is yet tender (young), and putteth forth leaves (grows), ye know that summer is nigh: So likewise ye, when ye shall see all these things, know that it (margin, he) is near (*eggus*, **at hand**), even at the **doors** (symbol of the two Raptures[73]). Verily I say unto you, This generation shall not pass, till all these things be fulfilled.

Modern Israel was a young nineteen-year-old when she grew four leaves, Gaza Strip, Golan Heights, Sinai, and

West Bank, in the Six-Day War of 1967. Summer was nigh. The War began June 6. Summer began June 21. At that time, both Raptures, when believers will enter the kingdom of God, became "at hand." This period when the Raptures are at hand is measured by a generation, demonstrated to be 40 years when Israel wandered in the wilderness 40 years while one generation died off. The Lord said, "ye shall bear your sins forty years, and ye shall know my fierce anger."[74]

Nothing remains to be fulfilled before the door opens and the Rapture takes place. It probably has been "at hand" ever since 1967. This period probably coincides with "the time of the end" when "knowledge shall be increased."[75]

During the Six-Day War, something else significant happened. Not only did Israel grow four times as large as she was before the war, she got all of Jerusalem, ending the times of the Gentiles. Luke 21:24 says,

> And they shall fall by the edge of the sword, and shall be led away captive into all nations: and Jerusalem shall be trodden down of the Gentiles, until the times of the Gentiles be fulfilled.

Since the times of the Gentiles are fulfilled, we must use the Jewish calendar in preference to ours in figuring possible dates that end-time events might take place. Ours would be close, but theirs is exact. One reason for the difference is because their New Year is in the fall, either in our September or October. Another reason is that the Jews use inclusive reckoning. They count the first year as number one.

Keep in mind that Job 11:6 said that "the secrets of wisdom...are double to that which is," and think about circumstances at the time of the Exodus. After the Israelites came out of Egypt, a census was taken of males 20 and over. The youths nineteen and under were not counted. They were the younger generation. After wandering in the desert 40 years while the older generation, except Joshua and Caleb, died off, those who had been nineteen and under were the remnant who went in to possess their promised land.

Those same numbers carry over to the fig-tree nation of our days. Modern Israel was born as a nation May 14, 1948. Nineteen years later, in 1967, she entered the 40-year probationary period that corresponds to her wilderness wandering. (The number 40 means probation and testing.) After these 40 years have run their course and the older generation has died off, the remnant of those who were nineteen and under in 1967 will be the ones who will literally inherit all of the land promised to Abraham. Those 40 years run out when this age ends and the Millennium begins. God is trying to tell us something if only we have ears to hear.

When the Pharisees asked for a sign, Jesus told them none would be given but the sign of the prophet Jonah. Jesus was three and a half days in the heart of the earth just as Jonah was three days and three nights in the whale's belly.[76] However, Jonah told Nineveh, "Yet forty days, and Nineveh shall be overthrown."[77] Do you realize that Jerusalem was destroyed 40 years after the Crucifixion? That foreshadows an end-time destruction after 40 years of probation.

Jonah's message has overtones that reverberate down the corridor of time. After 40 time periods, Jerusalem was burned. In our days, 40 years after the Jews took possession of Jerusalem in the Six-Day War, Jerusalem will be salted with coals of fire. Ezekiel 10:2 says,

> Go in between the wheels (orbits), even under the cherub (Satan), and fill thine hand with coals of fire from between the cherubims (planets), and scatter them over the city.

In Zechariah 13:9, the Lord says, "I will bring the third part through the fire." Israel will be hit by flaming coals, the Mediterranean will be hit by a great mountain, Babylon by the main asteroid. Isaiah 42:25 (Concordant) says,

> He will pour out the fury of His anger on him (Israel), And strengthen the battle. And it (the asteroid) will **set him aflame** round about. Yet he will not know that it shall consume among them. Yet they will not lay it to heart.

91

For the Jews, their 40 years of probation should end as the Millennium begins on Tishri 1, the Feast of Trumpets at the end of the 2,300-day Shortened Tribulation. Those who believed in Yeshua will have gone to Heaven in the Raptures. Those who are left will suffer the catastrophe, realize that the Bible is true, and the remnant nation will be born in a day.[78]

Both Raptures should take place during the 40-year probationary period. Pentecost means 50. If Rapture I is to happen on Pentecost Sunday, 50 years after Israel became a nation in May, 1948, it will take place May 31, 1998. If the Rapture of the Tribulation Saints is to occur on the Feast of Trumpets at the end of the Shortened Tribulation, it will happen on September 13, 2007, just before the catastrophe hits. That is the first day of the Jewish year 5768. If that Feast of Trumpets is the end of the Shortened Tribulation, the 2,300 days would begin to be counted on the Feast of Weeks in the Jewish year of 5761, on our May 28, 2001.

The Feast of Weeks is a perfect time for the Seventieth Week of Daniel (the seven-year Tribulation) to begin. If the Rapture is on Pentecost and the Seventieth Week of Daniel begins on the Feast of Weeks, which is also called Pentecost, the four Jewish years between the Rapture and the beginning of the Tribulation are exact. The years would be 5758, 5759, 5760, and 5761, from Pentecost to Pentecost.

Let's look at this again and see how it works out on the Jewish Calendar. Modern Israel was born on Iyar 5, 5708. The year 5708 + 19 = 5727, when the Six-Day War took place. The year 5727 + 40 = 5767, the last day of which could be the last day of this age. If that is so, the Millennium will begin the next day, on Tishri 1, 5768.

Israel was born in the Jewish 5708 (our 1947/48). That year plus 50 is 5758 (our 1997/8), when it looks like the Rapture will take place. The Jewish 5758 is the 6,000th year since Adam left Eden. On our calendar, B.C. 4003 + 1998 A.D. - 1, because there is no zero year, = 6,000.

The church is called the Body of Christ. It began to be born on Pentecost in 30 A.D. As members died during the intervening years, they were expelled from Earth and went to Heaven. The two feet will be born into Heaven last, one foot exiting before the other. The two feet represent the two Raptures of LIVING members of the Body of Christ. The first foot could be born into Heaven on Pentecost Sunday Sivan 6, 5758. If the last foot is to endure tribulation ten years and be taken up on the Feast of Trumpets, then Rapture II would take place on Tishri 1, 5768, just before the catastrophe hits at noon.

The ten time periods were foreshadowed when Daniel was taken to Babylon. Wanting vegetables and water instead of the king's food, he said, "Please test your servants for ten days...So he...tested them for ten days."[79]

The shortened Tribulation lasts 2,300 days, according to Daniel 8:14. It includes the time they sacrifice at the Temple and the time that they don't because the Temple is desecrated. If the Feast of Trumpets in 2007 is the last day of the shortened Tribulation, and you count that day as the first day (using Jewish inclusive reckoning), then count backwards, you will find that the 2,300th day hits exactly on the Feast of Weeks in 2001.

That 2,300-day count is not a constant between the Feast of Weeks and the Feast of Trumpets in just any group of years because the Jewish Calendar is too irregular. There are now **only two times** before the 40 years are over that the count of days equals 2,300, from Sivan 6, 1997 to Tishri 1, 2003, and from Sivan 6, 2001 to Tishri 1, 2007. The first will not work because a Sunday Rapture on Pentecost would then be impossible. The **only** Sunday Pentecost left is May 31, 1998. Therefore, it seems that we are now locked into the 2001-2007 period for the shortened Tribulation.

Promise to overcomers

As Jesus continues his monologue, we hear him say,

> Thou hast a few names even in Sardis which have not defiled their garments; and they shall walk with me in white: for they are worthy. He that overcometh, the same shall be clothed in white raiment; and I will not blot out his name out of the book of life, but I will confess his name before my Father, and before

his angels. He that hath an ear, let him hear what the Spirit saith unto the churches.[80]

It looks like those who have defiled their garments are not over comers at the time of the Rapture, and their names will be blotted out of the book of life. However, during the Tribulation, they will wash their robes in the blood of the Lamb[81] and be reinstated. Not one true believer will be lost. They will go to heaven in the Translation of the Tribulation Saints, Rapture II, right after this age ends.

Jesus said that they will walk with him in white. There is no other way to go to Heaven. All Heaven's citizens will get there because they are arrayed in white.

A few of the names that will walk with him in white surely include Martin Luther; John Knox, who founded the Presbyterian church in Scotland; and John Calvin, who re-organized the Genevan church and aided a relative, Olivetan, in completing a translation of the Bible into French. Not to be forgotten are Desiderius Erasmus, who systematically examined Scripture manuscripts to prepare a new edition. (his meticulous notes became the basis for the best scientific study of Scripture during that period) and Ulrich Zwingli, founder of the Swiss Reformed church who taught that the Gospel alone should be the rule of faith and practice.

The great reformers were not always in agreement with each other on every point, but they were filled with the Holy Spirit and worked hard to eliminate errors that had crept in. They defended, and were willing to die for, the truth as they saw it. Where is that fire of enthusiasm today? What happened? Why did most of it die out?

We should take heed of Jesus' admonition, "Be watchful, and strengthen the things which remain, that are ready to die: for I have not found thy works perfect before God."

Compromise for the sake of unity is not the way to go. When the Rapture is at hand, some things are ready to die. Doctrines concerning Christ and salvation by faith are so very important, we should hang on with every fiber in us. Read the scriptures. Know what you believe. Be strong in the faith. Confess your sins. Hold fast. The time is short.

THE LORD'S MONOLOGUE: PART 6

Message to Philadelphia
In the viewfinder: the church that will be Raptured

The word Philadelphia means brotherly love. The city was founded by Attalus Philadelphus, king of Pergamos. At present, it is called *Allah Shair*, city of God, a good name since this is the group that has the open door set before them and who belong to the city of God, New Jerusalem.

In the last two messages, one to the Philadelphians and the other to the Laodiceans, the Lord does not mention church history. The reason: he is addressing LIVING individuals within the entire professing church today.

The Philadelphians represent one foot of the Body of Christ, the one that will exit the womb of Earth first. The Laodiceans represents the other foot, the one that will be born into a new world last.

When the Rapture is at hand, there are two basic kinds of Christians, those filled with the Holy Spirit (i.e., they have *agape* love) and those without enough of it. The Bride of Christ, who loves God and has his love, is going in Rapture I. The one who is not the Bride, who is indifferent, neither cold nor hot, is going to be left behind. Any bridegroom would make the same choice. There must be a love relationship between the Bride and Bridegroom.

There is a good reason why the Philadelphians are listed in sixth position. They represent the main body who will be Raptured, and the first Rapture is as the days of Noah.[82] Noah was 600 years old when he went up in the Ark, so it looks like the Rapture on the 6,000th year since Adam left Eden would fulfill the type. See *Exit: 2007, The Secret of Secrets Revealed* for more details.

The door to Heaven opens

> And to the angel of the church in Philadelphia write; These things saith he that is holy, he that is true, he that hath the key of David (as in the preview), he that openeth, and no man

> shutteth; and shutteth, and no man openeth; I
> know thy works: behold, I have set before
> thee an **open door**, and no man can shut it:
> for thou hast a little strength, and hast kept
> my word, and hast not denied my name.[83]

There are obvious differences between Sardis and
Philadelphia. One seems to be that the church of Sardis believed his word, but the church of Philadelphia believes and
obeys his word. They are zealous and demonstrate their faith
by their works. Sardis lost its strength. Philadelphia still has
a little strength. Laodicea is not zealous, either.

In our play, the door to Heaven above the sky-blue
curtain is now standing open. All is in readiness. Jesus has
already prepared a place for us. The Rapture will happen
quickly as soon as we hear his voice saying, "Come up
hither." In the meantime, we must be patient.

Love letter to the Bride

Jesus has a few words of encouragement for us while we are
waiting for the Rapture to take place.

> Behold, I will make them of the synagogue
> of Satan, which say they are Jews, and are
> not, but do lie; behold, I will make them to
> come and worship before thy feet, and to
> know that **I have loved thee**.[84]

Jesus is telling us something very special here. "I
have loved thee" are precious words spoken straight from
the heart of the Bridegroom to his chosen Bride. He chooses
those he loves who return his love.

What man in this country takes a bride without telling
her he loves her? What bride says, "Yes," to a marriage pro-
posal without telling him she loves him? If you truly love Jesus Christ, I suggest you tell him about it.

Be sure to confess any sin standing between you and
him. He will forgive you. Feel his fountain of love welling
up within you. Let his love fill you, flow through you, and
reach out to others to draw them closer to him.

He has made special promises to us. They are not the same as those made to Israel. He will keep every promise he made to the Jews. He hasn't forgotten them. It is as if he has them engraved on his hand. Their inheritance is intact. However, there is a special promise for us.

The Bridegroom's promise to the Bride

> Because thou hast kept the word of my patience (patient waiting), I also will keep thee **from** (*ek*, out of) the hour of temptation (*peirasmou*, adversity, trouble, trial; i.e., the ten years,[85] which includes the 2,300 days of the shortened Tribulation), which shall come (after the Rapture) upon all the world, to try (*peirasai*) them that dwell upon the earth.[86]

The faithful believers who are filled with the Holy Spirit and God's love are given this special promise not given to the other churches. Only to the church of Philadelphia does Jesus say that he will keep them from the hour of temptation.

The main part of this hour of temptation that we are to be kept out of is the seven-year Tribulation, which is shortened to 2,300 days. We say in the Lord's prayer, "lead us not into temptation (*peirasmon*, trial), but deliver (*rhuomai*, haul from danger, rescue) us from evil." The greatest trial, temptation, and evil will all be present during the Tribulation. In Matthew 26:41, the Lord said, "Watch and pray, that ye **enter not** into temptation (*peirasmon*, trial, adversity, trouble)."

One foot of the Body of Christ will be kept from the entire Tribulation. The other foot will only be kept from the great catastrophe. The first foot is the Bride of Christ. The second foot represents the friends of the Bride.

The Psalms have some very interesting passages that apply to the Rapture. Chapter 94:13 speaks of giving "rest **from** the days of adversity, until the pit be digged for the wicked." The days of adversity are the Tribulation. The pit will be dug for the wicked at the consummation of the age.

Psalm 12:1 in the NIV suggests that the faithful will just disappear. It says, "Help, LORD, for the godly are no more; the faithful have **vanished** from among men."

We will vanish, but the Rapture is not so secret that no one will see it happen. Look at what Psalm 40:1-3 has to say on the subject:

> I WAITED patiently (like the Philadelphians) for the LORD; and he inclined (bent down) unto me, and heard my cry. He brought me up (the Rapture) also out of an horrible pit, out of the miry clay (this body made from 'the dust of the ground'[87]), and set my feet upon a rock (Heaven), and established my goings. And he hath put a new song (sung after the Rapture[88]) in my mouth, even praise unto our God: **many shall see it, and fear, and shall trust in the LORD.**

Many shall see it. It may be a new thought, but there is a precedent. When Elijah was translated, Elisha saw it. He asked for a double portion of the Holy Spirit. Elijah told him, "Thou hast asked a hard thing: nevertheless, if thou see me when I am taken from thee, it shall be so unto thee; but if not, it shall not be so. And it came to pass, as they still went on, and talked, that, behold, there appeared a chariot of fire, and horses of fire, and parted them both asunder; and Elijah went up by a whirlwind into heaven."[89]

Elisha saw it happen. This sounds like we will go up by a whirlwind into Heaven too. It also suggests that the people who see the Rapture happen may be given a double portion of the Holy Spirit to see them through the hard times ahead. They will KNOW that the scriptures are true. This could wake them up and make a big difference in their lives.

Isaiah 57:1,2 says,

> The righteous perisheth, and no man layeth it to heart: and merciful men are taken away, none considering that **the righteous is taken away from the evil to come.** He

shall enter into peace: they shall rest in their beds, each one walking in his uprightness.

Paul told us of the millennial Day of the Lord:

That day shall not come, except there come a falling away (*apostasia*, defection from a state, separation, as in divorce; from the root *aphistemi*, to withdraw oneself, remove, go away, absent oneself from, **desert a station in life, depart**; i.e., the Rapture) **first**, and the man of sin be revealed, the son of perdition.[90]

He apostasia means "the departure" and was translated thus in early versions, The Geneva Bible, Tyndale's translation, Cranmer's version, the Great Bible, Breecher's Bible, the Coverdale Bible, and Beza's translation.

The man of sin cannot be revealed until the restraining Holy Spirit is removed when he takes the Bride to Heaven. It is as if every member of the Bride is hooked onto the Holy Spirit by being indwelt by him. Then, when he goes to Heaven, everyone that is hooked onto him goes also.

The False Prophet, who is the man of sin and the son of perdition, can be recognized when he and the Roman Beast sign the seven-year peace treaty. The departure (Rapture) has to take place **before** he signs that treaty at the beginning of the seven year Tribulation.

Hold fast the faith. Don't lose your crown. The Rapture can happen in a moment. Be wise virgins. Keep your lamps burning bright and hang on to the blessed hope that you will go in the Rapture.

Promise to overcomers

As he ends this segment, Jesus reassures the Philadelphians:

Behold, I come quickly (he comes quickly at the Rapture): hold that fast which thou hast, that no man take thy crown. Him that overcometh will I make a pillar in the temple of my

God, and he shall go no more out: and I will
write upon him the name of my God, and the
name of the city of my God, *which is* new
Jerusalem, which cometh down out of heav-
en from my God: and *I will write upon him*
my new name. He that hath an ear, let him
hear what the Spirit saith unto the churches.[91]

Our home is in New Jerusalem in the heavenly Sion.
We will get a glimpse of the city in Revelation 21:9,10,
which says, "Come hither, I will shew thee the bride, the
Lamb's wife. And he carried me away in the spirit to a great
and high mountain (Heaven), and shewed me that great city,
the holy Jerusalem, descending out of heaven from God."
John was shown it as if zooming in with a telescopic lens.

We must take heed of Christ's warning now. He tells
the Philadelphians, "Behold, I come quickly: hold that fast
which thou hast, that no man take thy crown." In Romans
13:10-14, Paul gives advice to those "knowing the time."

Love worketh no ill to his neighbour: therefore love is the fulfilling of the law. And that,
knowing the time, that now it is high time
to awake out of sleep: for now is our salvation nearer than when we believed. The night
is far spent, **the day is at hand** (the
Rapture): let us therefore cast off the works
of darkness, and let us put on the armour of
light. Let us walk honestly...put ye on the
Lord Jesus Christ, and make not provision
for the flesh, to fulfil the lusts thereof.

THE LORD'S MONOLOGUE: PART 7

Message to the Laodiceans
In the viewfinder: the church that is left behind

We have heard Jesus address "the church of Ephesus," "the
church in Smyrna," "the church in Pergamos," "the church
in Thyatira," "the church in Sardis," and "the church in Philadelphia." However, the last in this series is not a message

to the church in Laodicea, as we might expect. It is to "the church of the Laodiceans." These people are LIVING today, and they are scattered.

There is good reason why this is the seventh message. This is the church's **final wake-up call**. If they do not take heed, they will find themselves facing the terrible 2,300 days of Tribulation on Earth.

This group claims to be Christian, but it is hard to tell any difference in their lives. They hang on to the form of religion, but it has no power. Displaying no zeal to do Christ's work on Earth, yet they do not deny him. These Christians are not hot or cold, just lukewarm, like the baby's milk they feed on. They do not get into the strong meat of the Word, but go over the same basics over and over.

Laodicea fittingly means the rights of the people or people of judgment. This city, a banking center proud of its wealth, was named in honor of Laodice, the wife of Antiochus II (Antiochus Theos), who rebuilt it. Antiochus put her away to marry Bernice. Laodice deserved judgment because she killed Antiochus.

Just reading the name Antiochus Theos makes me shiver. Theos is the Greek word for God. Anti Theos would mean against or instead of God. Antiochus Theos sounds too much like the final Antichrist, the second beast of Revelation 13; and Laodice was the wife of Antiochus Theos.

These Laodiceans are in mortal danger and don't know it. They need a terrific jolt to wake them up right away so they will not swallow the big lie and become the bride of the Antichrist.

During the Tribulation, first the Beast of Rome and then the False Prophet of Israel will be the head of the world church as well as the head of the world government. We have been warned. Jesus said, "Beware of false prophets, which come to you in sheep's clothing, but inwardly they are ravening wolves."[92]

The Laodiceans are in danger of being sucked into the world church before they even realize what is going on. Satan has devised clever traps for the unwary. When they finally wake up and try to extricate themselves from his grasp, they could suffer martyrdom as in the Dark Ages.

Those days will cure them of their indifference and force them to be either hot or cold. It will separate the true believers from the mere professors. Jesus said,

> Not every one that saith unto me, Lord, Lord, shall enter into the kingdom of heaven; but he that **doeth** the will of my Father which is in heaven. Many will say to me in that day, Lord, Lord, have we not prophesied in thy name? and in thy name have cast out devils? and in thy name done many wonderful works? And then will I profess unto them, I never knew you: depart from me, ye that work iniquity.[93]

Be sure you are truly a born-again Christian. Pray and ask Christ to be your personal Saviour. Tell him you believe in him, and thank him for offering you the gift of salvation free of charge. Tell him you accept his offer. Record the date you are born into God's family. Then when you slip and sin, confess it to God immediately to get back in fellowship and be completely filled with the Holy Spirit.

Jesus has no words of commendation for the lukewarm Laodiceans. Listen carefully to what he tells them.

> And unto the angel of the church of the Laodiceans write; These things saith the Amen, the faithful and true witness (Christ), the beginning (*arche*, translated 'the prime source' in the NEB) of the creation of God.[94]

Amen means so be it. If this group does not take heed, so be it. Revelation 22:11 says the same thing.

Here is the creator, the source of all creation. In Revelation 1:8, he told us that he is "the beginning and the ending." The word "beginning" there is also *arche* in the Greek. It means origin, originator, the first person in a series, the leader, the person that commences, the extremity of a thing. John 1:3 is clear: "All things were made by him: and without him was not any thing made that was made."

Wake-up call

> I know thy works, that thou art neither cold
> nor hot: I would thou wert cold or hot. So
> then because thou art lukewarm, and neither
> cold nor hot, I will spue (*emesai*) thee out of
> my mouth.[95]

Here is a tragic spirit of indifference. These believers
are in Christ, but because of their lukewarmness, they are
not likely to be disturbed by heresy or to vigorously defend
the truth unless jolted into it. They don't care enough. However, they are about to get the shock of their lives. Jesus
doesn't mince words. *Emesai* means vomit. Though in
Christ, he will chuck them out. They are still in the stomach,
unassimilated. Their fate for the next decade hangs by a
thread. They are about to be cut off from the Bride of Christ
and become Tribulation saints because they are not worthy.

In John 15:1,2, Jesus said, "I AM the true vine, and
my Father is the husbandman. Every branch in me (believers
in Christ) that beareth not fruit **he taketh away.**"

In the sermon on the mount, Jesus said, "Ye are the
salt of the earth: but if the salt have lost his savour, wherewith shall it be salted? it is thenceforth good for nothing, but
to be cast out, and to be trodden under foot of men."

If we don't watch, he will come on us as a thief, and
we will not know what hour he will come.[96] The Laodiceans
are not watching and are in danger of being pruned from the
vine and cast out. Concerning the evil servant, Jesus said,

> The lord of that servant (believer) shall come
> in **a day** when he looketh not for him, and in
> **an hour** that he is not aware of, And shall
> cut him asunder, and appoint him his portion
> with the hypocrites: there shall be weeping
> and gnashing of teeth.[97]

Luke 12:46 says he **"will appoint him his portion with the unbelievers."** His portion with the hypocrites and unbelievers will be during the Tribulation. He

will go to heaven in Rapture II at the end of this age, but in the meantime, he will have to endure the terrible Tribulation.

If the evil servant can be cut off and appointed his portion with the unbelievers in a day and hour that he is not aware of, doesn't it sound like we should be aware and looking for him on a certain day and hour?

What day and hour? The clues are there if we only open our eyes and look for them. In the Olivet Discourse, when Jesus said, "But of that day and hour knoweth no man, no, not the angels of heaven, but my Father only,"[98] no man knew at that particular time. It applied to those early days, when Christ did not want them worrying about when he was coming. It could not apply forever. People will know during the Tribulation. It is different today too. The Sign of the End of the Age has already appeared. It made knowing the day possible. The Rapture is at hand.

The church in Sardis was told, "He that overcometh, the same shall be clothed in white raiment; and I will not blot out his name out of the book of life, but I will confess his name before my Father." Thus, the members of the church have their names written in the book of life, but under some circumstance, they can be blotted out. Blotting out names is similar to vomiting them out of his mouth. At this point, they must do something or be left behind. If they are to be part of the Bride of Christ, they must have white wedding garments, and "THE FINE LINEN IS THE RIGHTEOUS-NESSES OF SAINTS."[99] This includes Christ's imputed righteousness and our righteous acts after we believe.

Listen to what Jesus tells them.

Because thou sayest, I am rich, and increased with goods, and have need of nothing; and knowest not that thou art wretched, and mis-erable, and poor, and blind, and **naked**: I counsel thee to **buy of me** gold tried in the fire, that thou mayest be rich; and **white raiment**, that thou mayest be clothed, and *that* the shame of thy nakedness do not appear; and anoint thine eyes with eyesalve, that thou mayest see.[100]

In other words, **WAKE UP**, it will soon be too late. He wants the Holy-Spirit-deficient, spiritually-blind, people who are not wearing white robes to buy of him gold, a symbol of deity. To do this, they must repent, confess their sins, and be filled with his Holy Spirit. He loves them, but he will chastise them if that is what it takes.

> ## WARNING
> ## RAPTURE NEAR

Last chance to go for the gold

As many as I love, I rebuke and chasten (Jesus will chasten them during the Tribulation): be zealous therefore, and repent.[101]

They had better hurry to do what he says. This is their **last chance** to repent before the Rapture. This is their **last wake-up call.** The very next thing Jesus says is:

Behold, I stand at the door, and knock;[102]

SLAM! The Rapture is history. The door is shut.

Surprise! The Rapture flashed like lightning again. Suddenly it's too late. Like a garage door that pops its spring, the door slams down like crashing thunder. It happened quickly. It caught us unaware as it did in the preview. Christ and his Bride are now on the other side of the door.

The Philadelphians have vanished; the Laodiceans are left behind. They weep and gnash their teeth for what might have been. Yet, Jesus gives them encouragement:

if any man hear my voice, and open the door,
I will come in to him, and will sup with him,
and he with me[103] (they were not Spirit filled).

They have suddenly become saints that will have to go through the Tribulation to test their metal. They will not be kept "from the hour of temptation, which shall come upon all the world, to try them that dwell upon the earth." They have lost their crowns and position as one of the Bride. Now if they want him, they have to open the door to him, i.e., repent, confess their sins, and be filled with his Holy Spirit. They could have done it before the Rapture and been chosen as the Bride, but they would not listen and waited until it was too late. The choice was theirs.

Promise to the overcomers left behind
The explanation of the details of the Rapture will follow in Revelation 4:1, but first, Christ reassures the Laodiceans that if they over come, they can still sit with him in his throne, which is in Heaven.

To him that overcometh will I grant to sit
with me in my throne, even as I also overcame, and am set down with my Father in his
throne. He that hath an ear, let him hear what
the Spirit saith unto the churches.[104]

By the end of the Tribulation, the over comers will have washed their robes in the blood of Christ. In Revelation 7:14,15, we see a multitude from all nations in heaven. "These are they which came out of great tribulation, and have washed their robes, and made them white in the blood of the Lamb. Therefore are they before the throne of God.

Although some will be chastised, not a single overcomer will actually be lost. In John 6:39, John says,

And this is the Father's will which hath sent
me, that of all which he hath given me I
should lose nothing, but should **raise it up
again** (Rapture II) at the last day.

There is both a first day and a last day, a first Rapture and a second Rapture, a first trump and a last trump. The last day is the Translation of the Tribulation Saints, Rapture II. All living believers who do not go the first time will be taken to heaven the second time, which will take place when this age ends and the Millennium begins.

Those who go in the second Rapture will be invited, not to the marriage of the Lamb, but to the wedding reception, called the "marriage supper of the Lamb."[105] The Old Testament saints, like John the Baptist, are called friends of the Bridegroom.[106] The Tribulation saints are friends of the Bride.

Precious promises

Victors will be able to eat of the tree of life, which is in the midst of the paradise of God. The second death cannot hurt us. We will eat of the hidden manna and be given a white stone with a new name. We will be given the morning star, power over the nations, and white raiment.

Our names will not be blotted out of the book of life. The pillars of the church on Earth will become pillars in the temple of God in the heavenly New Jerusalem. We will also sit with Christ in his throne. We are a privileged group, and these are just a taste of the good things Christ has prepared for those that love him. This is the destiny of the faithful.

> Eye hath not seen, nor ear heard, neither have entered into the heart of man, the things which God hath prepared for them that love him.[107]

Do you truly love him? You should; just think of what he went through when he paid the supreme penalty—the death penalty—for our sins. He bought us with a price, and what a price. He must have loved us very much to do it.

Queen Esther is a type of the Bride of Christ. King Ahasuerus gathered many virgins, then chose Esther from among them. In this play, we saw Christ stand inspecting the churches to choose his Bride. Like other bridegrooms, he did not choose those who were indifferent to him, but those who loved him with all their hearts. We must have a love relationship with him. In Revelation 17:14, those "with him *are* called, and chosen, and faithful,"[108] like Esther.

Let all torchbearers take heed of the Lord's wake-up call. Keep your lamp's flame so bright that it can easily be seen, even at the midnight hour, if he comes at the time mentioned in the parable of the ten virgins. Then you will hear his voice like a trumpet saying, "Come up hither."

In Matthew 24:36, we find Jesus' statement, "of that day and hour knoweth no man." However, the next verse starts with **"But."** We are then given some clues. His next coming will be as the days of Noah. Noah was 600[109] when the Flood came, suggesting the 6,000th year. Midnight is mentioned a little later, in the parable of the ten virgins.

Matthew gives lots of information about the Rapture:

> Two women (two religious groups) shall be grinding at the mill; the one shall be taken (the Philadelphians), and the other left (the Laodiceans). Watch therefore: for ye (the one left?) know not what hour your Lord doth come. But know this, that if the goodman (leader) of the house (church) had known in what watch the thief (Christ) would come, he would have watched, and would not have suffered his house (church) to be **broken up**. Therefore be ye (Laodiceans?) also ready): for in such an hour as ye think not the Son of man cometh (Rapture II seems to be in the night[110])....The lord of that (evil) servant shall come in a day when he (the evil servant) looketh not for him, and in an hour that he is not aware of, And shall cut him asunder, and appoint him his portion with the hypocrites: there shall be weeping and gnashing of teeth. THEN shall the kingdom of heaven be likened unto ten virgins, which took their lamps, and went forth to meet the bridegroom. And five of them were wise (the Philadelphians), and five were foolish (the

Laodiceans). They that were foolish took their lamps, and took no oil with them: But the wise took oil in their vessels with their lamps. While the bridegroom tarried, they all slumbered and slept. And **at midnight** there was a cry made, Behold, the bridegroom cometh; **go** ye out to meet him. Then all those virgins arose, and trimmed their lamps. And the foolish said unto the wise, Give us of your oil; for our lamps are gone (margin, going) out. But the wise answered, saying, Not so; lest there be not enough for us and you: but go ye rather to them that sell, and buy for yourselves. And while they went to buy, the bridegroom came; and they that were ready (the Philadelphians) went in with him to the marriage: and **the door was shut** (as it slams shut on the Laodiceans). Afterward came also the other virgins, saying, Lord, Lord, open to us. But he answered and said, Verily I say unto you, I know you not. Watch therefore, for ye (foolish virgins, Laodiceans) know neither the day nor the hour wherein the Son of man cometh.[111]

We must be ready, for just as in the preview, the Rapture happens suddenly; it flashes without warning. By the time the thunder rolls, it is too late. The door has slammed shut. We must not delay.

Here in our play, as in the preview, the action comes first because it is such a sudden surprise. The explanation follows. We hear John explain what has happened as Revelation four begins.

Remember the twins, Jacob and Esau. Like the two feet of the Body of Christ, one was born before the other. Genesis 25:26 says that Isaac was 60 years old when they were born. The 60 years may be significant. Modern Israel was born in the Jewish 5708. The year 5708 plus 60 is 5768, the first day of which begins the Millennium. It also is the day of the birth of the other foot of the Body of Christ.

1 Revelation 2:7,11,17,29; 3:6,13,22
2 Daniel 8:14
3 Revelation 2:22-26
4 Revelation 3:3
5 Revelation 17:1-6
6 Revelation 13:11
7 Revelation 3:4
8 Revelation 7:14
9 Matthew 24:34
10 Matthew 25:1-12
11 Revelation 3:17
12 Revelation 1:19
13 Revelation 1:3
14 Daniel 10:5,6
15 Revelation 2:1
16 Revelation 2:2-4
17 Revelation 13:4
18 Revelation 13:11-18
19 NASB
20 Galatians 5:22
21 Revelation 2:5
22 John 7:38
23 Revelation 2:6
24 *Webster's New Twentieth Century Dictionary*, unabridged, 2nd ed., (Cleveland: World Publishing Co., 1960) p. 1210
25 Revelation 2:7
26 Revelation 12:1-4
27 Daniel 12:10
28 Revelation 6:11
29 Revelation 20:4
30 Revelation 7:13
31 Revelation 2:8,9
32 Revelation 2:10
33 Revelation 6:9
34 Revelation 17:16
35 Revelation 2:11
36 Revelation 20:14
37 Hutchings, Noah W. *Petra in History and Prophecy*. (Oklahoma City, OK, Hearthstone Publishing Ltd., 1991) pg. 76-79
38 Revelation 12:17
39 Matthew 24:21,22
40 Revelation 2:12
41 Revelation 2:13
42 Hosea 6:1-3

43 Zechariah 5:5-11
44 Matthew 24:21-26
45 Matthew 24:27
46 Isaiah 14:23
47 Revelation 2:14
48 Numbers 22:30-32
49 Hosea 13:4
50 Ezekiel 21:4,5,14-17
51 Numbers 25:1-3
52 Matthew 5:13
53 II Thessalonians 2:6,7
54 I Peter 4:17
55 Revelation 2:15-17
56 Revelation 2:17
57 Psalm 78:21-25
58 Revelation 2:18,19
59 *The Concordia Cyclopedia.* (St. Louis, MO: Concordia Publ. House, 1927) p. 564
60 Hains, Edmont. *The Seven Churches of Revelation.* (Winona Lake, IN: nd) p. 69-73
61 *The Concordia Cyclopedia.*, p. 580
62 Revelation 2:20
63 II Corinthians 4:4
64 Revelation 2:21,22
65 Revelation 2:23-25
66 Revelation 2:26-29
67 Romans 1:17
68 Isaiah 11:2
69 Revelation 3:1-3a
70 Revelation 3:3b
71 Matthew 16:3
72 Hosea 9:10; Joel 1:6,7; Ezekiel 36:8
73 Revelation 3:8; 4:1
74 Numbers 14:34, LXX
75 Daniel 12:4
76 Matthew 12:38,40
77 Jonah 3:4
78 Isaiah 66:8
79 Daniel 1:11,14 NIV
80 Revelation 3:4-6
81 Revelation 7:14
82 Matthew 24:37
83 Revelation 3:7,8
84 Revelation 3:9

[85] Revelation 2:10
[86] Revelation 3:10
[87] Genesis 2:7
[88] Revelation 5:9
[89] II Kings 2:10,11
[90] II Thessalonians 2:3
[91] Revelation 3:11-13
[92] Matthew 7:15
[93] Matthew 7:21-23
[94] Revelation 3:14
[95] Revelation 3:15,16
[96] Revelation 3:3
[97] Matthew 24:50,51
[98] Matthew 24:36
[99] Margin, Revelation 19:8
[100] Revelation 3:17,18
[101] Revelation 3:19
[102] Revelation 3:20a
[103] Revelation 3:20b
[104] Revelation 3:21,22
[105] Revelation 19:9
[106] John 3:29
[107] I Corinthians 2:9
[108] Revelation 17:14
[109] Genesis 7:6
[110] Luke 17:29-37
[111] Matthew 24:37-25:1-13

3

The Morning Star

Revelation 4 and 5

Lightning struck him twice and he lived to tell the tale. When he was young, ball lightning knocked my dad to his knees as it came in the open front door where he was standing. It rolled straight through that stately two-story house and out the back door. In self defense, that house, built by his dad from oak boards he had the saw mill cut from trees from his own woods, sprouted lightning rods.

In his later years, Dad was sitting on a wooden stool under his open garage door several miles from the old home place tinkering with his electronic equipment. He repaired TV sets in his spare time. Suddenly thunder crashed all around. Mom yelled for Dad to come in, that lightning had ruined the television in the house. He didn't come—or hear.

In spite of lightning arrestors and ground wires attached to six-foot copper rods driven deep into the Earth, the lightning he didn't see had knocked him off his stool. It's a good thing he was up on the high wooden stool and not grounded on the concrete when it struck. Mom found him on the floor of the garage, stunned out of his wits. It took some time for him to regain his senses and his equilibrium.

Even after he got to his feet, he tottered around for awhile jabbering gibberish incessantly as if the wiring in his brain was short circuited.

In our play, the Rapture happened too quickly for any explanation. Like the lightning that came in on the electric wires and hit Dad, it flashed unexpectedly and left the Laodiceans stunned on the wrong side of the door.

The fact that the door is already open in Jesus' message to the Philadelphians shows that the Rapture is at hand.

Since all of Revelation was written as if the Rapture was at hand, both the open door in the message to the Philadelphians and the closed door in the message to the Laodiceans appear at the time of the Rapture. The door opens and then bangs shut. It just takes longer to tell about it than for it to actually take place.

Our word Rapture is from the Latin *rapiemur*, which is derived from *raptus*, which means to seize by force. This is exactly what happened so quickly. Believers were suddenly snatched out of this world by the might of God. When the Holy Spirit went, those solidly attached to him went too.

Just as in the preview, the narrator of our play fills us in on what has happened right after it has taken place. First the action, then the description. It is like instant replay in slow motion with an accompanying explanation.

> "THE THINGS WHICH ARE, AND THE THINGS WHICH SHALL BE HEREAFTER"

The Rapture

In Revelation 3:20, the door suddenly slammed shut. There was no time to give the details. It happened too quickly for words. As Revelation four begins, John has already finished telling us about the things he had seen that concerned the state of the church when the Rapture was at hand.

Next, he will tell us of "the things which are," the Rapture itself. That will not take long because it happens so quickly. Just as we will, John will suddenly experience the Rapture himself. After being caught up to Heaven, he will report what he sees in Heaven. We listen carefully as he begins to speak, for this can happen to us.

> After these things I looked, and behold, a
> **door** *standing* **open** in heaven (NKJV).[1]

This door not only symbolizes the Rapture but the Lord Jesus Christ, who is the true door by which we enter Heaven. In John 10:9, he said, "I am the door: by me if any man enter in, he shall be saved, and shall go in and out, and find pasture (food)."

As John continues, he hears a voice:

> and the first (former) voice which I heard *was* as it were of a trumpet talking with me; which said, **Come up hither**, and I will shew thee things which must be hereafter (after the Rapture). And immediately I was (margin, became) in the spirit:[2]

The first voice John heard after the Rapture in the preview was the voice like a trumpet saying, "I am the Alpha and Omega, the first and the last."[3] Therefore, this voice like a trumpet is Christ. His voice is like a trumpet because it is a feast day. The door of the Temple was opened each morning with the sound of a trumpet. Here the door to Heaven is opened with the sound of a trumpet on a feast day. Pentecost is the most likely.

He trumpets, **"Come up hither,"** and John instantly becomes in the spirit and is transported quickly through the door into Heaven. This is the first of the two Raptures, one of the Philadelphians, the other of the Tribulation saints.

The Two Raptures
Some people believe in the Pre-Tribulation Rapture. Others think it will be just before Christ returns at the Second Advent. One reason for the confusion over when the Rapture will take place is because, in a way, both camps are right. The scriptures reveal that there are two Raptures, one of the Bride of Christ and one of the Tribulation saints.

All believers are part of the Body of Christ, but not all are of the same part of the body. Jesus Christ, the head, emerged from Earth and went to Heaven first. Afterward, as generation after generation of Christians died, the main part of the body has gradually been expelled from Earth and born into Heaven. Today, most of the Body of Christ has already been born into that new world.

We are living in the time of the end, when the feet are ready to come out. Set before you is the "blessed hope" that you will not have to die, that you can be transferred to Heaven alive by means of the Raptures. This last generation of living believers are the feet of the Body of Christ, and one foot will emerge from the womb slightly before the other.

It is important to understand this correctly so we will be watching for the right thing. I know of one man who says that those who are expecting Christ next will be fooled into accepting the Antichrist, because he is the next to appear. I do not believe that. The Bride of Christ is to watch for the Lord's appearing. Only the Tribulation saints will see the appearing of Antichrist before they see Christ coming.

Right now, we are not supposed to be looking for the appearance of the Antichrist, we are to be looking for our Lord and Saviour Jesus Christ's coming at the first Rapture. That is the next item on the prophetic agenda.

The Sign of the Son of Man that will be seen at the time of Rapture II will strike fear into the hearts of man, for "then shall all the tribes of the earth mourn."[4] At Rapture I, however, there will be a "glorious appearing." Titus 2:13 mentions this.

> Looking for **that blessed hope**, and **the glorious appearing** of the great God and our Saviour Jesus Christ.

Our blessed hope is that we will be chosen as the Bride of Christ and taken to Heaven in the first Rapture and won't have to go through that time of terrible testing that we call the Tribulation and the Seventieth Week of Daniel, but will be kept from it. In the end, those that are with him will be "called, and chosen, and faithful."[5]

The Rapture of the church saints takes place before the seven-year Tribulation begins. The second, the Rapture of the Tribulation saints, takes place at the end of the shortened Tribulation, on the 2,300th day, before the asteroid strikes Earth at noon. (See my book, *Exit: 2007, The Secret of Secrets Revealed*, for more details.)

The church is called the temple of the Holy Spirit. When it is raised up, construction on the literal temple in Jerusalem may be started. At least the altar has to be finished by the beginning of the Tribulation, because sacrificing begins then.[6] Revelation 11:1 mentions the temple at the beginning of the ministry of God's two witnesses. Therefore, I believe the temple will be finished by that time.

The first group to be raptured attends the Marriage of the Lamb. The second group are probably not present at the marriage ceremony, but they are the friends of the Bridegroom[7] who are invited to the reception after the wedding, called the Marriage Supper of the Lamb.

Revelation 19:7-9 reflects this. It says,

> Let us be glad and rejoice, and give honour to him: for the marriage of the Lamb is come, and his wife hath made herself ready. And to her was granted that she should be arrayed in fine linen, clean and white: FOR THE FINE LINEN IS THE RIGHTEOUSNESS OF SAINTS. And he saith unto me, Write, Blessed *are* they which are called unto the marriage supper of the Lamb.

I typed this when I wrote a letter to a friend and was awe struck as I looked back at what I typed. I did not intend to capitalize that phrase. This is the second time something like this has happened. Both times, I was blindly copying Scripture, looking at the Bible, not at my screen. The caps lock key is not above the shift key as on a typewriter, either. It's in the lower left corner where it is very awkward to hit even when I want to use it. The Lord must want me to emphasize this.

The Bride of Christ is already wearing white robes when Christ comes at the first Rapture. The Tribulation saints must have "washed their robes, and made them white in the blood of the Lamb"[8] before they can be admitted to Heaven. Thus, it is the righteousness of the saints that determines which Rapture they can take part in. The first Rapture is a prize to be earned.

The word "righteousness" in the scripture above is plural in the Greek. It includes the righteousness of Christ that is imputed to us plus our righteous acts. Most important of all is to confess our sins and therefore be filled with the Holy Spirit. Sin forms a barrier between us and God. The amount of the Holy Spirit in us is diminished. We have to be forgiven our sins to be completely filled.

This was the second time capitalization happened. The first time, my friend Yvonne, whom I have not met, but with whom I correspond, had written that she had received the interesting information that we are now on the horizon of a rendezvous of five planets and the moon, all in the vicinity of the sun—a rare event! The seven heavenly bodies will be coming together in a massing of the planets. Her sources said that it will occur May 5, 2000. She wanted to know if this could be the sign Jesus spoke about in Luke 21:25,26.

As I typed my answer, I said, "I don't know right off if the massing of the planets on May 5, 2000 is the sign Jesus spoke of in Luke 21:25,26, but it will be Friday, Nisan 30, 5760 on the Jewish Calendar. Since I grabbed a Bible at random and have the Lamsa Bible on my desk, I'll just quote what it says and see if I can get any idea on this. I'll start with the last of verse 24 and quote through 28:"

> Jerusalem will be trodden under the feet of the Gentiles until the time of the Gentiles comes to an end. AND THERE WILL BE SIGNS IN SUN AND MOON AND STARS; AND ON EARTH DISTRESS OF THE NATIONS, AND CONFUSION BECAUSE OF THE ROARING OF THE SEA; And upheaval that takes life out of men, because of fear of what is to come on earth; and the powers of the universe will be shaken. Then they will see the Son of man coming in the clouds with a large army and great glory. But when these things begin to happen, have courage and lift up your heads, because your salvation is at hand.

It looks like the Lord may have helped me get an idea on this. I was amazed the first time but awe-struck the second time this capitalization happened. Maybe Yvonne is right in thinking that the massing of the Sun, Moon and planets in May, 2000, could be a sign. Saturn will be among them.

Information that she sent gave several dates of interesting conjunctions in 2000. It says that on May 17, Venus will be in conjunction with Jupiter and with Saturn a few hours later. On May 27, Jupiter and Saturn will come together. A lot of interesting things happen in one month.

As you can see, my mail is very interesting. People have written from as far away as Kuala Lumpur, Malaysia.

Another correspondent of mine, George, ran the Expert Astronomer computer program and told me that the best massing of heavenly bodies would take place May 3, 2000, when Sun, Moon, Mercury, Venus, Mars, Saturn and Jupiter all line up, with the bonus of a partial solar eclipse.

Think about how our little Moon causes tides on the Earth. At that time we will have the Sun, Moon, Jupiter, Saturn, Mercury, Mars and Venus all on one side of us. This is the main mass of the solar system. The sun is huge in size. Jupiter and Saturn are giants. Will this cause some huge tides? The scripture mentioned "the roaring of the sea."

Also of interest, Saturn will travel through the constellations from Taurus to Leo from 2000 to 2007. These constellations are thought by many to tell the story of God's Wrath poured out on unbelievers. Taurus represents the Judge. Gemini, in the ancient zodiacs speaks of the Bridegroom and his Bride. Cancer stands for resurrection. Leo, the lion is pouncing on the many-headed serpent, Hydra.

Near August 29, 2007, Saturn and Regulus, the king star in Leo, will be in conjunction (appear close together) as Rosh Hashanah, the Jewish New Year and Feast of Trumpets approaches. Rosh Hashanah, Tishri 1, 5768 will be on September 13, 2007. It will start at 6:00 P.M. on our September 12. If these are meant to be signs, they will be good ones, especially this last conjunction. They seem to tell a connected story, and the dates are significant. It looks like Christ will be crowned with a golden crown on that Tishri 1.

I also wonder if the comet Hale-Bopp that was discovered July 23, 1995 is a sign. It travels nearly a million miles per day and did rendezvous with our planet in the spring of 1997.[9] It was a mere 85 million miles from the Sun at its closest approach on April 2, 1997. From March 8 through 10, it swept several degrees north of the galaxy NGC7331 in the constellation of Pegasus. It drew an arc in the sky above Saturn, the slow planet, which is now under the Great Square of Pegasus and moving lazily to the left toward Aries. It looks like Saturn will be entering Aries, the Ram, when the Rapture takes place.

The view of the comet Hale-Bopp was sensational. It stretches over 2.5 million kilometers, so it has a larger volume than the Sun. Its nucleus may span several dozen kilometers. It was spectacular and may have been a sign.

The times of the Gentiles came to an end when Israel took the rest of Jerusalem in the Six-Day War of 1967. Since then, the Rapture could have been "at hand."

I can't emphasize this enough. We should be sure to confess our sins and have them forgiven, so as to be wearing the wedding garment when the Rapture takes place. Otherwise we can be cast out. In the parable of the marriage feast, Jesus said,

> The wedding is ready, but they which were bidden were **not worthy**. Go ye therefore into the highways, and as many as ye shall find, bid to the marriage....And when the king came in to see the guests, he saw there a man which had not on a wedding garment: And he saith unto him, **Friend** (a Tribulation saint, friend of the Bride), how camest thou in hither not having a wedding garment? And he was speechless (he didn't know he was like the Laodiceans—"naked"[10]) Then said the king to the servants, Bind him hand and foot, and take him away, and cast him into outer darkness; there shall be weeping and gnashing of teeth. For many are called, but **few are chosen**.[11]

As in the parable of the ten virgins that Jesus told, some (like the Philadelphians) are wise and have enough oil of the Holy Spirit, others (like the Laodiceans) are not properly prepared. They are not yet worthy to be chosen, and "they that are with him (Christ) are called, and chosen, and faithful."[12]

Rapture I is as it was in the days of Noah. Only they were listed as being given in marriage, and their going up into the Ark preceded the flood by seven days[13] just as our going up precedes the seven-year Tribulation. Rapture II is as it was in the days of Lot when no marriage was listed and fire and brimstone fell that same day. Here are the scriptures.

> But as the days of Noe (Noah) were, so shall also the coming of the Son of man be. For as in the days that were before the flood they were eating and drinking, marrying and giving in **marriage**, until the day that Noe entered into the ark, And knew not until the flood came and took them all away; so shall also the coming of the Son of man be....Two women (religious groups, Philadelphians and Laodiceans) shall be grinding at the mill; the **one shall be taken, and the other left.**[14]

Above: one group, the Philadelphians, shall be taken in Rapture I—as the days of Noah. Below: another group, the Laodiceans, shall be taken in Rapture II—as the days of Lot.

> Likewise also as it was in the days of Lot; they did eat, they drank, they bought, they sold, they planted, they builded (**no marriage is listed**); But **the same day** that Lot went out of Sodom **it rained fire and brimstone from heaven**, and destroyed them all. Even thus shall it be in the day when the Son of man is revealed (this is the Sign of the Son of Man of Matthew 24:30 that is seen on the 2,300th day of the shortened Tribulation)...I tell you, in that night there shall be two men in one bed; the one shall be taken, and the other shall be left.[15]

There has been some confusion over when the Rapture is to take place because I Corinthians 15:52 mentions being changed "at the last trump." It has been suggested that this last trump is the last of the seven trumpet judgments. However, the Tribulation saints are seen in heaven before the seventh seal is opened, after which the seven trumpet judgments begin to sound. It seems that the trumpets that sound to call the redeemed to Heaven are separate from the trumpet judgments.

There are two times when the Lord calls in a voice like a trumpet for a group of saints to come up. The first Rapture takes place at the first trump, the second Rapture at the last trump.

Scriptures that apply to the first trump

> I would not have you to be ignorant, brethren (Christians), concerning them which are asleep (dead in Christ), that ye sorrow not, even as others which have no hope (we have this 'blessed hope'). For if we believe that Jesus died and rose again, even so them also which sleep in Jesus (the dead in Christ) will God bring with him. For this we say unto you by the word of the Lord, that we which are alive and remain unto the coming of the Lord (at the Rapture) shall not precede them which are asleep. For the Lord himself shall descend from heaven with a shout, with the voice of the archangel, and with **the trump of God** (the first trump): and the dead in Christ shall rise first: Then we which are alive and remain shall be **caught up together with them in the clouds, t o meet the Lord in the air**, and so shall we ever be with the Lord. Wherefore comfort one another with these words.[16]

> Because thou (the Philadelphians) hast kept the word of my **patience**, I also will keep

thee **from** the hour of temptation (the Tribulation), which shall come upon all the world, to try them that dwell upon the earth.[17]

Watch ye therefore, and pray always, that ye may be accounted **worthy to escape all these things that shall come to pass**, and to stand before the Son of man.[18]

THE righteous perisheth, and no man layeth it to heart: and merciful men are taken away, none considering that **the righteous is taken away from the evil to come**, He shall enter into peace: they shall rest in their beds, each one walking in his uprightness.... For thus saith the high and lofty One that inhabiteth eternity, whose name is Holy; I dwell in the high and holy place (Heaven), with him also that is of a contrite and humble spirit, to revive the spirit of the humble, and to revive the heart of the contrite (repentant) ones.[19]

(Type:) Enoch (meaning teacher) walked with God; and he was not; for God took him.[20]

I WAITED patiently for the LORD; and he inclined (bent down) unto me, and heard my cry. **He brought me up** also out of an horrible pit, out of the miry clay (out of this body of clay), and set my feet upon a rock (Heaven), and established my goings. And he hath put a new song in my mouth, even praise unto our God (a new song is sung after the Rapture[21]): many shall see it (Rapture I), and fear, and shall trust in the LORD.[22]

I press toward the mark for the prize (Rapture I) of the high calling of God in Christ Jesus.[23]

(In) Christ shall all be made alive, But every man in his own order (*tagmati*, rank).[24]

Scriptures that apply to the last trump

Behold, I shew you a mystery; We shall not all sleep, but we shall all be changed, In a moment, in the twinkling of an eye, at **the last trump** (the last call for the saints): for the trumpet shall sound (on the Feast of Trumpets, but before the seven trumpet judgments sound), and the dead shall be raised incorruptible, and we shall be changed, For this corruptible must put on incorruption, and this mortal must put on immortality.[25]

after that tribulation, the sun shall be darkened...And **the stars of heaven shall fall**...then shall they see the Son of man coming in the clouds (this is the Sign of the Son of Man)...Then shall he send his angels, and shall gather together his elect from the fourwinds, from the uttermost part of the **earth** (the Tribulation saints are gathered from Earth) to the uttermost part of **heaven** (the church saints are gathered in Heaven, where they were taken in Rapture I).[26]

Come, my people, enter thou into thy chambers, and **shut thy doors** (symbol of two Raptures) about thee: hide thyself as it were for a little moment, **until the indignation** (Day of God's Wrath) **be overpast.**[27]

But they that wait upon the LORD shall renew their strength; **they shall mount up with wings as eagles** (to join the rest of the Body of Christ[28]); they shall run, and not be weary; and they shall walk, and not faint.[29]

At the rebuke of the LORD, at the blast of the wind of his wrath, **He reached out from on high and grasped me;** he drew me out of the deep waters....and rescued me, because he loves me.[30]

(the LORD) will hide me in his abode (Heaven) **in the day of trouble**; He will conceal me in the shelter of his tent, **he will set me high upon a rock.**[31]

The prize, the first Rapture

If we do not want to be a castaway at the time of Rapture I, we must run the race. To go in the first Rapture is a prize worth working for. Look at what hard-working Paul said,

Know ye not that they which run in a race run all, but one receiveth **the prize.** So run, that ye may obtain. And every man that striveth for the mastery is temperate in all things. Now they do it to obtain a corruptible crown; but we an incorruptible (crowns are given at Rapture I, but are not mentioned at Rapture II). I therefore so run, not as uncertainly; so fight I, not as one that beateth the air: But I keep under my body, and bring it into subjection: lest that by any means, when I have preached to others, I myself should be **a castaway.**[32]

Some modern preachers wearing robes spotted by the flesh should take Paul's words to heart. Preachers can be cast out at the time of the first Rapture too. We must all strive for the prize. Salvation is absolutely free, but the prize of going to Heaven in Rapture I is not a certain thing if we do not run the race properly.

The Tribulation is the worst seven years since Adam was put on Earth. Satan will spring his trap and there will be many martyrs caught in it. Don't be one of them.

Proudly the wicked harass the afflicted, who
are caught in the devices the wicked have
contrived.[33]

To be filled with the Holy Spirit, believers must
confess sins that we have committed since we first accepted
Christ. Jesus said that if he did not wash Peter's feet, Peter
would have no part with him.[34] Remember I John 1:9:

If we confess our sins, he is faithful and just
to forgive us our sins, and to cleanse us from
all unrighteousness.

Heavenly Scene after the Rapture

In our play, we hear John's voice from heaven. He is describing events unfolding there:

and, behold, a throne was set in heaven, and
one (i.e., God) sat on the throne. And he that
sat was to look upon like a jasper and a sardine (sardius) stone:[35]

The jasper and sardius stones were the first and last
stones in the breastplate of the high priest.[36] This indicates
that the one sitting on the throne actually is the Almighty,
who is both the first (Yahweh) and the last (Jesus Christ).
This is the same one we heard in the preview saying, "Fear
not; I am the first and the last: I am he that liveth, and was
dead; and, behold, I am alive for evermore."[37]

However, Jesus is not emphasized here as the one
sitting on the throne because he is to be seen as the Lamb in
the midst of the throne, and because he is to receive his
golden crown the first day of the Millennium. It would be
confusing when we tried to figure out which day his coronation falls on. Here, it is Yahweh, who also is in Jesus, that
is to be highlighted.

The jasper is thought to be purple,[38] evidently deli-
cately colored and clear as crystal, representing the royalty
and perfection of the Lord. In the breastplate of the High

Priest, jasper stands for Reuben, firstborn of Jacob[39] Reuben means "viewing the son,"[40] and shows that this is a view of Jesus, the "firstborn son."[41] At first, it seems confusing, but it always was the son that had to do with mankind, first as Yahweh, the pre-incarnate Christ, later as Christ Jesus.

In the Old Testament, Yahweh said,

> I, even I, am the LORD; and beside me there is no saviour...I am God. Yea, **before the day was I am he.**[42]

In the New Testament, Jesus said,

> Neither pray I for these alone, but for them also which shall believe on me through their work; That they all may be one; as thou, **Father, art in me**, and I in thee, that they also may be one in us: that the world may believe that thou hast sent me. And the glory which thou gavest me I have given them; that they may be one, even as we are one: I in them, and **thou in me**, that they may be made perfect in one...thou lovedst me before the foundation of the world (margin, earth).[43]

The sardius is carnation red, suggesting his blood that was shed as an atonement for our sins. In the breastplate, this stone represents Benjamin, which means "son of my right hand," also referring to Jesus, who sits on the right hand of the Father.[44]

Just as Reuben and Benjamin were the first and last sons born to Jacob, the two colors that represent them in the breastplate, purple and red, are the first and last colors formed by the refraction of light through a prism. These things emphasize the fact that Christ is the first and the last.

In wonder, John continues his description,

> and *there was* a rainbow (*iris*) round about the throne, in sight like unto an emerald.[45]

The heavenly planet is much like the pupil of an eye, seen in the sky with an iris surrounding it like a halo. The *iris* John sees is a clear green because the emerald represents Judah in the breastplate. This ties in beautifully because the Lord is of the tribe of Judah, which means praise of God.

In ancient times, the emerald was considered a wedding stone,[46] and Jesus is the bridegroom.[47] This not only shows that the Bride of Christ has just been chosen, but it also suggests that the planet surrounded with an *iris* is not only the Lord's throne, but also where the Marriage of the Lamb will take place. Symbolically, the whole place is surrounded by an emerald wedding ring.

These various symbols help expand our understanding of the one who is both the Lord of the Old Testament and the Lord of the New Testament, the pre-incarnate Christ and the incarnate Christ. They also help us find the actual location of Heaven.

We listen attentively as John speaks. He has more to say about the scene on the heavenly planet:

> And round about the throne *were* four and twenty seats (*thronoi*, thrones): and upon the seats I saw four and twenty elders sitting, clothed in white raiment; and they had on their heads crowns (victors crowns) of gold. And out of the throne proceeded lightnings and thunderings and voices:[48]

The twenty-four elders are the twelve princes of Israel plus the twelve Jewish apostles of Jesus Christ. They represent all the over comers of both Israel and the church. Their names are on the twelve gates and the twelve foundations of the heavenly New Jerusalem.[49] Each one has earned his white robe, and therefore, has received his "crown of life, which the Lord hath promised to them that **love him**."[50]

In I Chronicles 24:1-19, we find that king David appointed 24 elders to represent the entire Levitical priesthood, which numbered into the thousands. The priests were divided into 24 courses. Each course served for two weeks at a time in the temple. When the 24 elders met, they represented the whole priesthood. Just as the 24 elders in those days stood for all the priests, the 24 elders we see here around the throne stand for all the over comers who receive crowns. We are all priests, represented before the throne by the elders.

We heard one reason why they wear crowns in Revelation 1:6. After the Rapture in the preview, the apostle John said that Jesus "hath (just moments before) made us (those taken to heaven in the Rapture) kings and priests unto God and his Father."

A crown of righteousness is also to be awarded at the Rapture. In 2 Timothy 4:8, the apostle Paul said that "there is laid up for me a crown of righteousness, which the Lord, the righteous judge, shall give me at that day: and not to me only, but unto all them also that **love his appearing**."

Here we see the proper attitude of the Bride. She loves him and his appearing. The Bridegroom loves her, and she returns his love. This kind of marriage lasts. Do you suppose this genuine love is what God was after all along? what our life is all about? why he lets us make our own decisions? It is obvious that he wants more than respect for his power; he could have that in an instant. He wants our love. Has he earned it? What more could he have done? In Proverbs 8:17, he said, "I love them that love me; and those that seek me early shall find me."

The crown of righteousness will be given by the Lord when he comes for his saints. In Revelation 22:12, he says, Behold, I come quickly, and my reward *is* with me." There cannot be crowned elders in Heaven until after Christ comes for his saints at the Rapture. Therefore, "Come up hither" has to represent the catching up of the elders who represent all the over comers who receive crowns.

The Rapture was probably prefigured when Moses climbed Mount Sinai and received the ten commandments on Pentecost. At that time, the voice of the trumpet was heard. Exodus 19:16-20 says,

> there were thunders and lightnings, and a
> thick cloud upon the mount, and the voice of
> the trumpet exceeding loud...And Moses

brought forth the people out of the camp to meet with God....mount Sinai was altogether on a smoke...**when the voice of the trumpet sounded long...the LORD called Moses up** to the top of the mount; and Moses went up.

Heaven is covered with clouds. Job 22:14 reveals that "Thick clouds are a covering to him." When Moses went up into the thick clouds, it was a type of the Rapture.

It seems that just as Christ arose in the night, the Rapture will take place on our Saturday night (Sunday on the Jewish calendar). Then as that joyous Sunday morning rolls around, we will attend church in New Jerusalem on the heavenly mount Sion (or Zion from the Hebrew). Hebrews 12:22-24 describes the scene that day:

> But ye are come unto mount Sion, and unto the city of the living God, the heavenly Jerusalem, and to an innumerable company of angels, To the general assembly and church of the firstborn, which are written in heaven, and to God the Judge of all, and the spirits of **just men made perfect**. And to Jesus the mediator of the new covenant.

Seven lamps before the throne

> and *there were* seven lamps of fire burning before the throne, which are the seven Spirits (*pneumata*) of God.[51]

The seven lamps of fire burning before the throne may have a dual meaning. First, they represent the sevenfold Holy Spirit. Isaiah 11:1,2 suggests this:

> AND there shall come forth a rod out of the stem of Jesse, and a Branch shall grow out of his roots: And the spirit of the LORD shall rest upon him, the spirit of wisdom and under-

standing, the spirit of counsel and might, the
spirit of knowledge and of the fear of the
LORD.

The possible secondary meaning of the lamps is an
interesting subject to pursue. It expands our knowledge and
raises our eyes to new horizons.

Since the tabernacle was symbolic, it is significant
that these seven lamps of fire are seen burning **before** the
throne. In the tabernacle, the seven-branched lampstand
burned just outside, or before, the Holy of Holies, which
represented God's throne in Heaven.

The Greek *pneumata* means spirit, wind, a movement of air, the breath of the mouth. It's possible that these
seven Spirits, which are seven lamps of fire burning before
the throne, represent seven spherical objects propelled by the
breath of God.

Zechariah 4:10 mentions seven and says that "those
seven; they are the eyes (orbs) of the LORD, which run to
and fro through (*shuwt*, whip about, roam around,[52] i.e., orbit) the whole earth."

A light or lamp can represent a heavenly body, such
as the sun or a planet. Genesis 1:16 says,

God made two great lights; the greater light to
rule the day, and the lesser light to rule the
night; he made the stars also.

Their appearance in the sky is said to resemble
lamps, torches, or burning coals. Ezekiel saw these in two
visions and said that

their appearance was like **burning coals of
fire,** and like the appearance of **lamps**[53] (or
torches, as in the NASB).

In Zechariah's vision of four chariots coming out
from between two mountains, we are told that the chariots
"are the four spirits of the heavens, which go forth from
standing before the Lord of all the earth."[54] If we count the

Lord's dwelling place, the two mountains, and the four spirits of the heavens, they total seven. They probably represent the same type of thing as the "seven lamps of fire burning before the throne, which are the seven Spirits of God" in Revelation 4:5—seven orbiting spheres.

The sea of ice crystals

As John continues, he gives us an important bit of information—a key piece to this puzzle. He says,

> And before the throne *there was* a sea of glass like unto crystal (*krustallos*, ice):[55]

Instead of crystal, the New English Bible translates *krustallos* as ice. It says,

> Burning before the throne were seven **flaming torches**, the seven spirits of God, and in front of it (the throne) stretched what seemed a sea of glass, **like a sheet of ice**.

The rainbow John sees around the throne seems to be a sea of ice, glass or crystal. What does this suggest? Where in our solar system can you find a shining sea of ice crystals? Multiple rings at least ten feet thick composed of orbiting ice crystals have been photographed through Earthbound telescopes and from space craft flying by Saturn, and it is the eighth luminary in our lineup.

We have (1) the Sun, (2) Mercury, (3) Venus, (4) Earth, (5) Mars, (6) Rahab, Satan's former planet which exploded and formed the Asteroid Belt,[56] (7) Jupiter and (8) Saturn. If heavenly spheres propelled by the breath of God are portrayed by these seven lamps, there would be seven before the throne with its surrounding sea of ice crystals.

New Jerusalem is at the heavenly Mount Sion (which means monumental guiding pillar). Could Mount Sion actually be the monumental Saturn? If our ringed-planet was Heaven, the Lord's throne would appropriately have a halo.

At one time, the Israelites worshipped Saturn—not the right thing to do. They disobeyed God's commandment against making images, were tricked by Satan, and ended up worshiping creation rather than the Creator. The Lord, "Whose hands created all the host of the heavens (said) Yet I did not show them to you that you should go after them."[57] In Amos 5:25,26 in the Jerusalem Bible, the Lord says,

> Did you bring me sacrifices and oblations those forty years in the desert, House of Israel? Now you must shoulder Sakkuth (a statue of human form with the head of an ox which represented the planet Saturn) your king and **the star of your God, Kaiwan** (*Kiyyun*, the planet Saturn[58]), those idols you made for yourselves; for I am about to drive you into captivity.

Be very careful not to make images of Heaven to worship them. Worship the creator, not the creation.

The Hebrew word translated star in the above quotation is *kowkab*. It means a shining, heaped-up, hilly, rolling globe, a good description of a planet. Could Saturn be the star of our God?

Ezekiel also saw a vision of the Lord upon his throne, but he saw more colors in the rings than John did. This is not surprising. If you look at a diamond in bright light, all the colors of the rainbow shoot from it as you turn it slightly. Sunlight on ice crystals can do the same thing. In Ezekiel 1:28, he said,

> As the appearance of the bow that is in the cloud in the day of rain, so was the appearance of the brightness round about. This was the appearance of the likeness of the glory of the LORD.

If Saturn is "the throne," it would be our heavenly destination too. It is a naked-eye planet, actually the last one visible to the naked eye, and it is covered with clouds.

I have a picture of it taken through an Earth-based telescope. In this picture, the planet looks like a frothy gold custard with a darker polar cap resembling the pupil of an eye. Surrounding the planet in the blackness of space are what appear to be two rings, a wide white inner ring and a thin greenish outer ring.

According to the angle of view, sometimes the rings actually look like handles or wings. Early astronomers described them this way, and David prayed, "Keep me as the apple of the eye, hide me under the shadow of thy wings."[59] It makes me wonder if this might have a dual meaning.

The four fliers of the heavens
As John continues, he gives us more clues:

> and in the midst of **the throne**, and round about the throne, *were* four beasts full of eyes before and behind (full orbs, i.e., spheres). And the first beast *was* like ("like" or "as" indicates figurative language) a lion, and the second beast like a calf, and the third beast had a face as a man, and the fourth beast *was* like a flying eagle.[60]

These four beasts are fliers of the heavens. Therefore, they too could actually be moving heavenly bodies, luminaries, or lamps. They are personified in our play, but they could be four orbiting planets surrounding the Lord's throne in Heaven. Jupiter orbits closer to the sun than Saturn. Uranus, Neptune, and Pluto orbit farther away from the sun than Saturn.

These spheres seem to be lined up with "the four spirits of the heavens, which go forth from standing before the Lord of all the earth" in Zechariah 6:5. The four in Zechariah's vision seem to represent Mercury, Venus, Earth, and Mars. They are before the Lord's throne. The four in Revelation 4:6 seem to represent Jupiter, Uranus, Neptune, and Pluto. They surround the throne.

The first four are terrestrial planets called Cherubim.[61] They are characterized as having four wings.[62] The last four are called Seraphim,[63] which means burners, suggesting that they too are lamps. They are characterized as having six wings. Both Cherubim and Seraphim have four faces—face all directions, because they are spheres.

The Israelite camp in the wilderness

The lion, calf, man and eagle represent the four directions. They were used on the standards placed at the compass points when the Israelites camped in a circle around the Tabernacle in the wilderness after they came out of Egypt.

Their camp in the wilderness probably depicted Heaven. Josephus, the Jewish historian, said that the Tabernacle represented heaven and that the priests camped in the first row around it. The rest of the Levites camped around the priests, and the remainder of the Israelites camped around the Levites. They built roads between the rows and set up booths along the roads to buy and sell goods.[64]

The whole thing would look like a giant phonograph record from the air, and this is exactly what Saturn's rings remind us of when we photograph them from our space vehicles. More than ever, it makes me wonder about Saturn.

The Seraphim

As John continues his narration, we hear him say,

> And the four beasts had each of them six wings about *him*; and *they were* full of eyes (full orbs, or spheres) within: and they rest not day and night (they rotate as they revolve in their orbit), saying, Holy, holy, holy, Lord God Almighty, which was (at the First Coming), and is (at the Rapture), and is to come (at the Second Coming).[65]

The six symbolic wings show that these are the Seraphim. Isaiah 6:1-3 also describes them for us:

> I saw also the Lord sitting upon a throne, high and lifted up (in Heaven), and his train (hem of his robe) filled the temple. Above it

stood the seraphims (*saraphim*, burners, i.e., lamps): each one had six wings; with twain he covered his face (two top quarters), and with twain he covered his feet (two bottom quarters), and with twain he did fly. And one cried unto another, and said, Holy, holy, holy, is the LORD of hosts (Hebrew, *Yahweh Sabaoth*): the whole earth is full of his glory.

Psalms 19:1-6 helps us understand this type of speech:

THE heavens declare the glory of God; and the firmament (vault of space) sheweth his handywork. Day unto day uttereth speech, and night unto night sheweth knowledge. There is no speech nor language where their voice is not heard. Their line is gone out through all the earth, and their words to the end of the world. In them (the heavens, our solar system) hath he set a tabernacle for the sun.

THE PLANETARY LINE

Mercury—Venus—Earth—Mars—Rahab/Asteroid Belt—Jupiter—Saturn—Uranus—Neptune—Pluto

The circuit of Heaven

Christ is the "Sun of righteousness" who shall "arise with healing in his wings" in Malachi 4:2. He is called the bridegroom who goes forth of his chamber in Joel 2:16. These help us realize that this passage in Psalms 19 switches from the literal to the figurative as verse five begins. It says,

Which is **as a bridegroom** coming out of his chamber, and rejoiceth **as a strong man** to run a race. His (Christ's) going forth is from the end of the heaven, and **his circuit** unto the ends of it: and there is nothing hid from the heat thereof (of his judgment).

In other words, the heavenly mount Sion (Saturn?), where Christ's throne is, orbits within our solar system the same way the sun makes its circuit.

How can we be sure it is within our own solar system? Only the sun and planets of our solar system make a **circuit** as seen against the stationary background stars. The stars are so far away that there is no apparent motion at all during one man's lifetime. We call this circuit where the sun, moon and planets travel across our sky the ecliptic.

It looks like the Lord Jesus Christ's heavenly throne orbits within our own solar system, and this means that our heavenly home does too. Like the moon, **"his circuit"** is visually from one end of the sky to the other end of it.

His throne—like the Sun, Moon, and Earth

There are scriptures that show that "his throne" is in our solar system, "as the sun," "as the moon," "like the earth," and even "as dusty earth," i.e., with soil.

> His (David's) seed (Jesus) shall endure for ever, and his throne **as the sun** before me. It shall be established for ever **as the moon**, and as a faithful witness in heaven (the sun and moon are both in our solar system).[66]

> (The Lord) built his sanctuary **like high palaces** (spheres), **like the earth** (a planet) which he hath established forever.[67]

> (Who) is he that numbers the clouds in wisdom, and has bowed the heaven...to the earth (from here, it looks like a rainbow surrounds it)? For it (Heaven) is spread out **as dusty earth**, and I have cemented it as one hewn stone to another (formed by coalescence).[68]

> A glorious **high throne** from the beginning is the place of our sanctuary (lit., palace).[69]

It is hard to be sure how far to carry out these like-nesses. Collectively, the common denominator seems to be that they are all spheres orbiting within the band called the ecliptic in our solar system.

However, since Heaven is "as the sun," can we say that it produces heat too? Strangely enough, astronomers have found that it does. It radiates three times as much heat as it receives from the sun.

It seems safe to say that since it is "like high palaces," it too is a sphere. All these things it is compared to are spheres. It is "as the moon," so it orbits around Earth. Actually, both Earth and Heaven orbit around the sun, but Heaven's orbit is outside Earth's. Therefore, it literally does orbit around Earth.

When we compare it to "dusty earth," are we to assume that Heaven has soil? It seems that it does. Manna, angel's food, is called "the corn of heaven."[70]

I think our astronomers are in for another surprise. They think that Heaven is too cold for things like that, but since they discovered that it gives off more heat than it receives from the sun, that puzzles them.

Our astronomers also think that our two Voyager spacecraft have discovered the boundary of our solar system, and just maybe they have. Where the plasma known as the solar wind slams into the interstellar cold and gasses at the edge, called the heliopause, the turbulence generates intense low-frequency emissions, the most powerful source of radio signals found in our solar system,[71] at least up to 1993. This heliopause may be the outer boundary around the planets that travel across our sky along the ecliptic.

The elders toss their crowns at Jesus feet

Feeling runs high in this group as John continues his description of the throne scene:

> And when those beasts (the Seraphim) give glory and honour and thanks to him (the first and the last, the Almighty) that sat on the throne, who liveth for ever and ever, The four and twenty elders fall down before him

that sat on the throne, and worship him that liveth for ever and ever, and cast their crowns before the throne, saying, Thou art worthy, O Lord, to receive glory and honour and power: for thou hast created all things, and for thy pleasure they are and were created.[72]

The Almighty, who is both Yahweh and Jesus Christ, is the creator. He is worthy of all glory and honor and is the one that deserves the crowns. He is all-powerful and can save us from destruction. According to John 14:2, he is preparing His Place for us so we can live where he is. His throne is on a royal planet surrounded by a halo. This is our destination when the Rapture takes place.

It may be surrounded by 24 moons. Astronomers already think there might be 23. They list the moons as 22+ and keep finding more as time goes on. Since there are 24 elders surrounding the throne, I won't be a bit surprised to find out that there are 24 moons around Saturn also.

Does Saturn fit the facts?

Assuming that Saturn is Heaven, how does it fit the facts? Around Saturn are the four Seraphim: Jupiter, Uranus, Neptune, and Pluto. The four terrestrial planets, Mercury, Venus, Earth, and Mars, are the heavenly fliers called Cherubim in Ezekiel 10:20. Their concentric orbits are the wheels within wheels Ezekiel saw in his visions of the heavens.[73] Ezekiel saw one of the wheels upon the earth,[74] so Earth is one of the four Cherubim.

Both Seraphim and Cherubim are personified and depicted as having powers of speech. Of the Cherubim, Ezekiel said, "I heard the noise of their wings, like the noise of great waters, as the voice of the Almighty, the voice of speech, as the noise of an host."[75] The Seraphim say, "Come and see" as the seals are broken in Revelation 6. (For more detailed information about the Cherubim, see *Exit: 2007*.)

There are nine planets at present. The four inner planets are called Cherubim. The four outer planets that surround the throne are called Seraphim. Saturn makes nine.

Saturn is a giant planet. This agrees with Psalms 118:5, which says, "I called upon the LORD in distress: the LORD answered me, and set me in a large place." Psalm 19:2-7 (NAB) also suggests that Heaven is a giant planet:

> The heavens declare the glory of God, and the firmament (vault of space) proclaims his handiwork. Day pours out the word to day, and night to night imparts knowledge...He has pitched a tent (tabernacle) there for the sun, which comes forth like the groom (Jesus Christ) from his bridal chamber and, **like a giant** (Heaven, a giant planet), joyfully runs its course. At one end of the heavens it comes forth, and its course is to their other end (its circuit along the ecliptic).

The morning star

To the over comers of Thyatira, Jesus said, "I will give him the morning star."[76] This probably indicates that the Rapture will take place before sunup, while the morning star can still be seen. In Revelation 22:16, he tells us, "I am the root and the offspring of David, and the bright and morning star." He calls himself this because his throne is on a morning star.

Saturn literally is a morning star when the Rapture takes place. Starting in the spring, we can see it in the morning sky for five months, then we can see it in the evening for five months. The other two months, it is not visible for it is swinging around on the other side of the sun. It will be a morning star if Rapture I is on Pentecost and an evening star if Rapture II is on the Feast of Trumpets. This is another reason Rapture I on Pentecost fits the facts.

The Title Deed of the Earth

John continues reading the script found in Revelation 5:1.

> AND I saw in the right hand of him that sat on the throne a book written within and on the backside, sealed with seven seals.

This is a scroll. It has been called the Title Deed of the Earth. It has to do with the redemption of the purchased possession. Ephesians 1:13,14 says that after "ye believed, ye were sealed with that holy Spirit of promise, Which is the earnest of our inheritance until the redemption of the purchased possession."

Under the laws of the Jews, it was impossible for the land to be lost to those who would rightfully inherit it. If someone sold his land because of poverty, it was returned to his estate in the year of Jubilee. The nearest of kin, called the kinsman redeemer, could also redeem it, or buy it back, at any time before the year of Jubilee. The purchase price was prorated according to the number of years left until the Jubilee year.

When an inheritance was sold, there were two scrolls made that specified the price and any other details of the transaction. One of these mortgage deeds was open, the other sealed. The sealed scroll represented a forfeited inheritance that could later be recovered on the terms therein.

> Jeremiah said, The word of the LORD came unto me, saying, Behold, Hanameel the son of Shallum thine uncle shall come unto thee, saying, Buy thee my field that is in Anathoth: for the right of redemption is thine to buy it....And I bought the field...and weighed him the money...So I took the evidence of the purchase, both that which was sealed according to the law and custom, and that which was open: And I gave the evidence of the purchase unto Baruch...in the sight of Hanameel mine uncle's son, and in the presence of the witnesses that subscribed **the book of the purchase**...And I charged Baruch before them, saying, Thus saith the LORD of hosts, the God of Israel; Take these evidences, this evidence of the purchase, both which is sealed, and this evidence which is open and put them in an **earthen** vessel, that they may continue many days.[7]

The scroll is The Book of the Purchase of Earth. Christ has purchased back the land, acting as the kinsman redeemer. However, he has not yet taken possession. Jesus will begin to break the seals after the Rapture. The seventh will be broken after the consummation of this age, which ends on the Preparation Day for the Feast of Trumpets that begins the Millennium. That Jewish Civil Year will begin on Tishri 1. The Jewish Regnal year will not begin until the following Nisan 1, but more about this later.

> And I saw a strong angel (maybe Gabriel) proclaiming with a loud voice, Who is worthy to open the book, and to loose the seals thereof? And no man in heaven, nor in earth, neither under the earth, was able to open the book, neither to look thereon. And I wept much, because no man (not even John) was found worthy to open and to read the book, neither to look thereon. And one of the elders saith unto me, Weep not: behold, the **Lion** (i.e., King) of the tribe of Juda (Yahweh-shua, Yeshua, Iesous, Jesus), the Root of David (Yahweh), hath prevailed to open the book, and to loose the seven seals thereof.[78]

This proves that Christ is God. He is both the Lion of Juda and the Root of David. He is not just the Son of David; he is also the root of David. He did what no other can do. He existed before David, and yet he lived after David.

No man in Heaven or Earth can open the scroll. If he were just a man, he couldn't open it either. Jesus Christ has two complete natures, man and God, both the Lamb and the Lion. As the Lamb, Jesus died on the cross and purchased the world. As the Lion, he will rule the world.

The Lamb of God
John's narration continues:

> And I beheld, and, lo, in the midst of the throne and of the four beasts, and in the

midst of the elders, stood a Lamb as it had
been slain, having seven horns and seven
eyes, which are the seven Spirits of God sent
forth into all the earth.[79]

The first and the last is the Almighty sitting on the
throne. He is both the Almighty and Jesus in one person.
Therefore, the symbol of a Lamb that has been sacrificed is
used to represent Jesus. He is standing, and therefore alive,
proving that he was resurrected. His seven horns represent
his omnipotence. Here, the seven eyes, or Spirits of God,
represent his omniscience.

When Abraham offered up his only son by his wife
Sarah, Isaac, the Lord stopped him and provided a ram for
the sacrifice instead, just as Christ was sacrificed in our
stead.

And Abraham called the name of that place
Jehovah-jireh (which means the Lord will be
seen): as it is said to this day, In the mount of
the LORD it shall be seen.[80]

Here in The Revelation of Jesus Christ, the substitutionary
ram is seen in the mount of the Lord—Heaven.

Next, we see Christ take the book:

And he came and took the book out of the
right hand of him that sat upon the throne.
And when he had taken the book, the four
beasts and four *and* twenty elders fell down
before the Lamb, having every one of them
harps, and golden vials full of odours
(margin, incense), which are the prayers of
saints. And they sung a **new song**, saying
Thou art worthy to take the book, and to
open the seals thereof: for thou wast slain,
and hast redeemed us to God by thy blood
out of every kindred, and tongue, and people, and nation; And hast (past tense) made
us (at the Pre-Tribulation Rapture) unto our

God kings and priests: and we shall (in the future) reign on (*epi*, over) the earth.[81]

The saints have already been redeemed, "bought with a price,"[82] and made kings and priests. All that remains is to redeem the Earth they are to reign over. The terms and conditions for redeeming it are written on the scroll.

We hear John saying,

> And I beheld, and I heard the voice of many angels round about the throne and the beasts and the elders: and the number of them was ten thousand times ten thousand, and thousands of thousands; Saying with a loud voice, Worthy is the Lamb that was slain to receive power, and riches, and wisdom, and strength, and honour, and glory, and blessing. And every creature which is in heaven, and on the earth, and under the earth, and such as are in the sea, and all that are in them, heard I saying, Blessing, and honour, and glory, and power, *be* unto him that sitteth upon the throne, and unto the Lamb for ever and ever. And the four beasts said, Amen. And the four and twenty elders fell down and worshipped him that liveth for ever and ever.[83]

The Bride of Christ is safe in Heaven as chapter five ends. As chapter six begins, the Tribulation starts on Earth.

The Rapture of the Church is the first trump but the second entry into the house of the Lord, for Jesus took the Old Testament saints to Heaven with him right after his Resurrection. That first entry only involved the believers who were dead. When Jeremiah came up out of the pit, he represented Rapture II, the last trump and the third entry. Jeremiah 38:14 says, "the king sent, and took Jeremiah...unto him into the **third entry** that is in the house of the LORD."

[1] New King James Version
[2] Revelation 4:1,2
[3] Revelation 1:10,11
[4] Matthew 24:30
[5] Revelation 17:14
[6] Daniel 8:13
[7] John 3:29
[8] Revelation 7:14
[9] "Comet Hale-Bopp is Coming." *Sky and Telescope*, Nov. 1995, p. 20-23
[10] Revelation 3:17
[11] Matthew 22:4-14
[12] Revelation 17:14
[13] Genesis 7:4
[14] Matthew 24:37-41
[15] Luke 17:29-34
[16] I Thessalonians 4:13-18
[17] Revelation 3:10
[18] Luke 21:36
[19] Isaiah 57:1,2,15
[20] Genesis 5:24
[21] Revelation 5:9
[22] Psalm 40:1-3
[23] Philippians 3:14
[24] I Corinthians 15:23
[25] I Corinthians 15:51-53
[26] Matthew 24:30,31
[27] Isaiah 26:20
[28] Matthew 24:28; Luke 17:37
[29] Isaiah 40:31
[30] Psalm 18:16,17,20, NAB
[31] Psalm 27:5, NAB
[32] I Corinthians 9:24-27
[33] Psalm 10:2, NAB
[34] John 13:8
[35] Revelation 4:2,3
[36] Exodus 28:17-20
[37] Revelation 1:17,18
[38] Seiss, Joseph A. *The Apocalypse*. (Grand Rapids: Kregel Publications) p. 102
[39] Genesis 29:32
[40] Seiss, *op. cit.*, p. 163
[41] Luke 2:7
[42] Isaiah 43:11,13

[43] John 17:20-24
[44] Matthew 22:44
[45] Revelation 4:3
[46] De Haan, M.R. *Revelation*. (Grand Rapids: Zondervan) p. 77
[47] Matthew 9:15
[48] Revelation 4:4,5
[49] Revelation 21:12-14
[50] James 1:12
[51] Revelation 4:5
[52] Green's *Interlinear Greek Hebrew English Bible*
[53] Ezekiel 1:13
[54] Zechariah 6:1-5
[55] Revelation 4:6
[56] For more information, see *Exit: 2007, The Secret of Secrets Revealed*, by M.J. Agee. p. 213,14
[57] Hosea 13:4, Concordant Version, also see the LXX
[58] *Gesenius Hebrew-Chaldee Lexicon*. p. 395
[59] Psalms 17:8
[60] Revelation 4:6,7
[61] Ezekiel 10:20
[62] Ezekiel 1:6
[63] Isaiah 6:2
[64] Whiston, William. *The Works of Josephus*. (Philadelphia: David McKay Co., nd), pg 111
[65] Revelation 4:8
[66] Psalms 89:36,37
[67] Psalms 78:69
[68] Septuagint, Job 38:37,38
[69] Jeremiah 17:12
[70] Psalm 78:24
[71] "Flights may have found edge of solar system." *The Orange County Register*, May 27, 1993, page A10
[72] Revelation 4:9-11
[73] Ezekiel 1 and 10
[74] Ezekiel 1:15
[75] Ezekiel 1:24
[76] Revelation 2:28
[77] Jeremiah 32:6-14
[78] Revelation 5:2-5
[79] Revelation 5:6
[80] Genesis 22:14
[81] Revelation 5:7-10
[82] I Corinthians 7:23
[83] Revelation 5:11-14

The Location of Heaven

THE SECRET GOD HID IN THE TABERNACLE

𝔚hen I began intensive Bible study, Dr. Whiting, of Dallas Theological Seminary, drew God's Plan of the Ages with a broken line just before the Tribulation. He said that there was nothing to show that the Rapture had to happen exactly when the Tribulation began. There could be a gap. I am convinced that there is a gap, shown by the four Jewish years Jesus mentioned in the parable of the barren fig tree.[1]

Since the Tribulation does not follow directly on the heels of the Rapture, this is a good time to have an Interlude and look at more scriptures that indicate where Heaven is located. This is the great secret that God hid in the tabernacle.

Three mysterious things found in the Bible have long defied complete explanation:

(1) "the chariot of the Cherubims"
(2) "the vengeance of his temple"
(3) "the secret of his tabernacle"

When we unravel these three mysteries, we can understand more clearly the clues that show where Heaven is. All three have to do with the tabernacle Moses built at Mount Sinai in the wilderness after the Israelites came out of Egypt or with the temple King Solomon built later on in Jerusalem.

The Lord's original instruction manual for building the tabernacle was detailed, and Moses was warned to make all things according to the pattern shown him on the mount. It was important that he follow the exact specifications because the tabernacle told a story. However, the last page of that scroll had not been unrolled until I wrote *Heaven Found, A Butter and Honey Star*.

To my great surprise, that book seemed to have a mind of its own. It quickly outgrew its space in this chapter. In a few short months, it became a book in its own right. The full story is told in the book, but some major points will be covered here. I chose the subtitle, *A Butter and Honey Star*, because Heaven actually looks like a ball of whipped butter that has been brushed with honey. Amber and butterscotch coloring is concentrated in bands that are whirled around the planet by tremendous upper-atmosphere winds. It is the most gorgeous thing in our entire solar system.

Many things about the tabernacle, its furnishings, and the feasts celebrated there point to Christ. Some of the more obvious associations are easy to make. Gold represents his deity. He is the bread of life, the light of the world, our Passover, the firstfruit, and the door by which we enter Heaven. However, more is depicted by the tabernacle than we ever thought possible, much more.

Have you wondered why God shrouded some information in so much mystery? why he used symbols, veiled figures, and layers of meaning that are difficult to fathom?

In Mark 13:23, Jesus said, "But take ye heed: behold, I have foretold you all things." He also said, "Nothing is secret, that shall not be made manifest: neither any thing hid, that shall not be known and come abroad."[2] All the clues we need had to be planted in Scripture, but some things were not meant to be understood immediately. Isaiah 28:13 shows us why. It says that the word of the Lord is here a little and there a little so the unbeliever will not understand and will therefore come into judgment.

The way of salvation is plain: "Believe in the Lord Jesus Christ, and thou shalt be saved."[3] Interpreting prophecy is harder. Faith in Christ must come first. When we first accept Christ as our Saviour, our sins are forgiven and we are filled with the Holy Spirit. Only then we can begin to understand the deeper things hidden in the pages of Scripture.

It takes the indwelling Holy Spirit to be able to fully comprehend what the tabernacle depicts. When you discover the secret it has been hiding all these years, you will be surprised. No!—probably shocked. It gave me goose bumps.

The Chariot of the Cherubim

Concerning the Cherub/Cherubim, under the heading "The Meaning," Unger's Bible Dictionary says, "The Cherubim seem to be actual beings of the angelic order," which is the usual interpretation. However, under "Form," it says,

> Undoubtedly we are to think of the cherub as at Byblos; that is, as a winged lion with human face. In any case, **they are celestial creatures belonging to the spiritual realm and not at all to be confounded with any natural identification.**

Celestial I can buy, but not to be confounded with any natural identification—that kind of thinking tends to turn down the power to our brains, so we won't try to find out if there is a secret embodied in the chariot of the Cherubim. In his effort to scramble our understanding, Satan strews confusing counterfeits along the path to truth. We can't look to those things for answers. We must let Scripture speak for itself. We must be open minded, curious, alert, and not let any thing close the door to inquiry, no matter how well intended. God meant for us to use the intelligence he gave us.

The Bible has many hidden things to disclose to us, but we have to search for clues and solve puzzles along the way. If we pray and keep on searching, it will yield secret after secret. No matter how high the step we are on, there always seems to be one more. In Mark 4:22-25, Jesus said that unto those who have, more will be given, for

> there is **nothing** hid, which shall not be manifested; **neither was any thing kept secret, but that it should come abroad.** If any man have ears to hear, let him hear. And he said unto them, Take heed

what ye hear: with what measure ye mete, it
shall be measured to you: and unto you that
hear shall more be given. For he that hath, to
him shall be given: and he that hath not, from
him shall be taken even that which he hath.

I believe the Cherubim have a natural identification.
Many have just failed to recognize what they represent.

Cherubim and a flaming sword are first mentioned in
Genesis 3:24. When Adam was exiled from Eden, God

drove out the man; and he placed at the east
of the garden of Eden Cherubims, and a
flaming sword which turned every way, to
keep the way (path) of (to) the tree of life.

Skipping to the last chapter in the Bible, we find that
the tree of life that disappeared from the earthly garden of
Eden is now in the heavenly Paradise. The earthly depicted
the heavenly. Therefore, the Cherubim and the flaming
sword do not have to be on Earth. This may come as a surprise, for it's been assumed that they were on Earth, but this
Scripture does not limit them to the Earth. They were merely
positioned east of Eden. That could include the sky. Actually, they can appear in the eastern sky anywhere between
Earth and the heavenly "throne of God and of the Lamb."

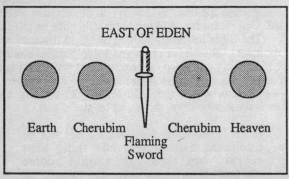

EAST OF EDEN

Earth   Cherubim   Cherubim   Heaven

Flaming
Sword

Chapter 4, The Location of Heaven

Both the Cherubim and flaming sword are symbols of real celestial objects. Most people have seen the brightest Cherubim. It stands out in the sky like a beacon—hard to miss. Several Cherubim are visible to the naked eye. All, even the flaming sword, can be seen with large telescopes.

Since the tree of life is now in Heaven, and nothing from Earth that defiles can enter Heaven, it seems that the flaming sword was set at the central crossroads between Earth and Heaven to keep the evil that had just been loosed on Earth from being transferred to Heaven. It was placed there to **guard** the pathway **to** the tree of life in Heaven.

Identifying the flaming sword is easier if we first figure out what the Cherubim represent. Unger's Bible Dictionary says that the chariot of the Cherubim probably means "the Cherubim as the chariot upon which God enters or is throned." That's an educated guess, but the picture is very hazy. By studying the tabernacle, we can get a clearer view.

However, it is not clear what the chariot of the Cherubim represents when it is mentioned in I Chronicles 28:18. This is one of those mysteries we have to solve. A pattern of the chariot of the Cherubim was in the temple, and therefore also in the earlier tabernacle that Moses built. When king David gathered the materials together for his son Solomon to use in building the temple in Jerusalem, he gave

> gold for **the pattern** (*tabniyth*) **of the chariot of the Cherubims**, that spread out their wings, and covered the ark of the covenant of the LORD. All this, said David, the LORD made me understand in writing by his hand upon me, even all the works (*melakah*) of this pattern.

The word *melakah* means works prescribed to. This pattern of the chariot of the Cherubim represented real heavenly things that have certain works prescribed to them. *Tabniyth* means pattern, model, figure, and likeness. The chariot of the Cherubim is a figure that symbolizes heavenly things.

According to the writer of Hebrews, the tabernacle contained "patterns of things in the heavens...which are the figures (*antitupa*, anti types, counterparts) of the true."[4] The Lord said, "by the hand of the prophets I will use likenesses."[5] Referring to the earthly tabernacle as "the example and shadow of heavenly things," Hebrews 8:1,5; 9:11 says,

> We have such an high priest (Jesus Christ, the Son of God), who is set on the right hand of the throne of the Majesty in the heavens; A minister of the sanctuary, and of the true tabernacle, which the Lord pitched, and not man....(Earthly priests) serve unto the **example and shadow of heavenly things**....But Christ (is) being come an high priest of good things to come, by a greater and more perfect tabernacle, not made with hands, that is to say, not of this building.

The Greek word translated building is *ktiseos* and means creation, as in Green's Interlinear Hebrew/Greek-English Bible. This creation refers to the renovation of planet Earth after it had been ruined by the asteroid impact that destroyed the huge animals like mammoths and saber-toothed tigers. This creation started with "Let there be light" in Genesis 1:3 and ended when God rested after creating Adam.

Earth and Heaven were originally formed long before this, in "the beginning," and as Isaiah: 45:18 says, "(He) created it not in vain (*tohuw*, an empty, waste, desolated surface), he formed it to be inhabited."

After the catastrophe that caused mass extinction, Earth became "without form (*tohuw*, an empty, waste, desolated surface), and void (*bohuw*, an empty, indistinguishable ruin)," as in Genesis 1:2. Then to make Earth habitable again for Adam, the Lord "renewest (*chadash*, repaired or restored) the face of the earth."[6] He will also renovate the heavens and the Earth after he returns as King of kings and Lord of lords. He will clear out the smoke of the asteroid impact as easily as "Let there be light: and there was light."

Our solar system was created "in the ancient (*qedem*, aforetime) days, in the generations (*dowr*, ages) of old."[7] The true tabernacle in the heavens is of that earlier creation.

The expanse of the heavens

The universe is enormous. Promised a heavenly home, where do we look for it? Is it just a shoulder-shrugging anywhere? or can we narrow it down to one particular place?

The word "heaven" itself is ambiguous. Birds fly in heaven. Planets orbit in heaven. Stars are in heaven. New Jerusalem is in heaven. Our search would be easier if we could narrow it down a bit.

The King James Version is very hard to understand when it says, "And God said, Let there be a firmament in the midst of the waters, and let it divide the waters from the waters. And God made the firmament, and divided the waters which were under the firmament from the waters which were above the firmament: and it was so. And God called the firmament Heaven" (literally, Heavens).

Do you know what that means? What is the firmament? A different translation can help. Genesis 1:6,7,16 in Green's Interlinear Hebrew/ Greek-English Bible says,

> God said, Let an expanse be in the midst of the waters, and let it divide the waters from the waters, And God made the expanse, and divided the waters which were under the expanse from the waters which were above the expanse....And **God called the expanse, Heavens**....And God made the two great luminaries: the larger light to rule the day, and the smaller light—and the stars to rule the night. And God **set them in the expanse of the heavens**, to give light on the earth.

This is easier to understand. The expanse of the heavens is where we send our space craft to explore our solar system. This expanse of space has in it both sun and moon, and is called heavens, an apt name because there literally is more than one orbiting body called heaven in it. We can be certain of this because Paul said,

> I knew a man in Christ above fourteen years ago, (whether in the body, I cannot tell; or

whether out of the body, I cannot tell: God knoweth;) such an one caught up to **the third heaven** (II Corinthians 12:2).

Believers in Christ will also be caught up to the third heaven. That is the Lord's throne. It probably is "the heaven of heavens" mentioned in II Chronicles 6:18.

In the last chapter, we found scriptures that show that "**his throne**" is in our solar system, because it is "as the sun," "as the moon," "like the earth," and "as dusty earth" plus a verse showing that this spherical "high throne" is the place of our palace too. These are worth repeating.

His (David's) seed (Jesus Christ) shall endure for ever, and **his throne as the sun** before me. It shall be established for ever **as the moon**, and as a faithful witness **in heaven** (both orbit in our solar system).[8]

(The Lord) built his sanctuary like high palaces (spheres), **like the earth** (a spherical **planet**) which he hath established forever.[9]

(Who) is he that numbers the clouds in wisdom, and has **bowed the heaven**...to the earth (as viewed from Earth)? For it (Heaven) is spread out **as dusty earth**, and I have cemented it as one hewn stone to another.[10]

A glorious **high throne** from the beginning is the place of our sanctuary.[11]

Since Satan's planet exploded and formed our Asteroid Belt, the spherical heavens in our solar system that go around Earth much like the Moon are: Mars, Jupiter, Saturn, Uranus, Neptune and Pluto. These all have orbits that are higher, or farther from the sun, than ours. It looks to me like one of these is the Heaven of heavens.

In Genesis 1:7, the waters under the expanse are easy to understand, we have oceans plus an atmosphere, even vapor rivers that have been discovered in the lower atmosphere that carry as much water as the Amazon,[12] but what about the waters which are above the expanse?

The expanse of space making up our solar system literally does separate waters above from waters below. Psalm 148:4 says, "Praise him, ye heavens of heavens, and ye **waters that be above the heavens.**"

Outside the orbit of Pluto are waters that are above the heavens (the planets). Orbiting out there in the Oort Cloud are comets of dust and water ice. This Oort Cloud is thought to reach out more than two light years from the Sun, halfway to the next star. Just maybe the object QB1 seen beyond Pluto's orbit in 1992 is one of these. Inside the Oort Cloud belt is the similar Kuiper Belt.[13]

According to Paul Recer, in "*Halo of comets circles solar system,*" (Press-Enterprise, Riverside, CA, June 15, 1995) the Hubble Space Telescope found "millions" of comets surrounding our solar system "like a halo of snowballs." That "millions" is a projected figure. They zeroed in on a small part of the Kuiper Belt and were able to see 30 objects. Based on the size of the total area and the density found in the sample area, they said that "there are at least 100 million and more like a billion or 10 billion out in the Kuiper Belt."

Besides the large showy comets that occasionally wander into the inner solar system, there are tiny water comets that have been discovered bombarding and replenishing our atmosphere daily. They are not large enough to be seen easily, but they just keep coming in and show up as dark dots on photographs I have seen.

No wonder Job 38:29,30 in the NAB asks,

> who gives the hoarfrost its **birth in the skies**, When the waters lie covered as though with stone that hold captive the surface of the deep? (the King James Version says, 'the face of the deep is frozen.')

Even when rivers and ponds are frozen over in the winter, there is moisture in the atmosphere above that has "its birth in the skies." God tends to our needs every day.

The tabernacle

The tabernacle, set up after the Lord gave Moses detailed instructions, was made up of two sections, the outer Holy Place and the inner Holy of Holies. In general, the outer Holy Place seemed to symbolize Israel's earthly worship of the heavenly God under the first covenant. Christ was prefigured by the shew bread and the golden candlestick. He is the true bread of life and the light of the world. What the Holy Place depicted has been thought to have been largely fulfilled in the first covenant that ended with the crucifixion and resurrection of Christ.

The veil that hung across the doorway leading from the Holy Place into the Holy of Holies was a type of the human body of Jesus. Hebrews 10:19,20 speaks of "a new and living way, which he hath consecrated for us, through the veil, that is to say, his flesh." As his flesh was sacrificed, that heavy veil was supernaturally ripped from top to bottom, and a new era began under a new covenant.

If we believe in him, we are said to be "in Christ."[14] Because God looks upon the church as being the body of Christ,[15] his perfect sacrifice atones for our sins, and we can go to Heaven to be with him where he is. He is truly the door[16] by which we enter Heaven.

When that veil split, the door opened for the Old Testament saints to go to Heaven. The door closed (and the veil was repaired) until it opens again for the Philadelphians.

The Holy of Holies represented Heaven. In the Bible, the Earth is referred to as being four-cornered,[17] not that it has corners, but it has four quarters. Heaven, as represented by the Holy of Holies is also foursquare. That cubicle had the same dimensions in all directions.[18] New Jerusalem is also said to be "foursquare, and the...length and the breadth and the height of it are equal."[19] As we saw in the last chapter, Heaven is like the sun, moon, and Earth, therefore Heaven is a sphere with equal dimensions in all directions.

In the beginning, God brought our solar system into being as part of his original creation of the universe. It helps us understand the end result if we imagine that God sat out in space on the orbit of the Earth, and pitched ten spherical flying heavenly bodies from his fingers, five from the left hand (Mercury, Venus, Earth, Mars, and Rahab, the planet that split and formed our Asteroid Belt), and five from the right hand (Jupiter, Saturn, Uranus, Neptune, and Pluto). Jupiter, and probably Rahab (which means large) were large like thumbs. Mercury and Pluto were small like little fingers. According to the force of the throw and the English put on each ball, some ended up in orbit nearby, others circled the sun farther away, but all orbited in the same direction.

Isaiah 48:13 lends itself to such a picture:

> Mine hand (His left hand) also hath laid the foundation of the earth (along with the other terrestrial planets, Mercury, Venus, Mars, and Rahab), and my right hand hath spanned (*taphach*, extended as a tent) **the heavens**: when I call unto them they stand up (*amad*, are established) together.

Here, the term "heavens" embraces five planets: Jupiter, Saturn, Uranus, Neptune, and little Pluto.

The planet Rahab split into pieces during ancient times, before Adam's day. A stray stone seems to have been hurled at it because of the sins of Satan.

A similar thing will happen to Earth at the end of the seven-year Tribulation (which is why it has to be shortened or no flesh would be saved; the asteroid must come in at just the right angle). Revelation 8:10 shows that a "star" (*aster*, star, luminous meteor, or asteroid) will impact Earth when the third trumpet judgment strikes, but unlike Rahab, Earth will not break up. The Lord will uphold its pillars—its supports. In Psalm 75:3 he said, "I bear up the pillars of it. Selah" (which means: pause and look at this, it's important).

The asteroid will crash into Earth because of a whirlwind. Isaiah 17:13 says that the nations "shall be chased as the chaff of the mountains before the wind, and like a rolling thing before the whirlwind." The rolling thing is the curse that Zechariah saw. It orbits "over the face of the whole earth."[20] In The Concordant Version, Micah 7:11 says that "In that day the delineating limit shall be put far off."

Satan's former planet, Rahab, was also shattered by a rolling thing before the whirlwind, because Job says that the heavens are cleared by his breath. Scripture says,

> And by His understanding He **shattered** Rahab. By His breath the heavens are cleared; His hand has pierced the fleeing serpent.[21]
> Thou hast **broken Rahab in pieces**, as one that is slain: thou hast scattered thine enemies with thy strong arm.[22]

> Awake, awake, put on strength, O arm of the LORD; awake, as in the ancient days, in the generations of old. Art thou not it that hath cut (*chatsab*, **split**) **Rahab**, and wounded the dragon? (Satan).[23]

The heavens are extended as a tent

When the Lord said in Isaiah 48:13, "my right hand hath spanned (*taphach*, extended as a tent) the heavens," he gave us an excellent clue. The heavens are extended as a tent. The ten planets were represented by the ten curtains that covered the tabernacle. Isaiah 40:22 uses figurative language and says the heavens are "as a curtain" and "as a tent."

> (It is God) that sitteth upon the circle (*chuwg*, circuit, i.e., orbit) of the earth...that stretcheth out the heavens **as a curtain**, and spreadeth them out **as a tent** to dwell in.

The tabernacle curtain

The curtain was made of ten widths of fabric, each embroidered with Cherubim. Two sets consisting of five widths each were coupled together. Moses was told to fasten the pair together with loops and taches (knobs) of gold "and it shall be one tabernacle (*mishkan*, dwelling, residence)."[24]

The whole curtain stands for our solar system. As if flung from God's left hand, five widths represent the terrestrial planets, Mercury, Venus, Earth, Mars and Rahab, the

_____

inner planets. As if flung from his right hand, the other five widths represent the giant planets, Jupiter, Saturn, Uranus, and Neptune plus tiny Pluto. These are the outer planets. The knobs even suggest the myriad of asteroids left orbiting in the Asteroid Belt after Rahab broke up.

The earthy tabernacle was the dwelling place of the Lord, and the heavenly realities it represented include the Lord's residence. In some way, God dwells inside the perimeter of the heavenly tent, and therefore within our solar system—on a planet, not the sun. Concerning the earthly tabernacle, he said, "Make me a sanctuary so that I can reside among them. You will make it all according to the design for the Dwelling and the design for its furnishings which I shall now show you."[25]

As explained on pages 209-211 in *Exit: 2007, The Secret of Secrets Revealed*, the Cherubim are symbols of the planets. Cherubim were embroidered on the ten widths covering the tabernacle to show us what they represent.

Burning coals of fire

The orbits of four Cherubim form the wheels within wheels that Ezekiel saw around the blazing sun in his visions when "the heavens were opened" to him in the first chapter of the book of Ezekiel. The flying heavenly bodies themselves looked "like burning coals of fire." Verse 13 is translated clearly in the New Scofield Bible: "As for the likeness of the living creatures, their appearance was like **burning coals** of fire."

Looking up at the sky, Ezekiel saw a whirlwind come out of the north (i.e., up) and form a great doughnut-shaped cloud representing our asteroid belt. In the center of that circle was a bright amber hub, our radiant sun. Verse four describes it as "a fire infolding itself, and (says) a brightness (Hebrew, *nogah*, **sunlight**) was about it." When we realize that this is actually talking about the sun, this obscure vision of Ezekiel's begins to make sense.

In the space between the central sun and the Asteroid Belt, Ezekiel saw four flying heavenly bodies whose complete orbits formed four high concentric rings (or full orbs) around the sun. According to verse 16, "their appearance and their work was as it were (figurative language) a wheel in the middle of a wheel." These are not literal wheels, they just have the appearance of wheels. They are actually orbits.

Surrounding the hub of the wheel, which is the central sun, Ezekiel saw the orbital ring of Mercury. Outside Mercury's orbit, he saw the orbit of Venus. Outside of Venus' orbit, he saw Earth's orbit. Outside of our orbit, he saw that of Mars. All planetary orbits in our solar system form concentric rings around the central sun.

The meaning of this mysterious vision is unlocked by the key phrase in verse 15: **"behold one wheel upon the earth."** This identifies the Earth as one of the flying bodies. Like the other planets, its wheel is its orbit.

Verse seventeen in the Concordant Literal Bible best reveals their circular orbits, "When they go, toward one of their four quarters are they going." To picture this, imagine an orange with its rind scored into four quarters. The only way to travel toward each quarter in turn is to go in a circle.

Their "appearance was like burning coals of fire," and according to verse 16, all "four had one likeness." Yet, verse five says, "And this was their appearance; they had the likeness of a man." The translation of the word adam as "man" has obscured the true meaning here.

The word adam means man, as being ruddy, but it basically means red earth, and that is what is referred to here. Adam was given this name because his body was formed from red clay.

In addition to the red clay located in different places upon the continents, fine red clay is found in the depths of our Pacific Ocean. Endlessly circulating in the oceanic mixing bowl, this rock flour, eroded from all continents, represents an average of the mineral makeup of the entire surface of this planet. Therefore, it is no big surprise to find the Earth characterized as being covered with red earth. When we saw photographs taken of the surface of Mars, it literally looked like red-orange earth. Some places on the Moon have orange coloring.

The four planets seen by Ezekiel all look like burning coals of fire when reflecting the sunlight, but they actually have red earth or clay soil on all four quarters. They are the terrestrial planets, Mercury, Venus, Earth, and Mars. Surely you have seen Venus. Next to the sun and moon, it is the brightest thing in the sky. There are even times when it can still be seen after dawn in the daylight near the ascending sun. When in the sky at twilight, it is the first star to appear.

Green's Interlinear Bible mentions the "four wings of the earth" in Isaiah 11:12, and Ezekiel 1:6 says of the Cherubim, "every one had four wings." The planets fly, but these are not actually wings but *kanaph*, the four quarters of each solid orb, or sphere. Two quarters are joined together covering half the body, and two are joined together covering the other half as on our orange with its rind scored in quarters. Concerning the wings, Scripture says,

> every one (of the Cherubim) had two, which
> covered on this side, and every one had two,
> which covered on that side, their bodies.[26]

Around 3000 B.C., the Sumerians listed ten planets. A cylinder seal, VA/243, at the State Museum in East Berlin depicts the solar system as it was known in those days. It consists of twelve celestial bodies, ten planets plus the Sun and Moon. They showed a planet between Mars and Jupiter that was larger than Mars and smaller than Jupiter.[27]

Western astronomers only knew of six until Uranus was discovered in 1781. Neptune was found in 1846, Pluto in 1930. It has only been possible since 1930 to figure out that the ten curtains covering the tabernacle represented the original ten planets in our solar system. Starting from the back, the ten curtains represented Mercury, Venus, Earth, Mars, Rahab, Jupiter, Saturn, Uranus, Neptune and Pluto.

The symbolic chariot

In the Holy of Holies was a rectangular chest called the ark of the covenant. Inside it were the ten commandments written on two "tables of stone." On top of the ark was a golden lid called the mercy seat. Connected to it on either side were two winged Cherubim made of beaten gold. Protruding through rings on either side of the ark were two shafts for carrying it that were never to be removed.

To get a mental picture of the chariot of the Cherubim, instead of thinking of these two Cherubim as winged creatures similar to pictures of angels, substitute some of the heavenly reality for the symbolic figures. A different image will emerge. The two Cherubim are two planets, each with its own orbit or wheel. Imagine **two wheels**, one protruding downward at each side of the mercy seat covering the ark and the two shafts protruding from the ark. There is your symbolic chariot, with its shafts, seat, storage compartment containing two stones, and wheels.

What its parts depict orbit in the heavens. Hebrews 9:5 in Green's Interlinear Bible says that above the ark were

> the Cherubim of glory over-shadowing the
> mercy-seat (of which we cannot now speak
> part by part). [The parenthetic portion above
> is part of the Scripture, not my comment.]

These things were not meant to be completely understood until the time of the end began in 1967, when Israel grew four leaves, the Gaza Strip, the Golan Heights, the Sinai, and the West Bank, and fulfilled the fig tree parable of Matthew 24:32-34. According to Daniel 12:4, knowledge would be increased in the "time of the end."

All kind of knowledge has been increased in our days, including the meaning of Bible prophecy. The first real computer, ENIAC, was built in 1946, two years before Israel became a nation.[28] We have become space explorers. We even sent two Voyager space vehicles out that photographed Saturn and its magnificent ring system in 1980 and 1981.

This chariot of the Cherubim has something to do with the Day of God's Wrath. Amos 6:1,3 in the Concordant Version says, "Woe to the tranquil in Zion...You are those isolating the day of evil, Yet you are bringing **the seat of violence** closer."

Other scriptures also mention a chariot or chariots:

> For, behold, the LORD will come with fire,
> and with his chariots like a whirlwind, to
> render his anger with fury, and his rebuke

---

with flames of fire. For by fire and by his
sword will the LORD plead with all flesh:
and the slain of the LORD shall be many.[29]

Come, behold the works of the LORD, what
desolations he hath made in the earth. He
maketh wars to cease unto the end of the
earth; he breaketh the bow (of the Beast[30]),
and cutteth the spear in sunder (splits the binary asteroid into two major pieces); **he
burneth the chariot in the fire**. Be still,
and know that I am God.[31]

Russian astronomers call the exploded planet Rahab
"Phayton," which means chariot. It's a good name.

The last sentence quoted above, "Be still, and know
that I am God," are the exact words I heard God say to me
one night. In the early morning, I woke suddenly—terrified—my heart beating like a little bird trying to get out. As
soon as I heard that masculine voice say, "Be still, and know
that I am God," my heart quieted instantly. I was still the rest
of the night, but nothing else happened.

It was about 20 years before I understood what took
place that night. When reading Job 33:15,16 in the Septuagint, it finally dawned on me that God opened my understanding that night. After that, I was able to figure out things
others seem not to have recognized in the Scripture. It said,

For when the Lord speaks once, or a second
time, sending a dream, or in the meditation of
the night; (as when a dreadful alarm happens
to fall upon men, in slumberings on the bed:)
then opens he the understanding of men.

The chariot of Israel

When Elijah was taken up to Heaven a chariot appeared,

a chariot of fire, and horses of fire, and parted them both asunder (as the binary asteroid
is parted asunder); and Elijah went up by a

whirlwind into heaven. And Elisha saw it, and he cried, My father, My father, the chariot of Israel, and the horsemen thereof.[32]

This chariot has something to do with the Lord's destroying weapon, the flaming sword, the sword of the Lord, or the arrow of the Lord's deliverance. When Elisha was sick just before he died, Joash the king of Israel, said,

O my father, my father, **the chariot of Israel**, and the horsemen (the Confraternity has 'guider') thereof. And Elisha said unto him, Take bow and arrows...Elisha put his hands upon the king's hands. And he said, Open the window **eastward**....Then Elisha said, **Shoot**. And he shot. And he said, **The arrow of the LORD'S deliverance**.[33]

The Lord is the driver of the chariot in the heavenly tabernacle. When whatever this arrow symbolizes is shot toward a land **east** of Israel, a hail of stones and coals of fire will fall. Psalms 18:10-13 says that the Lord

rode upon a cherub, and did fly...upon the wings of the wind. He made darkness his secret place; his pavilion (*cukkah*, tent, tabernacle) round about him were dark waters and thick clouds of the skies. At the brightness that was before him his thick clouds passed, hail stones and coals of fire.

Christ is more than the driver of the chariot, he is positioned there as our mercy seat. Scripture says that

all have sinned and come short of the glory of God, being justified as a free gift, by His grace, through the redemption which is in Christ Jesus. For God has set Him out **as a mercy seat** (*hilasterion*, mercy seat, propitiation) through faith in His blood.[34]

He is the propitiation (the atoning sacrifice)
for our sins: and not for our's only, but also
for the sins of the whole world.[35]

Sin lieth at the door

If we accept Jesus Christ as our Saviour, his blood that was
shed for us atones for our sins. His sacrifice applies to us,
and we can enter Heaven's door. If we try to get in by any
other route, "sin lieth at the door." Romans 6:23 is very
clear, "For the wages of sin is death: but the gift of God is
eternal life through Jesus Christ our Lord." Acts 4:12 adds
the important warning, "Neither is there salvation in any other: for there is none other name under heaven given among
men, whereby we must be saved."

    If we do not avail ourselves of the Lord Jesus
Christ's free offer of salvation, we probably will still be on
Earth during the worst times to hit since Adam was put on
this planet. It is not worth waiting. Get right with God now.

The Vengeance of His Temple

Something in the tabernacle and later in the temple, symbolized the Lord's vengeance. The "arrow of the LORD'S deliverance" and "coals of fire" refer to the Lord's device that
administers the vengeance of his temple. It will land east of
Jerusalem and destroy Babylon. Jeremiah 51:11 says his

device is against Babylon (the literal city), to
destroy it; because it is the vengeance of the
LORD, **the vengeance of his temple.**

    We were meant to understand these things in the lat-
ter days. Jeremiah 30:23,24 says,

Behold, the whirlwind of the LORD goeth
forth with fury, a continuing whirlwind (like
the 'strong east wind' that blew all night to
divide the sea when the Israelites came out of
Egypt): it shall fall with pain upon the head of
the wicked (the wicked one, i.e., the False
Prophet). The fierce anger of the LORD shall

not return, until he have done it, and until he have performed the intents of his heart: **in the latter days** (the days in which we live) **ye shall consider** (*biyn*, **understand**) it.

In the Septuagint, Jeremiah 37:23 says, "For the wrathful anger of the Lord has gone forth...**in the latter days ye shall know these things**." We are living in the latter days. It is the proper time for the deep things to surface. The Lord warns,

> **Flee out of the midst of Babylon**, and deliver every man his soul: be not cut off in her iniquity; for this is the time of the LORD'S vengeance...Babylon is suddenly fallen and destroyed...We would have healed Babylon, but she is not healed: forsake her...go every one into his own country: for **her judgment reacheth unto heaven, and is lifted up even to the skies.**[36]

The "flaming sword (*chereb*, destroying weapon) which turned every way," is still rotating and orbiting in the skies. It is the asteroid that Satan has lived on since his planet split apart, and it will destroy the city of Babylon immediately after this age ends. Revelation 18:21 says,

> And a mighty angel took up a **stone** like a great millstone, and cast *it* into the sea, saying, Thus with violence shall that great city Babylon be thrown down, and shall be found no more at all.

The ten commandments were not written on stone for nothing. Another idol will be made and placed in the temple even though the commandments in Exodus 20:4 include, "Thou shalt not make unto thee any graven image." Remember how Moses smashed the original stone tablets on the ground in a flash of anger because the Israelites made the golden calf while he was on Mount Sinai? Immediately after this age ends, those who do not believe in Jesus and do not obey the commandments inscribed on those tablets will be literally stoned. Two large stones plus a hail of others weighing around 100 pounds each will fall on them.[37]

Keep in mind that this judgment is for unbelievers only. Christ will take all believers to Heaven before this happens. The church saints will go in the Rapture between now and the beginning of the seven year Tribulation. The rest will go in Rapture II just before the asteroid impacts Earth.

In a vision, Zechariah saw this broken chunk of rock, a flying rolling thing twice as wide as it is long.

> This is **the curse** that is going forth over the face of the whole land: surely everyone who steals will be purged away according to the writing on one side (as if it were the stone with the commandments on it), and everyone who swears will be purged away according to the writing on the other side.[38]

The curse seems to be a binary asteroid. It will split apart, releasing the hail of smaller stones. The smaller mountain-sized asteroid will strike the northeastern sector of the Mediterranean Sea. The larger "star" will hit Babylon.

The Lord is against Satan and therefore his abode. The Lord said, "Behold, I am against thee, **O destroying mountain**...and I will stretch out mine hand upon thee, and **roll thee down from the rocks**, and will make thee a burnt mountain."[39] It is an irregular broken piece of Satan's planet, Rahab, that was split because of his sin of wanting to be like the Most High.

Psalm 89:10 is now easy to understand. **"Thou hast broken Rahab in pieces**, as one that is slain; thou hast scattered thine enemies (the dragon, Satan, and his fallen angels) with thy strong arm. The heavens are thine."

The Sword of the Lord

The asteroid is to be destroyed the same way the planet Rahab was—by collision. Remember Isaiah 51:9:

Awake, awake, put on strength, O arm of the
LORD; awake, **as in the ancient days**, in
the generations of old. Art thou not it that
hath cut Rahab, and wounded (*chalal*, pierced
through) the dragon?

Satan was wounded as with a sword. The counterpart in our days is when the "flaming sword" of Genesis
3:24 will impact Earth at the end of this age and wound the
idol shepherd, the Satan-possessed False Prophet. Scripture
says,

(The) sword of the LORD shall devour from
the one end of the land (earth) even to the
other end of the land (earth): **no flesh shall
have peace.**[40]

Woe to the idol shepherd that leaveth the
flock (he will go to Babylon)! the sword shall
be upon his arm, and upon his right eye: his
arm shall be clean dried up, and his right eye
shall be utterly darkened.[41]

When a stone crashed into Rahab, the impact blast
whizzed this broken chunk of rock out into a cometary orbit
that crosses Earth's pathway regularly (maybe as often as
twice a year, as Icarus does). Like the sword of Damocles, it
is an ever-present threat. It is the "sword which turned every
way" of Genesis 3:24.

Satan lives on this asteroid. Isaiah 22:18,19 warns,

(The) LORD will carry thee away...He will
surely violently turn and **toss thee like a
ball** into a large country (into Babylonia,
now Iraq, not tiny Israel): there shalt thou
die, and there the **chariots** of thy glory
(Rahab and the asteroid called Wormwood in
Revelation 8:11) shall be the shame of thy
lord's house. And **I will drive thee from
thy station** (*matstsab*, spot where you

stood, military station, i.e., the orbit he was placed in to guard the path to the tree of life).

The asteroid will come from between the planets. This was symbolized in Ezekiel's second vision:

> Go in between the wheels (orbits), even **under the cherub** (Satan[42]), and fill thine hand with coals of fire from between the Cherubims (planets), and scatter them over the city (Jerusalem, lucky not to have to take the full force of the blast)....Take fire from between the wheels, from between the Cherubims.[43]

Collision course

At the end of this age in 2007, this asteroid and Earth will be on a collision course. In the Septuagint, Nahum 2:3,4 shows that these two chariots, the asteroid that Satan rides, and the Earth that we ride, will crash into each other. Both look like lamps of fire in the darkness of space. By that time, Satan and the False Prophet will have destroyed

> the arms of their power from among men, their mighty men sporting with fire (taken military power from nations and given it to the world government): the reins (controls) of their chariots shall be destroyed in the day of his **preparation**, and the horsemen shall be thrown into confusion in the ways (plural of *derek*, paths, i.e., in their orbital paths), and **the chariots** (Earth and the asteroid) **shall clash together**, and shall be entangled in each other in the broad ways (in space): **their appearance is as lamps of fire.**

I believe that the day of preparation is September 12, 2007, the last day of this age. It is the day before the Feast of Trumpets that begins the Millennium.

What does "the reins of their chariots shall be destroyed" remind you of? This has been dramatized for us before. Remember what happened to the Egyptian chariots when they pursued the Israelites into the dried up path through the sea? The Lord "took off their chariot wheels, that they drave them heavily: so that the Egyptians said, Let us flee from the face of Israel; for the LORD fighteth for them against the Egyptians."[44]

In those days, he "caused the sea to go back by a strong **east wind** all that night."[45] At the end of this age, he will again use wind.

> Behold, a **whirlwind** of the LORD is gone forth in fury, even a grievous whirlwind: it shall fall grievously upon the head of the wicked. The anger of the LORD shall not return, until he have executed, and till he have performed the thoughts of his heart: in the latter days (we live in the latter days) ye shall consider (*biyn*, **understand**) **it perfectly.**[46]

Nahum 1:5,6 describes the Lord's vengeance on the day the flaming sword of the Lord strikes Earth:

> The mountains quake at him, and the hills melt, and **the earth is burned** at his presence, yea, the world, and all that dwell therein. Who can stand before his indignation? and who can abide in the fierceness of his anger? his fury is poured out like fire, and **the rocks are thrown down by him.**

This is when the seven trumpet judgments will strike Earth in quick succession. A great star (*aster*, star, flaming meteor, or asteroid) will fall from heaven "burning **as it were a lamp.**" A fiery mountain-sized piece will split off and be cast into the sea,[47] so the asteroid is probably a binary like Toutatis. Zechariah said the curse was twice as long as it is wide.[48]

In the tabernacle, the chariot of the Cherubim concealed the mystery of the vengeance of his temple in the stone tablets placed inside the ark. The stone was between the Cherubim. The asteroid, Wormwood, will orbit until God's pent up wrath is unleashed on the city of Babylon.

This is not literally how it will take place, but it is as if the chariot of the Cherubim orbits in space for a long time, then as the seventh millennium begins on the Feast of Trumpets, the first day of the seventh month of the Jewish sacred year, the Lord will fly a bombing run and drop the stone tablet that will destroy the rebuilt city of Babylon on the Euphrates River. Psalm 17 (18):8-16 (Septuagint) reflects this:

> There went up a smoke in his wrath, and fire burst into a flame at his presence: coals were kindled at it. And he bowed the heaven (the rainbow around his throne), and came down: and thick darkness was under his feet. And he **mounted on cherubs** (the chariot of the Cherubim) **and flew**: he flew on the wings of winds. And he made darkness his secret place: round about him was his tabernacle (as the chariot of the Cherubim was in the tabernacle), even dark water in the clouds of the air. At the brightness before him the clouds passed, hail and coals of fire. The Lord also thundered from heaven (the seven thunders,[49] the noise heard round the world[50]), and the Highest uttered his voice. And **he sent forth his weapons** (stones), and scattered them; and multiplied lightnings, and routed them. And the springs of waters appeared, and the foundations of the world were exposed, at thy rebuke, O Lord, at **the blasting** of the breath of thy wrath. He sent from on high and **took me, he drew me to himself** (Rapture II) out of many waters (nations[51])....And he brought me out into a **wide place** (a giant planet with a halo).

The explosions of the coals of fire cause the noise heard round the world. This is "the noise of his tabernacle" mentioned in Job 36:29. When iniquity has come to a head, the Lord will roar like a lion in his wrath. Jeremiah 25:29-33 shows this. The Lord says,

> I will call for a sword (the sword of the Lord[52]) upon all the inhabitants of the earth, saith the LORD of hosts....The LORD shall roar from on high, and utter his voice from his holy habitation (Heaven); he shall mightily roar upon his habitation; he shall give a shout, as they that tread the grapes, against all the inhabitants of the earth. A noise shall come even to the ends of the earth; for the LORD hath a controversy with the nations... he will give them that are wicked to the sword (those who live by the sword must die by the sword[53])...And the slain of the LORD shall be at that day from one end of the earth even unto the other end of the earth.

This Feast of Trumpets was prefigured when the Israelites orbited Jericho seven days carrying the ark. On the seventh day, they went around seven times blowing their trumpets. When they shouted, the walls fell down flat, and they burned the city, just as Babylon will be obliterated by fire. Every "wall shall fall."[54] The harlot Rahab, echoing the name of the harlot planet, and her family were saved "so as by fire"[55] as a type of Rapture II when the last believers will be pulled out of the harlot church before it is destroyed.

Since the Crucifixion, mankind stands at the door of the Holy of Holies facing the ark. If you enter with sin on your head, you will die.

Set before you is the way of life and the way of death. Life and death, righteousness and judgment, are embodied in the mercy seat (standing for Christ and life) and the ark (*aron*, coffin, i.e., death). Which do you choose?

The Secret of His tabernacle

This is the big one. As if the mysteries of the chariot of the Cherubim and the vengeance of his temple weren't enough, the tabernacle contains another astonishing secret, one that we never dared hope to have revealed to us ahead of time, the location of Heaven.

In Psalms 27:4, the Tribulation saints say, "For in the time of trouble ("time of Jacob's trouble,"[56]) he shall hide me (Rapture II) in his pavilion (Heaven): in the secret of his tabernacle shall he hide me; he shall set me up upon a rock."

The phrase about hiding them in his pavilion is parallel to the one about hiding them in the secret of his tabernacle. It is the same thing restated in different terms. Therefore, if his pavilion is Heaven, the secret of his tabernacle also refers to Heaven, and they are both "up" upon a celestial rock. In Hebrew, the word translated pavilion is *cok*, meaning pavilion, tabernacle, tent, or house. The Lord's palace is on this rock.

Our Heaven is not an unknown place. It is another orbiting stone out there in his heavenly tent, similar to Earth. In the Septuagint, Job 38:37,38 asks,

> (Who) is he that numbers the clouds in wisdom, and has **bowed the heaven**...to the earth (i.e., as viewed from Earth)? For it (Heaven) is spread out **as dusty earth**, and I have cemented it as one hewn stone to another (probably formed by coalescence).

Since Earth is a planet, and Heaven is "as dusty earth," Heaven is also a planet. As the abode of the Lord, it is fitting that it has a rainbow, or halo, around it.

The sapphire clue

After the Exodus, when Moses climbed up Mount Sinai and saw God, "there was under his (God's) feet as it were a paved work of **a sapphire stone**, and as it were **the body of heaven** (heavenly body) in *his* clearness."[57] The sapphire stone symbolizes the Lord's throne on a flying heavenly body and furnishes us an excellent clue to its location.

Ezekiel, in his second vision of the Cherubim, said,

> (In) the firmament (vault of space) that was **above the head of the Cherubims** there

appeared over them (in an orbit farther out in space than Mars) as it were **a sapphire stone** (another planet), **as the appearance of the likeness of a throne.**[58]

And the Cherubims (heavenly bodies, the planets) lifted up their wings (figurative language indicating flight), and mounted up from the earth in my sight: when they went out, the wheels (orbits) also were beside them, and every one stood at the door of the **east** gate of the LORD'S house (just as the Cherubim were placed to the east of Eden in Genesis 3:24); and the glory of the God of Israel was over them above. This (the higher planet where the Lord's glory resides) is the living creature (lively heavenly body, or flying planet) that I saw **under the God of Israel** by the river of Chebar; and I knew that they (those four plus the one under the God of Israel) were the Cherubims.[59]

Therefore, the Lord's throne is on one of the ten heavenly bodies in our solar system, in his heavenly tent. Psalm 80:2 in the New American Bible says, **"From your throne upon the cherubim, shine forth."** Daniel 3:55,56 (NAB) says, **"from your throne upon the cherubim...Blessed are you in the firmament of heaven."**

Heaven is farther out in space than Mars. It is probably one of the giant planets. Psalm 19:2-7 (NAB) says,

The heavens declare the glory of God, and the firmament proclaims his handiwork. Day pours out the word to day, and night to night imparts knowledge...He has pitched a tent (tabernacle) there for the sun, which comes forth **like the groom** (Jesus Christ) from **his bridal chamber** (Heaven) and, **like a giant,** joyfully runs its course. At one end of

the heavens it comes forth, and its course is
to their other end; nothing escapes its heat.

The Hebrew is clear that this "course" is an orbit. Green's
Interlinear has "He goes forth from the end of the heavens,
and **his orbit** to their ends; and nothing is hidden from his
heat." Heaven, where the Bridegroom is, must be a giant
planet that orbits like our sun in the heavenly tabernacle.

In Ezekiel 1:22,26-28, the sapphire throne is mentioned with another important clue added. There is a ring of
radiance around the throne. The New English Bible says,

> Above the heads of the living creatures (the
> Cherubim) was, as it were, a vault glittering
> like a sheet of **ice**...Above the vault over
> their heads there appeared, as it were, a **sap-
> phire** in the shape of a throne, and high
> above all, upon the throne, a form in human
> likeness. I saw what might have been brass
> **(golden clouds)** glowing like fire in a fur-
> nace from the waist (equator) upwards; and
> from the waist (equator) downwards I saw
> what looked like fire (i.e., a lamp) **with en-
> circling radiance. Like a rainbow** in the
> clouds on a rainy day was the sight of that
> encircling radiance; it was like the appearance
> of the glory of the LORD.

The King James Version describes the encircling radiance as "the brightness round about." We do have one
unique planet in our solar system that stands out from all the
rest because of its golden clouds surrounded by a spectacular
halo of ice rings around the equator.

In Ezekiel 28:12-18, God spoke to Satan as the king
of Tyrus ("rock"). Evidently, Satan was king of the rock
Rahab in the past and is still king of an asteroid, a broken
chunk of the planet Rahab. Addressing Satan, the Lord said,

> Thou hast been in Eden the garden of God;
> every precious stone (planet) was thy cover-

ing (surroundings), the sardius (Mercury), topaz (Venus), and the diamond (Earth), the beryl (Mars), the onyx (Rahab), and the jasper (Jupiter), the **sapphire (7—Saturn)**, the emerald (Uranus), and the carbuncle (Neptune), and gold (Pluto).[60]

When wondering if these stones could represent the planets, I casually looked up sapphire in my desk dictionary[61] and got an electrifying shock. Sapphire is derived from the Sanskrit *sanipriya*, from *Sani*, **Saturn**, plus *priya*, dear. The name sapphire does have a concrete connection with Saturn, and it is certainly dear—it's Paradise. It is appropriately listed in the seventh place, for seven is God's number of perfection. Heaven is perfect.

Warning

The Lord hid the clues so well that we would need his guidance to unravel them, for he did not want us to figure it out until the Rapture was at hand. This is because he does not want us to revere creation instead of the Creator. Never lose sight of this. In the Septuagint, he told Israel,

> I am the Lord thy God that established the heaven, and the whole host of heaven: but I shewed them not to thee that thou shouldest go after them...thou shalt know no God but me; and there is no Saviour beside me.[62]

Israel had enough problems with pagan worship without knowing where Heaven was. It was better that they didn't know. Satan tried hard to establish Saturn worship. At times, he was very successful, especially in Babylon and in Rome, where they celebrated the Saturnalia every year.

Sinai and the sapphire stone

Sani reminds me of Sinai (Sina in the New Testament). Because Moses climbed Mount Sinai and saw the Lord standing on the paved work of a sapphire stone as if it were the heavenly body on which he resides, it makes me wonder if the Hebrew Sinai and the Greek Sina are also derived from *Sani*—Saturn. Sinai's derivation is uncertain.

The passage in Ezekiel shows that Satan's planet was in the middle of the planetary lineup. The Lord said to Satan,

> Thou art the anointed cherub that covereth (*cakak*, guards): and I have set thee so: thou wast upon the holy mountain of God (when the 'sons of God' presented themselves); thou hast walked up and down in the midst of the stones of fire....thou hast sinned: therefore I will cast thee as profane out of the mountain of God (Saturn): and I will destroy thee, O covering cherub, from the midst of the stones of fire (from the planet Rahab)....I will bring thee to ashes upon the earth.[63]

This reveals a three-step judgment against Satan. (1) Satan is cast off the Lord's planet. (2) He is cast off his own planet, Rahab. (3) He and his fallen angels are cast down to Earth, and their asteroid Wormwood follows soon afterward to destroy what they have engineered here.

At times, the truth peeks out between the chinks in pagan writings and reveals Satan's prior knowledge. One is in the Babylonian "Epic of Creation." It seems to speak of Satan's planet, which the Bible calls Rahab, as planet NIBIRU, which means point of crossing. It was like a crossing guard set halfway between Earth and God's Heaven.

> Planet NIBIRU: The Crossroads of Heaven and Earth he shall occupy. Above and below, they shall not go across.

Mars looks reddish, and when we sent a probe out to photograph it, the ground looked strange. In one photo, the soil is reddish-orange, and it has many sharp broken rocks strewn on the surface. An ancient Mesopotamian text tells us that the next planet out from Mars appeared dark red.

The great planet: At his appearance, dark red.
The Heavens he divides in half and stands as
Nibiru.

Also, an instance that reveals Satan's prior knowledge of where God's planet orbits is found in an ancient Sumerian astronomical text.

The *kakkab* (star) of the Supreme Scepter is
one of the sheep (Sun's wandering planets)
in *mulmul* (Sumerian for our solar system).[64]

NEAs, Near Earth Asteroids

When the planet Rahab blew up, the impact blast shot a broken piece out into a cometary orbit. This asteroid may threa-
ten us about twice a year as it crosses our orbit.

Our astronomers have found about 310 NEAs. They
have even found an unsettling number, about 50, between us
and our moon. The flaming sword (*chereb*), a hunk of a
former Cherubim, is out there threatening us all right.

The astronomers now realize that the other heavenly
bodies we have seen are all cratered. This is why the symbolic Cherubim in the tabernacle were made of beaten gold.
Even our moon is pockmarked, and Earth is not immune.

In 1991, at San Juan Capistrano, California, during a
meeting with prominent astronomers from around the world,
we were told that they definitely expect an asteroid to crash
into Earth sometime, maybe within the next 30 years. About
a dozen experts from around the world were already working on a missile system to try to deflect an incoming asteroid. Half of them were at that meeting.

After the 21 spectacular string-of-pearl pieces of
Comet Shoemaker-Levy 9 slammed into Jupiter in July,
1994, Representative Ralph Hall of Texas, chairman of the
House space subcommittee said,

> If a comet or asteroid the size of the one we
> have been watching hit Jupiter this week
> were to hit the Earth, it would cause a major
> global catastrophe....If a head-on collision is

coming, there is a remedy: Hit the intruder
with a nuclear missile. Or, given time, send
up a spacecraft to nudge it off course.[65]

Scripture shows that their efforts will be in vain. Hall also
said that "each day, an asteroid the size of a house passes
within the distance between the Earth and the moon....Each
month, one the size of a football field." The threat is real,
and one of 0.7 mile diameter could wipe out civilization.

The analysis of six of the impacts on Jupiter was
presented in Bethesda, Maryland, on the following Halloween at the annual meeting of the Division of Planetary Sci-
ences of the American Astronomical Society. The G frag-
ment that smashed into Jupiter caused a fireball 5 miles in diameter that had a temperature greater than the sun, at least
14,000 degrees Fahrenheit, about 4,073 degrees hotter than
the sun. The fireball expanded within one and a half minutes
to hundreds of miles across.[66] The energy released by the
impacts on Jupiter had a force of over 20 million megatons.

These impacts taught us something. Collisions are
not impossible here, and if we were to take a hit, the devastation could well be global. The lesson was sobering.
Strange that the first piece slammed into Jupiter on Tisha
Be'Av (our July 16), a Jewish fast commemorating the last
day, Av 9, that both Solomon's and Herod's temples stood.
They were both burned on Av 10.[67] Jeremiah recorded that in

the fifth month, in the tenth day of the month,
which was the nineteenth year of Nebuchadrezzar king of Babylon, came Nebuzar-
adan, captain of the guard, which served the
king of Babylon, into Jerusalem, And burned
the house of the Lord.[68]

There may be a reason this happened on that particular day.
Was the Lord trying to get our attention? Was he trying to
get us to face the reality that something like this would happen to Earth at the end of this age? Was it a sign? Luke 21:25
says, "And there shall be signs in the sun, and in the moon,
and in the stars." What better example do we need?

The alternative

If this kind of destruction is inevitable on Earth, what options do we have? The same Lord that told of the catastrophic events that we face also offered us a way out. He promised that even with temptations, he will "also make **a way to escape.**"[69] He has given us a test. We must make our choice. It's either lose or choose Christ. We can't sit on the fence. We must exercise our will and choose him. If we believe in him, we can be with him where he is. He said,

> ye believe in God, believe also in me. In my Father's house are many mansions: if it were not so, I would have told you. I go to prepare a place for you. And if I go and prepare a place for you, I will come again, and receive you unto myself; that where I am, there ye may be also. And **whither I go ye know**, and the way ye know. Thomas saith unto him, Lord, we know not whither thou goest; and how can we know the way? Jesus saith unto him, I am the way, the truth, and the life: no man cometh unto the Father, but by me. If ye had known me, ye should have known my Father also: and from henceforth ye know him, and have seen him...he that hath seen me hath seen the Father.[70]

Lamps of fire

Can we know for sure where Heaven is? Yes! Jesus said, "And **whither I go ye know.**" This means that this place was familiar to Thomas even though he did not recognize that it was Heaven. The place is knowable. The ancients knew about Saturn. It is visible with the naked eye. At present, it is under the two lower stars in the Great Square of Pegasus, forming a triangle with them. Is it really Heaven? Let's see what clues we have found so far.

In Revelation 4, John was taken to Heaven. The first thing he saw there was a throne. It sounds like it could be on Saturn. He that sat on the throne was "like a jasper and a sardine stone." These are the first and last stones in the breast-plate worn by the high priest. This signifies that Jesus is the first and the last as he told us in Revelation 1:17 and 22:13. This means that he is both Yahweh (or Jehovah) of the Old Testament and the Lord Jesus Christ of the New Testament.

John continues reading Revelation 4:3-6, saying,

> and *there was* a **rainbow round about the throne,** in sight like unto an emerald (the stone in the breastplate that stood for Judah, the tribe of Jesus)....and *there were* **seven lamps of fire burning before the throne,** which are the seven Spirits of God. And before the throne *there was* **a sea of glass like unto crystal.**[71]

The rainbow around the throne and the sea of glass like crystal (or ice, as in the New English Bible) sound like the rings around Saturn, but what are the seven lamps of fire (flaming torches, in the NEB) burning before the throne? Here they are called Spirits of God.

Since they are lamps or torches, and before the throne instead of in the midst of it, they may not be the same as the Spirits of God of Revelation 5:6. There, the Lamb is "in the midst of the throne" and has "seven horns (representing Christ's omnipotence) and seven eyes (his omniscience), which are the seven Spirits of God (his omnipresence) sent forth into all the earth." These stand for the complete perfect Spirit of God residing in Christ. "For it pleased the Father that in him should all fulness dwell."[72]

However, if the lamps before the throne stand for something else, what do they represent? Could these spirits represent the same things as the flying creatures that looked like lamps that Ezekiel saw in his visions? Ezekiel 1:21 says that "the spirit of the living creature was in the wheels." The word translated spirit is *ruwash*, and means wind or current of air. There was a propelling current of air in the orbits.

The four Cherubim are characterized as living creatures with four wings, yet "their appearance was like burning coals of fire, and like the appearance of lamps"[73] orbiting in the sky. They were not actually alive, but lively *planetes*, wanderers. They did not have wings, but flew. They were not lamps, but looked like lights. They did not have eyes, but were themselves spheres or full orbs, just as the Latin *orbis terrarum* applies to the globe of the Earth.

They did not have high rings full of eyes, but high orbits. They did not have actual wheels within wheels, but concentric orbits. They were not burning coals, but planets reflecting the sunlight. They did not have four faces, but faced four directions; the same faces were on the banners at the compass points around Israel's wilderness camp.

Ezekiel saw what looked like lamps or coals of fire orbiting the sun, and John saw what looked like seven lamps or flaming torches. Is it possible that they could stand for the same things? Could both represent planets? Are these lamps of fire before the throne Mercury, Venus, Earth, Mars, Rahab, Jupiter, and Saturn, standing for the same planets that the first seven precious stones in Ezekiel 28:13 represent?

The Seraphim

Revelation 4:6,8 and Isaiah 6:1-3 describe four beasts that sound like the Cherubim, except they have six wings.

> ...in the midst of the throne, and round about the throne, *were* four beasts full of eyes (full orbs) before and behind (they are spheres)... And the four beasts had each of them six wings about *him*; and *they were* full of eyes within: and they rest not day and night, saying Holy, holy, holy Lord God Almighty.

> (He) saw also the Lord sitting upon a throne, high and lifted up, and his train (hem, robe of light) filled the temple. Above it stood the Seraphims: each one had six wings...And one cried unto another, and said, Holy, holy, holy, is the LORD of hosts.

These four Seraphim do not have to actually be alive to utter this kind of speech for Psalms 19:1 says that the heavens declare the glory of God; and the firmament sheweth his handiwork. Day unto day uttereth speech, and night unto night sheweth knowledge. There is no speech nor language, where their voice is not heard. Their line is gone out through all the earth, and their words to the end of the world. In them (the heavens) hath he set a tabernacle for the sun.

Literally, the mention of the sun limits this tabernacle to our solar system. Symbolically, this entire solar system is for Christ, who is called "the Sun of righteousness."[74]

In the King James Version quoted above, the four Seraphim are described as in the midst and round about the throne. They could be the planets, Jupiter, Uranus, Neptune, and Pluto, that orbit near Saturn. The word translated midst is *meso*, which means among, between or before them. That gives us another clue. Since Jupiter's orbit is closer to us, it is before them, before Saturn and the other outer planets. The orbits of the other three planets are outside Saturn's orbit, so they orbit around Saturn.

Similar to the Amplified Bible and Vincent's translation, the Berkeley Version says,

> Around the throne, in the center of each side, there were four living beings full of eyes in front and behind; the first...like a lion, the second like a bullock, the third with a man-like face and the fourth like a flying eagle.[75]

That the heavenly bodies were symbolically positioned in the center of each side around the throne makes sense because the four flags placed at the cardinal compass points around the tabernacle had on them the faces of a lion, a bullock, a man and an eagle. In Ezekiel's first vision of the heavens, each of the Cherubim had the same four faces.[76]

The Israelites camped in a circle around the tabernacle. The Holy of Holies represented Heaven. The priests camped closest to the tabernacle. Outside of their circle, the rest of the Levites built their camps. Around them bivouacked the remainder of the Israelites. According to Josephus,[77] they even built roads between the rows, making concentric circles that remind us of the rings around Saturn.

The symbolism of the tabernacle is important. The picture is getting clearer. Many things seem to point to Saturn, but we want to explore every possibility to be sure.

On the tabernacle curtains, all ten original planets were depicted as Cherubim. However, after we learn that Satan's planet Rahab was split apart and became the asteroid belt, another picture emerges. Omitting Rahab from the five terrestrial planets leaves the four present Cherubim, Mercury, Venus, Earth and Mars. These were what Ezekiel saw when he looked and said that "the heavens were opened."[78]

It seems that the throne of the Lord is an outer planet. Saturn is the second largest. Around it are four planets. With respect to distance from the sun, Jupiter precedes Saturn, and Uranus, Neptune, and Pluto follow it. Do the four six-winged Seraphim around the throne of the Lord represent Jupiter, Uranus, Neptune, and Pluto?

Evidently, all the planets can be designated as Cherubim, as were embroidered on the tabernacle curtains. Or, taking into consideration that Rahab split and the asteroid belt now separates the inner from the outer planets, the inner ones can be called Cherubim and the outer ones surrounding the throne can be called Seraphim. Since the word Seraphim means burners, they also have "the appearance of lamps."[79]

The Cherubim in Ezekiel 1 and 10 may have been characterized as having four wings because they are the first four planets—Mercury, Venus, Earth and Mars. The Seraphim in Isaiah 6:1,2 and Revelation 4:6,8 may have been given six wings because there were six remaining planets in the original lineup (Rahab, Jupiter, Saturn, Uranus, Neptune, and Pluto) even though only four of them were mentioned in the immediate context. Rahab had already been blown to bits and the remaining four (Jupiter, Uranus, Neptune, and Pluto) surrounded the throne on Saturn.

According to the New English Bible, John saw the Lamb "inside the circle of living creatures."[80] Thus, the four planets are around the throne just as Jupiter, Uranus,

Neptune, and Pluto orbit on one side or the other of the planet Saturn.

There is another question that keeps popping into my mind. In Revelation 4:4, we see 24 elders sitting on lesser thrones around the Lord's throne. Does this have any connection with Saturn's moons? So far, by using the Hubble Telescope, astronomers have identified 22,[81] but some think there are 23. I will not be surprised if they find 24 moons.

The Lord "sitteth between the Cherubims"

When the Lord is crowned and begins to reign, he will start to judge. Psalms 99:1 says, "let the people tremble, **he sitteth** *between* **the Cherubims**; let the earth be moved ("The earth shall reel to and fro like a drunkard."[82]

If the King James is translated correctly, and "he sitteth between the Cherubims," his throne could be between Jupiter and Uranus. However, Green's Interlinear says, "(He) sits (on) the Cherubim," and the Jerusalem Bible has "he is enthroned on the winged creatures." First Samuel 4:4 (RSV) speaks of "the LORD of hosts, who is **enthroned on the Cherubim**." First Chronicles 13:6 (Green) says, "God Jehovah, who dwells among the cherubs."

Both II Samuel 22:11 and Psalm 18:10 say that "**he rode upon a cherub**, and did fly: yea, he did fly upon the wings of the wind.

It seems that the Lord is enthroned on one of the ten Cherubim, but between two other Cherubim, therefore not on the first or the last. This quickly eliminates the two smallest planets, Mercury and Pluto. We have already eliminated the terrestrial planets anyway, so the only possibilities left are the giant planets, Jupiter, Saturn, Uranus, and Neptune.

Saturn is shrouded in light golden clouds. We have never seen its surface. This ties in. Psalms 104:1-3 says,

> O LORD...Who coverest thyself with light as with a garment: who stretchest out the heavens like a curtain (of the tabernacle): Who layeth the beams of his chambers ("upper rooms"[83]) in the waters (there is water in Heaven[84]): **who maketh the clouds his**

chariot: who walketh (orbits) upon the wings of the wind.

Not only does Saturn have water on the planet, it seems to float in a sea of ice crystals. Also, our astronomers say that Saturn's density is so little, .07, that it would actually float on water, which has a density of 1.0.

Saturn has an equatorial diameter of 74,600 miles. It's year is long, its day short. It circles the Sun once in 29.5 years and spins once on its axis in 10.2 hours. Its Mass is 95 times that of Earth, its volume 755 times ours. In 1993, it was listed as having "22+" moons.[85]

Heaven is visible to the naked eye

Job 36:32;37:18-22 in the Septuagint indicates that Heaven has to be visible to some from the Earth:

> He has hidden the light in his hands, and given charge concerning it to the interposing cloud....the foundations for the ancient heavens? they are strong as a molten (cast) mirror...But **the light** is not visible to all: it **shines afar off in the heavens**...From the north (i.e., up) come the **clouds shining like gold**: in these great are the glory and honour of the Almighty (it is his throne).

The golden clouds limit the possibilities. Not everyone has seen it, but Saturn is visible to the naked eye in clear skies. Some astronomers have picked out Uranus, but Neptune cannot be seen with the naked eye at all and is therefore eliminated as a possibility. The "clouds shining like gold" zero in on the planet Saturn like a guided missile. Jupiter is reddish, and Uranus looks bluish to some and greenish to others. The picture is getting clearer. Let's review the clues and see if there is anything else we should consider.

The circuit of heaven

We know that the Lord's dwelling place orbits, suggesting that it is a planet. The Lord not only "walketh upon the wings of the wind," but he "walketh in the circuit of heaven." Job 22:12-14 says,

> Is not God in the height of heaven?...thou sayest, How doth God know? can he judge through the dark cloud? Thick clouds are a covering to him, that he seeth not; and he walketh **in the circuit of heaven**.

The Hebrew word translated "walketh" is *halak*. It means walk, move forward, to and fro or up and down, or whirl. This aptly describes Heaven's orbit.

The "circuit of heaven" is an important clue. Only the sun, moon, planets, asteroids, and comets circle in front of the stationary field of stars, which are too far away for us to detect any orbital movement at all during one man's lifetime. This "circuit of heaven" is the ecliptic, the track through the stationary stars that the sun, moon, and planets travel.

The third heaven

What is the third heaven? Paul said,

> I knew a man in Christ...(whether in the body, I cannot tell; or whether out of the body, I cannot tell: God knoweth;) such an one caught up to **the third heaven**.... caught up into **paradise**.[86]

This makes sense if the first heaven is now Mars, the second Jupiter, and the third Saturn. The Paradise of God seems to be on Saturn no matter which way we approach it or which clues we examine; we seem always to somehow come back to Saturn.

We saw that Scripture places the Lord's throne in our solar system like the Sun, Moon and Earth, which are visible spheres. He

> **built his sanctuary like high palaces** (spheres), **like the earth** (a spherical planet) which he hath established for ever.[87]

187

His seed (Jesus) shall endure for ever, and his throne **as the sun** (a body in our solar system) before me. It shall be established for ever **as the moon** (another heavenly body in this solar system) and **as a faithful witness** (therefore visible) **in heaven.**[88]

The morning star

When Rapture I is at hand, Jesus calls himself **"the bright and morning star"** in Revelation 22:16. When the Second Coming is in view, he calls himself "the Sun of righteousness that will arise with healing in his wings" in Malachi 4:2. Why the difference? The Rapture happens before the Second Advent, just as the morning star is seen before sun up, but there is more to it than that. It looks like he has planned to snatch us up on Pentecost when HEAVEN IS A BRIGHT AND MORNING STAR. Saturn is a morning star five months out of every year and an evening star five months.

I did not intend to capitalize that. The Lord must have caused it. Neither the shift key nor the caps lock key was down. This is the ninth time something has come out in caps automatically as I typed. It never starts or ends in the middle of a word. It is always a complete word, phrase, or thought.

The first Rapture will, I believe, take place on Pentecost (when we, as the firstfruits[89] of the dough[90] are to be a wave offering), when Saturn is a morning star , and the second Rapture will take place on the Feast of Trumpets, when Saturn is an evening star. However, Jesus did not mention anything about being an evening star. This could be because there is too much smoke in the sky to see the stars when Rapture II takes place.

However, in his monologue to the seven churches, Jesus said of the over comers of Thyatira,

> **I will give him the morning star.** He that hath an ear, let him hear what the Spirit saith unto the churches.[91]

There is an important message here for believers that have ears to hear. Jesus is not referring to himself as the morning star that he will give over comers because these are believers, members of the church. They already have Christ in their hearts. He has already given himself to them. This morning star is Heaven, where his throne is located.

Saturn is also bright. It can be seen more clearly than seems warranted in slightly hazy skies. It's steady light seems to burn through. Because of its distance from us, it is third in brilliance among the planets. Venus is brightest. Jupiter is next. Both are closer to us than Saturn.

Our space exploration found a few thin faint rings around the other giant planets, but Saturn is the only planet marked with such a resplendent royal halo. The many rings look like ice crystals. This is the "sea of glass," "the likeness of an expanse like the sparkle of awesome ice."[92]

Satan's original home planet, Rahab, was also a morning star. Any planet seen in the morning is a morning star. The Septuagint says,

> How has Lucifer, that rose in the morning (or **'shining star, son of the morning,'** Green), fallen from heaven! He that sent orders to all the nations is crushed to the earth. But thou saidst in thine heart...I will be like the Most High.[93]

> (When) the angels of God came to stand before the Lord...the devil came with them. And the Lord said to the devil, Whence art thou come? And the devil...said, **I am come from compassing (orbiting) the earth,** and walking up and down in the world.[94]

No matter where we look, Scripture, in the original editions, always portrays truth. Satan's planet, Rahab, had an orbit that was outside Earth's, farther from the sun than ours. Therefore, Rahab orbited around Earth.

Because "Joshua" from the Hebrew is "Jesus" from the Greek, the Septuagint brings out the real meaning of Zechariah 3:1-10. The English translation of the Greek version makes it easy to recognize Jesus for who he really was.

the Lord shewed me **Jesus the high priest** standing before the angel of the Lord, and the Devil stood on his right hand to resist him... If thou wilt walk in my ways, and take heed to my charges, then shalt thou judge my house (all God's judgment is committed to the Son[95]): and if thou wilt diligently keep my court, then will I give thee men to walk in the midst of these that stand here. Hear now, Jesus the high priest, thou, and thy neighbors that are sitting before thee: for they are diviners (*mowpheth*, men who shadow forth future events[96]), for, behold, I bring forth my servant The Branch. For as for **the stone which I have set before the face of Jesus, on the one stone are seven eyes** (orbs, i.e., spheres).

The stone that is set before the face of Jesus is marked with the number seven, God's number of completion and perfection. The planet set before Jesus is perfect. It's Paradise. The seven spheres, could be diagramed thus:

OOOOOO<u>O</u>

Could this be a celestial map indicating that the throne of Jesus will be on the seventh rock, or planet— Mercury, Venus, Earth, Mars, Rahab, Jupiter, then Saturn? We put a similar celestial map in our spaceships so someone could figure out that the vehicle came from the third planet.

The golden candlestick

The seven-branched golden candlestick in the tabernacle not only represents Christ as the light of the world, but it could indicate where his throne is located with respect to the Earth. There were seven bowls and seven lamps in the bowls that were to be lit in the evening.[97] If the middle lamp represents Saturn, the three on the left would represent Mars, next outside Earth's orbit, then Rahab and Jupiter. The three lamps on the right would represent Uranus, Neptune, and Pluto.

These lamps depict the planets well for the sun only lights up the near side of each planet. More than anything else, they resemble spot lights screwed into bowl-shaped fixtures. Also, the branches of the candlestick form semi circles, suggesting their concentric orbits.

However, the candlestick may represent planets plus the sun. Josephus described the candlestick thus:

> It was made with its knops, and lilies, and pomegranates, and bowls (which ornaments amounted to seventy in all); by which means the shaft elevated itself on high from a single base, and spread itself into **as many branches as there were planets, including the sun** among them. It terminated in seven heads, in one row, all standing parallel to one another; and these branches carried **seven lamps**, one by one, **in imitation of the number of the planets.**[98]

If the sun is included, the luminaries depicted would be: the Sun, Mercury, Venus, Earth, Mars, Jupiter, and Saturn. However, the Sun seems to be lit in the daytime, the planets at night. When the one is up, the other is not. Exodus 30:7,8 says that "Aaron lighteth the lamps at even." Yet, the seven circles on the one stone set before Jesus put His Place in the seventh position. Saturn was the seventh in the original lineup of planets: Mercury, Venus, Earth, Mars, Rahab, Jupiter, Saturn.

Paradise was in "the third heaven"[99] when Paul wrote about it in the first century A.D. This favors the Earth-**Mars**-**Jupiter**-**Saturn**-Uranus-Neptune-Pluto lineup. It is incredible, but it seems that no matter how you look at it, the candlestick tells a true story. Originally, Saturn was the seventh **planet**. Since Rahab split into pieces, Saturn is the seventh **luminary** and our third **heaven.**

Zechariah had a vision of a golden candlestick. When asked, "What seest thou?" he answered, "I have looked, and behold a candlestick **all of gold** (symbol of deity), with a bowl upon the top of it, and his seven lamps thereon." Instead of a "bowl," the literal Concordant Version has "globe." That globe seems to represent the golden Saturn.

The tabernacle curtains tell their own story. Imagine standing inside, near the middle of the tabernacle, looking heavenward at the curtains with Cherubim embroidered on them. The five rear curtains on our left, toward the west, represent Mercury, Venus, Earth, Mars, and Rahab. The five front curtains on our right, toward the east, stand for Jupiter, Saturn, Uranus, Neptune, and Pluto. Both sets are hooked together unifying our planetary solar system.

When the ten curtains are spread out over the supporting boards of the tabernacle, two and a half curtains hang down the back and seven and a half cover the top. Thus the one that folds down over the upper back corner represents Earth, and the rest of the top represents the same planets as the candlestick in the tabernacle, if we think of it as pointing to the third heaven.

The symbolism of the tabernacle was carried over to the temple. So when Ezekiel 9:3 says that "the glory of the God of Israel was gone up from the cherub which stood on the corner of the house,"[100] the glory had gone up from the Earth. When Ezekiel 10:18[101] mentions that "the glory of the LORD departed from the corner of the temple, and stood over the Cherubim," we know that the glory departed from the Earth and stood above at least two planets. Thus, the glory of the Lord returned to the third heaven—its source.

The identification of Earth with the corner is one reason why Psalm 118:22 says, "The stone which the builders refused is become the **head stone of the corner.**" Christ will be King over the Earth. He will also be King over Heaven. In the parable of sums of money, Jesus said,

> A man of noble birth (Jesus Christ, Son of God) went to a faraway country (Heaven) to become **its king**, and then return.[102]

When we understand the significance of the "corner," Psalm 144:11,12 takes on new meaning too. It says, "Rid me, and deliver me from the hand of strange children (the asteroid impact will do that)...that our daughters (the Jews during the Millennium) may be **as corner stones** (earthly leaders under Christ the King of kings and Lord of lords), polished (*chatab*, carved, i.e., formed) after the similitude of a palace" (in a government set up on Earth, as it is in Heaven). No wonder the Lord Jesus Christ taught us to pray, "Thy will be done in earth, as it is in heaven."[103]

Evidently, the third, fifth and seventh planets were assigned respectively to Adam, Satan and the Lord Jesus Christ for their thrones. Satan, not content with his own kingdom, took dominion away from Adam and tried to be "like the Most High." His hope is in vain, his time short.

Ash colored horses

In Zechariah 6:1-8 in the LXX, the asteroids are aptly depicted as ash colored horses. Many are clinkers produced when the planet Rahab blew up. Zechariah said,

> I...lifted up my eyes...four chariots coming out from between two...brazen mountains. In the first chariot were red horses: and in the second chariot black horses, and in the third chariot white horses, and in the fourth chariot piebald and ash-colored horses....These are the four winds (or spirits, as in Revelation 4:5) of heaven, and they are going forth to stand before the Lord of all the earth.

If the two brazen mountains are Mercury and Jupiter, the four chariots between them represent Venus, Earth, Mars, and Rahab, and they are all before the Lord's planet, Saturn. "And the ash colored went out," Zechariah continued, "and looked to go and compass the earth: and he said, **Go, and compass** (*shuwt*, **whip around**, i.e., orbit) **the earth.**" These are the Near Earth Asteroids. Everything is set up for the coming collision.

Rescue is available

Since there is a way of getting out of here before the NEA called Wormwood[104] destroys civilization as we know it, we should take advantage of the opportunity set before us. Jesus is willing to rescue you if you trust him. Ask him to be your Saviour. "How shall we escape, if we neglect so great salvation?" There are two Raptures when Jesus will gather his believers and take them to Heaven. The first is described in I Thessalonians 4:16,17:

> (The) Lord himself shall descend from heaven with a shout, with the voice of the archangel, and with the trump of God: and the dead in Christ shall rise first: Then we which are alive and remain shall be **caught up** together with them in the clouds, **to meet the Lord in the air**: and so shall we ever be with the Lord.

He promised, "Because thou hast kept the word of my patience, I also will keep thee from the hour of temptation (the seven year Tribulation), which shall come upon all the world, to try them that dwell upon the earth."[105]

It may come as a surprise, but it looks as if many will see the Rapture take place. Psalm 40:1-3 in the New English Bible says,

> I waited, waited for the LORD, he bent down to me and heard my cry. **He brought me up** out of the muddy pit, out of the mire (Earth) and the clay (body made of clay); he set my feet on a rock (the heavenly planet) and gave me firm footing; and on my lips he put a new song (sung after the Rapture[106]), a song of praise to our God. **Many when they see will be filled with awe and will learn to trust in the LORD.**

The King James Version has "many shall see it, and fear, and shall trust in the LORD." The message is consistent in other versions.[107] Many will see the Rapture take place, fear, and then believe in Christ. People will also see God's two witnesses, Moses and Elijah taken up to Heaven.

The month when Israel became a nation may actually be another indication as to when Rapture I will take place. Also, Israel grew leaves when summer was near. In Mark 13:28,29, Jesus said,

> Now learn a parable of the fig tree; When her branch (modern Israel) is yet tender, and putteth forth leaves (she grew in the Six-Day War), ye know that **summer is near**: So ye **in like manner**, when ye shall see these things (Israel reborn and growing) come to pass, know that it (or he) is nigh, even **at the doors** (symbol of the two Raptures).

Will a Rapture door open in May, when summer is near, just as Israel was born in May and grew leaves when summer was near? If so, Pentecost fits. In 1998, Pentecost will fall on Sunday, May 31, before summer arrives on June 21.

When the coming of the Lord is "at hand," Jesus is stationed "at the doors" to judge who is to be brought to Heaven when the first door opens. James said,

> Be patient, therefore, brethren, until the coming of the Lord (he comes for the brethren at the Rapture). Behold, the farmer waits for the precious fruit of the earth, being patient over it until it receives the early and the late rain. You also be patient. Establish your hearts, for **the coming of the Lord is at hand**. Do not grumble, brethren, against one another, that you may not be judged; behold, **the Judge is standing at the doors** (James 5:7-9, RSV).

At Rapture II, the Tribulation saints will be "saved; yet so as by fire,"[108] They will just barely escape before the Arrow of the Lord's deliverance hits Earth. Scripture says,

> The LORD thundered from heaven...he sent out arrows...the channels of the sea ap-

peared, the foundations of the world were discovered, at the rebuking of the LORD, at the blast of the breath of his nostrils (the whirlwind). He sent from above, **he took me**; he drew me out of many waters (nations[109]); He delivered me...**in the day of my calamity** (day of Jacob's trouble)... **He brought me forth also into a large place** (i.e., a giant planet).[110]

For in the time of trouble (just before the asteroid impact) **he shall hide me in his pavilion** (in Heaven): **in the secret of his tabernacle** (which reveals where Heaven is located) shall he hide me; **he shall set me up upon a rock** (a planet).[111]

It looks to me like the secret of his tabernacle reveals that the giant planet Saturn is Heaven, where neither moth nor rust doth corrupt, and thieves do not break through and steal. Nothing will ever be allowed to defile the seventh stone, the perfect Paradise, the "sapphire" planet. That is why Sapphira died when she lied to the Spirit of the Lord.[112] She was made an example. Her name means "that relates or tells." It did have a story to tell us. Revelation 21:27 agrees:

there shall in no wise enter into it any thing that defileth, neither *whatsoever* worketh abomination, or *maketh* a lie: but they which are written in the Lamb's book of life.

In the Lord Jesus Christ "dwelleth all the fulness of the Godhead bodily,"[113] but God cannot be contained in one place, not even on the sapphire throne. The Lord was present in the tabernacle and will sit on the throne of David on Earth at his Second Advent. He will sit on his throne in Heaven, but there is more to it than this. The universe is enormous, and "All things were made by him."[114] God is spirit.[115] "For in him we live, and move, and have our being."[116] There is a heaven of heavens, but in I Kings 8:27, Solomon revealed that even "the heaven and heaven of heavens cannot contain thee."

Sometimes, Saturn's rings present themselves to us edge-on and seem to disappear, as they have lately. Then, Saturn hangs there like a great pearl in the sky, revealing the meaning of the parable of the pearl of great price.

Jesus said that **"the kingdom of heaven is like** unto a merchant man, seeking goodly pearls: Who, when he had found **one pearl of great price**, went and sold all that he had, and bought it."[117]

This "pearl" is larger than Earth. Job 11:5-9 says,

> But oh that God would...show you the se-
> crets of wisdom...Do you know the height of
> the heaven? Or the depth of Sheol?...The
> measure thereof (of Heaven) is longer than
> the earth, and (of Sheol) broader than the sea.

Satan's planet, Rahab, was closer to the sun than Heaven. Job 9:13 in the Berkeley version reflects this. It says, "God lets His indignation have full sway; **beneath Him** Rahab's helpers tremble."

In retrospect, many clues indicate that the Lord's throne is on Saturn, originally the seventh planet from the sun. It is among the planets flung from God's right hand, for he said in Isaiah 48:13, "my right hand hath spanned the heavens."

The "paradise of God" is in "the third heaven" on a pearl-like heavenly body in our solar system, "as the sun," "as the moon," and "like the earth." It has beautiful "clouds shining like gold" and an iridescent halo befitting the palace of deity, the golden-crowned King of kings and Lord of lords. While effectively shielding his great brightness from us, Saturn still "shines afar off in the heavens" "as a faithful witness in heaven" and is known by our astronomers to radiate three times more heat than it receives from the sun.

1. Luke 13:6-9
2. Luke 8:17
3. Acts 16:31
4. Hebrews 9:23,24
5. Hosea 12:10, Concordant Version
6. Psalms 104:30
7. Isaiah 51:9
8. Psalm 89:36,37
9. Psalm 78:69
10. Septuagint, Job 38:37,38
11. Jeremiah 17:12
12. Schmid, Randolph E.. "Vapor rivers detected above Earth." *The Orange County Register*, Jan. 22, 1993
13. Kerrod, Robin. *The Star Guide*. (N.Y.: Prentice Hall, 1993), p. 132
14. Galatians 3:28
15. Romans 12:5
16. John 10:9
17. Isaiah 11:12
18. I Kings 6:20
19. Revelation 21:16
20. Zechariah 5:1-3
21. Job 26:12, NASB
22. Psalms 89:10
23. Isaiah 51:9
24. Exodus 26:6
25. Exodus 25:8,9, Jerusalem Bible
26. Ezekiel 1:23
27. Sitchin, Zecharia. *The 12th Planet*. (N.Y., Avon Books,1976)
28. "Can Machines Think." *Time*, March, 1996, p. 50
29. Isaiah 66:15,16
30. Revelation 6:2
31. Psalm 46:8-10
32. II Kings 2:11,12
33. II Kings 13:14-17
34. Romans 3:23-25, Green's Interlinear
35. I John 2:2
36. Jeremiah 51:6-9
37. Revelation 16:21
38. Zechariah 5:3, NASB
39. Jeremiah 51:25
40. Jeremiah 12:12
41. Zechariah 11:17
42. Ezekiel 28:14

[43] Ezekiel 10:2,6
[44] Exodus 14:25
[45] Exodus 14:21
[46] Jeremiah 23:19,20
[47] Revelation 8:8,10
[48] Zechariah 5:2,3
[49] Revelation 10:3
[50] Jeremiah 25:31
[51] Revelation 17:15
[52] Isaiah 34:6
[53] Revelation 13:10
[54] Ezekiel 38:20
[55] I Corinthians 3:15
[56] Jeremiah 30:7
[57] Exodus 24:10
[58] Ezekiel 10:1
[59] Ezekiel 10:19-21
[60] Ezekiel 28:13
[61] *Webster's Seventh New Collegiate Dictionary*. (Springfield, MA, G. & C. Merriam Co., 1966) p. 763
[62] Hosea (Osee) 13:4
[63] Ezekiel 28:14-18
[64] Sitchin. op. cit., p. 237, 242, 203
[65] "Lawmaker aims for Earth to avoid the fate of Jupiter." *The Orange County Register*, July 22, 1994
[66] Allen, Jane E. "Comet created a fireball hotter than sun's surface." *The Orange County Register*, November 16, 1994
[67] Josephus. *Wars of the Jews*. Book 6, Ch. 4, sect. 5
[68] Jeremiah 52:12,13
[69] I Corinthians 10:13
[70] John 14:1-9
[71] Revelation 4:3-6
[72] Colossians 1:19
[73] Ezekiel 1:13
[74] Malachi 4:2
[75] Revelation 4:6,7
[76] Ezekiel 1:10
[77] William Whiston. *The Works of Josephus*. (Philadelphia, David McKay Co., nd), chap. XII, page 111
[78] Ezekiel 1:1
[79] Ezekiel 1:13
[80] Revelation 5:6
[81] *Astronomy*, Nov. 1995, p. 26
[82] Isaiah 24:20

[83] Green's Interlinear
[84] Revelation 22:1
[85] Robin Kerrod, *op. cit.*, p. 133
[86] II Corinthians 12:2
[87] Psalm 78:69
[88] Psalm 89:36,37
[89] James 1:18
[90] Numbers 15:18-21, LXX
[91] Revelation 2:28,29
[92] Ezekiel 1:22, NWT
[93] Isaiah 14:12-14
[94] Job 1:6,7
[95] John 5:22
[96] Gesenius' Lexicon
[97] Exodus 30:8; II Chronicles 13:11
[98] Josephus. *Antiquities of the Jews.* Book 3, Chap. VI, pg 98,99
[99] II Corinthians 12:2
[100] Lamsa translation
[101] *Ibid.*
[102] Luke 19:12, New American Bible
[103] Matthew 6:9,10
[104] Revelation 8:11
[105] Revelation 3:10
[106] Revelation 5:9
[107] NIV, RSV, Berkeley, New Jerusalem, Amplified, Lamsa, and Confraternity
[108] I Corinthians 3:15
[109] Revelation 17:15
[110] II Samuel 22:5-20
[111] Psalm 27:5
[112] Acts 5:1-10
[113] Colossians 2:9
[114] John 1:3
[115] John 4:24
[116] Acts 17:28
[117] Matthew 13:45,46

5

*B*ook of *P*urchase *U*nsealed

Revelation 6 and 7

𝔅uy it, Jeremiah was told, "the right of inheritance is thine, and the redemption is thine; buy it."

Jeremiah means grandeur of the Lord. When that prophet bought the field of Hanameel, which means gift of God, it was a type of the sealed book given to Christ by his Father after the Rapture of the Church.

This deed was "the book of the purchase." Two copies were made, one sealed, one open. Both were put "in an earthen vessel, that they may continue many days."[1]

The two copies remind us of the book of Daniel, which was sealed, and Revelation, which is open. Both have information concerning the end times, and Daniel was to be opened in "the time of the end." Revelation is written as if the time of the end and the Rapture are at hand. It helps us understand Daniel, and Daniel adds spice to Revelation.

Jeremiah's "book of the purchase" shows us what the book handed to Christ is called. It was put "in an earthen vessel" to make the type even clearer. Christ is holding the sealed Book of the Purchase of Earth.

As the next scene in our play opens, Christ begins to break the seals, and the Tribulation, called the Seventieth Week of Daniel[2] and the hour of trial,[3] begins immediately.

When our Lord takes official ruler ship of Earth near the end of the seven-year Tribulation, evil will be purged and lasting peace will come, but during the 2,300-day shortened

Tribulation, evil comes to a head and must be dealt with. Therefore, this Book of the Purchase of Earth, and also a book that was given to Ezekiel, are filled with woe.

The latter book, also written on both front and back, adds details to the outline given in Revelation. Ezekiel 2:9,10 shows us what to expect to find in these little books, "lamentations, and mourning, and woe."

We saw mourning mentioned before. The Tribulation saints will mourn. In fact, there will be weeping and gnashing of teeth when they get left behind because they are not worthy when Jesus says, "Come up hither" and Rapture I takes place. At that time, he will also say,

> I tell you, I know you not whence ye are; depart from me, all ye **workers of iniquity**. There shall be weeping and gnashing of teeth, when ye shall see Abraham, and Isaac, and Jacob, and all the prophets, in the kingdom of God, and you yourselves thrust out.[4]

> The lord of that servant will come in a day when he looketh not for him, and at an hour when he is not aware, and will cut him in sunder (cut him off), and will appoint him his **portion with the unbelievers**. And that servant, which knew his lord's will, and prepared not himself, neither did according to his will, shall be beaten with many stripes.[5]

> See that ye refuse not him that speaketh. For if they escaped not who refused him that spake on earth, much more shall not we escape, if we turn away from him (Jesus) that speaketh from heaven[6] (at the Rapture).

We better pay close attention to what this says. We have to prepare ourselves, repent, confess our sins, wash our robes in the blood of Christ, be certain that our light is not becoming shadow, and "love his appearing."[7] We must be perfect in God's eyes, filled to the brim with his Holy

Spirit, wearing a spotless wedding garment, or we risk being cut off and having to go through the Tribulation with the unbelievers.

I wrote a correspondent friend and told her about the Lord talking to my son David when he stepped out into the hall. What stuck in his mind afterward was that we must be perfect to go in the Rapture. I like what she wrote back,

> The minute I read Dave's vision I headed for Vines and Strongs to check out perfect. I like this best, "...those who abide in God, giving them to be possessed of the very character of God, by reason of which 'as He is, even so are they in this world.'"

Two betrayers of mankind

During the Tribulation, two rulers will reign over the world consecutively. Revelation 13 calls the first "the beast" and the second "another beast." Revelation 20:10 calls them "the beast and the false prophet." Daniel 7:8,11 refers to them as "the beast" and "another little horn." Thus, "another beast" and "another little horn" are both designations for the "false prophet." I refer to them as the Beast and the False Prophet.

Both men are ultimately controlled by Satan. The first sits on Satan's throne during the first three and one half years, 1,260 days, of the Tribulation. The second occupies Satan's throne during the last part, the remaining 1,040 days of the Shortened Tribulation. He is deposed on the 2,300th day, the Feast of Trumpets that kicks off the Millennium, called the Day of the Lord. Yet, he still has the power to gather the nations together to fight Christ when he returns.

The Beast is Satan-obsessed. The False Prophet is Satan-possessed. This False Prophet is the final Antichrist who will speak "as a dragon,"[8] because Satan will enter into him, as he entered into Judas Iscariot, who betrayed Christ.[9] This man will betray all mankind. Jeremiah 8:15 explains, "We looked for peace, but no good came; and for a time of health, and behold trouble!"

In Revelation 13:11, the False Prophet has "two horns like a lamb" (i.e., like Christ, the Lamb of God, who comes twice). A horn stands for power or a king. During this age, there are two times when Satan comes to power.

Satan came three and one half years before the Crucifixion and tempted Jesus. At that time, Satan promised to give Jesus all the kingdoms of the world if he would fall down and worship him.[10] That didn't work, so as those three and a half years were running out, Satan entered into Judas and betrayed Jesus.

About three and one half years before Christ returns as the King of kings and Lord of lords, Satan will be cast down from heaven to Earth. He will find a man that will accept his offer of all the kingdoms of the world. At that time, he will enter into the False Prophet, who will then become a king of kings and lord of lords, because he will head up both the world government and the world church. Therefore Satan, residing in the False Prophet, will actually command all the kingdoms of the world, both religious and secular.

Satan meant it when he said, "I will be like the most High."[11] He will be as much like Christ as he can manage. The public ministry of Jesus Christ lasted three and one half years. The public ministry of Judas lasted three and one half years, and that of Satan and the False Prophet will too.

Christ, as the Lamb of God, is seen with seven horns when his omnipotence is being represented in Revelation 5:6. In Revelation 13:11, he is referred to as having two horns because he comes twice and is both man and God. The False Prophet is also described as having two horns, because he comes twice and is both man and Satan. As powerful as he is, he could never even come close to mimicking the Lord as being seven horned, or omnipotent.

The False Prophet is called "another little horn" himself and is inhabited by the "little horn" who is Satan. This gives him two horns also.

Daniel 8:8-10 speaks of Satan as a little horn:

> the four winds (spirits, breaths, orbits) of heaven. And out of one of them (the planet Rahab) came forth a little horn, which waxed exceeding great, toward the south and toward the east, and toward the pleasant land

(Israel). And it waxed great, even to the host of heaven; and it cast down some of the host (one third of the angels) and of the stars to the ground, and stamped upon them.

These four winds of heaven probably represent the four orbiting spheres that were originally on either side of the Earth, Mercury, Venus, Mars, and Rahab. Out of one of them, Rahab, came forth Satan. His planet was split apart because of his sin. Today, we call it the Asteroid Belt.

Both the Beast and False Prophet, who head up world government during the Tribulation, are wolves in sheep's clothing. They wear the robes of the clergy.

Beware of false prophets, which come to you in sheep's clothing, but inwardly they are ravening wolves. Ye shall know them by their fruits.[12]

And thou profane wicked prince of Israel, whose day, even an end, is come in a season of iniquity (the Tribulation), thus saith the Lord; **Thou hast taken off the mitre and put on the crown**, it shall not have such another after it...woe...until he comes to whom it belongs.[13]

The Beast is an idol shepherd based in Rome, but the False Prophet is the foolish idol shepherd of Israel spoken of in Zechariah 11:15-17:

Take unto thee yet the instruments of a foolish shepherd. For, lo, I will raise up a shepherd in the land (Israel), which shall not visit those that be **cut off** (Tribulation saints that did not go to Heaven in the first Rapture), neither shall seek the young one, nor heal that that is broken, nor feed that that standeth still: but he shall eat the flesh of the fat (take their money), and tear their claws in pieces (disarm them). Woe to the idol shepherd (he has them make "the image of the beast"[14]) that leaveth the flock (he will move to Babylon)! the sword (Sword of the Lord) shall be upon his arm, and upon his right eye: his arm shall be clean dried up, and his right eye shall be utterly darkened.

Zechariah 5:4 gives us more insight into the character of these two beasts. In the consummation of this age, the Sword of the Lord, the curse, will destroy both their houses. The Beast is called "him that sweareth falsely by my name." Like Judas Iscariot, the other son of perdition, the False Prophet is a thief.

I will bring it forth (the curse, the asteroid), saith the LORD of hosts, and it shall enter into the house of **the thief** (False Prophet, who steals the world church and leads it during the last half of the Tribulation), and into the house of him that **sweareth falsely by my name** (the Beast of Rome, who heads up the world church during the first half of the Tribulation): and it shall remain in the midst of his house, and shall consume it with the timber thereof and the stones thereof.

In Scripture, inanimate objects are sometimes personified and given speech. For instance, in Revelation 16:7, the altar speaks. The NASB translates it thus: "I heard the altar saying, 'Yes, O Lord God, the Almighty, true and righteous are Thy judgments." In our play, we are about to hear the Seraphim speak.

As the curtain draws back, and we listen to John describing it for us, we realize right away that we are looking at a heavenly scene. The throne of the Almighty is set on a heavenly body surrounded by a beautiful iridescent rainbow of ice crystals, as if it is floating in a crystal sea.

As we zoom in for a closeup, Christ, as the Lamb of God, is about to open the first seal on the little book. As soon as it separates, a personification of one of the four Seraphim is given a voice like celestial thunder because he is a heavenly body.

First seal, man on the white horse
John begins his narration here with a strong steady voice. His script is found in Revelation 6:1,2.

> AND I saw when the Lamb opened one of the seals, and I heard, as it were the noise of thunder, one of the four beasts (Seraphim) saying, Come and see. And I saw, and behold a white horse: and he that sat on him had a bow: and a crown was given unto him: and he went forth conquering, and to conquer.

"AND" hooks this to the previous chapter. There, we saw the Lamb given the "book written within and on the backside, sealed with seven seals." That scene was in Heaven. Here, we are going to see the effect on Earth as the seals are opened in Heaven. John is still in Heaven, but given a vision of events on Earth.

A charismatic white-haired man wearing beautifully wrought vestments rides onto the earthly stage. Upon his head are "blasphemous names,"[15] such as Vicar of Christ, Vicar of God, successor of St. Peter, Supreme Pontiff, and **supreme sovereign over the church and the world.**

He is mounted on a white horse, mimicking Christ, who will return the second time as the Prince of Peace riding on a white horse.[16] This is the Beast of Revelation 13:4-10, presenting himself to the world as a prince of peace on the first day of the seven-year Tribulation.

His horse is of a different type than the one Jesus Christ rides. In Revelation 9:7, the shapes of the locusts, which are actually demon spirits, "were like unto horses prepared unto battle." Isaiah 31:3 says of the Egyptians, "their horses flesh, and not spirit." Therefore, a horse can be a symbol of a spirit. Christ is guided by the Holy Spirit; therefore he rides a white horse. This man is influenced by a demon spirit, and worse, for "the dragon gave him his power, and his seat, and great authority."[17] His horse represents a powerful guiding and controlling influence under him, an indwelling unclean demon that he has swallowed up.

It has been said that we should not offer Satan a ride, for we will find that he will want to drive. It is like that in this case too. This man will sit on a spirit horse, and he will find that his horse has more control over the speed and direction in which he travels than he does. Only if the horse wants to go in the direction the rider indicates will it head for that quarter. Where it wants to go, it will go, regardless.

There is an unholy trinity of the end times, the Beast, the False Prophet, and the dragon, which is Satan himself. We can be sure that they have unclean spirits in them for Revelation 16:13,14 says,

> And I saw three unclean spirits like frogs *come* out of the mouth of the dragon, and out of the mouth of the beast, and out of the mouth of the false prophet. For they are the spirits of devils.

These unclean spirits are said to be like frogs because these greenish amphibians live a double life, both on land and in the sea, which stands for the nations.[18] The one coming out of the mouth of the dragon is Satan. In the book of Job, he is called "leviathan"[19] in the King James Version and *drakonta* , translated "serpent"[20] in the Septuagint.

The LXX also says that "His lair (his asteroid) is formed of sharp points (it is a broken section of his planet Rahab); and all the gold of the sea under him is as an immense quantity of clay...There is nothing upon the earth like to him, formed to be sported with by my angels. He beholds every high thing: and he is king of all that are in the waters"[21] (i.e., nations). The KJV says that "When he raiseth up himself, the mighty are afraid: by reason of breakings (crashes) they purify themselves....he is a king over all the children of pride."[22] "I will," Satan said in Isaiah 14:14, "be like the most High." However, he is a counterfeit and cannot actually be like the Lord. Satan and his henchmen, the Beast and False Prophet, also counterfeits, try hard though.

In Revelation 13:7,8, power is given to the Beast "over all kindreds, and tongues, and nations. And all that dwell upon the earth shall worship him, whose names are not written in the book of life of the Lamb." Thus, he seems to be the head of world religion who is also elected leader of the world government. The Popes have always done their best to rule from both the throne and the altar. This Tribulation Pope will have his way. His headquarters in Rome will be moved to literal Babylon on the Euphrates River in Iraq.[23]

We can imagine an elaborate ceremony taking place as this Pope of the Tribulation is crowned head of this one-world government. He is handed a bow, but is given no arrows, demonstrating that he now controls the armies of the United Nations, but has no arrows, no actual armaments, of his own. Yet, he "reigneth over the kings of the earth."[24]

Signing the Peace Treaty

After his coronation, a seven-year peace treaty is signed by the Beast of Rome and the False Prophet of Israel. The treaty will be signed by others also, for Daniel 9:27 says, "And he (the Roman prince whose people destroyed Jerusalem and burned the temple in 70 A.D.) shall confirm the covenant with many for one week (of years)."

This treaty of Rome is an international media event. Virtually all television and newspapers, plus many magazines around the world will give this election lots of coverage and will herald the signing of the covenant of peace.

Countdown to disaster

Today is the Jewish Feast of Weeks, the first day of the final 2,300-day[25] countdown to disaster. This is the beginning of the Seventieth Week of Daniel, the final seven years of the prophecy in Daniel 9:24-27.

The Temple in Jerusalem, I believe, has already been rebuilt during the four Jewish years between the Rapture and the present time. The sacrificing at the Temple begins today and will end at Mid-Tribulation. Daniel 8:13,14 sets up the count of the days. They start on the Feast of Weeks and end on the Feast of Trumpets. This scripture says,

> How long shall be the vision concerning the daily sacrifice, and the transgression of desolation, to give both the sanctuary and the host to be trodden under foot? And he said unto me, Unto two thousand and three hundred days; then shall the sanctuary be cleansed.

The time when they offer the daily sacrifice at the Temple is during the first three and one half years of the Tribulation. The transgression of desolation is at the midpoint of the entire seven years, on the 1,260th day. At that time, the idol, called the "abomination of desolation" in Matthew 24:15 and the "abomination that maketh desolate" in Daniel 12:11, will be placed in the Temple in Jerusalem. The False Prophet will also sit in the Temple playing God.

This will stop the sacrificing for the remainder of the 2,300 days. One thing the Israelites have learned is not to have anything to do with idols. The days when they sacrifice (1,260) plus the days when they do not (1,040) equal the 2,300-day Shortened Tribulation.

The count of days is literal. If you start in the right year on the Jewish Calendar, there are exactly 2,300 days from the Feast of Weeks at the beginning of the Tribulation to the Feast of Trumpets that begins the Millennium. There must also be seven Jewish months from Tishri 1 to Nisan 1 in the last year. Therefore the last year has to be a leap year. From 5761(our 2000/1) to 5768 (our 2007/8) is the only segment that works out before this last generation ends.

The Beast out of the Sea

This ancient and reputable clergyman of Rome is the head of the world church after the Rapture. (At the present time, we do not know for sure if he is already in office at the time of the Rapture or if he is elected immediately afterward.) Whoever he is, he obviously was left behind at the Rapture, tarnishing his honor, but the world at large pays no attention to that fact. They heap him with honors in spite of it.

In his book, "Keys of This Blood," Dr. Malachi Martin states that it is the belief of Pope John Paul II that there will be a second Fatima, the Illumination, and because of it, all religions will accept him as God's Vicar on Earth.[26]

If a second Fatima take place just before the Rapture, this apparition could be the Jezebel of Revelation 2:20. Addressing the church of Thyatira, the Lord Jesus Christ says,

> ...I have a few things against thee, because thou sufferest that woman Jezebel, which calleth herself a prophetess, to teach and to seduce my servants to commit fornication, and to eat things sacrificed unto idols. And I gave her space to repent...and she repented not. Behold, I will cast her into a bed, and them that commit adultery (join) with her into great tribulation, except they repent of their deeds. And I will kill her children with death; and all the churches shall know that I am he which searcheth the reins (minds) and hearts... But...as many as have not this doctrine, and which have not known the depths of Satan, as they speak; I will put upon you none other burden...hold fast till I come.

The Beast is the sixth head of the beast out of the sea in Revelation 13:1. (The False Prophet is the seventh.) According to Revelation 17:15, the sea represents "nations, and tongues." This Beast is not necessarily a Roman by birth. He comes out of the nations, but takes office in Rome.

Hopes for world peace will surge like a storm tide. They will think they have done the right thing to bring peace. The Tribulation Pope, now also Secretary General of the United Nations, mounts his white horse and parades down the streets of Rome. He is going forth to conquer those hold-outs who have not yet embraced his peace program.

In San Francisco, from September 27 to October 1, 1995, Mikhail Gorbachev convened his Global Forum think tank to discuss how the world would be governed in the next century. His opening speech was titled, "The Birth of the

First Global Civilization." His vision is a one-world government under the United Nations. "Toward a New Civilization: Launching a Global Initiative" was the theme for the State of the World Forum. Among those attending was George Bush and Margaret Thatcher.[27] During Operation Desert Storm, we heard President Bush mention the new world order.

In our play, we can almost see God's two witnesses, Moses and Elijah, in the background, clothed in sackcloth, explaining things to come to a group of followers. They understand what is coming upon the world and will prophesy 1,260 days.[28] They witness during the first half of the Tribulation, because the last part is shortened to 1,040 days.

Second seal, man on a red horse

When Christ opens the second seal, we see the Beast being influenced by a different steed. The red horse symbolizes another unclean spirit under him, bringing bloodshed and war. This is outright trickery, masterminded by Satan. Daniel warned that "by peace shall (he) destroy many."[29] What happened to the peace? Right after the Beast signs the peace treaty, we see war brewing. Any peace during the Tribulation is very short-lived, as we hear in Revelation 6:3,4:

> And when he (the Lamb of God) had opened the second seal, I heard the second beast (Seraphim) say, Come and see. And there went out another horse *that was* red: and *power* was given to him that sat thereon to take peace from the earth, and that they should kill one another: and there was given unto him a great sword.

Red, speckled, and white horses are identified for us in Zechariah 1:7-11, and a specific date is given. Since Scripture is especially written for us at the end of this age,[30] the chances are good that Shevat 24 in the second year is given to show us how long the peace of the Tribulation lasts, from the Jewish Sivan 6, 5761 to Shevat 24, 5762 (which is our Wednesday, February 6, 2002). Scripture says,

Upon the four and twentieth day of...Sebat (Shevat), in the second year of Darius, came the word of the LORD...I (the angel of the LORD that stood among the myrtle trees) saw by night, and behold a man riding upon a **red horse**, and he stood among the myrtle trees that were in the bottom; and behind him were there **red horses, speckled, and white**. Then said I, O my lord, what are these?...**These are they whom the LORD hath sent to walk to and fro through the earth**. And they answered the angel of the LORD that stood among the myrtle trees, and said, We have walked **to and fro** through the earth, and, behold, all the earth sitteth still, and is at rest.

This ties in with Job 2:1,2, which shows that these horses are symbols of angels, spirits. It says,

AGAIN there was a day when the sons of God (angels) came to present themselves before the LORD, and Satan came also among them to present himself before the LORD. And the LORD said unto Satan, From whence comest thou: and Satan answered the LORD, and said, From going **to and fro** in the earth, and from walking up and down in it.

This pseudo prince of peace will speak peace, but will go to war, maybe with the declared intention to end war by this means. Whatever his intentions, Satan's intentions are to kill people before they can be saved.

Yet men will say, "who is able to make war with him?"[31] He is not only the leader of world religion, but the man who controls all the armies of the world. His watchword is control. He has reins of the whole world between his thumb and first finger, yet he is controlled by demons himself. The promised peace is as elusive as a tiny bar of soap in a tub of aerated soapy water. The great sword given the Beast is a symbol of the army of all nations united together under his leadership.

Here he is, the Pope, the revered head of world religion, and who do you think he attacks? Who would Satan like to attack? He is the ultimate controlling entity. It is awful to contemplate, but Scripture tells us that it is "given unto him (the Beast) to make war with the **saints**, and to overcome them."[32] Does he label them heretics to justify his actions against them as the Roman church did in the middle ages?

We grimace as the reality that many people of this day and age can be martyred for their faith, even beheaded, strikes deep and lights the smoldering flame of dread. We should resolve not to be here during those days because Jesus has set before us the blessed hope that we can be in Heaven with him when this takes place. We must repent, confess our sins, and stand before him wearing white robes. We want to be perfect in our standing with our holy God.

Third seal, man on a black horse

Choking dust is stirred up by the hoof beats of an approaching black horse, for there has been no rain since the Tribulation began. The bare ground is tiled with millions of uneven shapes. The two witnesses have "shut heaven, that it rain not in the days of their prophecy."[33] Therefore, famine is hard upon the land by the time Christ opens the third seal.

We hear John's narration in Revelation 6:5,6:

> And when he had opened the third seal, I heard the third beast (Seraphim) say, Come and see. And I beheld, and lo a black horse; and he that sat on him had a pair of balances in his hand. And I heard a voice (probably from Heaven, Saturn) in the midst of the four beasts (Seraphim, which stand for Jupiter, Uranus, Neptune, and Pluto) say, A measure of wheat for a penny (literally, a denarius), and three measures of barley for a penny; and see thou hurt not the oil and the wine.

This time, we see the Beast of Rome, who has moved to Babylon, seated on a different mount. Therefore, he is ruled by yet another spirit. Like those used in funerals, this black horse suggests that times are bad, the economy is failing, some with shrunken limbs and swollen tummies are starving, death threatens.

A denarius represents one days work. The drought is bringing on famine so severe that it already costs a full day's pay for one day's food. There is nothing left to apply to other necessities like clothing and shelter. Although grain is scarce, the olive trees and grape vines are still producing, unhurt by the drought.

This Beast is holding scales in his hand to weigh out the grain. There is probably a long unruly line of desperate people waiting to purchase food. Hunger is such a powerful force, it drives people to atrocious measures.

It looks like what happened years ago in Egypt may be played out again. Remember the consequences? When Joseph sold them grain, first of all, he got all their money. When that failed, he got their cattle. Then in **the second year** (i.e., the Jewish 5762, our 2002) they said to him,

> We will not hide it from my lord, how that our money is spent; my lord also hath our herds of cattle; there is not ought left in the sight of my lord, but our bodies, and our lands...so the land became Pharaoh's.[34]

Pharaoh means the destroyer, and the two evil leaders of the end times, the Beast and the False Prophet, will certainly bring on destruction. Remember what Isaiah 9:15,16 says,

> The ancient and honourable, he is the head (the sixth head of the beast out of the sea in Revelation 13:1); and the prophet that teacheth lies (the seventh head), he is the tail (indwelt by Satan, the tail of the dragon). For the leaders of this people cause them to err; and they that are led of them are destroyed.

MID-TRIBULATION

Fourth seal, second rider

The Tribulation began with high hopes for peace, but it was elusive. As Christ opens the fourth seal, the False Prophet, the second man mentioned by Isaiah, rides onstage. He is called Death and swallows up Satan, who is cast out of Heaven at this time.

It is the middle of the Tribulation, when this Satan possessed man puts an idol in the temple in Jerusalem and sits there passing himself off as God, thus touching off an uproar among the people. To quell the uprising, he kills Moses and Elijah. Non-believers rejoice while those who know their Bibles flee the city, heading for the ancient city Esau's descendants carved out of the rose-red sandstone, Petra in Jordan.

John tells of the False Prophet in Revelation 6:7,8:

> And when he had opened the fourth seal, I heard the voice of the fourth beast (Seraphim) say, Come and see. And I looked, and behold a pale (sickly green) horse: and his name that sat on him was Death, and Hell (Satan) followed with him. And power was given unto them (Satan in the False Prophet) over the fourth part of the earth, to kill with sword, and with hunger, and with death, and with the beasts of the earth.

This sickly green horse is the same as the unclean spirit like a frog which is also greenish, seen coming out of the mouth of the dragon.[35] It represents Satan himself.

The Satan-possessed man riding this horse is the leader of Israel. A Jew, maybe of Assyrian background, he is the final Antichrist. He proceeds to kill as many as he can with warfare, introduced by the red horse, then with hunger, introduced by the black horse, later with death and beasts.

Ezekiel 5:17 recorded the Lord's words concerning the coming famine, beasts, pestilence and sword. He said,

> I will send upon you famine and evil beasts, and they shall bereave thee; and pestilence and blood shall pass through thee; and I will bring the sword upon thee, I the LORD have spoken it.

Other details about the False Prophet are found in Habakkuk 2:5,6. He is not elected to office, but he "gathereth unto him all nations."

> Yea also, because he transgresseth by wine (there is plenty of wine), he is a proud man (like Satan), neither keepeth at home (he moves to Babylon), who enlargeth his desire as hell (Satan, the controlling influence in him), and is as death, and cannot be satisfied, but **gathereth unto him all nations**, and heapeth unto him all people...Woe to him that increaseth that which is not his (he is a thief like Judas)! how long? (three and one half years) and to him (Satan) that ladeth himself with thick clay (he inhabits this body made from clay of the earth)!

Suddenly, the first Beast has an accident that incapacitates him for awhile. Revelation 13:12,14 says he has a deadly wound "by a sword" and is healed.

The False Prophet seizes the reins of world government and stuns the nations with his miraculous powers. No one has the immediate capability to do anything about his coup. He has already robbed the nations of their potential to resist him. How did he take over so quickly?

He obtains it by smooth talk and arms. Daniel 11:21-23 explains this and shows that the Beast is wounded. There

> shall stand up a vile person, to whom they shall not give the honour of the kingdom: but he shall come in peaceably, and obtain the kingdom by flatteries. And with the arms of a flood (probably of soldiers) shall they be

overflown from before him, and shall be **broken; yea, also the prince of the covenant** (the Beast). And after the league (the seven-year peace treaty) made with him he shall work deceitfully: for he shall come up, and shall become strong with a small people (probably from a small country, Israel).

The takeover was carefully planned. The Beast had an accident engineered by Satan, and the False Prophet grabbed the reigns of world power away from him so quickly that it was done before the world realized what was happening. He wrenched leadership of world government and religion away from the incapacitated Beast in one stroke.

And he exerciseth **all the power** of the first beast before him, and causeth the earth and them which dwell therein to worship the first beast, whose deadly wound was healed.[36]

This Satan possessed man is probably of the tribe of Dan for Genesis 49:17 says, "Dan shall be a serpent by the way, an adder in the path, that biteth the horse heels, so that his rider shall fall backward." Revelation 13:14 says that the Beast had a "wound by a sword, and did live."

Confirmation that he is of the tribe of Dan seems to be found in Jeremiah 8:15-17:

We looked for peace, but no good came; and for a time of health, and behold trouble (the Tribulation)! The snorting of his horses (i.e., evil spirits) was heard from **Dan**: the whole land trembled at the sound of the neighing of his strong ones; for they are come, and have devoured the land, and all that is in it; the city, and those that dwell therein. For, behold, I will send serpents, cockatrices, among you, which will not be charmed, and they shall bite you, saith the LORD.

The Beast may be wounded by his own ornamental sword when his horse rears up causing him to fall backward, or this may only be symbolic. Whatever his accident, after he is incapacitated, the False Prophet immediately takes over his official duties.

The wounding of the Beast probably takes place at the same time that the False Prophet and ten kings burn the harlot church and the False Prophet kills Moses and Elijah. It all seems to have something to do with the False Prophet's takeover coup and Satan's frenzy to wipe out Christianity.

In Isaiah 28:18, the Lord warned Israel that "your covenant with death (the False Prophet) shall be disannulled, and your agreement with hell (Satan inhabiting the False Prophet) shall not stand: when the overflowing scourge shall pass through, then ye shall be trodden down by it."

Daniel 7:20-26 fills in details and shows how long the False Prophet will hold the reins of this ailing world. He is called "another" in Revelation 13:11. Here he is referred to as the "other" little horn and "another" king. He follows in the footsteps of the Beast and makes war on the saints.

> the **other**...had eyes, and a mouth that spake very great things ('he spake as a dragon'[37]), whose look was more stout than his fellows (Satan looks out through his eyes)...the same horn made **war with the saints**...Until the Ancient of days (Christ the Almighty) came...The...fourth kingdom (which is the feet of Nebuchadnezzar's image)...which shall be diverse from all kingdoms...shall devour the whole earth...out of this kingdom are ten kings (the ten toes) that shall arise (at the beginning of the Tribulation): and **another** (the False Prophet) shall rise after them (Mid-Tribulation); and he shall be diverse from the first (the Beast), and he shall subdue three kings. And he shall speak great words against the most High...and think to change times and laws: and they shall be given into his hand until a time and times and the divid-

ing of time (three and a half years). But the judgment shall sit (Christ's Judgment of the Nations at the end of the seven-years), and they shall take away his dominion (the False Prophet's and Satan's), to consume and to destroy it unto the end (of Armageddon).

Daniel 8:23-25 also describes the False Prophet, who by peace shall destroy many.

when the transgressors are come to the full, a king of fierce countenance, and understanding dark sentences, shall stand up. And his power shall be mighty, but not by his own power (by Satan's): and he shall destroy wonderfully, and shall prosper, and practise, and shall **destroy the mighty** (Moses and Elijah) **and the holy people** (Christians). And through his policy also he shall cause craft to prosper in his hand; and he shall magnify himself in his heart, and **by peace shall destroy many**: he shall also stand up against the Prince of princes (Christ); but he shall be broken without hand.

Second Thessalonians 2:3-12 in the New KJV describes the action of that fateful day in the middle of the Tribulation when the Satan-possessed False Prophet will sit in the Temple as God, and end up killing the two witnesses:

Let no man deceive you by any means: for that day (Day of the Lord, the Millennium) shall not come unless the falling away (departing, Rapture I) comes first, and the man of sin is revealed, the son of perdition, who opposes and exalts himself above all that is called God or that is worshiped, so that **he sits as God in the temple of God**, showing himself that he is God....And now you know what is restraining, that he may be revealed in his own time. For the mystery of lawlessness is already at work; only He (the Holy Spirit) who now restrains will do so until He is taken out of the way (at the Rapture). And then **the lawless one will be revealed**, whom the Lord will consume with the breath of His mouth and destroy with the brightness of His coming. The coming of the lawless one is **according to the working of Satan**, with all power, signs, and lying wonders, and with all unrighteous deception among those who perish, because they did not receive the love of the truth, that they might be saved. And for this reason God will send them strong delusion, that they should believe the lie (that he is the Messiah), that they all may be condemned who did not believe the truth but had pleasure in unrighteousness.

These scriptures are like film clips shown as he is introduced on the world scene. They show us what kind of a man he is. He will be around until the end of Armageddon.

Fifth seal, martyrs speak
As the fifth seal breaks, John reads Revelation 6:9-11:

And when he (our Lord Jesus Christ) had opened the fifth seal, I saw under the altar the souls of them that were slain for the word of God, and for the testimony which they held: And they cried with a loud voice, saying, **How long, O Lord, holy and true, dost thou not judge and avenge our blood on them** that dwell on the earth? And white robes were given unto every one of them; and it was said unto them, that they should rest yet for a little season, until their fellowservants also and their brethren, that should be killed as they *were*, should be fulfilled.

There will be more war against the saints during the reign of the False Prophet. Revelation 12:17 says that he "went to make war with the remnant of her (Israel's) seed, which keep the commandments of God, and have the testimony of Jesus Christ."

The answer to the "How long" is till the 1,040 days of the Great Tribulation are over. The last day of the 1,040 is the 2,300th day of the Shortened Tribulation.

> ### THE END OF THIS AGE AND THE
> ### BEGINNING OF THE MILLENNIUM

Sixth seal, Day of God's Wrath
John, the narrator, continues with Revelation 6:12-17:

> And I beheld when he (Christ) had opened the sixth seal, and, lo, there was a great earthquake; and the sun became black as sackcloth of hair, and the moon became as blood; And the **stars of heaven fell** unto the earth, even as a fig tree casteth her untimely figs, when she is shaken of a mighty **wind.** And the heaven departed as a scroll when it is rolled together; and every mountain and island were moved out of their places (earthquake). And the kings of the earth, and the great men, and the rich men, and the chief captains, and the mighty men, and every bondman, and every free man, hid themselves in the dens and in the rocks of the mountains; And said to the mountains and rocks, Fall on us, and hide us from the face of him that sitteth on the throne (they see the Sign of the Son of Man[38]), and from the wrath of the Lamb: For **the great day of his wrath is come;** and who shall be able to stand?

I believe this age ends and the Millennium begins at 6 P.M., as Tishri 1, 5768 begins. That is the dividing line between civilization as we know it and total chaos. Among other things taking place that day, Tishri 1 is the Jewish New Year, the Feast of Trumpets, and the Day of God's Wrath.

Two main stones hit the Earth along with many smaller rocks. A mountain-sized piece of the asteroid hits first in the Mediterranean Sea. This seems to be what is happening under the sixth seal. It causes Earth to shake and the smoke from the impact blast blanks out the sun and moon.

Like scared moles, the leaders of the nations dash for their underground emergency headquarters. All others hide in bomb shelters or scramble for the mountains because they know that another larger stone is coming.

They look up and see a vision of Christ on his throne. It is his Coronation Day in Heaven. It is also the day of the Judgment Seat of Christ, when rewards will be handed out, good or bad, whatever is deserved.

Rapture Two, Day of God's Wrath

Revelation 7 is a parenthetic section. John describes the picture he sees. The time is just before the stone strikes the Mediterranean Sea. His script is found in Revelation 7:1-3.

> AND after these things (after the Day of God's Wrath has arrived) I saw four angels standing on the four corners (quarters) of the earth, holding the four winds of the earth, that the wind should not blow on the earth, nor on the sea, nor on any tree. And I saw another angel ascending from the east, having the seal of the living God: and he cried with a loud voice to the four angels, to whom it was given to hurt the earth and the sea, Saying, **Hurt not the earth, neither the sea, nor the trees, till we have sealed the servants of our God in their foreheads.**

Although Tishri 1, the Day of God's Wrath, started at 6:00 P.M., we are now shown what has to be sandwiched in before the stars of heaven strike Earth at noon. The judgment has to be restrained long enough for Rapture II to take place. Earth cannot be hurt until the Tribulation saints are safe in Heaven.

Some things under the sixth seal take place before Rapture II, which happens on the first day of the millennial Day of the Lord. Joel 2:31,32 says,

> The sun shall be turned into darkness, and the moon into blood, **before** the great and terrible day of the LORD come. And it shall come to pass, that whosoever shall call on the name of the LORD shall be delivered (*malat*, **escape**): for in mount Zion and in Jerusalem shall be deliverance.

In Micah 7:9, we hear the voice of the Tribulation saints. They come so close to being on Earth when the asteroid hits that the sun is already darkened by smoke. They must wait until Christ receives his golden crown in Heaven on Tishri 1 and begins to judge. Then, as eagles, they fly to Heaven immediately to join the rest of the Body of Christ.

> I will (say the Tribulation saints) bear the indignation of the LORD, because I have sinned against him, **until he plead my cause**, and execute judgment for me: he will bring me forth (out of the darkness) to the light, and I shall behold his righteousness.

Rapture I was as the days of Noah, but Rapture II is as the days of Lot. This is the day of the fire fall. Genesis 19:15-22 says,

> And when the morning arose, then the angels hastened Lot, saying, Arise, take thy wife, and thy two daughters...and they brought him forth, and set him without the city...Escape for thy life...Haste thee, escape thither; for I cannot do any thing till thou be come thither....when Lot entered into Zoar. Then the LORD rained upon Sodom and upon Go-

morrah **brimstone and fire from the
LORD out of heaven.**

The Tribulation saints truly are saved yet so as by
fire. They get pulled out of the fiery furnace as flames are
kindled in the atmosphere. When the incoming stones strike
the atmosphere, a flame ignites and blazes before them and
smoke trails behind them.

Luke 17:29-37 tells us more about the days of Lot.
The fire fell the same day he escaped.

> But **the same day** that Lot went out of Sod-
> om it rained fire and brimstone from heaven,
> and destroyed them all. Even thus shall it be
> in the day when the Son of man is revealed
> (when the Sign of the Son of Man is seen[39]).
> In that day, he which shall be upon the
> housetop, and his stuff in the house, let him
> not come down to take it away: and he that is
> in the field, let him likewise not return back
> (they cannot take anything to Heaven). Re-
> member Lot's wife. Whosoever shall seek to
> save his life shall lose it; and whosoever shall
> lose his life shall preserve it. I tell you, **in
> that night** (i.e., in the early morning while
> it is still dark), there shall be two men in one
> bed; the one shall be taken, and the other
> shall be left....And they...said unto him,
> Where, Lord: And he said unto them, Where-
> soever the body (of Christ) is (in Heaven),
> thither will the **eagles** (high flyers, i.e.,
> Tribulation saints) be gathered together.

Isaiah 40:31 ties in with the above. Speaking of the
Tribulation saints, it says,

> But they that wait upon the LORD shall re-
> new their strength; they shall mount up with
> wings as **eagles**; they shall run, and not be
> weary; and they shall walk, and not faint.

Again, it takes longer to tell about some things than for them to take place. We now find that there are 144,000 Jews that will be part of this translation. After that, we will see the saints from all nations, including those just sealed of the 12 tribes of Israel, in Heaven.

Sealing 144,000 Israelites

John tells us that these 144,000 are "children of Israel." They are literal Jews. In Revelation 7:4-8, he says,

> And I heard the number of them which were sealed: *and there were* sealed an hundred *and* forty *and* four thousand of all the tribes of the children of Israel. Of the tribe of Juda *were* sealed twelve thousand. Of the tribe of Reuben *were* sealed twelve thousand. Of the tribe of Gad *were* sealed twelve thousand. Of the tribe of Aser *were* sealed twelve thousand. Of the tribe of Nepthalim *were* sealed twelve thousand. Of the tribe of Manasses *were* sealed twelve thousand. Of the tribe of Simeon *were* sealed twelve thousand. Of the tribe of Levi *were* sealed twelve thousand. Of the tribe of Issachar *were* sealed twelve thousand. Of the tribe of Zabulon *were* sealed twelve thousand. Of the tribe of Joseph *were* sealed twelve thousand. Of the tribe of Benjamin *were* sealed twelve thousand.

It is significant that two tribes, Dan and Ephraim, are omitted here that appear in other lists. Both had to do with idolatry. The names of Levi, which means joining, and Joseph, which means added, appear instead.

Many think the 144,000 Israelites are sealed as the Tribulation begins. I doubt it. Right after the sealing, all the Tribulation saints appear in Heaven. Therefore, it seems like the sealing will take place just before Rapture II, which is probably only hours before the main catastrophe hits.

Ezekiel had a vision of a slaying in Jerusalem. A mark was put upon the foreheads of the men that sighed and cried for all the abominations that were done in Jerusalem. There was no waiting. The slayers followed right behind the one who was marking. Ezekiel 9:4-6 says,

> And the LORD said unto him (like John, a man clothed with linen with a writer's inkhorn by his side), Go through the midst of...Jerusalem, and set **a mark** upon the foreheads of the men that sigh and that cry for all the abominations that be done in the midst thereof. And to the others he said in mine hearing, **Go ye after him through the city, and smite**...Slay utterly...but come not near any man upon whom is the mark; and begin at my sanctuary.

Tribulation saints arrive in Heaven

In our play, immediately after the 144,000 are sealed, we hear about the white-robed Tribulation saints out of all nations, including Israel, appearing in Heaven before the throne. They have palms in their hands, but no crowns on their heads. They appear there before the main catastrophe strikes. John describes them in Revelation 7:9-17:

> After this (the sealing) I beheld, and, lo, a great multitude, which no man could number, **of all nations**, and kindreds, and people, and tongues, **stood before the throne**, and before the Lamb, clothed with white robes, and palms in their hands; And cried with a loud voice, saying, Salvation to our God which sitteth upon the throne, and unto the Lamb. And all the angels stood round about the throne, and *about* the elders and the four beasts, and fell before the throne on their faces, and worshipped God, Saying, Amen: Blessing, and glory, and wisdom, and thanksgiving, and honour, and power, and might, *be* unto our God for ever and ever. Amen. And one of the elders answered, say-

ing unto me, What are these which are arrayed in white robes? and whence came they? And I said unto him, Sir, thou knowest. And he said to me, **These are they which came out of great tribulation, and have washed their robes, and made them white in the blood of the Lamb.**

When the sixth seal is broken, the four angels have to be restrained while the Israelites are sealed. Then the sealed immediately appear in Heaven with all the others who have washed their robes in the blood of the Lamb. Rapture II happened quickly like the first Rapture. They are on Earth as the Day of God's Wrath begins; then snap! they are in Heaven before the asteroid can impact Earth.

They are in his temple, Heaven itself, that of which the earthly temple spoke.

Therefore are they before the throne of God, and serve him day and night in his temple: and he that sitteth on the throne shall dwell among them. They shall **hunger no more, neither thirst any more; neither shall the sun light on them, nor any heat.** For the Lamb which is in the midst of the throne shall feed them, and shall lead them unto living fountains of waters: and God shall wipe away all tears from their eyes.[40]

The tears are understandable. On Earth, they were faced with the terror of terrors. Then suddenly they were snatched away to safety. That alone would cause tears to spurt. Tears of fear give way to tears of relief and joy.

The Rapture of the Tribulation saints precedes the opening of the last seal. As the sixth seal was opened, we heard, "FOR THE GREAT DAY OF HIS WRATH IS COME."

It happened again. I did not mean to capitalize the above. This is the third time. It just happened, and the caps lock key is not down. This must be very important to emphasize right here. The Day of God's Wrath starts on Tishri 1, as 6:00 P.M. introduces the Feast of Trumpets.

The dividing line

Six P.M. is the dividing line between the end of this age and the beginning of the Millennium. The asteroid will hit the next day at noon. Between 6:00 P.M. and noon, the Rapture of the Tribulation saints must take place.

> ## Doomsday Rock strikes at noon

In Amos 8:9,10, the Lord says, "I will cause the sun to go down **at noon**...I will turn your feasts into mourning." This is the Jewish Feast of Trumpets. The Lord also says, "I have brought for them a ravager **at noonday** ...(the) sun has gone down while it was yet day."[41]

Job 20:19-29 shows that the fury of God's Wrath will be dashed on the False Prophet while he is eating:

> Because he hath oppressed and hath forsaken the poor; because he hath **violently** taken away an house (Church) which he builded not...When he is about to fill his belly, **God shall cast the fury of his wrath upon him, and shall rain it upon him while he is eating**...The increase of his house shall depart, and his goods shall flow away **in the day of his wrath**. This is the portion of a wicked man from God.

This was foreshadowed when Babylon fell the day of the handwriting on the wall. Belshazzar had "made a great feast to a thousand of his lords."[42] Daniel interpreted the handwriting on the wall as meaning "MENE; God hath numbered thy kingdom, and finished it. TEKEL: Thou art weighed in the balances, and art found wanting. PERES: Thy kingdom is divided, and given to the Medes and Persians.[43]

The False Prophet will be deposed from office on the Day of God's Wrath. He will also be injured. Zechariah

11:17 says that "the sword (the Sword of the Lord) shall be upon his arm, and upon his right eye: his arm shall be clean dried up, and his right eye shall be utterly darkened."

It is strange that the previous Israeli Prime Minister's name is Shimon Peres. Daniel interpreted "PEREZ" as meaning "Thy kingdom is divided..." Israel is busy dividing the land. They have already given up Jericho and the Gaza Strip to the PLO and the Palestinians. That does not sound like the right thing to do. In Joel 3:2, the Lord said,

> I will also gather all nations, and will bring them down into the valley of Jehoshaphat (meaning Yah is judge), and will plead with them there for my people and for my heritage Israel, whom they have scattered among the nations, and **parted my land**.

When the Rapture of the Tribulation saints takes place, they already know what is coming. It reminds me of the "string of pearls" (broken pieces of the Comet Shoemaker-Levy 9) that smacked into Jupiter in July, 1994. Astronomers knew ahead of time that the pieces would hit Jupiter.

It probably was a sign to show us what would happen to Earth on the Day of God's Wrath. The first piece hit on Av 9, the last date two Temples, Solomon's and Herod's, still stood in Jerusalem. The next day they were destroyed. It seems planned. Maybe a similar "string of pearls" will hit Earth.

Rapture II is at the time of Jacob's trouble. Besides the living saints, there is resurrection of those martyrs who we saw wearing white robes. Daniel 12:1,2 says,

> There shall be a time of trouble such as never was since there was a nation even to that same time: and at that time thy people (the 144,000 of Israel that were sealed) shall be delivered, every one that shall be found written in the book. And many of them that sleep in the dust of the earth shall awake.

This agrees with Isaiah 26:19-21 (Scofield Bible margin). It says,

> Thy dead shall live: my dead bodies shall rise. Awake and sing, ye that dwell in dust...earth shall cast out the dead. **Come, my people** (the 144,000 Israelites), enter thou into thy chambers, and shut thy doors (symbol of a Rapture) about thee: **hide thyself** as it were for a little moment, **until the indignation be overpast**. For behold, the LORD cometh out of his place to punish the inhabitants of the earth for their iniquity.

It looks like the Tribulation saints are caught away in the early morning, while it is still night,[44] before the main asteroid strikes at noon. Rapture II takes place just before the seventh seal is broken. The saints in heaven are watching in awe as rocks burning with fire home in like guided missiles toward the earthly houses of the Beast and the False Prophet. We are reminded of the string of pearls (broken pieces of the Comet Shoemaker-Levy 9) that crashed into Jupiter in July, 1994.

It is a very close call for the Tribulation saints. They are saved from the fiery furnace at almost the last moment.

1. Jeremiah 32:8-14
2. Daniel 9:24-27
3. Revelation 3:10
4. Luke 13:27,28
5. Luke 12:46,47
6. Hebrews 12:25
7. II Timothy 4:8
8. Revelation 13:11
9. John 13:27
10. Matthew 4:8,9
11. Isaiah 14:14
12. Matthew 7:15,16
13. Ezekiel 21:25,26, LXX
14. Revelation 13:14,15
15. Revelation 13:1, Phillips
16. Revelation 19:11
17. Revelation 13:2
18. Revelation 17:15
19. Job 41:1
20. Job 40:20, LXX
21. Job 41:21-25, LXX
22. Job 41:34
23. Zechariah 5:5-11
24. Revelation 17:18
25. Daniel 8:14
26. Alston, Greg. *The Prophecy Post*. (Denver, CO, Apr. 1996)
27. Ibid.
28. Revelation 11:3
29. Daniel 8:25
30. I Corinthians 10:11
31. Revelation 13:4
32. Revelation 13:7
33. Revelation 11:6
34. Genesis 47:18,20
35. Revelation 16:13,14
36. Revelation 13:12
37. Revelation 13:11
38. Matthew 24:30
39. Matthew 24:30
40. Revelation 17:15-17
41. Jeremiah 15:8,9, Green's Interlinear
42. Daniel 5:1
43. Daniel 5:25-28
44. Luke 17:29-37

6

Jesus' Long Day

Revelation 8 — 11

FEAST OF TRUMPETS

Silence in Heaven

"AND when he had opened the seventh seal, there was silence in heaven about the space of half an hour."
(Revelation 8:1)

Silence on Earth

"But the LORD is in his holy temple: let all the earth keep silence before him." (Habakkuk: 2:20)

Silence in the Isles

"KEEP silence before me, O islands (maybe Cherubim, planets); and let the people (the Tribulation saints) renew their strength: let them come near; then let them speak: let us come near together to judgment."
(Isaiah 41:1)

Today is Jesus' birthday. This day is unique, no other day is like it—ever. Joel 2:2 says that "there hath not been ever the like, neither shall be any more after it." In it the "mystery of God" will be finished, as he has declared to the prophets.[1] Today, men see the "sign of the Son of man in heaven."[2]

On Earth, this is Jesus' Long Day, of which Joshua's Long Day was a type. It is Tishri 1, the Feast of Trumpets, the last day of the Shortened Tribulation and the first day of the millennial Day of the Lord. In both Heaven and Earth, this day is packed to overflowing with momentous events that only happen once.

Between its beginning at 6:00 P.M and now, just before noon, some unparalleled events have taken place. Heaven has witnessed the splendid Royal Coronation of Jesus Christ and the long-awaited Marriage of the Lamb.

> ## "THE LORD REIGNETH,
> ## HE IS CLOTHED WITH MAJESTY."[3]

THE LORD reigneth; let the people tremble: he sitteth between the cherubims (Jupiter and Uranus); let the earth be moved[4] (judgment).

The Cherubim on either side of the Mercy Seat represent the planets that orbit on either side of the Lord's planet. Soon after he is seated on his own throne, we hear of judgment, "let the earth be moved." The judgment will be terrible when it hits, but the intense effects will be temporary. Afterward, the Lord will return and put things right again.

Christ, wearing his golden crown, is now seated on his own throne. "Alleluia: for the Lord God omnipotent reigneth."[5] The Bride of Christ has become his Queen at the Marriage of the Lamb. Overcomers sit with him, for he said,

> To him that overcometh will I grant to sit with me in **my throne**, even as I also overcame, and am set down with my Father in **his throne** (Revelation 3:21).

Christ has been awarded dominion over Earth and installed as judge. Daniel saw these things happen. He said,

the Ancient of days (the Father) did sit,
whose garment was white as snow, and the
hair of his head like the pure wool...the judgment was set, and the books were opened
...one like the Son of man (Jesus Christ)
came with the clouds of heaven, and came to
the Ancient of days...And there was given
him dominion, and glory, and a kingdom,
that all people, nations, and languages,
should serve him.[6]

"Thou didst cause judgment to be heard from
heaven; the earth feared, and was still. When
God arose to judgment" (Psalm 76:8,9).

Judgment Seat of Christ, now in session

In our play, the Judgment Seat of Christ is now in session.
The "Father judgeth no man, but hath committed all judgment unto the Son."[7] He "was ordained of God to be the
Judge of quick and dead"[8] "at his appearing and his
kingdom."[9]

Today, men on Earth will see the Sign of the Son of
Man in the heavens.[10] They will say "to the mountains
(plural) and rocks, Fall on us, and hide us from the face of
him that sitteth on the throne, and from the wrath of the
Lamb: For the great day of his wrath is come; and who shall
be able to stand?"[11]

The "LORD...hath prepared his throne for judgment."[12] The "LORD'S throne is in heaven: his eyes behold,
his eyelids try, the children of men....Upon the wicked he
shall rain snares, fire and brimstone, and an horrible tempest: this shall be the portion of their cup."[13]

The whole courtroom, including Earth and Heaven,
was respectfully silent while the King of kings and Honor-
able Judge Jesus Christ was seated at the bench.

The jurors have been summoned, the witnesses
called. The Old Testament and Church saints have been

gathered from "the uttermost part of heaven," the Tribulation saints from "the uttermost part of the earth."[14] Psalm 50:4,5 has come to pass.

> He shall call to the heavens from above, and to the earth, that he may judge his people. Gather my saints together unto me; those that have made a covenant with me by sacrifice. And the heavens shall declare his righteousness: for God is judge himself.

The testimony of the witnesses has been heard. Psalm 94:1-7 is an example:

> O LORD God, to whom vengeance belongeth ...**shew thyself**. Lift up thyself, thou judge of the earth: render a reward to the proud. LORD, how long shall the wicked...triumph? How long shall they utter and speak hard things? and all the workers of iniquity boast themselves? They break in pieces thy people, O LORD, and afflict thine heritage. They slay the widow and the stranger, and murder the fatherless. Yet they say, The LORD shall not see, neither shall the God of Jacob regard it.

This is the day that the Sign of the Son of Man will be seen in the sky. Scripture says,

> And then shall **appear** the sign of the Son of man in heaven: and then shall all the tribes of the earth mourn, and they shall see the Son of man coming in the clouds of heaven with power and great glory.[15]

> And the LORD shall be **seen** over them, and his arrow shall go forth as the lightning: and the Lord GOD shall blow the trumpet, and shall go with whirlwinds of the south. The LORD of hosts shall defend them (Israel).[16]

I will rain upon him (Gog)...and upon the
many people that are with him, an overflowing rain (shower, i.e., tsunami), and great
hailstones, fire, and brimstone. Thus will I
magnify myself, and sanctify myself; and I
will be known in the eyes of many nations,
and they shall know that I am the LORD.[17]

"The LORD shall not see, neither shall the God of
Jacob regard it" is one of Satan's lies. Those who believe it
will soon find out if he watches and pays attention to what
he sees. The triumph of the wicked will end today. The Lord
will fight for Israel.

In court, the verdict has been read. Believers were
found not guilty by reason of their faith in Christ, for "to
him give all the prophets witness, that through his name
whosoever believeth in him shall receive remission of
sins."[18] Unbelievers were found guilty of their sins.

Sentence is being pronounced. The saints will receive rewards for their faith and good works at the same time
that those on Earth receive their "reward"[19] for their unbelief
and evil works.

After judgment is pronounced, the Marriage Supper
of the Lamb will be celebrated with gifts, food, and fireworks on a grand scale, fireworks that can be seen for millions of miles. It is the grand finale of the ages.

Mid-day approaches. The climax of the Day of
God's Wrath will come at the very apex of the day, noon.
Earth is already hurtling through space toward its rendez-
vous with a death star. Joel 1:15 sets the tone of the day:

Alas for the day! for the day of the LORD is
at hand, and as a destruction from the Almighty shall it come.

Second Peter 3: 7 gives us an inkling of what will
happen to the ungodly ones left on Earth when he speaks of

the heavens and the earth, which are now, by
the same word are kept in store, reserved

unto fire against the day of judgment and perdition of ungodly men.

On Earth, a great confederacy of all nations has banded together to destroy Israel, intending to literally wipe her off the map. "They have said, Come, and let us cut them off from being a nation; that the name of Israel may be no more in remembrance."[20] They strike from the north.

In Heaven, the Lord hears Israel blow the alarm with the trumpet when the huge United Nations army attacks, and his fury comes up in his face. This is the last straw. Look out! Ezekiel 38:8,16-20 tells us that

> in the latter years thou (the great army of all nations[21] led by Gog, chief prince of Meshech and Tubal) shalt come (out of the north) into the land that is brought back from the sword, and is gathered out of many people, against the mountains of Israel...I will bring thee against my land...And it shall come to pass at the same time when Gog shall come against the land of Israel, saith the Lord GOD, that **my fury shall come up in my face**....in the fire of my wrath have I spoken...in that day (Tishri 1, 5768) there shall be a great shaking in the land of Israel: So that the fishes of the sea...and all the men that are upon the face of the earth, shall shake.

This large army attacks Jerusalem before the Lord returns. At first they are successful. Zechariah 14:2,3 says,

> I will gather **all nations** (U.N.) against Jerusalem to battle; and the city shall be taken, and the houses rifled, and the women ravished; and half of the city shall go forth into captivity, and the residue of the people shall not be cut off from the city. Then shall the LORD go forth, and fight against those nations as when he fought in the day of battle.

Jesus' Long Day

The Lord will fight against all these nations "as when he fought in the day of battle" refers to the battle at Gibeon on Joshua's Long Day, when more were killed by falling rocks than were killed by the Israelites.[22] Joshua's Long Day is a type. The name Jesus, from the Greek, is Joshua in Hebrew. It is the same name. Today is Jesus' Long Day.

This is the day the Lord will bring to pass "his strange act," the collision of two orbiting bodies in the orderly flight patterns of space. It looks like a binary asteroid will crash into Earth, one piece hitting the Mediterranean, the other impacting at Babylon. Isaiah 28:21,22 says,

> For the LORD shall rise up as in mount Perazim, he shall be wroth as in the valley of Gibeon, that he may do his work, his strange work; and bring to pass his act, **his strange act**. Now therefore be ye not mockers, lest your bands be made strong: for I have heard from the Lord GOD of hosts a consumption, even determined **upon the whole earth**.

Perazim means interval or gap. It represents the ten-year interval between the sixth and seventh millenniums of time since man became mortal. This ten years was indicated when Jesus told the church in Smyrna that they would "have tribulation ten days."[23] The Greek word translated "days" is *hemeron*. It means days, periods, ages, times, whiles, or years. I believe that there are ten years between the two Raptures, from the Jewish 5758 to 5768 (our 1998 to 2007).

This decade also covers the time from the Rapture to the end of the 2,300-day Shortened Tribulation. It seems that all three 2,000-year ages, the Age of the Gentiles, the Age of the Jews, and the Age of the Church have extensions that run concurrently and end together in a grand finale with a great earthquake and fireworks as the Millennium begins.

Paul showed us that the ends of more than one single age is to come at the same time—a photo finish. First Corinthians 10:11 in the New Scofield Reference Bible says,

Now all these things happened unto them (Israel) for examples, and they are written for our admonition, upon whom the **ends of the ages** are come.

The Lord showed us that there was an interval between the sixth and seventh millenniums in a very subtle but effective way. He inserted parenthetic portions between the sixth and seventh seals, between the sixth and seventh trumpets, and between the sixth and seventh vials. He also made a division between the sixth and seventh things he hates in Proverbs 6:16.

Jesus' Long Day does not represent the Second Coming in glory. It is as in Isaiah 63:1-6, where the Lord trods the wine press alone and says, "their blood shall be sprinkled upon my garments...For the day of vengeance (Tishri 1) is in mine heart, and the year (5768, first of the Millennium) of my redeemed is come." He also said, "Vengeance belongeth unto me, I will recompense."[24]

The record of Joshua's Long Day shows what will happen in Jesus Long Day. The only difference is in the intensity. Joshua 10:9-15 says,

Joshua therefore came unto them suddenly, and went up from Gilgal (circle, revolution of the wheel, i.e., orbiting sphere) all night. And the LORD discomfited them before Israel, and slew them with a great slaughter at Gibeon...as they fled from before Israel, and were in the going down to Beth-horon (house of wrath or the hole), that **the LORD cast down great stones from heaven upon them** unto Azekah, and they died: they were more which died with hailstones than they whom the children of Israel slew with the sword. Then spake Joshua to the LORD...he said...Sun, stand thou still upon Gibeon; and thou, Moon, in the valley of Ajalon (ruin). And the sun stood still, and the moon stayed, until the people had avenged themselves upon their enemies...So **the sun stood still** in the midst of heaven, and hasted not to go down about a whole day. And there was no day like that before it or after it, that the LORD hearkened unto the voice of a man: for **the LORD fought for Israel**. And Joshua returned...unto the camp to Gilgal.

Today, no man will ask for the sun to stand still, but the Lord will cause it to happen. As before, today will be almost as long as two days.

Many think the Second Advent will be on the day the Lord fights for Israel. There are too many dead bodies in Israel for a glorious coming. They must have seven months to bury the bodies and cleanse the land before he returns. Therefore, today, like Joshua, Jesus will return to his camp.

Seven trumpets readied for action

In our play, John resumes his narration in 8:2:

And I saw the (*tous*) seven angels which stood before God; and to them were given seven trumpets.

Since the article *tous* is given, these are THE seven angels. In Scripture, when the article is used, it usually means that we have been introduced to the subject before and should be able to identify it. Therefore, these must be the seven stars Jesus had in his hand at the Rapture of the Bride of Christ. He told us plainly that "The seven stars are the angels of the seven churches."[25]

Psalm 149:1-9 shows that the saints will set in motion the judgment written. This honor is given to all saints.

PRAISE ye the LORD. Sing unto the LORD a new song (sung after the Rapture[26]), and his praise in the congregation of saints....Let the saints be joyful in glory (in Heaven): let them sing aloud upon their beds. Let the high praises of God be in their mouth, and a twoedged sword in their hand; To execute vengeance upon the heathen, and punishments upon the people; To bind their kings with chains, and their nobles with fetters of iron; To execute upon them the judgment written: this honour have all his saints.

Paul told the Corinthians, "Do ye not know that the saints shall judge the world?"[27] Since "all his saints" have this honor, it includes the Tribulation saints who have just arrived in heaven. Isaiah 41:1 says,

KEEP silence before me, O islands; and let the people (Tribulation saints) renew their strength: let them come near; then let them speak: let us come near together to judgment.

The Tribulation saints have had their tears wiped away and have renewed their strength. They take part in the judgment process the same day they arrive in Heaven.

Fire cast down to Earth

We listen with bated breath as John describes in 8:3-5 what is going to happen to this beautiful planet called Earth.

And another angel came and stood at the altar, having a golden censer (globe shaped); and there was given unto him much incense, that he should offer *it* with the prayers of all saints upon the golden altar which was before the throne. And the smoke of the incense, *which came* with the prayers of the saints, ascended up before God out of the angel's hand. And the angel took the censer, and filled it with fire of the altar, and cast *it* into the earth: and there were voices, and thunderings, and lightnings, and an earthquake.

This being called "another angel" must be the Lord Jesus Christ himself as the Angel of the Lord. He is the

High Priest who has the right to officiate at the golden altar. He is the one that has all the prayers that have ever been offered up "in Jesus' name." Here, the angel casts fire down to the Earth, and Jesus said, "I came to cast fire upon the earth."[28] Today, this is coming to pass in your ears.

The Old Testament parallel is Isaiah 22:17-19. It is the Lord who will toss the asteroid into the Earth.

> Behold, **the LORD** will...violently turn and **toss thee** (Satan's home on the asteroid called Wormwood) **like a ball** into a large country (Babylonia, now Iraq, not tiny Israel)...and...drive thee from thy station.

At his first coming, Jesus said, "Think not that I AM COME TO SEND PEACE ON EARTH: I came not to send peace, but a sword."[29] (That phrase came out capitalized on its own. I had no intention of doing it. This is the fourth time that has happened.) When Jesus will come to send peace on Earth will be at his second coming. Seven Jewish months before that, expect the sword.

Remember that Jesus will actually toss the asteroid by means of a whirlwind. It is as if he will blow with the breath of his mouth and tick its orbit over into a collision course with Earth. Luke 21:26 in the Good News for Modern Man version says that **"the powers in space will be driven from their course."** The Satan possessed False Prophet is powerless to stop it in spite of any attempts to nudge it off course with nuclear missiles.

"David lifted up his eyes, and saw the angel of the LORD stand between the earth and the heaven, having a drawn sword in his hand stretched out over Jerusalem."[30] Balaam and his ass "saw the angel of the LORD standing in the way, and his sword drawn in his hand."[31] Jeremiah 47:6 calls it the "sword of the LORD." Psalm 149:6 says that a two edged sword is also in the hands of the saints.

We are told that a mountain falls into the sea and that a star falls. This probably represents a binary asteroid like Toutatis. The two main pieces will break apart. Other pieces will split off as it divides and smashes into our atmosphere. A hail of stones weighing 100 pounds each will fall.

Isaiah 24:1,5,6 shows that the earth will be turned upside down. It also explains why this curse will destroy on Earth, leaving a very small remnant alive.

> BEHOLD, the LORD maketh the earth empty, and maketh it waste, and **turneth it upside down,** and scattereth abroad the inhabitants....because they have transgressed the laws, changed the ordinance, broken the everlasting covenant. Therefore hath the curse devoured the earth, and they that dwell therein are desolate: therefore the inhabitants of the earth are burned, and few men left.

The sun and moon will in effect stand still as the smooth regular rotation of this globe is disturbed. Earth will stagger with drunken footsteps. Habakkuk 3:10-13 says,

> The mountains...trembled: the overflowing of the water (tsunami) passed by: the deep uttered his voice, and lifted up his hands on high. The sun and moon stood still in their habitation: at the light of thine arrows they went, and at the shining of thy glittering spear. Thou didst march through the land in indignation, thou didst thresh the heathen in anger. Thou wentest forth for the salvation of thy people, even for salvation with thine anointed; thou woundedst the head (the False Prophet) out of the house of the wicked.

This beautiful blue and white planet will even be jarred out of her usual orbit in space. Not only the Earth, but the heavens themselves will be effected. Isaiah 13:13 says,

> I will shake the heavens...the earth shall remove out of her place, in the wrath of the LORD of hosts...the day of his fierce anger.

Full cycle

All this is not without precedent. The days before "the last Adam," Christ, returns are similar to the days before "the first man Adam"[32] came on the world scene.

In the beginning, God created Earth perfect. He "created it not in vain (*tohuw*, ruin), he formed it to be inhabited."[33] Yet, by the second verse in the Bible, we find that Earth had become a chaotic ruin stamped with mass extinction. The second verse in the Concordant Version makes it clear. The "earth **became** a chaos and vacant, and darkness was on the surface of the **submerged** chaos." The New American Bible adds that "a mighty wind swept over the waters." All the land was under water. Psalm 104:5-9 says,

> Who laid the foundations of the earth, that it should not be removed for ever. Thou coveredst it with the deep as with a garment: the **waters stood above the mountains**. At thy rebuke they fled; at the voice of thy thunder they hasted away. They go up by the mountains; they go down by the valleys unto **the place** (the Pacific Basin) which thou hast founded for them. Thou hast set a bound that they may not pass over; that they turn not again to cover the earth.

Something terrible happened between the first two verses of Scripture. It effected both the heavens and the Earth. Because of divine judgment against Satan, a wayward stone destroyed Satan's planet and formed the Asteroid Belt. As a result of that explosion, Earth was hit by a piece of Satan's planet Rahab. It dug out our Pacific Basin and punched up convoluted mountains elsewhere on the globe bringing land up out of the sea as the waters dashed into the Pacific Basin. One side of Mars was pelted badly too. Maybe this is why her waters and atmosphere have all but disappeared.

I looked up the pertinent verses concerning the catastrophe before Adam was created in all the various versions of the Bible in my collection. Some translations are clearer than others. I will quote the ones that tell this story in terms that are the easiest to understand. If not noted otherwise, they are from the King James Version.

Job 26:11-14 in the Jerusalem Bible says,

> The pillars of the heavens tremble, awe-struck at his threats. By his power, **he has whipped up** (*raga*, tossed suddenly and violently, broken, divided) **the Sea**, by his skill, **he has crushed Rahab**. His breath has made the heavens luminous (the blackness of space lit up by the impact explosions), his hand transfixed the Fleeing Serpent (Satan). This is only a fraction of what he has done and all we catch of it is the feeblest echo. But who can conceive the thunder of his power (i.e., the noise of the explosions)?

We know that the Lord decreed a "severe sentence"[34] against Satan because of his sins. The New English Bible translation of Isaiah 51:9-16 shows that the Lord had a couple of other reasons for choosing the form of judgment he did. He split Rahab and divided the sea so he could fix the heavens in place and form the Earth as a potter molds the clay. This passage in Isaiah says,

> Awake, awake, put on your strength, O arm of the LORD, awake as you did long ago, in days gone by, Was it not you who **hacked the Rahab in pieces** and ran the dragon through?...**I cleft the sea** and its waves roared, **that I might fix** (*nata*, fasten) **the heavens in place and form the earth.**

At that time God's Heaven ended up being the third heaven, Mars, Jupiter, Saturn, as later depicted in the Tabernacle. The Amplified ends the above with "that I may fix the *new* heavens **as a tabernacle**, and lay the foundations of a *new* earth?"

This is interesting. The new heavens and new Earth mean the renovation of existing things. This was necessary just before Adam was created. It will also be necessary after Christ returns, and for the same reason, a stone will come out of the heavens and impact Earth. The source of both stones is the split planet Rahab, which means proud or borders of a kingdom, a perfect name for proud Satan's planet. One stone hit before the first Adam arrived. The other will hit before the "second Adam" comes back.

Psalm 89:9,10 also tells us of the raging sea and the broken planet Rahab. It says,

> Thou rulest the **raging of the sea**: when the waves thereof arise, thou stillest them. Thou hast **broken Rahab in pieces**, as one that is slain; thou hast scattered thine enemies with thy strong arm. The heavens are thine, the earth also.

First the Lord created the heavens and the Earth. Later, he split Rahab into pieces. This spread out the heavens because a planet was missing. A result of the explosion on Rahab was the hammering Earth took. Isaiah 42:5 in the Jerusalem Bible explains it well:

> Yahweh, who created (*bara*, to create a new thing) the heavens and **spread them out**, who **hammered into shape the earth**.

In spite of what those who do not believe the Bible say, all things have not continued as they were from the beginning of creation. Before long, these will change their minds. There was a catastrophe before Adam and there will be another before the Second Adam returns. Peter said,

> Knowing this...there shall come in the last days scoffers...saying, Where is the promise of his coming? for since the fathers fell asleep, all things continue as they were from the beginning of the creation. For this they willingly are ignorant of, that by the word of God the heavens were of old, and the earth

standing out of the water and in the water:
Whereby **the world that then was, being overflowed with water perished:**
But the heavens and the earth, which are now, by the same word are kept in store, reserved unto fire against the day of judgment and perdition of ungodly men.[35]

After the land became a submerged chaos, the New American Bible shows clearly that the mountains rose as the seas gathered into a single basin:

'Let the water under the sky be **gathered into a single basin, so that the dry land may appear.'** And so it happened: the water under the sky was gathered into its basin, and the dry land appeared. (Genesis 1:9)

With the ocean, as with a garment, you covered it; above the mountains the waters stood. At your rebuke they fled, at the sound of your thunder (the impact explosion) they took to flight; **As the mountains rose, they went down the valleys to the place you had fixed** for them. (Psalm 104: 6-8)

Psalm 74:12-17 indicates that the moon was thrown up at the same time that the sea was divided. It also shows that the stone that hit Earth came from Rahab, because the heads of the dragons were smashed on the waters, and that summer and winter dates from that same time, because this globe's axis was knocked into a tilted position.

God...Thou didst divide the sea by thy strength: thou brakest the heads (*rosh*, beginnings, chiefs, rulers) of the dragons **in the waters** (JB, 'on the waters'). Thou brakest the heads of leviathan ('the crooked serpent,'[36]) in pieces...Thou didst cleave the fountain and the flood: thou driedst up mighty rivers...thou hast prepared (*kuwn*, **erected, stood perpendicular, set up, heaped up**; i.e., thrown up) **the light** (*maor*, light giver, as in Genesis 1:16, 'the lesser light;' Confraternity, **'the moon'**) and the sun. Thou hast set (*natsab*, put in place) all the borders (*gebuwlah*, regions) of the earth: thou hast made summer and winter.

Can we know when this happened? We know that the first chapter in the Bible says that about a week before ADAM WAS CREATED, IT WAS DARK, THERE WAS A MIGHTY WIND, AND THE SEA HAD NOT YET RUN INTO ITS PREPARED PLACE, SO IT WAS NEAR THAT TIME. Job 26:7-14 in the New American Bible gives us one more necessary fact. (I did not mean to put the above in caps. The Lord emphasized it himself, so it was near that time. This is the eleventh time this has happened.) Job says,

> He stretches out the North over empty space (astronomers found a tunnel through the stars in the north), and suspends the earth over nothing at all; He binds up the waters in his clouds, yet the cloud is not rent by their weight (it rained later, in Noah's day); **He holds back the appearance of the full moon** by spreading his clouds before it.... The pillars of the heavens tremble and are stunned at his thunderous rebuke; By his power he **stirs up the sea,** and by his might he **crushes Rahab;** With his angry breath he **scatters the waters,** and he hurls the lightning against them relentlessly; His hand pierces the fugitive dragon (Satan) as from his hand it strives to flee. Lo, these are but the outlines of his ways, and how faint is the word we hear!"

Since the full moon was there at the time of the catastrophe and the first new moon, when God rested, was

Tishri 1 in 4043 B.C., the catastrophe could have happened about Elul 14 in 4043 B.C., two weeks before the Sabbath when God rested.

There will be a replay of this catastrophe in our days, but with some differences. There will be more destruction from fire than water. Also, the Lord will not allow the Earth to fly apart as the planet Rahab did. He will "bear up the pillars of it."[37] Psalm 78:69 mentions "the earth which he hath established for ever." When it waxes old, it will be renewed.

The order fixed before Adam was created is still in effect today. Jeremiah 31:35,36 in the NEB says,

> These are the words of the LORD, who gave the sun for a light by day and the moon and stars for a light by night, who cleft the sea and its waves roared; the LORD of Hosts is his name: If this **fixed order** could vanish out of my sight, says the LORD, then the race of Israel too could cease.

The arm of the Lord is said to have scattered his enemies. Psalm 89:10 tells this story:

> Thou hast broken Rahab in pieces, as one that is slain: thou hast scattered thine enemies (Satan and his angels) with thy strong arm.

When Israel walked dry-shod through the divided Red Sea, it was a shadow of what happened just before Adam was created. Nehemiah 9:10,11 says,

> And shewedst signs and wonders upon Pharaoh (which means: destroyer, king, that disperses or spoils; i.e., a type of Satan)...they (Egyptians) dealt proudly against them (Israelites)...And thou didst divide the sea before them, so that they went through the midst of the sea on the dry land; and their persecutors thou threwest into the deeps, **as a stone into the mighty waters.**

Back to our play and the echo of the catastrophe that happened just before Adam was created. In Revelation 8:5, the globe shaped censer with fire in it represents the main asteroid (*aster*, star, asteroid) that is cast down to Earth seven Jewish months before Christ returns. It actually does go into the earthen cellar; it is the key that opens Hell's trapdoor.

As the asteroid smashes into this planet, it encounters resistance, stops abruptly, and explodes with almost unimaginable force, thus digging the pit for the wicked.[38] The energy created at the instant of impact is greater than all the atomic bombs ever made. The whole planet will reverberate like a bell. The earthquake generated will be worldwide. Even the fish will shake.[39] The dead will lay around the Earth.

William J. Broad's article, "Earth's early-warning effort," in The Press-Enterprise of May 14, 1996 informs us that the Air Force and NASA have teamed up to hunt for "objects that might strike the planet and cause a catastrophe." Only four months into the project, headed by Eleanor Helin of NASA's Jet Propulsion Laboratory, they have already discovered four more Earth-crossers by using an Air Force telescope in Hawaii usually used for surveillance of spacecraft and satellites. Mr. Broad said,

> To produce a planetary disaster...an asteroid or comet would probably have to have a diameter of at least a kilometer, or six-tenths of a mile...up to 1,700 of those crossing Earth's path might be big enough to wreak global havoc....Both asteroids and comets of sufficient size can cause extraordinary damage on Earth because of their enormous speeds, typically many thousand of miles an hour. On impact, the kinetic energy of such objects is converted instantaneously to heat, making them explode with a force equivalent to that of millions of nuclear weapons.

When Sodom, Gomorrah, and the cities of the plain were destroyed, the crust of this planet split for 5,000 miles, from Turkey to Lake Nyasa in Africa, forming the Great Rift

Valley. The Earth still shivers there at times. The strike of
the Sword of the Lord today will be twice as bad as that one.

Let the sword be doubled the third time

Ezekiel gives us important details of what is coming upon
this world. It shows us that this asteroid impact is not an ac-
cidental collision. The point of the Sword of the Lord has
long been aimed at a certain target—Babylon. Adam was
banished from Eden/Eridu, south of Babylon, near Ur. The
builders of the Tower of Babel were scattered. God warns.
Yet, men return to that area. Ezekiel 21:9-15,25-27 says,

> A sword, a sword is sharpened...to make a
> sore slaughter...let the sword (the flaming
> sword set to the east of Eden[40]) be **doubled
> the third time**, the sword...of the great
> men that are slain, which entereth into their
> privy chambers. I have set the **point of the
> sword** against all their gates (Babylon's),
> that their heart may faint, and their ruins be
> multiplied: ah! it is made bright...for the
> slaughter....thou, profane wicked prince of
> Israel (the False Prophet who has moved to
> Babylon), whose day is come, when iniquity
> shall have an end...**take off the crown**
> (depose him)...exalt him that is low (Christ is
> crowned today), and abase him that is high
> (Satan). I will overturn, overturn, overturn,
> it: and it shall be no more, until he (Christ)
> come (seven Jewish months later[41]) whose
> right it is; and I will give it him.

The Hebrew *chereb*, sword, often represents a broken section of Satan's Cherubim, the terrestrial planet Rahab, that blew up in the Asteroid Belt in ancient times.

The sword is doubled the third time. According to
Ezekiel 21:16,18 in the Confraternity version, God gave this
sword "over to the burnisher" (Lucifer, light bearer, Satan)
and "the sword has been tested." Large asteroids have hit
Earth before. The three times **since** Adam was created are

when Sodom and Gomorrah were destroyed, at Gibeon on Joshua's Long Day, when more died with hailstones than the Israelites killed,[42] and when Babylon is annihilated today, Jesus' Long Day.

We also know that the sword was tested when Rahab exploded. It does seem as if some enormous sword took a swashbuckling slash into our solar system and upset the perfect order a bit. We now find odd things like Uranus traveling around its orbit tipped over on its side, Venus rotating in a clockwise direction when all other planets rotate counter-clockwise, Mars losing most of its water and atmosphere, and Pluto crossing inside Neptune's orbital ring, where it is now and will be until 1999.

The destruction of Babylon cannot compare in intensity with the mass extinction before Adam was created. Today, Tishri 1, 5768 (our September 13, 2007) the Lord will actually thresh from Babylon to Egypt,[43] but the effects will be felt worldwide. In the NEB, Isaiah 27:12,13 says,

> On that day the LORD will beat out the grain, from the streams of the Euphrates to the Torrent of Egypt; but you Israelites will be gleaned one by one. On that day a blast shall be blown on a great trumpet (it is the Feast of Trumpets).

The prognosis for the inhabitants of wounded Earth is not good. Psalm 75:3 in the Amplified version says,

> I will call for a sword upon all the inhabitants of the earth, saith the LORD of hosts....The LORD shall roar from on high, and utter his voice from his holy habitation (Heaven): he shall mightily roar upon his habitation; he shall give a shout, as they that tread the grapes, against all the inhabitants of the earth. A noise shall come even to the ends of the earth (the impact explosion)...evil shall go forth from nation to nation, and a great whirlwind shall be raised up from the coasts of the

earth. and the slain of the LORD shall be at that day from one end of the earth even unto the other end of the earth.

The noise that shall be heard around the world is likened to a lion's roar because at that time Christ will already be crowned King of kings. The Lamb of God has now become the Lion of the tribe of Judah, and he is furious because his land of Israel is being attacked by the army of the united nations.

The Lord Almighty will use a whirlwind, an east wind, to actually execute the judgment. Hosea 11:9 says," I will not execute the fierceness of mine anger...the LORD: he shall roar like a lion: when he shall roar, then the children shall tremble from the west" (the United States included).

Recompenses for the controversy of Zion

We are about to hear seven trumpets of judgment sound on this Feast of Trumpets. Like cause and effect, lightning and thunder, as they sound in Heaven, the effect appears on Earth. The devastation flares outward from the strike zone quickly, the consequences to this planet growing worse and worse in a domino effect. Be glad that we do not have to experience this. We are with John, watching from Heaven. This is Egypt just before the Exodus all over again, but the plagues are intensified almost beyond our comprehension.

SEVEN TRUMPET JUDGMENTS

First trumpet: hail, fire, blood

Ears tuned, we listen attentively as John begins to tell us about the trumpet judgments. These things are going to happen to our Earth, maybe to our friends or family.

And the seven angels which had the seven trumpets prepared themselves to sound. The first angel sounded, and there followed hail and fire mingled with blood, and they were cast upon the earth (Seiss says the best MSS add **'and the third of the earth was**

**burned'): and the third part of trees was
burnt up, and all green grass was burnt up."[44]**

Think of this globe. One third of it is scorched earth
before the second trumpet sounds. This had its parallel in
Egypt. "Moses stretched forth his rod toward heaven: and
the LORD sent thunder and hail, and the fire ran along the
ground."[45] Imagine the serious and far-reaching consequences of just one part of this. The main parts of the asteroid
have not even hit, yet the preceding rain of fire has already
spread wildfires that have destroyed all grass. Animals de-
pendent upon pasturage cannot find food. Since hay and
other vegetation will burn along with the grass, domestic animals cannot find food. What will happen to man's food
supply? and these are just the preliminaries.

Second trumpet: mountain splashes into sea

As the second judgment strikes, a mountain-sized rock
smashes into the Mediterranean Sea, causing a huge tidal
wave that radiates rapidly from the epicenter, causing appall-
ing damage. Listen as John continues in Revelation 8:8,9:

> And the second angel sounded, and as it were
> a **great mountain** burning with fire was
> cast into the sea: and the third part of the sea
> became blood; And the third part of the
> creatures which were in the sea, and had life,
> died; and the third part of the ships were de-
> stroyed.

This is the first stone of large size to fall. Since this
is the sea, we should be able to identify it. The Mediterranean (meaning middle of the earth), fits the criteria because
there are scriptures that tell of the damage to the cities along
Israel's coast. In Jeremiah 47:2-7, the Lord says,

> waters rise up out of the north, and shall be
> an overflowing flood, and shall overflow the
> land, and all that is therein; the city, and them
> that dwell therein...men shall cry, and all the

inhabitants of the land shall howl...Baldness is come upon Gaza; Ashkelon is cut off with the remnant of their valley...O thou sword of the LORD...be still. How can it be quiet, seeing the LORD hath given it a charge against Ashkelon, and **against the sea shore? there hath he appointed it.**

The army attacking Israel is to be rinsed out of her hair right away. The Lord fights for them today. He says,

I will plead against him (the invading army) with pestilence and with blood; and I will rain upon him...and upon the many people that are with him, an overflowing rain (literally, shower, i.e., tsunami), and great hailstones, fire, and brimstone. Thus will I magnify myself, and sanctify myself; and I will be known in the eyes of many nations (they will see the Sign of the Son of Man today[46]), and they shall know that I am the LORD.... Thou shalt fall upon the mountains of Israel, thou, and all thy bands.[47]

Other scriptures also mention these overflowing waters that are temporarily expelled from their basin and the cities that are hit. Both stones hit at noon.

O Israel....prepare to meet thy God...For, lo...what is his thought, that maketh the morning darkness...The LORD, The God of hosts, is his name....Seek him that maketh the seven stars (Pleiades[48]) and Orion, and turneth the shadow of death into the morning, and maketh the day dark with night: that calleth for the waters of the sea, and poureth them out upon the face of the earth.[49]

For Gaza shall be forsaken, and Ashkelon a desolation: they shall drive out Ashdod at the

> noon day, and Ekron shall be rooted up.
> Woe unto the inhabitants of the sea coast...
> the word of the LORD is against you; O Ca-
> naan, the land of the Philistines. I will even
> destroy thee, that there shall be no inhabitant.
> And the sea coast shall be dwellings and cot-
> tages for shepherds, and folds for flocks.
> And the coast shall be for the remnant of the
> house of Judah.[50]

It is up to us to figure out where in the Mediterranean the mountain will fall to cause waters to rise up north of Ashkelon and Gaza. The northeast corner seems most likely.

Third trumpet: death star strikes

In our play, under the third judgment, the second great stone falls. It is a death star, the doomsday rock named Wormwood. John relates in Revelation 8:10,11,

> And the third angel sounded, and there fell a
> **great star** (*aster*) from heaven, burning as it
> were a lamp (or torch), and it fell upon the
> third part of the (*ton*) rivers, and upon the
> fountains of waters: And the name of the star
> is called Wormwood: and the third part of the
> waters became wormwood (bitter); and many
> men died of the waters, because they were
> made bitter.

Not only is the food supply affected, now the drinking water is poisoned. Since this asteroid is to hit at Babylon, the rivers are probably those mentioned in Genesis 8:10-14, the Pison, Gihon, Hiddekel (Tigris), and Euphrates. The fountains of waters sound like the river that went out of Eden. Verse 10 says, "and a river went out of Eden to water the garden; and from thence it was parted, and became into four heads."

This great star is a stone that descends at thousands of miles per second. Its incoming roar is loud as it burns furiously in the atmosphere. Since this is the only one of the rocks that has a name, it must be Satan's home. The Lord said, "I will smite the winter house (the Satan possessed False Prophet's in Babylon, in the desert) with the summer house (Satan's asteroid)."[51]

Fourth trumpet: thick darkness

As the fourth trumpet sounds, dense smoke smites the sun, moon, and stars with darkness. This is the day of eerie thick darkness. Joel and Zephaniah both told us that this would happen:

> BLOW ye the trumpet in Zion, and sound an alarm in my holy mountain: let all the inhabitants of the land tremble: for the day of the LORD cometh, for it is nigh at hand: A day of darkness and of gloominess, a day of clouds and of thick darkness.[52]

> The great day of the LORD is near...the mighty man shall cry there bitterly. That day is a day of wrath, a day of trouble and distress, a day of wasteness and desolation, a day of darkness and gloominess, a day of clouds and thick darkness. A day of the trumpet and alarm.[53]

In Revelation 8:12,13, John tells us about the fourth trumpet judgment on the day of darkness.

> And the fourth angel sounded, and the third part of the sun was smitten, and the third part of the moon, and the third part of the stars; so as the third part of them was darkened, and **the day shone not for a third part of it**, and the night likewise. And I beheld, and heard an angel flying through the midst of heaven, saying with a loud voice, **Woe, woe, woe**, to the inhabiters of the earth by reason of the other voices of the trumpet of the three angels, which are yet to sound!

Fifth trumpet, first woe

It is not over. As if enough woe has not already arrived, there are yet three woes to come. It does not sound good. John tells us what is taking place. His script is in 9:1,2.

> AND the fifth angel sounded, and I saw a star (*astera*) fall (*peptokota*, fallen) from heaven unto the earth: and to him (Satan or his asteroid) was given the key of the bottomless pit. And he opened the bottomless pit (the molten core of the Earth); and there arose a smoke out of the pit, as the smoke of a great furnace; and the sun and the air were darkened by reason of the smoke of the pit.

There seems to be a double meaning here. Lucifer (day-star), "son of the morning"[54] has been cast down to the Earth. The asteroid, or key, that will open the abyss was given to him after his planet blew up.

Green's translation shows that this can also apply just to the asteroid. He said, "I saw a star which had fallen to the earth out of the sky. And there was given to it the key of the bottomless pit. And it opened the bottomless pit."

The asteroid which has already fallen is Wormwood. It fell when the third trumpet sounded. By the time the fifth trumpet blasted, the abyss was opened. This demonstrates how fast these trumpet judgments strike. Deuteronomy 32:22 shows that this pit is D E E P, really deep. It is a good thing the Lord is holding the Earth together.

> For a fire is kindled in mine anger, and shall burn unto **the lowest hell,** and shall consume the earth with her increase, and set on fire the foundations of the mountains.

All of these trumpet judgments, and the bowls of God's wrath too, drum the Earth in rapid succession on the same day. The trumpets show the initial effects; the bowls reflect the final effects. For instance, when the second trumpet sounds, a third part of the creatures in the Mediterranean

Sea die, but when the second vial, or bowl, is poured out, "every living soul died in the sea."[55]

After the abyss is opened at Babylon,[56] the Lake of Fire forms in a rush. Molten rock gushes out; its extent— 181.8 miles.[57] Smoke will go up from that site forever. Isaiah 34:8-10 is plain:

> For it is the day (Tishri 1) of the LORD'S vengeance, and the year (everything fits the Jewish 5768) of recompences for the controversy of Zion. And the streams thereof shall be turned into pitch, and the dust thereof into brimstone, and the land thereof shall become burning pitch. It shall not be quenched night nor day; the smoke thereof shall go up for ever: from generation to generation it shall lie waste; none shall pass through it for ever.

The "land thereof shall become burning pitch" sounds like the oil stored underground in the middle east is ignited too. We saw what that can be like when Saddam Hussein had hundreds of oil wells torched in Kuwait. It took over a year to put those fires out. This time the fire is on the invader's home territory. There is justice, after all.

Since the abyss is now open, the demons that have been imprisoned there fly free. These are "the angels which kept not their first estate (*archen*, first principality), but left their own habitation." They are the ones that took wives from among the daughters of men. Their hybrid children were the giants that had to be destroyed in Noah's Flood.[58] These fallen angels, the Lord "hath reserved in everlasting chains under darkness unto the judgment of the great day."[59] In Revelation 9:3,4, they are symbolized by locusts that do not eat green things, but torment men.

We listen as John describes the scene:

> And there came out of the smoke locusts (spirit locusts, demons) upon the earth: and unto them was given power, as the scorpions of the earth have power. And it was com-

manded them that they should not hurt the grass of the earth, neither any green thing, neither any tree; but only those men which have not the seal of God in their foreheads.

These men do not have the seal of the living God, so they probably have the seal of Satan, the mark of the beast, the 666, maybe even in its original three Greek letters, Chi, Xi, Sigma. The middle one looks like a serpent when written in lower case, $\chi\xi\varsigma$. The outer ones are, according to Seiss,[60] used to represent Christ. He thinks this addition of the serpentine letter marks the serpent messiah, the pseudo christ.

As John continues, we find a strange phenomenon, for five months, men will want to die and yet death flees.

And to them it was given that they should not kill them, but that they should be tormented five months: and their torment *was* as the torment of a scorpion, when he striketh a man. And in those days shall men seek death, and shall not find it; and shall desire to die, and death shall flee from them.[61]

The sting of a scorpion is extremely painful, affecting the nerves. The entrance of the stingers represent the entrance of these demons into the bodies of unregenerate men. Like literal locusts, these spirits stay around for five months.

Since the demons are released Tishri 1, the five Jewish months are Tishri, Cheshvan, Kislev, Teveth, and Shevat. There are two more, Adar and Adar II, before the return of Christ as the latter rain on Nisan 1, the beginning of the Jewish sacred and Regnal year. For there to be seven months between the catastrophe and the Second Coming, as shown in Ezekiel 39:12,13, that year has to be a Jewish leap year, and 5768 is a leap year. By these five months being mentioned as a time of torment for men, we can be sure that Christ does not return until after these five months are over.

He certainly could not return in glory the day of the catastrophe as so many teach. That is a day of thick darkness. Zechariah shows that he does not return on a dark day:

the LORD my God shall come, and all the saints with thee. And it shall come to pass in that day, that the light shall not be clear, nor dark: But it shall be one day which shall be known to the LORD (he knows when he will return), not day, nor night: but it shall come to pass, that at evening time it shall be light.[62]

God's land must be cleansed of the dead before Christ returns. Ezekiel 39:12,13 shows how long it takes.

And **seven months** shall the house of Israel be burying of them, that they may cleanse the land. Yea, all the people of the land shall bury them; and it shall be to them a renown the day (Sunday, Nisan 1) that I shall be glorified (Second Advent), saith the Lord God.

Horses symbolize spirits. These locusts are demon spirits with a king over them. Real "locusts have no king."[63] John continues his description in Revelation 9:7,8:

And the shapes of the locusts *were* **like** unto horses prepared unto battle; and on their heads *were* **as it were** crowns **like** gold, and their faces *were* **as** the faces of men. And they had hair **as** the hair of women, and their teeth were **as** *the teeth* of lions.

The repetition of the symbolic language, "like" and "as," tells us that this passage is symbolic and alerts us to look beyond these descriptions for the real meaning.

These being similar to horses prepared for battle reminds us of the red horse in Revelation 6:4. It too was a demon spirit, a fallen angel, and it had a rider. The two of them acted in conjunction.

These demon locusts have faces like men. Therefore, the demons enter into men when they strike them. Nahum 3:17 shows us that this is the correct interpretation. Addressing the king of Assyria (which is now Iraq), it says,

> Thy crowned are **as the locusts**, and thy
> captains as the great grasshoppers, which
> camp in the hedges in the cold day, but when
> the sun ariseth they flee away, and their place
> is not known where they are.

In Revelation 9, the crowns on their heads are not literal, but "as it were crowns like gold." They could represent the circlet emblems on the front of military leader's hats. They are pictured with hair of women to tie them in with the harlot Mystery Religion. Their teeth are as the teeth of lions to tie them in with Babylon, which was depicted as being "like a lion" in Daniel 7:4.

As John continues his narration in Revelation 9:9,10, we can see why some have thought that these locusts represent helicopters, except maybe helicopters do not have tail gunners like fighter planes.

> And they had breastplates, as it were breast-
> plates of iron; and the sound of their wings
> *was* as the sound of chariots of many horses
> running to battle. And they had tails like unto
> scorpions, and there were stings in their tails:
> and their power *was* to hurt men five months.

The breastplates of iron are to tie them in with the strength of the iron, which represented the might of Rome, in the feet of the image depicted in Daniel 2:31-40. Revelation 18:2 says that "Babylon the great...is become the habitation of devils, and the hold of every foul spirit." The harlot Mystery Religion of Babylon, at first headquartered in Rome, has been moved to Babylon before the catastrophe is to hit.

> And they had a king over them, *which is* the
> angel of the bottomless pit, whose name in
> the Hebrew tongue *is* Abaddon (destroyer),
> but in the Greek tongue hath *his* name Apol-
> lyon (destroyer). One woe is past; *and*, be-
> hold, there come two woes more hereafter.[64]

It does not say that this angel is in the bottomless pit at this time, but that he is "the angel of the bottomless pit," the one of whom it was said, who "shall ascend out of the bottomless pit, and go into perdition...the beast that was, and is not, and yet is."[65] He is the eighth beast of Revelation 17:11. He is not only the tail of the dragon, but the dragon himself. He is Satan (which means contrary, adversary, opponent, hater, a party in a process, an enemy, an accuser), but he is also the arch destroyer, the exact opposite of the Saviour. Satan is to be allowed to have all his forces at his disposal to fight the still future battle of Armageddon after Christ returns at the Second Advent.

It is not unusual for the Lord to give someone another more descriptive name. Satan is also called Lucifer, the Devil, the Dragon, Belial, Beelzebub, the Evil One, the Prince of this World, the Prince of the Power of the Air, and the God of this world.

Abram (father of height) became Abraham (father of a multitude). Sarai (my lady, my princess, contentious) became Sarah (lady, queen, princess, or the princess of the multitude). Jacob (supplanter, or heel-catcher), was called no more Jacob, but Israel (a prince with God, prevailing with God, one that wrestles with God, having power with God, God's fighter, or he will rule as God). Simon (that hears or obeys) was called Peter (Greek, *Petros*; Aramaic, *Sefas*, a rock). Saul (asked for, destroyer, sepulchre, death, hell) was changed to Paul (little, or worker).

There are many things that can be learned by looking up the names used in Scripture and thinking about types, or similitudes. For example: Abaddon means destroyer. Saul means asked for, **destroyer**, **death** and **hell**.

King Saul was the king the Israelites asked for. The Lord told Israel, "I gave thee a king in mine anger, and took him away in my wrath."[66] As a type, his wrath points directly to the end of this age. King Saul, who was troubled by an "evil spirit"[67] was followed by king David, then by the son of David, Solomon, called the wisest of men.

These things have parallels in the end times. In Revelation 6:8, the rider on the pale horse is named "Death, and Hell followed with him." He is the False Prophet riding Satan, an evil spirit, the ultimate destroyer. The False Prophet is the final king that will be taken away in God's wrath. King David will follow. David himself will be resurrected and put back on his throne as a prince under the greater King of kings, Jesus Christ, called the Son of David. Christ truly is the wisest of men. He is both God and the Son of God.

"For it pleased the Father that in him should all fulness dwell" (Colossians 1:19). "God giveth not the Spirit by measure unto him" (John 3:34). Psalm 45:6,7 says, "Thy throne, O God, is for ever and ever: the sceptre of thy kingdom is a right sceptre. Thou lovest righteousness, and hatest wickedness: therefore God, thy God, hath anointed thee with the oil of gladness (symbol of the Holy Spirit) above thy fellows." II Corinthians 5:18 is very plain. If we did not understand it before, we can now. It says that "God was in Christ, reconciling the world unto himself."

Sixth trumpet, second woe

As John reads Revelation 9:13-15, the scene changes.

> And the sixth angel sounded, and I heard a voice from the four horns of the golden altar which is before God, Saying to the sixth angel which had the trumpet, Loose the four angels which are bound in the great river Euphrates. And the four angels were loosed, which were prepared for an hour, and a day, and a month, and a year (Green: 'the hour and day and month and year'), for to slay the third part of men.

The one hour is probably 12:00-1:00 P.M., Tishri 1, 5768.

> And the number of the army of the horsemen *were* two hundred thousand thousand: and I heard the number of them. And thus I saw the horses in the vision, and them that sat on them, having breatplates of fire, and of jacinth, and brimstone: and the heads of the horses *were* as the heads of lions; and out of

their mouths issued fire and smoke and brimstone. By these three was the third part of men killed, by the fire, and by the smoke, and by the brimstone, which issued out of their mouths. For their power is in their mouth, and in their tails: for their tails *were* like unto serpents, and had heads, and with them they do hurt. And the rest of the men which were not killed by these plagues yet repented not of the works of their hands, that they should not worship devils, and idols of gold, and silver, and brass, and stone, and of wood: which neither can see, nor hear, nor walk: Neither repented they of their murders, nor of their sorceries (*pharmakeion*, drugs), nor of their fornication, nor of their thefts.[68]

These images "neither can see, nor hear, nor walk," but Satan is allowed to cause at least one to speak, and to kill those who will "not worship the image of the beast."[69]

We will hear more about this a little later in the play, but first we must be shown something like a film clip that fills in some necessary details of things that have already taken place, but have been skipped over in order to give us a connected story. Revelation 10:1 to 11:14 is parenthetical.

Christ and the little book
John is speaking. His script here is found in chapter 10.

AND I saw another mighty angel come down from heaven, clothed with a cloud: and a rainbow *was* upon his head, and his face *was* as it were the sun, and his feet as pillars of fire:

The one called "another mighty angel" is probably the same as "another angel" in Revelation 8:3. He is the Angel of the Lord that cast the fire-filled censer to the Earth. He is pictured with the rainbow to tie him in with the throne set in Heaven when the Lamb of God was given the little book.

John continues in Revelation 10:2-4. I find the part about where Jesus sets his feet intriguing.

> And he (the Angel of the Lord) had in his hand a little book open (the Book of the Purchase of Earth that was given to Christ, the Lamb of God[70]): **and he set his right foot upon the sea** (the Mediterranean), **and *his* left foot on the earth** (at Babylon), And cried with a loud voice, as *when* a lion roareth (the noise heard round the world): and when he had cried, seven thunders uttered their voices. And when the seven thunders had uttered their voices, I was about to write: and I heard a voice from heaven saying unto me, Seal up those things which the seven thunders uttered, and write them not.

Jesus walked on water, demonstrating that he has the power to stand on the sea. The Lamb of God has now become the King, The Lion of the Tribe of Judah. The seals are almost all broken, only one remains, and the Book of the Purchase of Earth, the title-deed, is just about open. He is ready to take possession.

Israel has been attacked, bringing his fury up into his face. This is when he roars, when the seven thunders utter their voices. The actual noise is produced when the mountain hits the sea and the death star falls on the land.

Symbolically, it is as if the Lord stomps down hard on the sea with his right foot and hammers the land with his left foot in his great wrath. Ezekiel 6:11 says,

> Thus saith the Lord GOD; Smite with thine hand, and **stamp with thy foot**, and say, Alas for all the evil abominations of the house of Israel! for they shall fall by the sword, by the famine, and by the pestilence. He that is far off shall die of the pestilence; and he that is near shall fall by the sword; and he that remaineth...shall die by the famine: thus will

I accomplish **my fury** upon them. **Then shall ye know** that I am the LORD.

"I am **trampling** peoples in My anger,"he declared in Isaiah 63:6 in the Concordant Version.

The seven thunders remind us of Psalm 29:3-10. We can now understand what it means.

The voice of the LORD is upon the waters: **the God of glory thundereth**: the LORD is upon many waters (the Mediterranean Sea). The voice of the LORD is powerful; the voice of the LORD is full of majesty (he is now King of kings and Lord of lords). The voice of the LORD breaketh the cedars...of Lebanon (with the impact blast in the Mediterranean). He maketh them also to skip like a calf; Lebanon and Sirion like a young unicorn. **The voice of the LORD divideth** (*chatsab*, splits) **the flames of fire** (he cuts the binary asteroid into two main chunks plus many smaller pieces). The voice of the LORD shaketh the wilderness; the LORD shaketh the wilderness of Kadesh (where Israel camped when the spies went into the promised land). The voice of the LORD... discovereth the forests ('twists the oaks and strips the forests'[71]): and in his temple (in Heaven) doth every one speak of his glory. The LORD sitteth upon the flood ('is enthroned above the flood'[72]); yea, **the LORD sitteth King for ever.**

"Because of the thunder, the nations are scattered," Isaiah 33:3 in the Concordant Version tells us. This is the noise heard around the world.

The fate of the army that attacked Israel is sure:

Behold, I am against thee, O Gog, the chief prince of Meshech and Tubal: And I will turn thee back, and leave but the sixth part of thee, and will cause thee to come up from the north parts, and will bring thee upon the mountains of Israel...Thou shalt fall upon the mountains of Israel, thou, and all thy bands, and the people that is with thee: I will give thee unto the ravenous birds of every sort, and to the beasts of the field to be devoured...And I will send a fire on Magog...and the heathen shall know that I am the LORD, the Holy One in Israel. Behold, it (the asteroid) is come, and **it is done**, saith the Lord GOD; this is the day whereof I have spoken....a great sacrifice upon the mountains of Israel...So the house of Israel shall know that I am the LORD their God from that day and forward.[73]

There is another passage that shows that the Tribulation saints are snatched up as the mountain falls into the Mediterranean Sea. II Samuel 22:7-21 says,

In my distress I called upon the LORD...and he did hear my voice out of his temple (Heaven)...Then the earth shook and trembled; the foundations of heaven moved and shook, because he was wroth. There went up a smoke out of his nostrils, and fire out of his mouth devoured: coals were kindled by it. He bowed the heavens also, and came down; and darkness was under his feet. And he rode upon a cherub, and did fly: and he was seen upon the wings of the wind (the Sign of the Son of Man[74]). And he made darkness pavilions round about him...Through the brightness before him were coals of fire kindled. The LORD thundered from heaven, and the most High uttered his voice. And he sent out arrows, and scattered them; lightning, and discomfited them. And the channels of the sea appeared, the foundations of the world were discovered, at the rebuking of the LORD, at the blast of the breath of his nostrils. He sent from above, he took me; he drew me out of many waters (the tsunami); He delivered me from my strong enemy...He brought me forth also into a large place (Heaven): he delivered me, because he delighted in me. The LORD rewarded me according to my righteousness.

The channels of the sea appeared as when the Israelites left Egypt. An east wind blew hard all night and Israel crossed dry shod. The Egyptian forces followed into the channel, but the water crashed back and drowned them all.

A similar phenomenon will take place in the northeastern section of the Mediterranean Sea. The bottom will be excavated to a depth not seen before and the water hurled away from the center by the force of the impact blast. Much of the water will shoot up into the stratosphere. Later, the sea will smack its hands then rush away again to scour the surrounding countries with a towering wall of water.

And the angel (Angel of the Lord) which I saw stand upon the sea and upon the earth lifted up his hand to heaven, And sware by him that liveth for ever and ever, who created heaven, and the things that therein are, and the earth, and the things that therein are, and the sea, and the things which are therein, that there should be time (delay) no longer: But in the days of the voice of the seventh angel, when he shall begin to sound, **the mystery of God should be finished**, as he hath declared to his servants the prophets.[75]

Since there is no greater than he, the Angel of the Lord swore by himself, as in Hebrews 6:13,14, which says,

For when God made promise to Abraham, because he could swear by no greater, he sware by himself, Saying, Surely blessing I will bless thee, and multiplying I will multiply thee.

This mystery of God that has been woven so adroitly throughout the fabric of Scripture will be understood on Tishri 1 as the seventh trumpet begins to be heard. Christ is the Almighty and he will rule. Paul wanted us to understand. He mentioned "the mystery of God, and of the Father, and of Christ: In whom are hid all the treasures of wisdom and knowledge."[76] As Isaiah 9:6,7 says, Christ is "The mighty God, The everlasting Father, The Prince of Peace. Of the increase of his government and peace there shall be no end." This ties in with what is said as the seventh trumpet is blown. Chapter 11:15 says that "there were great voices in heaven, saying, The kingdoms of this world are become the kingdoms of our Lord, and of his Christ; and he shall reign for ever and ever."

John continues reading in Revelation 10:8,9:

And the voice which I heard from heaven spake unto me again, and said, Go *and* take the little book which is open in the hand of the angel (the Angel of the Lord) which standeth upon the sea and upon the earth. And I went unto the angel, and said unto him, Give me the little book. And he said unto me, Take *it*, and eat it up; and it shall make thy belly bitter, but it shall be in thy mouth sweet as honey.

Here, it is the judgments of the Lord that are as sweet as honey. We should pay attention to Psalm 19:8-11.

The statutes of the LORD are right, rejoicing the heart: the commandment of the LORD is pure, enlightening the eyes. The fear of the LORD is clean, enduring for ever: the judgments of the LORD are true and righteous altogether. More to be desired are they than

gold, yea, than much fine gold: sweeter also
than honey and the honeycomb. Moreover by
them is thy servant warned: and in keeping of
them there is great reward.

Prophesy again

In Revelation 10:10,11, John is told to prophesy again.

And I took the little book out of the angel's
hand, and ate it up; and it was in my mouth
sweet as honey: and as soon as I had eaten it,
my belly was bitter. And he said unto me,
Thou must prophesy again before many peoples, and nations, and tongues, and kings.

Parenthetic section

Between the sixth and seventh seals, trumpets and vials are
parenthetic sections. The story moved along certain lines,
but there are other things that must be told. Here, John starts
again, back at the beginning of the Tribulation, to fill us in
on some important details. He has been in Heaven. Now it is
as if he again stands on Earth to tell us what has been happening in the meantime on this planet.

Zoom to the Beginning of the Tribulation

John begins the script in chapter 11, but the Angel of the
Lord actually starts speaking when he says, "Rise." The
Rapture is already past when John is to measure the temple
at the start of the Tribulation. From the 1,260 days listed for
the two witnesses to prophecy, we can be certain that this is
the beginning of the first half of the 2,300-day Tribulation.
The last part is shortened to 1,040 days.

AND there was given me a reed like unto a
rod: and the angel stood, saying, Rise, and
measure the temple of God, and the altar, and
them that worship therein. But the court
which is without the temple leave out, and
measure it not; for it is given unto the Gen-

tiles: and the holy city shall they tread under foot forty *and* two months (also referred to as 1,260 days or 3 1/2 years).

This seems to indicate that the temple is already there when the Tribulation begins. It could be built between the Rapture on Pentecost, May 31, 1998 and the signing of the Seven-Year Peace Treaty on the first day of the Tribulation, Pentecost/Feast of Weeks, Monday, May 28, 2001.

On December 3, 1995, the Chicago Sun-Times ran an article by Robin Wright, "Peres' Aim: Total Peace in Mideast By 2000." Shimon Peres, the former prime minister of Israel, said that he sought one last job: "to bear the burden of peacemaking." He still intends to work for peace.

I received two interesting newsletters, both dated February 1996, that tie in with what John is saying here. One, from Jerusalem Ministries International, states that Peres was determined to Internationalize Jerusalem. It also states that the Pope is calling for all three monotheistic religions to worship in the city of Jerusalem in 2000 A.D.

The other newsletter is the Prophetic Observer. Page three is especially interesting. Under the heading "The World Looks to 2000," it says that Dr. Malachi Martin, in his latest book, *The Keys of This Blood*, indicates that

Pope John Paul II believes that by the year 2000 there will be a second Fatima, the Illumination, and **all religions will accept him as God's vicar on Earth**. In the Sunday, April 3, 1994, edition of *Parade* magazine, Pope John Paul II is quoted:

We trust that with the approach of the year 2000, Jerusalem will become the city of peace for the entire world and all the people will be able to meet there, in particular the believers in the religions that find their birthright in the faith of Abraham.

The pope hopes that all people will come together in worship in Jerusalem by A.D. 2000, and in particular, adherents to **Judaism, Islam, and Christianity**. The pope has recently been quoted in the news media as remaining firm in his position that he alone must be the head of any ecumenical religious structure and retain his authority which entails infallibility. Therefore, it seems obvious that the pope expects the great Illumination to come in, or before, A.D. 2000 when he will become the head of an international religious entity. (emphasis mine)

It looks as if all the necessary ingredients are ready for the final mix. If Jerusalem is Internationalized according to this plan, it will put Jerusalem under the protection of the world government. Israel will agree to it only if he/they will guarantee the peace of Jerusalem. It will also pave the way for the Pope to be elected head of the world government.

In our play, those that worship in the temple are the Jews. Those that worship in the court that is without the temple could be the Christians and those who adhere to the tenets of Islam.

God's two witnesses identified
The Angel of the Lord continues in Revelation 11:3-6.

And I will give *power* unto my two witnesses, and they shall prophesy a thousand two hundred *and* threescore days, clothed in sackcloth. These are the two olive trees, and the two candlesticks standing before the God of the earth. And if any man will hurt them, fire proceedeth out of their mouth, and devoureth their enemies: and if any man will hurt them (the False Prophet will), he must in this manner be killed. These have power to shut heaven, that it rain not in the days of their prophecy: and have power over waters

to turn them to blood, and to smite the earth
with all plagues, as often as they will.

One of these two witnesses is Elijah. In the next to
the last verse of the Old Testament, Malachi said, "Behold, I
will send you Elijah the prophet before the coming of the
great and dreadful day of the LORD."[77] The other witness is
Moses. Some have thought he was Enoch, but Enoch was a
Gentile who was "translated that he should not see death."[78]
Both of these witnesses are Israelites and will be killed.

"These are the two olive trees (two Jews[79]), and the
two candlesticks standing before the God of the earth."
"These are the two anointed ones, that stand by the Lord of
the whole earth."[80] Both Moses and Elijah stood by Jesus at
the Transfiguration to show us exactly who these two witnesses are. Matthew 17:3 says, "And, behold, there appeared unto them Moses and Elias talking with him." Also,
as candlesticks, Moses and Elijah belong **inside** the Temple. Enoch would have to be outside since he was a Gentile.

The things these two do also point to who they are.
They still have the powers they were given before. In the
days of wicked king Ahab and his wife Jezebel, who introduced Baal worship, Elijah prayed that it not rain, and it did
not rain for three and a half years. Moses was instrumental
in the smiting of Egypt with plagues, just as he will let loose
plagues this time around.

Moses and Elijah will explain exactly what is coming. Jeremiah said,

For who hath stood in the counsel of the
LORD, and hath perceived and heard his
word? (Moses and Elijah at the Transfiguration) who hath marked his word, and heard
it? Behold, a whirlwind of the LORD is gone
forth in fury, even a grievous whirlwind: it
shall fall grievously upon the head of the
wicked. The anger of the LORD shall not return, until he have executed, and till he have
performed the thoughts of his heart: in the
latter days ye shall consider it perfectly.[81]

Who is the wise man, that may understand this? (both Moses and Elijah understand) and who is he to whom the mouth of the LORD hath spoken, that he may declare it, for what the land perisheth and is burned up like a wilderness, that none passeth through?[82]

In our play, the Angel of the Lord continues telling us about the two witnesses in Revelation 11:7-10:

And when they shall have finished their testimony (after their ministry of three and one half years), the beast that ascendeth out of the bottomless pit (Satan, who at that time enters into the False Prophet) shall make war against them, and shall overcome them, and kill them. And their dead bodies *shall lie* in the street of the great city (Jerusalem), which spiritually is called Sodom (symbol of immorality) and Egypt (symbol of materialism), where also our Lord was crucified. And they of the people and kindreds and tongues and nations shall see their dead bodies three days and an half, and shall not suffer their dead bodies to be put in graves. And they that dwell upon the earth shall rejoice over them, and make merry, and shall send gifts one to another; because these two prophets tormented them that dwelt on the earth.

The False Prophet will think he has won this battle. However, he is going to get an unexpected surprise.

It looks like the occasion that triggers these murders is when the False Prophet sits in the temple in Jerusalem playing God. Second Thessalonians 2:3,4 says of "that man of sin...the son of perdition; Who opposeth and exalteth himself above all that is called God, or that is worshipped... he as God sitteth in the temple of God, shewing himself that he is God." The two witnesses preach against him and refuse to worship the image. Therefore, they are killed.[83]

Resurrection and ascension

As the Angel of the Lord continues in Revelation 11:11,12, we find out right away that Death did not win.

> And after three days and an half the spirit of
> life from God entered into them, and they
> stood upon their feet: and great fear fell upon
> them which saw them. And they heard a great
> voice from heaven saying unto them, Come
> up hither. And they ascended up to heaven in
> a cloud; and their enemies beheld them.

This is a mini resurrection in the middle of the Tribulation. It demonstrates that when the Lord says, "Come up hither," an actual resurrection from the dead and an ascension take place. Thus we can be absolutely sure that this also happens when he says "Come up hither" at Rapture I. The dead stand upon their feet, hear the "Come up hither," and ascend to Heaven. Notice what else it says, "and their enemies beheld them." There will be some who will see the Rapture take place too.[84]

Similar to Jesus' "three days and three nights in the heart of the earth,"[85] these two witnesses will also be dead three and one half days before their resurrection.

In Revelation 11:13, the Angel of the Lord adds other things that happen in the middle of the Tribulation.

> And the same hour was there a great earth-
> quake, and the tenth part of the city fell, and
> in the earthquake were slain of men seven
> thousand: and the remnant were affrighted,
> and gave glory to the God of heaven.

It is too bad that some people have to be shaken up before they will give glory to God. At least these finally did it.

Seventh trumpet, third woe

Having finished giving us the information about the two witnesses, the play picks up the thread of the story again when the seventh trumpet is about to sound. We are in Heaven listening to John read Revelation 11:14,15.

> The second woe is past; *and*, behold, the third woe cometh quickly. And the seventh angel sounded: and there were great voices in heaven, saying, The kingdoms of this world are become *the kingdoms* of our Lord, and of his Christ; and he shall reign for ever and ever.

Remember what Revelation 10:7 said, that "in the days of the voice of the seventh angel, when he shall begin to sound, the mystery of God should be finished, as he hath declared to his servants the prophets"? What is declared as soon as the seventh angel sounds? that the "kingdoms of this world are become the kingdoms of our Lord, and of his Christ." This is the beginning of Christ's reign as King of kings and Lord of lords. We listen to Revelation 11:16,17.

> And the four and twenty elders, which sat before God on their seats, fell upon their faces, and worshipped God, Saying, We give thee thanks, O Lord God Almighty, which art (at the Judgment Seat of Christ), and **wast (at the Rapture)**, and art to come (the Second Advent); because thou hast taken to thee thy great power, and hast reigned.

The grand Coronation ceremony in Heaven is past. the elders give thanks that Christ has already begun his reign as King of kings. However, the Second Advent is still future. John reads Revelation 11:18:

> And the nations were angry (angry enough to send the great army to wipe Israel off the map), and thy wrath is come (his fury has come up in his face), and the time of the dead, that they should be judged (at the Judgment Seat of Christ), and that thou shouldest

> give reward unto thy servants the prophets,
> and to the saints, and them that fear thy
> name, small and great; and shouldest destroy
> them which destroy the earth.

Saints and sinners get whatever rewards they deserve at the same time, good in Heaven, bad on Earth.

> And the temple of God was opened in heav-
> en, and there was seen in his temple the ark
> (container) of his testament (*diathekes*, cov-
> enant, contract): and there were lightnings,
> and voices, and thunderings, and an earth-
> quake, and great hail.[86]

In the Ark are the two stone "tables of the coven-
ant,"[87] which was not kept by those on Earth. Therefore, two stones were dumped out on Earth, and the effects of the con-
cussions continue. Just as the two stone tablets were con-
tained in the Ark, the two stones cast into the Earth were bound together in a binary asteroid called the curse.

The Curse

The last verse of the Old Testament says,

> And he (Elijah) shall turn the heart of the fa-
> thers to the children, and the heart of the
> children to their fathers, lest I come and smite
> the earth with a curse.

This curse is described in Zechariah 5:1-4. The prophet had just seen the vision of the golden candlestick and the two olive trees. The olive trees represented Moses and Elijah, "the two anointed ones, that stand by the Lord of the whole Earth" (they stood by Jesus at the Transfiguration). Since his vision of the curse followed that of Moses and Elijah, its actual manifestation is after their testimony.

> THEN I turned, and lifted up mine eyes, and
> looked, and behold a flying roll (*megillah*,

rolling thing). And he said unto me, What seest thou? And I answered, I see a flying roll (rolling thing); the length thereof is twenty cubits, and the breadth thereof ten cubits (twice as long as wide). Then said he unto me, This is **the curse** (the binary asteroid) that goeth forth (orbits) over the face of the whole earth: for every one that stealeth shall be cut off as on this side (one piece hits the Mediterranean Sea) according to it; and every one that sweareth shall be cut off as on that side (the other piece hits Babylon) according to it. I will bring it forth, saith the LORD of hosts, and it shall enter into the house of the thief (the False Prophet), and into the house of him that sweareth falsely by my name (the Beast): and it shall remain in the midst of his house, and shall consume it with the timber thereof and the stones thereof.

A binary asteroid like Toutatis would fit the description here. It looks like two big potatoes stuck together. It also seems to be loosely bound, as if two pieces collided and are barely held together by their own gravity. It would be very easy for it to break apart on the way in. Chances are good that it would start to break up at the Roche limit, about 11,000 miles out.

There could easily be two large pieces plus a rain of smaller stones released upon the separation. Besides the stones released upon separation, all pieces would be subject to further breakup. Rocks under a certain size would burn up in the atmosphere, creating celestial fireworks on a scale never seen by man before.

All of this has taken place in one momentous day. Jesus was crowned, married, and presided at the Judgment Seat of Christ. Afterward, those at the Marriage Supper of the Lamb were able to watch the stupendous fireworks.

1 Revelation 10:7
2 Matthew 24:30
3 Psalm 94:1
4 Psalm 99:1
5 Revelation 19:6
6 Daniel 7:9-14
7 John 5:22
8 Acts 10:42
9 II Timothy 4:1
10 Matthew 24:30
11 Revelation 6:16,17
12 Psalm 9:7
13 Psalm 11:4,6
14 Mark 13:27
15 Matthew 24:30
16 Zechariah 9:14,15
17 Ezekiel 38:22,23
18 Acts 10:43
19 Obadiah 15
20 Psalm 83:4
21 Revelation 20:8
22 Joshua 10:10-14
23 Revelation 2:10
24 Hebrews 10:30
25 Revelation 1:20
26 Revelation 5:9
27 I Corinthians 6:2
28 Luke 12:49, RSV
29 Matthew 10:34
30 I Chronicles 21:16
31 Numbers 22:23
32 I Corinthians 15:45
33 Isaiah 45:18
34 Isaiah 51:9,10, Lamsa
35 II Peter 3:3-7
36 Isaiah 27:1
37 Psalm 75:3
38 Psalm 94:13
39 Ezekiel 38:20
40 Genesis 3:24
41 Ezekiel 39:12
42 Joshua 10:11
43 Jeremiah 51:33; Habakkuk 3:12
44 Revelation 8:6,7

[45] Exodus 9:23
[46] Matthew 24:30
[47] Ezekiel 38:22,23; 39:4
[48] Lamsa translation
[49] Amos 4:12,13; 5:8
[50] Zephaniah 2:4-6
[51] Amos 3:15
[52] Joel 2:1,2
[53] Zephaniah 1:14-16
[54] Isaiah 14:12
[55] Revelation 16:3
[56] Revelation 18:21
[57] Revelation 14:20
[58] Genesis 6:1-4
[59] Jude 6
[60] Seiss, *op. cit.*, pg. 347
[61] Revelation 9:5,6
[62] Zechariah 14:5,6
[63] Proverbs 30:27
[64] Revelation 9:11,12
[65] Revelation 17:8
[66] Hosea 13:11
[67] I Samuel 16:14
[68] Revelation 9:20,21
[69] Revelation 13:15
[70] Revelation 5:5-8
[71] New American Bible (NAB)
[72] Ibid
[73] Ezekiel 39:1-8,17,22
[74] Matthew 24:30
[75] Revelation 10:5-7
[76] Colossians 2:2,3
[77] Malachi 4:5,6
[78] Hebrews 11:5
[79] Jeremiah 11:16
[80] Zechariah 4:11-14
[81] Jeremiah 23:18-20
[82] Jeremiah 9:12
[83] Revelation 13:15
[84] Psalm 40:1-3
[85] Matthew 12:40
[86] Revelation 11:19
[87] Hebrews 9:4

7

The Woman and
the Dragon

Revelation 12

The Mystery of God has been revealed. Jesus Christ is the Almighty, the Lord of glory, and he will rule over the Earth.

Colossians 2:2,3 speaks of "the mystery of God, and of the Father, and of Christ; In whom are hid all the treasures of wisdom and knowledge." In I Corinthians 2:7,8, Paul said,

> But we speak the wisdom of God in a mystery, even the hidden wisdom, which God ordained before the world unto our glory: Which none of the princes of this world know: for had they known it, they would not have crucified the Lord of glory.

He was crowned King of kings and Lord of lords on his birthday, the Feast of Trumpets. Like king Solomon, the son of David, his mother probably was given the honor of crowning him on his wedding day. Song of Solomon 3:11 in the New American Bible says,

> In the crown with which his mother has crowned him on the day of his marriage, on the day of the joy of his heart.

The kingdoms of this world now legally belong to the greater Son of David, our Almighty Lord Jesus Christ.

He has married his Bride, who was appropriately a "virgin"[1] clothed in white.[2] Gifts, rewards, have been given out, and they celebrated at the Marriage Supper of the Lamb.

The judgment on unbelievers that also was meted out at the Judgment Seat of Christ has fallen on Earth. The myriad prophecies of "that day," the first day of the millennial Day of the Lord are fulfilled and understood.

However, Christ has not yet arrived on Earth. There are seven Jewish months between Tishri 1, 2007, when he received his golden crown in Heaven and Nisan 1, when he will return to Earth in glory on the first day of the Jewish Regnal year. He will wait for the dead to be buried in Israel to cleanse the land so his return can be truly glorious.

The Jewish remnant was born again the day of the catastrophe. That day, when they saw the Sign of the Son of Man and all the prophesied events coming to pass, they realized that the New Testament was true and that Jesus was their Messiah after all. They suddenly understood what the Lord had been trying to show them for so long. Isaiah 66:7,8 says,

> Before she travailed, she brought forth; before her pain came, she was delivered of a man child. Who hath heard such a thing? who hath seen such things? Shall the earth be made to bring forth in one day? or shall a nation be born at once? for as soon as Zion travailed, she brought forth her children.

Just as it said, the nation was born at once. As soon as her labor pains began, Israel brought forth her children. The reluctant fig tree finally has ripe fruit dangling from all its branches.

The Jews will mourn as never before throughout the Days of Awe between the Feast of Trumpets and the Day of Atonement, when the Jubilee year will be announced. The Jubilee will begin the following Nisan 1, when Christ will return at the beginning of their sacred and Regnal year. On the preceding Day of Atonement, Tishri 10, they will be accepted by the Lord because they have accepted Jesus Christ.

Starting the 15th, they will celebrate the seven-day Feast of Tabernacles in booths. This time it will be necessary because their houses will have sustained extensive damage from war, asteroid impact blast, falling stones, tornado winds, fire, tsunami, and earthquake. The cities of the nations have fallen.[3] Even Jerusalem had coals of fire sprinkled over her. In Ezekiel's vision, a man clothed with linen said,

> Go in between the wheels (planetary orbits), even under the cherub (Satan), and fill thine hand with coals of fire from between the cherubims (from the Asteroid Belt between the planets Mars and Jupiter), and scatter them over the city.[4]

When listening to the reading of the scriptures during the seven-days of the Feast of Tabernacles, the Israelites will understand as never before.

They will realize that they should cleanse the land for the return of Christ. Ezekiel tells us about this,

> And seven months shall the house of Israel be burying of them (the dead), that they may cleanse the land. Yea, all the people of the land shall bury them; and it shall be to them a renown the day that I shall be glorified (on Nisan 1, the beginning of their Regnal year), saith the Lord GOD.[5]

In our play, while we wait for ISRAEL TO BURY THE DEAD, our playwright goes back to fill us in on some details that have been left out. This time, we are taken back to the middle of the Tribulation and hear our narrator begin a new subject.

(The words capitalized above are the Lord's doing, not mine. I had no intention of putting anything in caps. Neither the caps lock key or the shift key is down. I was going to add "and for the smoke to clear away." I know now to leave that off. The one who said, "Let there be light: and there was light" does not have to wait while smoke clears.)

Sign of the woman in Heaven

John sees a great sign in Heaven and paints a beautiful word picture for us:

> AND there appeared a great wonder (*se-meion*, supernatural sign) in heaven; a woman clothed with the sun, and the moon under her feet, and upon her head a crown of twelve stars: And she being with child cried, travailing in birth, and pained to be delivered.

This is a great sign. Therefore it symbolizes something remarkable that the Lord wants to teach us. There are those who think this is the constellation Virgo. Some think this woman represents Israel. The twelve stars fit the twelve tribes of Israel. Others think she symbolizes the Church. The twelve stars fit the twelve apostles. Both camps have merit.

Those who think she represents Israel cite the Old Testament account of Joseph's dreams. That record is found in Genesis 37:5-10:

> Joseph dreamed...and, behold, the **sun** and the **moon** and the eleven **stars** made obeisance to me (Joseph makes twelve). And he told it to his father...and his father rebuked him, and said unto him, What is this dream that thou hast dreamed? Shall I and thy mother and thy brethren indeed come to bow down ourselves to thee to the earth?

The twelve sons of this family were the progenitors of the twelve tribes of Israel. The woman represents Israel because not only is she linked to the sun, moon, and stars right at the beginning, but Isaiah 66:5,7,8 locks Israel into the same type of figure we see in Revelation. Scripture has to be interpreted by Scripture. The Lord shows us what his signs represent. This passage in Isaiah says,

> Hear the word of the LORD...Before she (Israel) travailed, she brought forth (Jesus

Christ, the head of the Body of Christ); before her pain came (the Tribulation), she was delivered of a man child (the Body of Christ taken in Rapture I). Who hath heard such a thing? who hath seen (past tense) such things? (some will see the Rapture[6]) Shall (future tense) the earth be made to bring forth in one day? (Rapture II) or shall a nation be born at once? (Israel's remnant) for as soon as Zion travailed, she brought forth her children (more than one child, one group for Heaven, the other for Earth).

Genesis 3:15 introduced the seed of the woman, and Galatians 3:16 shows that this seed is Christ. Respectively, these scriptures say,

I will put enmity between thee (Satan) and the woman, and between thy seed (the False Prophet) and her seed (Christ); it (the flaming sword placed to the east of Eden[7]) shall bruise thy head ('his right eye...utterly darkened'[8]), and thou shalt bruise his (Christ's) heel (the Crucifixion bruised his heel).

Now to Abraham and his seed were the promises made. He saith not, And to seeds, as of many; but as of **one**, And to thy seed, **which is Christ**.

The seed is Jesus Christ, yet, the last verse of Revelation 12 talks about "the remnant of her seed," showing that more is in view than just Christ. However, before the Tribulation arrives, Israel will have already given birth to both Jesus Christ, who is the head of the Body of Christ, the dead in Christ and the part, one foot, of the Body of Christ that goes to Heaven in the first Rapture. The other foot is still to be born a little later on.

The earth will give birth to the other foot on Tishri 1, when the last rank of saints will be expelled from Earth and be born into a new world, Heaven, in Rapture II. Afterward, Israel's remnant will be born again on Earth the same day, the day of God's Wrath.

As soon as she travails, she brings forth children, some for Heaven, others for Earth. During this time of Jacob's trouble,[9] the Jewish remnant finally realizes that Jesus Christ is their true Messiah. They will live on Earth at the beginning of the Millennium. God never leaves himself without a witness on Earth.

Notice that the twelve stars on the woman's head have already been crowned. When does that happen? at Rapture I. Revelation 4:4 says that the elders sat on thrones, "and they had on their heads crowns of gold." Twelve of the elders are the progenitors of Israel, Joseph and his brothers. (The other twelve are the Jewish apostles.) Therefore, the Rapture is past. That foot of the Body of Christ was born into Heaven "before her pain came," before the Tribulation began.

The fact that this great sign is seen in Heaven shows that a great number of the saved of Israel are already in Heaven. This includes both Old Testament and the Hebrew Christians among the Church saints. Does this woman then represent the Church also? I think not, because she does not have 24 stars on her head, only twelve. We are talking about Israel.

The time here is the middle of the Tribulation, when Satan is cast down to Earth and the seventh head of the dragon, the False Prophet, is crowned. Verses 6 and 14 show that there are yet three and one half years of the seven left.

Israel's labor pains intensify greatly at this point. She still has more children to bring into the fold.

The sign of the dragon in Heaven

John sees another sign in Heaven, but it is not a "great" one. He describes it and then shows how it interacts with Israel.

> And there appeared another wonder (sign) in heaven; and behold a great red dragon, having seven heads and ten horns, and **seven crowns** upon his heads. And his tail drew

the third part of the stars of heaven, and did
cast them to the earth: and the dragon stood
before the woman which was ready to be delivered, for to devour her child as soon as it
was born.[10]

Red is Satan's color for he was a murderer from the
beginning.[11] He caused Cain's blood to be shed. The great
red dragon is Satan himself. The seven heads represent sev-
en world empires and their kings that are stained with red
because they are energized and controlled by the dragon and
his fallen angels.

All seven heads are crowned, so the last empire,
headed up by the False Prophet, is now in power. It is the
middle of the Tribulation.

The third part of the stars of heaven that are cast
down are the fallen angels, the demons. They arrive in the
middle of the Tribulation and turn savagely on Israel, trying
to annihilate her. The duration and intensity of her birth
pains pick up abruptly. "Death, and Hell," the Satan possessed False Prophet, that we heard about in Revelation 6:8
begin an immediate campaign against Christians and Israel.

Daniel 8:8-10 is the Old Testament passage that parallels Revelation 12:4.

And out of one of them (the four winds of
heaven) came forth a little horn (Satan),
which waxed exceeding great, toward the
south, and toward the east, and toward the
pleasant land. And it waxed great, even to the
host of heaven (the angels); and it cast down
some of the host (one third) and of the stars
to the ground, and stamped upon them.

Who is not the man child
Remember that the time in view is Mid-Tribulation as John
continues telling us about the woman:

And she brought forth a man (neuter gender)
child, who was to rule all nations with a rod

289

of iron: and her child was caught up unto
God, and *to* his throne.

Some think this man child is Christ. Psalm 2:9 says
of Christ, "Thou shalt break them with a rod of iron; thou
shalt dash them in pieces like a potter's vessel." However,
this is the middle of the Tribulation, not 30 A.D., when
Christ returned to Heaven.

Others think the man child represents the over
comers of the Church. Revelation 2:26,27 says of the
Church,

And he that overcometh, and keepeth my
works unto the end, to him will I give power
over the nations: And he shall rule them with
a rod of iron; as the vessels of a potter shall
they be broken to shivers: even as I received
of my Father.

Before deciding between Christ and the Church
saints, as if those are our only options, think about this. Israel is in labor. It is the middle of the Tribulation.

Isaiah 66:7 says, "**Before** she travailed, she brought
forth; before her pain came, she was delivered of a man
child." Christ was born **before** her pain started. Therefore,
this is not talking about Christ. The same goes for the
Church saints. They too were born into Heaven before Israel's labor pains began during the Tribulation.

Who is the man child?

We do not have far to go to find the answer. By our playwright's design, to make the identification of the man child
easy, we were just introduced to this group in the preceding
chapter, Revelation 11.

They are the Lord's two witnesses, Moses and Elijah, both Israelites, killed after three and one half years of
the Tribulation, resurrected after three and one half days, and
called up to Heaven. They are a very small group, but "they
heard a great voice from heaven saying unto them, Come up
hither. And they ascended up to heaven in a cloud."

Because they are believers, they are over comers and are included in the group to which Jesus said, "he that overcometh, and keepeth my (Christ's) works unto the end, to him will I (Christ) give power over the nations: And he shall rule them with a rod of iron."[12]

The sands of time

Next, John gives us an important piece of information concerning time that locks this into the middle of the seven years. He adds,

> And the woman (Israel) fled into the wilderness, where she hath a place prepared of God, that they should feed her there a thousand two hundred *and* threescore days.

This 1,260 days is the same as "a time, and times, and half a time" in 12:14. It is three and a half years, the last half of the complete seven-year, 2,520-day Tribulation.

Revelation 12:14 tells us that the woman will be nourished three and a half years "from the **face** of the serpent." Therefore, the woman's wilderness stay coincides with the ministry of Satan in the False Prophet during the last three and a half years of the Tribulation.

These 1,260 days end the day of the Judgment of the Nations, the day dominion is legally taken from Satan, the day the battle of Armageddon begins.

Who is told to flee to the wilderness, Israel or the Church? Matthew 24:15-22 says,

> When ye therefore shall see the abomination of desolation (the idol), spoken of by Daniel the prophet, stand in the holy place (in the temple)...Then **let them which be in Judaea flee** into the mountains....But pray ye that your flight be not in the winter, neither on the sabbath day: For then shall be great tribulation, such as was not since the beginning of the world to this time, no, nor ever shall be. And except those days (the 1,260)

should be shortened, there should no flesh be saved: but for the elect's sake those days shall be shortened (to 1,040).

It is Israel that is to flee, not the Bride of Christ. The Bride is not on Earth at this time. They went to Heaven in Rapture I, before the Tribulation began. The believers during this period are called Tribulation saints. They are the last foot of the Body of Christ, but not the part called the Bride of Christ, which is the first foot to be born into Heaven.

The last half of the seven-years is called the Great Tribulation. It is shortened to 1,040 days (Daniel 8:14's 2,300 - 1,260), which run out on the Day of God's Wrath. The elect, the Tribulation saints, the last foot of the Body of Christ, are taken to Heaven then. However, the full 1,260 days of the last half end the day Armageddon begins. Christ must be on Earth before that battle can begin. John saw

the beast, and the kings of the earth, and their armies, gathered together to make war against him (Christ) that sat on the horse, and against his army.[13]

First, the confederated army attacks Israel on the Feast of Trumpets on the 1,040th day after the middle of the Tribulation. The Lord stops them that same day with what is called the Sword of the Lord, the asteroid. Then, they re-group to attack Christ himself at the end of the full 1,260 days of the last half of the Tribulation. That last battle starts at the full end of the seven years, at the end of the 2,520th day (1,260 + 1,260 = 2,520), which is the end of Satan's official reign. Dominion is taken from him that day. And what will he do about it?—fight. It will be his last ditch stand. Job 41:9 says, "Behold, the hope of him is in vain!"

War in Heaven

In our play, the scene changes again to give us a more detailed explanation of how the angels were cast down to the Earth in the middle of the Tribulation, 1,260 days after the Seven-Year Peace Treaty was signed. John continues,

And there was war in heaven: Michael and his angels fought against the dragon; and the dragon fought and his angels, And prevailed not; neither was their place found any more in heaven. And the great dragon was cast out, that old serpent, called the Devil, and Satan, which deceiveth the whole world: he was cast out into the earth, and his angels were cast out with him.

Michael is "the archangel,"[14] the "great prince which standeth for the children of thy people"[15] (Israel). He commands two thirds of the angels. When the time comes to drive Satan and his one third of the angels out of Heaven, it is an uneven match, two to one. The deed is quickly accomplished.

Satan lost his planet, and he would very much like to have ours. He has tried to take over ever since he wrested dominion away from Adam. It is ironic that in the end, he will get his wish; he will spend eternity in Hell, in the bowels of this planet. He will not be free to roam the face of the Earth, only to possess her insides. What he coveted will become his prison. If he prayed for the Earth, his prayer will be answered, but in an unexpected way. It is too bad, but he is an incorrigible.

This casting down will be accomplished in stages. Ezekiel 28:13-19 gives more details about the destiny of the tail:

Thou (Satan) hast been in Eden the garden of God...Thou art the anointed cherub that covereth; and I have set thee so: thou wast upon the holy mountain of God (Heaven): thou hast walked up and down in the midst of the stones of fire (on Satan's planet Rahab, where our Asteroid Belt is now)....thou hast sinned: therefore **I will cast thee as profane out of the mountain of God**: and I will destroy thee, O covering cherub, from the midst of the stones of fire....**I will cast**

thee to the ground, I will lay thee before
kings, that they may behold thee (he will inhabit the body of the False Prophet). Thou
hast defiled thy sanctuaries (Rahab, Wormwood, and Babylon) by the multitude of thine
iniquities...therefore will I bring forth a fire
(the star called Wormwood) from the midst
of thee (from Rahab), it shall devour thee,
and I will bring thee to ashes upon the earth.

Rejoicing in Heaven

In our play, we hear "rejoice, ye **heavens** (*ouranoi*, plural),
and ye that dwell in **them** (plural)." The ones who now
dwell in the heavens include two thirds of the angels. Those
who dwell in The Heaven include the Old Testament saints,
the Bride of Christ, and God's witnesses, Moses and Elijah.

This passage mentions the power of his Christ, but
he is not yet sitting on his own throne. That comes on the
Feast of Trumpets that begins the Millennium. John says,

And I heard a loud voice saying in heaven
(*ourano*), Now (Concordant, '**Just now**,'
i.e., Mid-Tribulation) is come salvation, and
strength, and the kingdom of our God (the
Father), and the power of his Christ: for the
accuser of **our brethren** (Christians) is cast
down, which accused them before our God
day and night. And **they overcame him
by the blood of the Lamb**, and by the
word of their testimony; and they loved not
their lives unto the death. Therefore rejoice,
ye **heavens**, and ye that dwell in **them**.

The accuser is not to be allowed in Heaven any
more. God is probably very tired of listening to these accu-
sations day in and day out for around 6,000 years.

Woe to Earth dwellers

As John continues, we find out what Satan's reaction is to
the catching up of God's two witnesses, Moses and Elijah.

Woe to the inhabiters of the earth (especially Babylon where one foot of Christ will stamp) and of the sea (especially the Mediterranean where the other foot will stamp)! for the devil is come down unto you, having **great wrath**, because he knoweth that he hath but a short time. And when the dragon saw that he was cast unto the earth, **he** persecuted the woman (Israel) which brought forth the man *child* (God's two witnesses).

Satan's great wrath boils over in the middle of the Tribulation. He really has it in for Israel. When he goes too far and tries to annihilate her, God's fury will come up in his face. That is when He will stamp first with one foot and then with the other. The mountain will hit the sea and the death star will hit Babylon. Do you want to be on Earth at that time and get caught in the crossfire between God and Satan? At that time, it would be far better to be "ye that dwell in them" (the heavens), than to be "the inhabiters of the earth."

Her Place

Believers in Israel, and especially in Judaea, have a special place prepared for them to flee to. It must be Petra, a city Esau or his descendants cut out of rose-red Nubian sandstone in the Wady Musi, southeast of the Dead Sea. It has a deep narrow two-mile long entrance through the rock that is easily defended. John says,

And to the woman were given two wings of a great eagle, that she might fly into the wilderness, into **her place**, where she is nourished for a time, and times, and half a time (three and a half years), from the face of the serpent (Satan looking out through the eyes of the False Prophet).

Petra has amazing temples and other buildings carved out of the 200 to 400-foot-high cliffs. Outside, they are beautifully ornate. Inside each architectural facade are extensive caves in which one could be secure. There is a road, a High Place and an outdoor Amphitheater.

Standing in the city, you can look for about a mile in any direction and see sandstone cliffs carved with the exteriors of theaters, palaces, temples, dwellings and tombs. One temple-like tomb near the entrance has four tall pyramidal obelisks above the doorway.[16]

New Testaments have been placed in Petra for the Israelites to find upon their arrival. They need the scriptures badly.

If anyone is planning a trip to Petra, please contact me c/o Archer Press, 8641 Sugar Gum Rd., Riverside, CA 92508, (909) 653-4110, FAX (909) 697-8960. I would like to send copies of my books, "Exit 2007, The Secret of Secrets Revealed," "Heaven Found, A Butter and Honey Star," and "Revealtions 2000," to be placed there also.

This is one way I can leave a legacy to these persecuted people. It is the only way I can speak to them at the very time that they need understanding the most. They should prepare themselves to go in Rapture II, for the Lord has said that "over Edom will I cast out my shoe."[17] This refers to the time when he will stamp the other foot on the earth at Babylon. A smaller rock will fall somewhere on Edom.

In fact, the indignation is on all nations and upon the federated army attacking Israel, but Edom will come in for her share. Isaiah 34:1-8 says,

> COME near, ye nations...let the earth hear... For the indignation of the LORD is upon all nations, and his fury upon all their armies: he hath utterly destroyed them....For my sword shall be bathed in heaven: behold, it shall come down upon Idumea (Edom), and upon the people of my curse (Babylon), to judgment....for the LORD hath a sacrifice in Bozrah, and a great slaughter in the land of Idumea.....For it is the day of the LORD'S vengeance (Tishri 1), and the year (5768) of recompences for the controversy of Zion.

The Dragon's flood

The Lord will feed the people left in Petra after Rapture II until the 1,260 days are over. There will be 220 days left (2,520 - 2,300 = 220) (or 1,260 - 1,040 = 220). He will even use the Earth to help her. As John continues, we find out that an astonishing thing happens:

> And the serpent cast out of his mouth water as a flood after the woman, that he might cause her to be carried away of the flood. And the earth helped the woman, and the earth opened her mouth, and swallowed up the flood which the dragon cast out of his mouth.

This water could represent soldiers. Isaiah 59:19 says, "When the enemy shall come in like a flood, the Spirit of the LORD shall lift up a standard against him." If it does represent soldiers, they would be demon-possessed.

Water represents the Holy Spirit welling up within us. In John 4:14, Jesus says,

> But whosoever drinketh of the water that I shall give him shall never thirst; but the water that I shall give him shall be in him a well of water springing up into everlasting life.

Could water itself represent spirits, both bad and good? the good spirit coming out of Christ's mouth and the bad spirits coming out of Satan's mouth? One thing that makes this seem possible is Revelation 16:13,14. We can be certain that unclean spirits can come out of the mouth of the Great Red Dragon.

> And I saw three unclean spirits like frogs (leaping) *come* **out of the mouth of the dragon**, and out of the mouth of the beast, and out of the mouth of the false prophet. For **they are the spirits of devils**, working miracles, *which* go forth unto the kings of the

earth...to gather them to the battle of that great day of God Almighty (Armageddon).

The unclean spirits probably go into bodies of the unsaved to do Satan's bidding, so it looks like the "water as a flood" can be soldiers. Whether literal water or demon-possessed soldiers, the earth will open her mouth and swallow the flood.

It is also possible that this splitting of the Earth is because of the earthquake that happens the same hour that the two witnesses ascend up to heaven. As soon as Israel's "man child," the two witnesses, are "caught up unto God," we are told that the "woman fled into the wilderness." She is given "two wings" to fly into the wilderness, where she is to be nourished three and a half years. This places the serpent's flood in the middle of the Tribulation.

Earth has opened her mouth before. Numbers 16:30-33 tells us of the time the earth swallowed up Korah (bald), Dathan (rites), and Abiram (a high father, father of fraud) because they intruded into the priestly office when "no man taketh this honour unto himself, but he that is called of God, as was Aaron."[18] Notice how even the meaning of their names tells a story. With bald rites (worthless rituals), a fraudulent high father intruded into the priestly office.

The kingdom was taken away from Saul (destroyer) and given to David (beloved) because Saul intruded into the priestly office[19] and consulted the witch of Endor.[20] It will have its parallel in the time of the end.

During the Tribulation, both the Beast and False Prophet will appropriate titles that they have no right to. The Beast will be called Pope, High Father, Pontifex Maximus, Vicar of Christ, Vicar of God, sovereign over the church and the world, etc. The False Prophet will probably claim to be God incarnate. He will actually be Satan possessed.

Of Korah's group, Moses said,

But if the LORD make a new thing, and the earth open her mouth, and swallow them up, with all that appertain unto them, and they go down quick into the pit; then ye shall under-

> stand that these men have provoked the
> LORD. And it came to pass...the ground
> clave asunder that was under them: And the
> earth opened her mouth, and swallowed them
> up, and their houses, and all the men that ap-
> pertained unto Korah, and all their goods.
> They...went down alive into the pit, and the
> earth closed upon them (Numbers 16:30-33).

We can be certain that this will also have its parallel during the last half of the Tribulation, called the Great Tribulation.

War against the saints
Satan is furious when the earth opens her mouth. Who does he take it out on? Hebrew Christians.

> And the dragon was wroth with the woman,
> and went to make war with the remnant of
> her seed, which keep the commandments of
> God, and have the testimony of Jesus Christ.

Living believers will go to Heaven in Rapture II, when the last foot of the Body of Christ is expelled from planet Earth.

1 Matthew 25:1-10
2 Revelation 19:8
3 Revelation 16:19
4 Ezekiel 10:2
5 Ezekiel 39:12,13
6 Psalm 40:1-3
7 Genesis 3:24
8 Zechariah 11:17
9 Jeremiah 30:7
10 Revelation 12:3,4
11 John 8:44
12 Revelation 2:26,27
13 Revelation 19:19
14 Jude 9
15 Daniel 12:1
16 Thompson, Frank Charles. *The New Chain-Reference Bible*, 4th ed. (Indianapolis, B.B. Kirkbride Bible Co., Inc., 1964) p. 352
17 Psalm 108:9
18 Hebrews 5:4
19 I Samuel 13:8-10
20 I Samuel 28:7-17

𝒯wo 𝒲ild ℬeasts

Revelation 13

𝕆ur wonderful playwright, the Lord Jesus Christ, takes us back now to the very first of the Tribulation. In this scene, the Church saints are already in heaven for verse six says that the first beast blasphemes "them that dwell in heaven." These two beasts are crowned some time after the Rapture has taken place.

Jesus wants to tell us more about the two principal leaders that will rule during the Tribulation, the Seventieth Week of Daniel. Since they are both wild and evil, he calls them by the descriptive title "*therion*," wild beast.

The first, the Beast, will rule 42 months, 1,260 days, the first three and a half years of the seven. The 1,260 days run from Sivan 6, 5761 (May 28, 2001) to Cheshvan 23, 5765 (November 7, 2004). The second beast, the False Prophet, will operate 1,260 days during the last half of the Tribulation. They will each have a ministry of the same duration as Jesus Christ did in 30 A.D. It looks like the second beast will be deposed on the 1,040th day, the Day of God's Wrath, but he will still rally the leaders of the nations together to attack Christ when he returns. Both men will be present to face Christ at Armageddon for Revelation 19:20 says,

> And the beast was taken, and with him the false prophet...These **both** (two different men) were cast alive into a lake of fire.

The first beast is demon possessed. The second is Satan possessed. Satan dwells in him from Mid-Tribulation on. He is the final Antichrist in a string of antichrists. He is the pseudo christ, a god man, where Christ is the God man. There is a vast difference between these two extremes.

The False Prophet does some miracles, "denieth the Father and the Son," and commands men to worship an idol. Christ says to worship God, his Father, and not to worship idols. Men will have to choose whom they will serve in the hardest of times when many will be martyred for their faith. In those days Bibles, churches, and Christians will be tarred with the same brush and set on fire. Satan will attempt to wipe out all vestiges of Christianity from the face of the Earth.

The False Prophet is a liar. First John 2:22 says, "Who is a liar but he that denieth that Jesus is the Christ? He is antichrist, that denieth the Father and the Son."

Second John 7 says that "many deceivers are entered into the world, who confess not that Jesus Christ is come in the flesh. This is a (margin, the) deceiver and an (the) anti-christ." The article is there in the Greek in both instances. Therefore, we have a good chance of being able to identify the deceiver (Satan) and the antichrist (False Prophet).

Some say the first beast dies and is resurrected to become the second beast. This cannot be true. The second is different from the first. Daniel 7: 24 says that the one called another, the False Prophet, "shall be diverse from the first." They are two different men. The first is a leader in Rome, the second the leader of Israel. Both sign the seven-year peace treaty.[1] Both are cast alive into the Lake of Fire.

The pair have bilateral power, ecclesiastical and political, and will move their base of operations to the literal city of Babylon on the Euphrates River. It seems that the first leader of the world empire will move to Babylon in temporary quarters to oversee the construction of the permanent buildings. As soon as they are finished, the second man will pull off a coup and take over as the Supreme Ruler of the Church and the World.

The beast out of the sea

As this section of the play begins, we see John standing on a sandy beach. The waves of the Mediterranean surge and ebb, busily sculpting the sand into the patterns it likes. It is the first day of the Tribulation, the Feast of Weeks in 2001.

John continues his narration. His script is found in Revelation 13:1.

> AND I stood upon the sand of the sea, and saw a beast rise up out of the sea, having seven heads and ten horns, and upon his horns **ten crowns**, and upon his heads the name of blasphemy.

This beast actually rises out of all nations because the sea represents all nations. Revelation 17:15 explains that

> The waters which thou sawest, where the whore (the Mystery Religion of Babylon) sitteth, are peoples, and multitudes, and nations, and tongues.

The harlot religion is connected with this beast. They both are seen in the water. She is already sitting on him as he rises out of the water. Both are energized by the great red dragon.

The main name of blasphemy that is upon all seven heads of this beast is Pontifex Maximus. This is the title of the great high priest of the Mystery Religion of Babylon.

In his book, The Book of The Revelation, William R. Newell says,

> When the Babylonian cult of the Magians was driven out of Babylon, they found a haven at Pergamum, and Pergamum's king, Attalus III (B.C. 133), willed his kingdom and title into the hands of the Romans (Justin p. 364, Strabo). The title of the Magian high priest was, 'Chief Bridge Builder,' meaning the **one who spans the gap between** *mortals* and *Satan* and **his hosts.** In Latin, this title was written, *Pontifex Maximus.*[2] (the bold emphasis is mine)

That the Pontifex Maximus was the chief bridge builder between mortals and Satan and his fallen angels is astonishing when you stop and think about it. If this was true in ancient Babylon, it will probably be true in Babylon III also. This gives us more insight into the meaning of Revelation 2:24, which mentions "the depths of Satan, as they speak." Infallible? I think not.

As John continues, we find that the descriptions of this beast refer us back to Daniel 7, where Daniel saw four great beasts also come up from the sea (nations). John says,

> And the beast which I saw was like unto a leopard (Greece[3]), and his feet were as *the feet* of a bear (Media-Persia[4]), and his mouth as the mouth of a lion (Babylon[5]): and the dragon gave him his power, and his (Satan's) seat (throne), and great authority.[6]

The dragon's throne is the seat of the ruler of the world empire. This throne will be occupied by Satan when he indwells the False Prophet in the middle of the Tribulation, but first he allows six other leaders to sit on it. Four heads are described in Daniel 7:2-8,17:

> And four great beasts came up from the sea (nations), diverse one from another. The first was like a lion (Babylon[7])...a second, like to a bear (Media-Persia[8])...another, like a leopard (Greece[9])...After this...a fourth beast (Rome[10]), dreadful and terrible, and strong exceedingly; and it had great iron teeth: it devoured and brake in pieces, and stamped the residue with **the feet** (the end time world empire) of it: and it was diverse from all the beasts that were before it; and it had ten horns (kings)....there came up among them another little horn (the False Prophet), before whom there were three of the first horns plucked up by the roots: and, behold, in this horn were

eyes like the eyes of man, and a mouth speaking great things....These great beasts... are four kings, which shall arise out of the earth.

In Daniel, the ten kings appear during the time of the feet of the fourth beast, which represents Rome. These ten kings receive their crowns in Revelation 13:1. The two passages can be put together to enlarge our picture. It sorts the three world empires into their proper order and identifies the feet of Rome as the empire in view during the reign of the ten kings. We know this is correct because the legs of the image in Nebuchadnezzar's dream represent Rome and there are ten toes on the feet.[11]

Since the beast seen in Revelation 13:1-3 comes out of the nations, and is like Greece, Media-Persia, and Babylon, it represents world empires. It's seven heads and seven kings are listed below. Revelation 17:10-14 shows that at the time of the Rapture,

there are seven kings; five are fallen, and one **is,** *and* the other is not yet come...ten kings, which have received no kingdom as yet; but receive power as kings one hour with the beast....These shall make war with the Lamb...and they that **are** with him (Christ) *are* called, and chosen, and faithful.

AT THE TIME OF THE RAPTURE

Five kings are fallen

(1) Babylon I	Tower of Babel begun	Nimrod
(2) Babylon II		Nebuchadnezzar
(3) Media-Persia		Cyrus
(4) Greece		Alexander the Great
(5) Roman Empire		Caesars

One king is

(6) Ecclesiastic Rome		The Pope

One king is yet to come

(7) Babylon III	Tower of Babel finished	False Prophet

At the beginning of the Tribulation, I believe the Tribulation Pope will be elected Secretary General of the United Nations. When he receives that "crown," he will become the Beast of Revelation 13:4-10. Then ten sub-regents will be chosen to help him rule the world.

As Revelation 13 begins, we are viewing this beast at the very beginning of the Tribulation, when the sixth world empire elects the Tribulation Pope Secretary General of the United Nations and the ten subordinate kings receive their crowns. This chart changes slightly from the one above.

AT THE BEGINNING OF THE TRIBULATION

Five kings are fallen

(1) Babylon I   Tower of Babel begun   Nimrod
(2) Babylon II   Nebuchadnezzar
(3) Media-Persia   Cyrus
(4) Greece   Alexander the Great
(5) Roman Empire   Caesars

One king is

(6) United Nations   The Roman Beast
                ten sub-regents

One king is yet to come

(7) Babylon III Tower of Babel finished   False Prophet

The False Prophet will not be crowned until the middle of the Tribulation, when the seventh head is crowned. This beast that represents the world empires is like a costume donned by the great red dragon, who is Satan, the one energizing and controlling all these world empires. When we saw the great red dragon in Revelation 12:3,4, he had

> seven heads and ten horns, and **seven crowns** upon his heads, And his tail drew the third part of the stars of heaven, and did cast them to the earth.

The casting down of the fallen angels comes in the middle of the Tribulation. Revelation 12:6,14 fixes the time that the seventh crown is put on the False Prophet's head.

Revelation 17:3,8 gives us more information about Satan, the great red dragon. It says,

> I saw a woman (this is the harlot Mystery Religion of Babylon) sit upon a **scarlet** coloured beast (i.e., the great red dragon), full of names of blasphemy, having seven heads and ten horns....The beast that thou sawest was (in Judas Iscariot), and is not (in man now); and **shall ascend out of the bottomless pit**, and go into perdition.

Before the Flood

Satan controlled the bulk of mankind before Noah's Flood, but that was before the first head of the great red dragon as depicted here. Babel was the first world empire and the mother of the Mystery Religion of Babylon.

In the days before the Flood, the fallen angels took human wives of all whom they chose, and hybrid children of giant stature were born that had to be destroyed by the Flood.[12]

In our days, the demons would have us believe that they are producing hybrid children of small stature. Since the fallen angels who took human wives before the Flood were put in prison,[13] the demons had to figure out a different way of compromising humanity. The UFO literature is full of what is supposed to be their modern-day hybridization program. It also demonstrates the demon's abilities to appear, disappear, fly, and change their appearance at will. Another thing that is clearly apparent is their ability to exercise mind-control over their victims. They can use this ability to control people whether they are seen or remain invisible.

Our only defense against them is Christ. I know personally that we, in our own strength, are totally powerless against their greater strength. I have been tested.

One Halloween night years ago, I left a Christian tract someone had given my children on the kitchen table. From the picture and caption on the cover, you could not tell that it was Christian. It said something about the Devil. In the wee hours of that night, the demons decided to test me.

I awoke suddenly, only to realize that something was holding me down. I could not move a muscle. It was like several people were sitting on me, but I could not see them. I tried to scream for Christ to make them stop and quickly found out that even my tongue was paralyzed. Panic struck when I found out that I was totally paralyzed. I couldn't breathe. It felt like someone had a pillow over my face and was trying to suffocate me too. I was terrified and thought they were trying to kill me.

I started doing the only thing left to me, screaming in my mind words something like this: "Christ, make them stop, in the name of Jesus, stop." Then I thought of a scripture verse, which I can't remember at the moment, but it probably is in the Gospels. It just flew into my brain at the exact moment when I needed it. As soon as I recited it in my thoughts, they released me and I caught my breath in relief. The paralysis was gone. The episode had seemed a lot longer than it actually lasted. I certainly do not want anything to do with the demons. Their strength is too terrifyingly real.

Babel

After Noah's Flood, the seven heads of the dragon started with the Tower of Babel at Babylon I. Nimrod was king. He was the first wild beast of the seven. This is when the harlot Mystery Religion of Babylon first mounted the great red dragon. It will end with another Tower of BABEL and the False Prophet, "and when he cometh, he must continue a short space."

I did not intend to capitalize Babel above; it just happened. The Lord did it. This is the sixth time that a word or phrase has come out capitalized without either the shift key or the caps lock key staying down. Sometimes, it seems that he wants to emphasize something so I will know I am on the right track. Other times, he seems to do it so I will add more emphasis to something important, as when he capitalized THE FINE LINEN IS THE RIGHTEOUSNESS OF SAINTS. We must confess our sins and be filled with the Holy Spirit to go to Heaven in Rapture I. We have to be wearing the white wedding garment. The Bride always wears white. Others will go to Heaven in Rapture II.

When the Rapture takes place, "one is"[14] in office, the Pope of Rome. When the Tribulation starts four Jewish years later, the Tribulation Pope becomes the Beast of Revelation 13:4-10. He is elected Secretary General of the world empire, Babylon III. After 1,260 days, the False Prophet wrests rulership of Babylon III away from the Beast. It seems likely that it will be as soon as construction of three towers, the twin towers of the United Nations plus the Tower of Babel, are completed.

As demonstrated for us at the original Tower of Babel, there will be a babel of languages at Babylon III, both in the world church and in the UN. At the present time, the United Nations has six official working languages, English, Chinese, French, Russian, Spanish and Arabic.

It is significant that construction of the headquarters in New York began in September, 1948, after Israel became a nation on May 14, 1948. She is a member too. The Secretariat Building was ready for occupancy in the middle of 1950. By the spring of 1951, that location became the official address of the United Nations. However, during the Tribulation, the world government headquarters will be moved to Babylon on the Euphrates River in Iraq.

Satan indwells the False Prophet and this god man controls not only the world empire, but world religion for a short time, exactly 1,040 days, until the wrath of Christ, the God man, is poured out on Babylon III.

At that time, the False Prophet will be wounded. His "arm shall be clean dried up, and his right eye shall be utterly darkened,"[15] fulfilling Genesis 3:15's "it shall bruise thy head." However, even after that, he will have enough power to gather the armies of the Earth to fight Christ when he returns.

The wound that healed

In our play, as John continues reading the script, we find that one head of this beast has been symbolically wounded and healed. John says,

> And I saw one of his heads **as it were** wounded to death; and his deadly wound was

healed: and all the world wondered after the beast.[16]

The head of this beast, representing a world empire, does not have to be actually wounded here, although he may be. It took me a long time to realize this. The scripture says **"as it were** wounded to death." That is figurative language. Verse twelve in the Lamsa translation gives us a clue as to what this represents:

> And all the power of the first wild beast before him (the False Prophet) was exercised by him, and he caused the earth and those who dwell therein to worship the first beast, whose deadly wound was healed.

The very **first wild beast** in this series was Nimrod at the Tower of Babel—Babylon I. The **first beast whose deadly wound was healed** was Nimrod's son, Tammuz. According to Ezekiel 8:14,18, God's fury is to be poured out on **"women weeping for Tammuz,"** who was worshipped as the sun god. He was a counterfeit Son of God in the harlot Mystery Religion of Babylon set up, under Satan's direction, by Nimrod and queen Semiramis at Babel.

When the last vestiges of Christianity are stripped from the Christian-pagan mixture that is today's Roman religion, the underlying pagan worship of Tammuz may be revealed. The pictures used of the Saviour show him with light hair like Tammuz. Christ was Jewish and had black hair, which Rembrandt must have realized, since he painted him with black hair. The Song of Solomon 5:10-16 actually describes Jesus Christ. A lot of it is symbolic, but the part about his hair is unmistakable. It is an interesting passage. Maybe you can unravel the meaning of more of the symbols.

> My beloved is white and ruddy, the chiefest among ten thousand. His head is as the most fine gold (symbol of deity), **his locks are bushy, and black as a raven**. His eyes are as the eyes of doves (symbol of the Holy

Spirit) by the rivers of waters, washed with milk, and fitly set. His cheeks are as a bed of spices, as sweet flowers: his lips like lilies, dropping sweet smelling myrrh. His hands are as gold rings set with the beryl: his belly is as bright ivory overlaid with sapphires (sapphire means Saturn plus dear). His legs are as pillars of marble, set upon sockets of fine gold: his countenance is as Lebanon (white), excellent as the cedars (tall and stately). His mouth is most sweet: yea, he is altogether lovely. This is my beloved, and this is my friend, O daughters of Jerusalem.

The Mystery Religion of Babylon went underground and donned the robes of Rome, but it will throw them off again after the Rapture is past. During the Tribulation years, both the Beast and the False Prophet will move their base of operations to the literal city of Babylon on the Euphrates River in Iraq. It will be the capitol city of the world, and will be the headquarters of world religion.

All nations will have ambassadors there. They will also set up booths for displaying items for international trade.

Right now, Christians who understand the scriptures are the salt that keeps all this from happening. The Holy Spirit that is dwelling in them is the ultimate restraining influence. Babylon III and the Tower of Babel can only come to pass when the proper date comes on God's Blueprint of Time.

God has complete overall control. He is gathering them together under Christ's two feet for destruction. Matthew 22:44 says, "The LORD said unto my Lord, Sit thou on my right hand, till I make thine enemies thy footstool."

When the time is ripe, Christ will stamp one foot on the Mediterranean Sea. Immediately, a falling mountain will destroy the army invading Israel. He will stamp with the other foot on Babylon and a falling star will destroy the world empire housed at Babylon. The Lord Jesus Christ will also drop his "shoe" (i.e., a smaller stone) on Edom.[17]

The Roman Beast

There is a clever and progressive switch-over in the script of Revelation thirteen. First, we got a glimpse of the great world empires that the great red dragon has put on like a costume, and then, suddenly, the sixth head takes on the features of a man. He is the Beast, the leader during the first half of the Tribulation.

We may even have a double reference in verse three. The first head was symbolically wounded and healed, but the sixth head may also be wounded and healed. It is hard to tell for sure. The two views are merging. One grows out of the other.

It is easy to see that verse four progressively zeros in on this particular man that is the first leader of Babylon III. John says,

> And they worshipped the dragon (Satan) which gave power unto the beast (world empire): and **they worshipped the beast** (the sixth head of world empire), saying, Who *is* like unto the beast? (no other is like the Tribulation Pope) who is able to make war with him?

No one feels that they can make war with him. This man heads up both world religion and world government. His bilateral powers give him CONTROL. He is the same man we saw riding the white, red, and black spirit horses in Revelation six. He was given a great sword, which represented control over the armies of the entire world.

As John continues, we find out exactly how long the Beast continues in office.

> And there was given unto him a mouth speaking great things and blasphemies; and power was given unto him to continue forty *and* two months.

One of his many blasphemies is his claim that he is infallible. This mouth is like the mouth of a lion, meaning that he is now sounding like Nebuchadnezzar from the city of Babylon on the Euphrates River.

Nebuchadnezzar said, "Is not this great Babylon, that I have built for the house of the kingdom by the might of my power, and for the honour of my majesty?" He honored himself, not God. As that was rolling off his tongue, Nebuchadnezzar became like a beast for seven years. Just as Nebuchadnezzar was like a beast, this man will be the Beast for seven years.

He probably resides in temporary quarters in Babylon while the twin towers and the Tower of Babel are being built. Isaiah 30:25 shows that towers will be destroyed on the Day of God's Wrath:

> And there shall be upon every high mountain,
> and upon every high hill, rivers and streams
> of waters (seas are out of control) in the day
> of the great slaughter, when the towers fall.

This first beast will remain in power during the first half of the Tribulation, the same period during which God's two witnesses, Moses and Elijah, prophesy.

As John continues, the Beast shows his true colors.

> And he opened his mouth in blasphemy
> against God, to blaspheme his name, and his
> tabernacle, and them that dwell in heaven.

At this point, the Rapture is past. Those dwelling in Heaven include the Church. We have to be sure we are in this group. Get right with God, for look what John tells us next, and this is during the first half of the Tribulation.

> And it was given unto him (the Tribulation
> Pope) to make **war with the saints, and
> to overcome them**: and power was given
> him over all kindreds, and tongues, and na-
> tions (all the world). And all that dwell upon
> the earth shall worship him, whose names are
> **not** written in the book of life of the Lamb

slain from the foundation of the world. If any man have an ear, let him hear. He that leadeth into captivity shall go into captivity: he that killeth with the sword must be killed with the sword (be patient, there is justice). Here is the patience and the faith of the saints.

What will the Beast claim that will allow him to go to war with the saints? probably that they are heretics because they protest against some of his teachings that do not jibe with Scripture. (That is what the Popes claimed in the middle ages.) This is where some of the martyrs we saw when the fifth seal was broken came from. They "were slain for the word of God, and for the testimony which they held."[18]

In Jesus' long monologue, he warned,

> I have a few things against thee, because thou sufferest that woman Jezebel (worshiper of Baal), which calleth herself a prophetess, to teach and to seduce my servants to commit fornication (join with the world), and to eat things sacrificed unto idols. And I gave her space to repent of her fornication; and she repented not. Behold, I will cast her into a bed, and them that commit adultery with her into **great tribulation**, except they repent of their deeds. And I will kill her children with death; and all the churches shall know that I am he which searcheth the reins and hearts.[19]

The Israeli beast, the False Prophet

Here, the script of our play begins to tell us about a different man, called "another." He is the False Prophet, the seventh head of the great red dragon, who comes to power in the middle of the Tribulation. Here is the main player, the Satan-possessed man for whom Babylon and the Tower of Babel are rebuilt. He will take the world by storm and occupy Satan's throne.

This man is also referred to as "another" in the Old Testament. Those passages tie in with Revelation 13:11:

> And I beheld **another** beast coming up out
> of the earth (Israel, God's land); and he
> (Satan in the False Prophet) had two horns
> (Satan's two comings to power) like a lamb
> (Christ, the Lamb of God), and he spake as a
> dragon (Satan).

As far as we know, this is the second time Satan is allowed to inhabit the body of a man. The first time was when he entered into Judas Iscariot to betray Christ. That time, Satan was able to bruise Jesus' heel and destroy Judas. This time, he will not be able to touch Christ, so he will take his rage out on the remnant of Israel's seed.[20]

The False Prophet, Satan's robotic body, takes complete control away from Satan's puppet, the Beast. The False Prophet is a Jew. If he were not, Israel would not accept him. Jesus said "I am come in my Father's name, and ye receive me not: if **another** shall come in his own name, him ye will receive." Zechariah 11:16,17 says, "For, lo, I will raise up a shepherd **in the land**...Woe to the idol shepherd." This is that idol shepherd "that leaveth the flock" and goes to Babylon.

As John continues, we see that the script can reach back beyond the Beast, back to the first head, Nimrod. Chances are good that this is a double reference and refers to Nimrod, Tammuz, and the sixth head of the world empire.

> And he exerciseth all the power of **the first
> beast** (Nimrod at the Tower of Babel) before
> him, and causeth the earth and them which
> dwell therein to worship **the first beast,
> whose deadly wound was healed**
> (Nimrod's son, Tammuz).

History repeats itself, by the Master's design. At Babel, Semiramis said that Tammuz was killed by a wild boar and came back to life. Not only will the Tower of Babel be rebuilt, but under Satan's guidance, the Mystery Religion of Babylon will become the leading religion of the world. What was started at Babylon I will be finished at Babylon III.

It won't work. One evening long ago, when tired of typing all day, I threw myself down across the bed saying to myself, "What am I doing all this work for? It probably won't be published anyway." My Bible flew open in my hand and I saw a rectangle of light on Jeremiah 50:2. In awe, I read,

> Declare ye among the nations, and publish, and set up a standard; publish, *and* conceal not: say, Babylon is taken, Bel is confounded, Merodach (Marduk) is broken in pieces; her (Babylon's) idols are confounded, her images are broken in pieces.

Bel, meaning ancient, the patron god of Babylon, was Baal, meaning lord, to the Hebrews. He was identified with Marduk, head of the Babylonian pantheon. However, in the verse above, Bel seems to refer to the Satan-possessed False Prophet. Soon both he and Satan will be confounded, the Mystery Religion done away with, and all idols broken.

Jeremiah 51:44 says,

> I will punish Bel in Babylon, and I will bring forth out of his mouth that which he hath swallowed up: and the nations shall not flow together any more unto him: yea, the wall of Babylon shall fall.

Daniel 11:21-23 says that the vile person obtains the kingdom by flatteries, or fraud, and with the arms of a flood:

> And...shall stand up a vile person, to whom they shall not give the honour of the kingdom: but he shall come in peaceably, and obtain the kingdom by flatteries. And with the arms of a flood shall they be overflown from before him, and shall be **broken; yea, also the prince of the covenant** (the Beast). And after the league (the seven-year peace treaty) *made* with him he shall work deceit-

fully: for he shall come up, and shall become strong with a small people.

Instead of "flatteries," the Lamsa translation says that "he shall come suddenly and seize the kingdom by fraud."

The False Prophet comes in peaceably and is subordinate to the Beast at the first of the Tribulation, but this flood seems to represent armed forces. They attack in the middle of the Tribulation. When the initial skirmish is over, the False Prophet has pulled off his coup and is wearing the crown.

The Beast will be broken. He will lose his kingdom and may also be wounded physically. If he was to be hurt badly, it could incapacitate him long enough for the False Prophet to take over the reins of world government.

The False Prophet will probably be of the tribe of Dan, which means judgment, one of the tribes omitted in Revelation 7:4-8 (the other is Ephraim). Genesis 49:17 says that "Dan shall be a serpent by the way, an adder in the path, that biteth the horse heels, so that his rider shall fall backward." The Beast who came on the scene riding a white horse may have an accident engineered by Satan.

Daniel 8:23-25 gives us more details of what the Satan possessed False Prophet will do.

> when the transgressors are come to the full, a king (the False Prophet) of fierce countenance, and understanding dark sentences (riddles, hidden sayings), shall stand up. And his power shall be mighty, but not by his own power (by Satan's): and he shall destroy wonderfully, and shall prosper, and practise, and shall destroy the mighty (God's two witnesses) and the holy people (the Tribulation saints). And through his policy also he shall cause craft to prosper in his hand; and he shall magnify himself in his heart, and by peace shall destroy many: he shall also stand up against the Prince of Princes; but he shall be broken without hand.

The Beast started war against the saints in the first half of the Tribulation. The False Prophet kills God's two witnesses as soon as he comes to power and then the dragon goes to war against the remnant of Israel "which keep the commandments of God, and have the testimony of Jesus Christ."[21] The False Prophet and Satan are trying to wipe out what is left of Christianity. There are many martyrs at this time.

There are so many things that this deceiver does in such a short time that it is hard to see how he could accomplish them so quickly, except that underneath, he is Satan and has one third of the angels under his direction. He works fast and furious for he knows his time is short. The world will hardly know what hit them. Things will fall apart in a hurry. Jeremiah 8:15-17, in the Septuagint, explains why:

> We assembled for peace, but there was no prosperity; for a time of healing, but behold anxiety. We shall hear the neighing of his swift horses out of Dan...and he (the False Prophet of the tribe of Dan) shall come, and devour the land and the fulness of it; the city, and them that dwell in it. For, behold, I send forth against you deadly serpents, which cannot be charmed, and they shall bite you mortally with the pain of your distressed heart.

In Revelation 13:11, he is "another beast." In Daniel 7:8, he is "another little horn." Daniel 7:23-26 gives some more information about this vile man called "another."

> And the ten horns out of this kingdom (world government, Babylon III) are ten kings that shall arise (at the first of the Tribulation): and **another** (the False Prophet) shall rise after them (Mid-Tribulation); and he shall be diverse (different) from the first (Beast), and he shall subdue three kings. And he shall speak great words against the most High (Christ),

and **shall wear out the saints of the most High**, and think to change times and laws: and they (the saints) shall be given into his hand until a time and times and the dividing of time (three and one half years). But the judgment shall sit, and they shall take away his dominion (both Satan's and the False Prophet's), to consume and to destroy it unto the end (of the battle of Armageddon).

In the middle of the Tribulation, the False Prophet will place an image in the Temple in Jerusalem and command that people worship it. Second Thessalonians 2:4 shows that he also "sitteth in the temple of God, shewing himself that he is God." Daniel 8:10-14 also speaks of those days:

And it (Satan, the little horn) waxed great, even to the host of heaven (angels); and it cast down some (one third) of the host and of the stars to the ground, and stamped upon them. Yea, he (Satan in the False Prophet) magnified himself even to the prince (Christ) of the host (of heaven), and by him (the False Prophet) the daily sacrifice was taken away (Mid-Tribulation), and the place of his (the Lord's) sanctuary (the Temple in Jerusalem) was cast down. And an host was given him against the daily sacrifice by reason of transgression, and it cast down the truth to the ground; and it practised, and prospered.... How long shall be the vision concerning the daily sacrifice (during the first half of the Tribulation), and the transgression of desolation (when he sits in the Temple showing that he is God), to give both the sanctuary and the host to be trodden under foot? (the last half of the Tribulation) And he said...Unto two thousand and three hundred days (the Shortened Tribulation); then shall the sanctuary be cleansed (on the Feast of Trumpets).

There are exactly 2,300 days, by Jewish inclusive reckoning, from the Feast of Weeks in 2001 to the Feast of Trumpets in 2007. This count is not true in just any set of years. Only twice, from 1997 to 2003 and from 2001 to 2007, do the days add up to the necessary 2,300. If the Rapture is to take place on a Pentecost Sunday, 1997 to 2003 would not work. Therefore, I believe we are now locked into the 2001 to 2007 period for the Shortened Tribulation.

Instead of "his sanctuary was cast down," the Lamsa Bible says, "and demolished the place of his sanctuary."

Daniel 12:7 shows that he will scatter the power of the holy people all during the last three and one half years of the seven-year Tribulation.

> it shall be for a time (one year), times (two years), and an half; and when he shall have accomplished to scatter the power of the holy people (the saints), all these things shall be finished.

From Daniel 11:28-39, we find out that war (but not Armageddon, which must follow Christ's return) will break out in the middle of the Tribulation. It says that

> his (the False Prophet's) heart shall be against the holy covenant (the seven-year peace treaty); and he shall do exploits, and return to his own land (Israel)...And **arms shall stand on his part,** and they shall pollute the sanctuary of strength (the Temple), and shall take away the daily sacrifice, and they shall place the abomination that maketh desolate (the idol). And such as do wickedly against the covenant shall he corrupt by flatteries....

The flatteries are better understood as smooth talk. Psalm 55:22 in the New American Bible is enlightening: "Softer than butter is his speech, but war is in his heart; His words are smoother than oil, but they are drawn swords."

Chapter 8, Two Wild Beasts

The rest of our passage in Daniel adds some interesting facts about the False Prophet, leader of Israel:

> And the king shall do according to his will; and he shall exalt himself, and magnify himself above every God....in his estate shall he honour the God of forces (*maowz*, a fortified place, a rock; i.e., Satan, as the king of Tyre, the rock): and a god whom his fathers knew not shall he honour with gold, and silver, and with precious stones, and pleasant things.... and shall divide the land for gain.

Today, we have seen Israel give back pieces of their land gained in the Six-Day War of 1967. They have been doing it in the hopes that by so doing, they can have peace. However, the land should not be divided. Joel 3:2 says,

> I will also gather all nations, and will bring them down into the valley of Jehoshaphat, and will plead with them there for my people and for my heritage Israel whom they have scattered among the nations, and **parted my land**.

The image put in the Temple is not just an ordinary idol. As John continues his script in Revelation 13, he says,

> And he (the False Prophet) doeth great wonders, so that he maketh fire come down from heaven on the earth in the sight of men, And deceiveth them that dwell on the earth by *the means of* those miracles which he had power to do in the sight of the beast; saying to them that dwell on the earth, that they should make an image to the beast, which had the wound by a sword, and did live.

It is not easy to figure out what this image will be. Some think it will be of the Beast. It could be an image like

Nebuchadnezzar set up in the plain of Dura.[22] However, it might be of Tammuz. He was worshipped at the Tower of Babel. Ezekiel was taken "in the visions of God to Jerusalem, to the door of the inner gate that looketh toward the north; where was the seat of **the image of jealousy, which provoketh to jealousy.**" He said,

> behold northward at the gate of the altar this **image of jealousy** in the entry....Then he brought me to the door of the gate of the LORD'S house which was toward the north; and, behold, there **sat women weeping for Tammuz**....and they (men) worshipped the sun toward the east....they have filled the land with violence, and have returned to provoke me to anger: and, lo, they put the branch to their nose. Therefore will I also deal in fury.[23]

As John relates the rest of this section of Revelation thirteen, it is hard to imagine that these things could actually take place in our times, but since this play was written by Jesus Christ himself, we know that every tiny detail will happen exactly as planned. He is the Almighty. John starts reading verse fourteen.

> And he (Satan in the False Prophet) had power to give life (*pneuma*, wind, breath, spirit) unto the image of the beast, that the image of the beast should both speak, and cause that as many as would not worship the image of the beast should be killed.

This is a trick. The image has no life in it, but Satan is allowed to give it a voice. Spirits can even speak out of the ground. Speaking to Ariel (Jerusalem), Isaiah 29: 4 says that

> thy voice shall be, as of one that hath a familiar spirit, **out of the ground**, and thy speech shall whisper out of the dust.

Jeremiah 10:14 assures us that "every founder is confounded by the graven image: for his molten image is falsehood, and there is no breath in them. They are vanity, and the work of errors: in the time of their visitation they shall perish."

Habakkuk 2:18-20 says,

> What profiteth the...molten image, and a teacher of lies...Woe unto him (the teacher of lies, the False Prophet) that saith to the wood, Awake; to the dumb stone, Arise, it shall teach! Behold, it is laid over with gold and silver, and there is no breath at all in the midst of it. But the LORD is in his holy temple: let all the earth keep silence before him

The silence is when the judge is being seated at the bench. It is the Judgment Seat of Christ. Destruction is imminent.

The mark of the beast

Next, we hear about the well-known mark of the beast. If anyone takes this mark, he cannot buy or sell, but worse than death itself, he cannot be saved. Revelation 14:9-11 says,

> If any man worship the beast and his image, and receive *his* mark in his forehead, or in his hand, The same shall drink of the wine of the wrath of God, which is poured out without mixture into the cup of his indignation; and he shall be tormented with fire and brimstone in the presence of the holy angels, and in the presence of the Lamb: And the smoke of their torment ascendeth up for ever and ever: and they have no rest day nor night, who worship the beast and his image, and whosoever receiveth the mark of his name.

John continues with the enigmatic information about the mark of the beast. In Revelation 13: 16-18, he says,

And he causeth all, both small and great, rich and poor, free and bond, to receive a mark in their right hand, or in their foreheads: And that no man might buy or sell, save he that had the mark, or the name of the beast, or the number of his name. Here is wisdom. Let him that hath understanding count the number of the beast: for it is the number of a man; and his number *is* Six hundred three score *and* six.

Many people have tried to figure out what this mark of the beast means. In Greek, letters have numerical equivalents, and the Pope's title, Vicarius Filei Deus (Vicar of the Son of God) adds up to 666, so does Teitan, a name for Satan. The Roman Numeral System itself adds up to 666 (I = 1, V = 5, X = 10, L = 50, C = 100, and D = 500) (DCLXVI = 666).

The gold that came to Solomon in one year was 666 talents.[24] This may tie in for the False Prophet will be in charge of the world bank and control all buying and selling.

Six is our universal computer code for international communications, and this will certainly be world government using computers for international communications and world banking.

Babylon's math system was based on the six. We can hear the overtones reverberating yet today. We have 360 degrees in a circle, 36 inches in a yard, and 60 minutes in an hour. The six could easily stand for Babylon, and the 666 for Babylon III. We had Nimrod's Tower of Babel, Nebuchadnezzar's Neo-Babylonian Empire, and will have a final world empire headquartered in rebuilt Babylon on the Euphrates River in Iraq. The Tower of Babel will be rebuilt.

"Nebuchadnezzar made an image of gold, whose height was threescore (60) cubits, and the breadth thereof six cubits: he set it up in the plain of Dura, in the province of Babylon."[25] The 60 plus 6 equals 66, and that was Babylon II.

The False Prophet will also set up an image, this time in the temple in Jerusalem. If it is gold, remember that the number of talents of gold that Solomon received was 666.

Whatever else the mark is, six is the number of man, and the False Prophet will say, "I am a God, I sit in the seat of God, in the midst of the seas; yet **thou art a man, and not God**, though thou set thine heart as the heart of God."[26]

The mark may even be used as it appears in the Greek, Chi, Xi, Sigma, *χξς*. The middle letter even resembles a serpent, as Seiss pointed out in his book, *The Apocalypse*.[27] He said,

> The 'mark' itself is at once a number and a name. The Apostle tells us what it is. As he gives it, it is made up of two Greek characters which stand for the name of Christ, with a third, the figure of a crooked serpent, put between them...the name of God's Messiah transformed into a Devil sacrament.

It could be like the Chinese chop, a mark that represents a person's name made into a stamp similar to our rubber stamps. My niece had her chop made on her trip to Taiwan and Hong Kong. She used her initials. The mark of the beast is also made up of three letters. It is possible that the initials of the False Prophet could be used.

The terrible part is that no man is to be allowed to buy or sell unless he has the mark "or the name of the beast." Even obtaining food every day would be difficult.

[1] Daniel 9:27

[2] William R. Newell. *The Book of The Revelation*. (Chicago: Moody Press, 1935) p. 48

[3] Daniel 7:6

[4] Daniel 7:5

[5] Daniel 7:4

[6] Revelation 13:2

[7] Daniel 2:38

[8] Daniel 5:30-31

[9] Daniel 8:20,21

[10] Daniel 9:26

[11] Daniel 2:31-35

[12] Genesis 6:1-4

[13] Jude 6

[14] Revelation 17:10

[15] Zechariah 11:17

[16] Revelation 13:3

[17] Psalm 60:8; 108:9

[18] Revelation 6:9

[19] Revelation 2:20-23

[20] Revelation 12:17

[21] Revelation 12:17

[22] Daniel 3:1

[23] Ezekiel 8:3,5,14,16,18

[24] II Chronicles 9:13

[25] Daniel 3:1

[26] Ezekiel 28:2

[27] Seiss, pg. 347

9

Seven Last Plagues

Revelation 14 — 16

Today is the Feast of Trumpets, 1,040 days after the rider on the pale horse, the False Prophet, pulled off his coup as the white horse bucked and threw its rider, the Beast. The False Prophet still holds the reins of world government and world religion, but not for long. It is not yet noon.

This is the day of darkness, a day without dawn. Isaiah 8:21,22 in the New American Bible says,

> He shall look upward, but there shall be strict darkness without any dawn; He shall gaze at the earth, but there shall be distress and darkness, with the light blacked out by its clouds (caused by the incoming asteroid). Then his yoke shall be removed from them, and his burden from their shoulder. This is the plan proposed for the whole earth.[1]

The Douay Version agrees that "they shall not have the morning light." In Isaiah 13:10, the KJV has "the sun shall be darkened in his going forth" and the LXX says, "it shall be dark at sunrise."

Zoom to Rapture II

Suddenly, before John can even say anything, he finds himself and the 144,000 Jews standing in Heaven as if Rapture II had just snapped them up. The scene changes because today is when Rapture II actually takes place. Our script is picking up where it left off in chapter seven to give us more information about the 144,000 Jews that have the seal of

God in their forehead. When we left them, they had just arrived in Heaven and were standing before the throne of God. The last words we heard were about wiping away all their tears.

As John describes the scene in Heaven right after Rapture II, it is easy to see that it is very much like what took place right after Rapture I. Listen with that in mind as he begins to read the script found in Revelation fourteen.

> AND I looked, and lo, a Lamb (Christ before he roars like a Lion) stood on the mount Sion (Heaven), and with him an hundred forty *and* four thousand, having his Father's name written in their foreheads (i.e., Hebrew Christians). And I heard a voice from heaven as the voice of many waters, and as the voice of a great thunder:[2]

This is the voice of the Almighty, and Christ revealed himself as the Almighty at the first Rapture. Ezekiel 1:24 describes this voice as "the noise of great waters, as the voice of the Almighty, the voice of speech." The great waters represent the Holy Spirit of God, who is symbolized by water throughout the Bible, as in John 4:14, where Jesus said,

> But whosoever drinketh of the water that I shall give him shall never thirst; but the water that I shall give him shall be in him a well of water springing up into everlasting life.

After Rapture I, the Bride of Christ sang "a new song."[3] Here, we find out that the 144,000 Hebrew Christians have their own special adaptation of that song. Since it has been performed before by a different group, it is "as it were a new song." Listen as John continues reading the script.

> and I heard the voice of harpers harping with their harps: And they sung as it were a new song before the throne, and before the four

beasts (the Seraphim), and the elders (those who went to Heaven in the first Rapture): and no man could learn that song but the hundred *and* forty *and* four thousand, which were redeemed from the earth.[4]

To be admitted to Heaven, we must be as pure virgins, without fault. This is also true of the 144,000 Hebrew Christians. John says,

These are they which were not defiled with women (symbol of harlot religions); for they are virgins (i.e., undefiled). These are they which follow the Lamb whithersoever he goeth. These were redeemed from among men, *being* the firstfruits unto God and to the Lamb. And in their mouth was found no guile: for they are **without fault** before the throne of God.[5]

Past sins versus present sins

This is such an important lesson for us. We must be "without fault" to go to Heaven. It does not mean that we have never sinned. That is impossible. What it means is that (1) we have trusted Christ as our Saviour and he has washed our PAST sins away, and (2) when we have sinned AFTER salvation, we have confessed those sins to God and asked him to forgive us for those sins.

It is as the time Jesus washed Peter's feet. Peter did not want him to wash his feet. Jesus told him that he would understand later and said, "If I wash thee not, thou hast no part with me." Jesus washes away our past sins at the moment of salvation. At that time, our whole body is clean. However, as we walk the dusty road of life, our feet get dirty. Christ must wash away those sins also.

This is the lesson the foolish virgins and Laodiceans have not learned. I feel like shouting, "**Selah!**" which means pause, pay attention, this is important. It can make the difference in which Rapture you go to Heaven. It can make the difference in whether you keep your crown or lose it.

Remember what Jesus said in Revelation 3:11: "Behold, I come quickly: hold that fast which thou hast, that no man take thy crown." Those who go to Heaven in Rapture II are in the Body of Christ, but are not part of the Bride of Christ. To go to Heaven in Rapture I, we must be wearing white robes. We must confess our known sins to God and stand before him sinless, as wise virgins.

In his first epistle, John said,

> God is light, and in him is no darkness at all. If we say that we have fellowship with him, and walk in darkness, we lie, and do not the truth: But if we walk in the light, as he is in the light, we have fellowship one with another, and the blood of Jesus Christ his Son cleanseth us from all sin. If we say that we have no sin, we deceive ourselves, and the truth is not in us. If we confess our sins, he is faithful and just to forgive us our sins, and to cleanse us from all unrighteousness. If we say that we have not sinned, we make him a liar, and his word is not in us.[6]

Fellowship between Christians is very real. The current of the Holy Spirit flows between us, plugging us all into the Body of Christ and tugging at our heartstrings. We should not strain the connection.

The hour of judgment is come

Do you remember when Jesus told the Pharisees, "I tell you that, if these should hold their peace, the stones would immediately cry out"?[7] The Lord never leaves himself without a witness.

In the first half of the Tribulation, he even sends Moses back from the dead to witness for him. He gives mankind every chance to believe in him.

After Rapture II, when the Body of Christ is all in Heaven, what happens? The Lord tries another kind of witness. An angel preaches the gospel to all those left on Earth. People get one last chance to believe (and live on into the

Millennium). Look what happens right after Rapture II. John continues reading the script:

> And I saw another angel fly in the midst of heaven, having the everlasting gospel to preach unto them that dwell on the earth, and to every nation, and kindred, and tongue, and people, Saying with a loud voice, Fear God and give glory to him; for **the hour of his judgment is come**: and worship him that made heaven, and earth, and the sea, and the fountains of waters. And there followed another angel, saying, **Babylon is fallen**, is fallen, that great city, because she made all nations drink of the wine of the wrath of her fornication.[8]

The angel preaches and warns of the judgment, and boom! Figuratively, Jesus stamps the Earth with his other foot. The first foot stamped on the Mediterranean Sea. Now, the main asteroid hits Babylon. In one hour, noon to 1:00 P.M., she is totally destroyed, never to be rebuilt.

As John goes on, we find out what happens to those who worship the False Prophet. If you don't want to be in this group, do not take the mark of the beast.

> And the third angel followed them, saying with a loud voice, **If any man worship the beast and his image, and receive *his* mark in his forehead, or in his hand, The same shall drink of the wine of the wrath of God**, which is poured out without mixture into the cup of his indignation; and he shall be tormented with fire and brimstone in the presence of the holy angels, and in the presence of the Lamb: And the smoke of their torment ascendeth up for ever and ever: and they have no rest day nor night, who worship the beast and his image, and whosoever receiveth the mark of his name.[9]

Watching from Heaven

As John says, "Here," remember that "Here" is in Heaven. We are figuratively with him, watching from Heaven.

> Here is the patience of the saints: here *are* they that keep the commandments of God, and the faith of Jesus. And I heard a voice from heaven saying unto me, Write, Blessed *are* the dead which die in the Lord from henceforth: Yea, saith the Spirit, that they may rest from their labours; and their works do follow them.[10]

Instant replay, the first reaping

Both Raptures happen too fast for the description to be written right then. Just as lightning flashes and thunder follows, the action flashes and the explanation follows.

John now describes what has actually taken place just moments before at Rapture II. Notice one major difference between the second Rapture and the first one. When the Church saints saw Christ, he was not wearing a crown. Here the Tribulation saints see him wearing a golden crown, which he has just received earlier today.

> And I looked, and behold a white cloud, and upon the cloud *one* sat like unto the Son of man (Christ, both Lamb and Lion), having on his head a **golden crown**, and in his hand a sharp sickle. And another angel came out of the temple, crying with a loud voice to him that sat on the cloud, Thrust in thy sickle, and reap: for the time is come (Tishri 1) for thee to reap; for the harvest (Tribulation saints) of the earth is ripe. And he that sat on the cloud thrust in his sickle on the earth: and the earth was reaped.[11]

This is Rapture II, the translation of the Tribulation saints. Christ gathers them just as he does the Church saints.

However, this time, he has on a golden crown. He has gone from Lamb to Lion this very day, which started at 6:00 P.M. the preceding evening, the exact dividing line between the Church Age and the millennial Day of the Lord.

The Rapture of the Church takes place in the Church Age. The trumpet blows, but does not sound an alarm. Numbers 10:7 says,

> But when the congregation is to be gathered together, ye shall blow, but ye shall not sound an alarm.

The Rapture of the Tribulation saints takes place the first day of the Millennium, the day the federated army attacks Israel. Then the trumpet sounds the alarm. Numbers 10:9 says,

> And if ye go to war in your land against the enemy that oppresseth you, then ye shall blow an alarm with the trumpets; and he shall be remembered before the LORD your God, and ye shall be saved from your enemies.

Christ comes with a **white** cloud and meets them in the air. This white cloud is in stark contrast to the dark clouds that are also in the sky on this day of darkness and destruction. This is the day without a dawn. The sun is already darkened when it should be seen rising.

The second reaping

As John continues, we hear about another sharp sickle, this one wielded by an angel.

> And another angel came out of the temple which is in heaven, he also having a sharp sickle. And another angel came out from the altar, which had power over fire; and cried with a loud cry to him that had the sharp sickle, saying, Thrust in thy sharp sickle, and gather the clusters of the vine of the earth;

for her grapes are fully ripe. And the angel thrust in his sickle **into the earth,** and gathered the vine of the earth, and cast *it* into the great winepress of the wrath of God. And the winepress was trodden without the city (to the east of Jerusalem), and blood came out of the winepress, even unto the horse bridles, by the space of a thousand *and* six hundred furlongs.[12]

Christ reaps the first group. The angels take care of the second. These are not taken to Heaven. They are cast into the winepress at Babylon. What appears to John to be blood is probably blood mixed with red-hot molten rock spreading out over the land to form the Lake of Fire after the abyss is opened and the pit dug for the wicked. This lake[13] is 181.8 miles across. That is huge. No volcanic lake that we have ever seen is anything like that size. The smoke will go up from it forever.[14] This shows that it is not just blood. Blood would not smoke forever.

Jesus explained this reaping when he expounded the second mystery of the kingdom to his disciples. He said,

He that soweth the good seed is the Son of man; The field is the world; the good seed are the children of the kingdom; but the tares are the children of the wicked one (the False Prophet); The enemy that sowed them is the devil; the harvest is the end of the world (*aionos*, age); and **the reapers are the angels.** As therefore the tares are gathered and burned in the fire; so shall it be in the end of this world. The Son of man shall send forth his angels, and they shall gather out of his kingdom all things that offend, and them which do iniquity; And shall cast them into a furnace of fire: there shall be wailing and gnashing of teeth. Then shall the righteous shine forth as the sun in the kingdom of their Father. Who hath ears to hear, let him hear.[15]

Seven angels and seven bowls of wrath

As the play proceeds, the script is found in Revelation fifteen. We listen as John describes another sign.

> AND I saw another sign in heaven, great and marvellous, seven angels having the seven last plagues; for in them is filled up the wrath of God.

These last plagues are called vials in the King James Translation and bowls in some other translations. They literally are bowls or cups, which is true to the picture being painted for us. A bowl sounds like it holds a lot of plague, and that is just what these do. The "cup" is poured out on Babylon in Revelation 18:6. These bowls or cups are poured out on the day of the catastrophe, but they predict the final effects of the asteroid impacts. For instance, if at first only one third of the living things in the sea died, now all of them are dead.

It takes some time before the one third expands and becomes the whole. This is another reason Christ does not return at once. However, the main reason is that Israel must bury the dead and cleanse the land so he can return in glory.

Isaiah 16:4,5 in the New American Bible shows that there is a span of time in which the ruin becomes complete before Christ returns to set up his throne on Earth.

> When the struggle is ended, the ruin complete, and they have done with trampling the land, A throne shall be set up in mercy, and on it shall sit in fidelity [in David's tent] A judge upholding right and prompt to do justice. (the brackets are in the NAB)

As John continues, we are reassured again that the Tribulation saints are in Heaven before the plagues are poured out. He says,

> And I saw as it were a sea of glass mingled with fire: and them that had gotten the victory

over the beast, and over his image, and over his mark, *and* over the number of his name, stand on the sea of glass, having the harps of God.[16]

These are the Tribulation saints that were on earth during the reign of the False Prophet. The sea of glass probably represents Saturn's ring system. It literally is a sea of ice crystals. Here we see it reflecting the fireworks going on in the distance.

John continues:

And they (the Body of Christ) sing the song of Moses the servant of God (showing that Israelites are there), and the song of the Lamb (showing that Christians are there), saying, Great and marvellous *are* thy works, Lord God Almighty; just and true *are* thy ways, thou **King** of saints ('nations' in the better MSS). Who shall not fear thee. O Lord, and glorify thy name? for *thou* only *art* holy: for all nations shall come and worship before thee; for thy judgments are made manifest.[17]

The song of Moses

The song of Moses was sung right after the Lord saved Israel from the Egyptians. The complete song is found in Exodus 15:1-19. Here are some interesting excerpts that show that the events of today were foreshadowed then.

Before looking at the words of the song, think about types. The horse and rider suggest the False Prophet riding the pale horse in Revelation 6:8. According to the Syriac, Pharaoh means destroyer, which fits the picture perfectly. The Red Sea reminds us of the Lake of Fire, where both the Beast and False Prophet are cast after Armageddon.[18] The stone represents the asteroid. The Lord's right hand dashed in pieces the enemy, just as the Lord's hand is suggested in Isaiah 51:9 as the means of wounding the dragon. The redeemed Israelites being led forth and being guided in the Lord's strength to his holy habitation are a type of the

144,000 Israelites taken to Heaven in Rapture II. The mountain and "the place" tie in with "a place" Jesus has gone to prepare for us in Heaven.[19] This type is a good one. The song is quite long. The meat of what Moses sang follows:

> I will sing unto the LORD, for he hath triumphed gloriously: the horse and his rider hath he thrown into the sea. The LORD (Yahweh) is my strength and song, and he (as Yahwehshua, Yeshua, Iesous, Jesus) is become my salvation: he is my God...I will exalt him....Pharaoh's chariots and his host hath he cast into the sea: his chosen captains also are drowned in the Red sea....they sank into the bottom as a stone....thy right hand, O LORD, hath dashed in pieces the enemy....the earth swallowed them. Thou in thy mercy hast **led forth the people which thou hast redeemed: thou hast guided them in thy strength unto thy holy habitation** (i.e., Heaven, of which Sinai was a type)....Thou shalt bring them in, and plant them in the mountain of thine inheritance, in the place, O LORD, which thou hast made for thee to dwell in, in the Sanctuary, O Lord, which thy hands have established. **The LORD shall reign** for ever and ever.

This shows that Rapture II takes place when the Lord is beginning his reign, although he is still in Heaven.

When "Moses went up unto God" at Sinai, the Lord said, "Ye have seen what I did unto the Egyptians, and how I bare you on eagles' wings, and brought you unto myself."[20] That also portrayed a Rapture, the first one, the one that takes place on Pentecost. Then Moses had to go back down and wait until the third day (representing the third millennium after Israel went into captivity) and **come up again**. This ascent represented the second Rapture. It will take place in the morning before the asteroid strikes at noon.

And it came to pass on the third day **in the morning**, that there were thunders and lightnings, and a **thick cloud** upon the mount, and the voice of the trumpet exceeding loud: so that all the people that was in the camp trembled. And Moses brought forth the people out of the camp to meet with God... And mount Sinai was altogether on a smoke, because the LORD descended upon it in fire: and the smoke thereof ascended as the smoke of a furnace, and the whole mount quaked greatly. And when the voice of the trumpet sounded long, and waxed louder and louder, Moses spake, and God answered him by a voice....and the LORD called Moses up to the top of the mount; and Moses went up.[21]

The song of the Lamb

The song of the Lamb here must be almost like the new song that the participants in Rapture I sang when they fell down before the Lamb. At that time, they sang as follows:

And they sung a new song, saying Thou art worthy to take the book, and to open the seals thereof: for thou wast slain, and hast redeemed us to God by thy blood out of every kindred, and tongue, and people, and nation; And hast made us unto our God kings and priests: and we shall reign on (or over) the earth.[22]

Right after Rapture II, Christ has not yet returned to Earth. However, all his people are already with him in heaven preparing for the journey, both the saved of Israel and the saved of the Gentiles.

My guess is that part of the remaining time before the Second Advent will be spent instructing the saints as to what their duties are to be. They need to know what is expected of them immediately after the Second Advent, during the battle of Armageddon, and for the remainder of the Millennium.

The ark is seen in the heavenly temple

John continues the account of what is taking place in Heaven. Verse five says,

> And after that I looked, and, behold, the temple of the tabernacle of the testimony in heaven was opened:

This ties in with Revelation 11:19, when the temple was opened in Heaven after the seventh trumpet sounded, and the pronouncement was made that "thy wrath is come."

> And the temple of God was opened in heaven, and there was seen in his temple the ark of his testament: and there were lightnings, and voices, and thunderings, and an earthquake, and great hail.

The ark held the two stones on which were written the ten commandments. They represented the two main stones that would be dashed to pieces on Earth because the commandments were broken. One stone would strike the sea, the other the earth.

Moses pictured this for us when he dashed the first tablets to pieces because the Israelites made the golden calf after he went up on Sinai. This is similar to the image being made after Rapture I and to the two stones being dashed in pieces as a result.

Exodus 32:19,20 describes the smashed stones:

> And it came to pass, as soon as he (Moses) came nigh unto the camp, that he saw the calf, and the dancing: and Moses' anger waxed hot, and he cast the tables out of his hands, and brake them beneath the mount. And he took the calf which they had made, and burnt it in the fire, and ground it to powder, and strawed (cast) it upon the water, and made the children of Israel drink of it.

When the asteroid hits Earth at Babylon, it too will be cast upon the water. It will hit "the third part of the rivers"[23] and the waters will be poisoned.

Seven last plagues
John continues his narration:

> And the seven angels came out of the temple, having the seven plagues, clothed in pure and white linen, and having their breasts girded with golden girdles. And one of the four beasts (Seraphim) gave unto the seven angels seven golden vials (or bowls) full of the wrath of God, who liveth for ever and ever.[24]

Since Jupiter is one of the four Seraphim, and since a Seraphim gives the seven bowls to the seven angels, I wonder if the tremendous gravitational field of Jupiter is instrumental in perturbing the orbit of the asteroid so that it comes ever closer to Earth. It even seems possible that the bowls represent seven orbs like those that hit Jupiter in July, 1994.

The asteroid could be a binary, broken apart and hurled into a trajectory that would intersect Earth's orbit by Jupiter's gravitational field. Maybe Earth will get hit with two major pieces, seven smaller pieces and a great hail of smaller stones. It seems that the pieces crashing into Jupiter could be a sign and an example of what faces Earth. We are told that there are to be signs in the sun, moon and stars.[25]

There also could be five stones like David picked up out of the brook. One slung at Goliath killed the giant.

> And the temple was filled with smoke from the glory of God, and from his power; and **no man was able to enter into the temple**, till the seven plagues of the seven angels were fulfilled.[26]

At this point, there will be no more Raptures. The unregenerated left behind will feel the effects of the plagues.

The command to pour

John now tells us what happens when the command to pour is given. His script is found in Revelation sixteen.

> AND I heard a great voice out of the temple saying to the seven angels, Go your ways, and pour out the vials of the wrath of God upon the earth.

First plague: sores

> And the first went, and poured out his vial upon the earth; and there fell a noisome and grievous sore (*helkos*, ulcer) *upon* the men which had the mark of the beast, and upon them which worshipped his image.[27]

This reminds us of when Moses threw up ashes of the furnace, and boils broke out on the Egyptians, both on men and beasts.[28] Some of these plagues are very similar to what happened to Egypt when Pharaoh did not "let the people go."[29]

Second plague: another dead sea

> And the second angel poured out his vial upon the sea; and it became as the blood of a dead *man*: and every living soul died in the sea.[30]

When Moses lifted up the rod, and smote the waters of the Nile river, "all the waters that were in the river were turned to blood. And the fish that was in the river died."[31] This time, the Mediterranean Sea will become the grave of every person on every ship in the whole sea, and all the fish will die.

Hosea 4:1-6 explains why this will happen:

> HEAR the word of the LORD, ye children of Israel: for the LORD hath a controversy with

the inhabitants of the land, because there is
no truth, nor mercy, nor knowledge of God
in the land. By swearing, and lying, and killing, and stealing, and committing adultery,
they break out, and blood toucheth blood.
Therefore shall the land mourn, and every
one that dwelleth therein shall languish, with
the beasts of the field, and with the fowls of
heaven; yea, the fishes of the sea (the Mediterranean) also shall be taken away....There-
fore shalt thou fall in the day, and the prophet
(False Prophet) also shall fall with thee in the
night (he will be wounded and deposed from
office), and I will destroy thy mother.

Thy "mother" has a double meaning here. It not only
means the harlot religion of Babylon, but Abraham came
from the city of Ur, which is not far from Babylon. Destruction will hit all that area—and more. Isaiah 11:15,16 in the
New American Bible says,

The LORD shall dry up the tongue of the Sea
of Egypt, and wave his hand over the Euphrates in his fierce anger And shatter it into
seven streamlets, so that it can be crossed in
sandals.

The King James Version says that "men go over dryshod."

Third plague: blood
As John goes on, we find rivers being affected. This echoes
the third trumpet judgment.

And the third angel poured out his vial upon
the rivers and fountains of waters; and they
became blood. And I heard the angel of the
waters say, Thou art righteous, O Lord,
which art (at Feast of Trumpets), and wast (at
Rapture I), and shalt be (at Second Coming),
because thou hast judged thus. For they have

shed the blood of saints and prophets, and
thou hast given them blood to drink; for they
are worthy. And I heard another out of the altar say, Even so, Lord God Almighty, true
and righteous *are* thy judgments.[32]

This ties with the harlot Mystery Religion of Babylon. Revelation 17:6 says, "I saw the woman drunken with
the blood of the saints, and with the blood of the martyrs of
Jesus." Of the Beast, Revelation 13:7 said, "And it was
given unto him to make war with the saints, and to overcome
them." The False Prophet killed Moses and Elijah.[33] Satan
went to war with the Hebrew Christians after Israel fled to
the wilderness.[34] The judgments are righteous.

Fourth plague: fire and heat
Next, John tells us what happens as the fourth plague is
poured out. Some areas now seem free of dark clouds.

And the fourth angel poured out his vial upon
the sun: and power was given unto him to
scorch men with fire. And men were
scorched with great heat, and **blasphemed
the name of God**, which hath power over
these plagues: and they repented not to give
him glory.[35]

Since the Lord Jesus Christ has power over these
plagues, it is not a good time to blaspheme his name. Yet,
they do and repent not.

Fifth plague: thick darkness
John mentions blasphemy again and repeats that they do not
repent of their deeds:

And the fifth angel poured out his vial upon
the seat of the beast (Babylon); and his kingdom was full of darkness; and they gnawed
their tongues for pain, And blasphemed the

God of heaven because of their pains and their sores, and repented not of their deeds.[36]

Egypt was hit with "a thick darkness in all the land of Egypt three days"[37] as a type of this day of darkness. I wonder if this thick darkness will last three days also.

Sixth plague: the Euphrates dried up

As John goes on, we get word of destruction in the area of Babylon:

> And the sixth angel poured out his vial upon the great river Euphrates; and the water thereof was dried up, that the way of the kings of the east might be prepared.[38]

This is where human history began, in the wide flats of the Euphrates valley. Eden (Eridu), Ur, Larsa, Kish (clean water-laid clay layer found in the midst of stratified rubbish in this first city rebuilt after the Flood), and Babel were all in that general area. During operation Desert Storm to free Kuwait, we got to see some of that land on television.

All the nations will be gathered to the battlefield near the Mount of Megiddo in Israel to try to withstand Christ when he returns. The kings of the east can cross the Euphrates riverbed dry shod on their way. Previously, it was scarcely fordable anywhere.

Parenthetic section

The Lord is consistent. He put in a parenthetic section between the sixth and seventh trumpets. Here, between the sixth and seventh bowls, is another parenthetic section suggesting that trumpets and bowls are closely aligned in time.

The Lord also put in parenthetic sections between the sixth and seventh because there is a ten-year interval in between the sixth and seventh 1,000-year days. In it are the Rapture and the 2,300-day Shortened Tribulation. This furnishes us one more confirmation that we understand his timing correctly. He does not miss a chance to give us clues.

Some sections of the script of Revelation are not in chronological order. However, there are always clues, like registration marks, to show us exactly where a particular segment fits.

In the parenthetic section at hand, the Lord takes this opportunity to fill in a few details that we need to know. As John continues, think about the bold faced section thrown in the middle of this. It is a break in subject matter, by the Lord's matchless design, to show us where this fits.

And I saw three unclean spirits like frogs (green like the pale green spirit-horse the False Prophet rides) *come* out of the mouth of the dragon, and out of the mouth of the beast, and out of the mouth of the false prophet. For they are the spirits of devils, working miracles, *which* go forth unto the kings of the earth and of the whole world, to gather them to the battle of that great day of God Almighty. **Behold, I come as a thief. Blessed *is* he that watcheth, and keepeth his garments, lest he walk naked, and they see his shame.** And he gathered them together into a place called in the Hebrew tongue Armageddon.[39]

The reason the Lord did this is to show us the order of these events. First, the False Prophet comes to power. Later, Christ comes as a thief at Rapture II. The battle of Armageddon is after Rapture II. From other sections, we know that there is some space between the three events.

The spirits coming out of their mouths was prophesied in Jeremiah 51:44. The Lord said,

I will punish Bel (or Baal, the national god of Babylon; i.e., the False Prophet) in Babylon, and I will bring forth out of his mouth that which he hath swallowed up: and the nations shall not flow together any more unto him: yea, the wall of Babylon shall fall. My peo-

ple, go ye out of the midst of her, and deliver
ye every man his soul from the fierce anger
of the LORD.

Since the Tribulation saints were already in Heaven
in Revelation 15:2, and the seven angels holding the bowls
were told to pour in 16:1, we can be certain that 16:13-16 are
parenthetic verses. Because the spirits of devils are working
miracles, this section starts out in the middle of the Tribulation when the False Prophet begins doing great wonders,
even making fire come down from heaven.[40]

Armageddon (literally Harmageddon, the Mount of
Megiddo) means the Mount of Slaughter. It is from a Hebrew root that means to cut off, to slay. That is enough right
there to show that the Lord will win that battle.

The area where the troops will assemble is near this
mountain, in the great plain of Jezreel. This battlefield gir-
dles Israel from the Mediterranean to the Jordan. It has long
been a place of slaughter. Battles were fought there in Debo-
rah and Barak's time as well as in king Josiah's time.

Seventh plague: It is done
Next, we hear John saying,

And the seventh angel poured out his vial
(bowl) into the air; and there came a great
voice out of the temple of heaven, from the
throne, saying, **It is done.**[41]

At the Crucifixion, Jesus said, "It is finished." Now,
we are to another stage in God's plan. Here the cup of the
Lord's indignation is poured out. It too is finished.

Just as the seventh trumpet was to sound, we heard
that "when he shall begin to sound, the mystery of God
should be finished." Then when the seventh bowl is poured
out, we hear a "great" voice proclaiming, "It is done." Both
the seventh trumpet and the seventh bowl actually begin to
take place at the same time.

At the completion of the crucifixion, a great sacrifice
was completed by which believers could be saved. This is

another great sacrifice, only of unbelievers. Those who do not avail themselves of the first could find themselves partakers of the second. Also, this is not the last sacrifice of unbelievers. After Armageddon, we will hear of another one.

John continues:

> And there were voices, and thunders, and lightnings: and there was a great earthquake, such as was not since men were upon the earth, so mighty an earthquake, *and* so great. And the **great city** (Babylon) was divided into three parts, and the cities of the nations fell: and **great Babylon** came in remembrance before God, to give unto her the cup of the wine of the fierceness of his wrath.[42]

Babylon is divided into three parts, reminding us that this is Babylon III. Some say that this great city is Jerusalem, but Babylon is called "that great city Babylon" in Revelation 18:10 and 18. Jeremiah 28:8 in the Septuagint says, "Babylon is fallen suddenly, and is **broken to pieces.**"

Jerusalem is called "the city" in Revelation 11:13. Matthew 4:5 calls her "the holy city." Jerusalem will also drink some of the cup of his fury, but it will not sustain a direct hit by a large rock. It is to have coals of fire cast over it,[43] but her judgment is limited.

Information about this cup is expanded in Psalm 11:6: "Upon the wicked he shall rain snares, fire and brimstone, and an horrible tempest: this shall be the portion of their cup."

Isaiah 51:17 says, "Awake, awake, stand up, O Jerusalem, which hast drunk at the hand of the LORD the cup of his fury; thou hast drunken the dregs of the cup of trembling, and wrung them out." He promised in verse 22,23, "Behold, I have taken out of thine hand the cup of trembling, even the dregs of the cup of my fury; thou shalt no more drink it again: But **I will put it into the hand of them that afflict thee.**" That points directly to Babylon.

We found those who received the mark of the beast mentioned in Revelation 14:10: "The same shall drink of the wine of the wrath of God, which is poured out without mixture into the cup of his indignation: and he shall be tormented with fire and brimstone in the presence of the holy angels, and in the presence of the Lamb."

Psalm 75: 8 depicts a cup in the Lord's hand. It says, "For in the hand of the LORD there is a cup, and the wine is red; it is full of mixture; and he poureth out of the same: but the dregs thereof, all the wicked of the earth shall wring them out, and drink them."

Jeremiah tells us more about the sign of the wine cup of fury in 25:15-33.

> For this saith the LORD...Take the wine cup of this fury at my hand, and cause all the nations, to whom I send thee, to drink it. And they shall drink, and be moved, and be mad, because of the sword that I will send among them. Then took I the cup at the LORD'S hand, and made all the nations to drink, unto whom the LORD had sent me...for I will call for a sword upon all the inhabitants of the earth, saith the LORD of hosts....And the slain of the LORD shall be at that day from one end of the earth even unto the other end of the earth.

The Sword of the Lord, the "flaming sword" of Genesis 3:24, is the asteroid. It will cause a worldwide earthquake. We hear John telling us some of its effects:

> And every island fled away, and the mountains were not found. And there fell upon men a great hail out of heaven, *every stone* about the weight of a talent (about 100 pounds) and men blasphemed God because of the plague of the hail; for the plague thereof was exceeding great.[44]

It is now easy to see that Adam was driven out of that area of the world because the flaming sword will strike nearby.

Registration marks

We find parenthetic sections between the sixth and seventh seals, between the sixth and seventh trumpets, and between the sixth and seventh bowls. That is too consistent and too obvious to be by accident. Are these parenthetic sections registration marks that indicate that the sixth and seventh seals, trumpets, and bowls are all closely aligned in time? Let's search for clues.

Under the sixth seal, a lot is already going on. We find "a great **earthquake**," darkness, stars of heaven falling like untimely figs, and every mountain and island moved out of their places. Christ is sitting on his throne, and the day of his wrath has come. We hear men saying to the rocks, "Fall on us." They already know what else is on its way.[45]

When the seventh seal breaks, there is silence in heaven while the judge is being seated at the bench. We see the seven angels with the seven trumpets, but before they can sound to tell us what happens, the Angel of the Lord throws a fire-filled censer that represents a rock named Wormwood into the Earth. There are "thunderings, and lightnings, and an **earthquake**."[46]

Then the trumpets sound to show us what happened. A great mountain falls into the sea and the "great star" named Wormwood falls upon one third of the rivers. There is darkness. Quickly spreading from the strike zone at the Euphrates River, within one hour one third of the population of Earth dies. The certain hour, day, month, and year must be noon to 1 P.M. on the Tishri 1 that begins the Millennium.

We are then told that when the seventh trumpet sounds, "the mystery of God should be finished, as he hath declared to his servants the prophets." When the seventh trumpet sounds, Christ is King and his "wrath is come." There are "thunderings, and an **earthquake**."[47]

Then the bowls full of plagues are poured out. We are told that "in them is filled up the wrath of God" and that Christ is King.[48] When the sixth bowl is poured out, we again hear of the Euphrates. This time the water is dried up.[49]

When the seventh bowl is poured out, we hear, "It is done. And there were...thunders, and lightnings; and there was a great earthquake such as was not since men were upon the earth, so mighty an earthquake....and the cities of the nations fell: and great Babylon came in remembrance before God, to give unto her the cup of the wine of the fierceness of his wrath. And every island fled away, and the mountains were not found."[50]

Did you find some registration marks? Christ is King and it is the Day of Wrath, but let's take a close look at one thing—the earthquake.

In 6:12 (sixth seal), "lo, there was a great earthquake." In 8:5 (seventh seal), we find "an earthquake." In 11:19 (seventh trumpet), we find "an earthquake." In 16:18 (seventh bowl), "there was a great earthquake, such as was not since men were upon the earth, so mighty an earthquake."

The first seal is broken at the beginning of the Tribulation. The fourth is opened in the middle of the Tribulation. However, the earthquake seen under the sixth and seventh seals, the seventh trumpet, and the seventh bowl tie these together in time. On this occasion, as at the Rapture, everything happens so fast that it is hard to tell the complete story as quickly as it takes place.

It looks like a binary asteroid comes flying in on a trajectory that intersects Earth's orbit. Probably as it previously passed within range of Jupiter's great gravitational system, it broke into pieces. If not broken before, it certainly will break when it hits Earth's Roche limit about 11,000 miles out. There will be two main pieces, one larger than the other, plus many other smaller chunks. All come down blazing fiercely and spitting out a hail of hot coals. One mountain sized piece strikes the Mediterranean Sea. The largest piece, the "star" Wormwood, hits the prearranged target where the point of the "flaming sword"[51] was aimed—Babylon.

As the Lord stamps one foot on the sea and the other on the Earth, the asteroid pieces crash on the sea and Earth. He said he would drop his shoe on Edom in the process, so a rock also hits Edom.[52] Jeremiah 49:12-21 says,

> For thus saith the LORD; Behold, they whose judgment was not to drink of the cup

have assuredly drunken...Bozrah shall become a desolation, a reproach, a waste, and a curse: and all the cities thereof shall be perpetual wastes....Edom shall be a desolation: every one that goeth by it shall be astonished, and shall hiss at all the plagues thereof. As in the overthrow of Sodom and Gomorrah...no man shall abide there, neither shall a son of man dwell in it....**who will appoint me the time?** (the Feast of Trumpets, Tishri 1)...The earth is moved at the noise of their fall, at the cry the noise thereof was heard in the Red sea.

There are many Old Testament prophecies that tell of "that day." Many of them take place on the Feast of Trumpets that starts the Millennium and line up with the seventh trumpet and the seventh bowl. When the seventh trumpet sounds, "the mystery of God should be finished, as he hath declared to his servants the prophets." When the seventh bowl is poured out, there comes "a great voice out of the temple of heaven, from the throne, saying, It is done."

Interesting parts of Jeremiah 50 and 51 follow. They concern Babylon. One evening many years ago, after I asked to understand everything that the Lord wanted man to know about the Bible, I saw a rectangle of light on the section in bold face type. I have been studying and writing ever since.

The word that the LORD spake against Babylon and against the land of the Chaldeans by Jeremiah the prophet. **Declare ye among the nations, and publish, and set up a standard; publish, and conceal not: say, Babylon is taken, Bel is confounded, Merodach is broken in pieces; her idols are confounded, her images are broken in pieces**...Because of the wrath of the LORD it shall not be inhabited, but it shall be wholly desolate: every one that goeth be Babylon shall be astonished,

and hiss at all her plagues...it is the vengeance of the LORD: take vengeance upon her;
as she hath done, do unto her....How is the
hammer of the whole earth cut asunder and
broken! how is Babylon become a desolation
among the nations!...The LORD hath opened
his armoury, and hath brought forth the weapons of his indignation...

The hammer, or pounder, of the earth is **"cut asunder and broken**. This clearly is the binary asteroid that the
Lord breaks apart.

it shall be no more inhabited for ever....At
the noise of the taking of Babylon the earth is
moved...Flee out of the midst of Babylon,
and deliver every man his soul: be not cut off
in her iniquity; for this is the time of the
LORD'S vengeance; he will render unto her a
recompence. Babylon hath been a golden cup
in the LORD'S hand, that made all the earth
drunken: the nations have drunken of her
wine; therefore the nations are mad. Babylon
is suddenly fallen and destroyed...her judgment reacheth unto heaven, and is lifted up
even to the sky...his device is against Babylon, to destroy it; because it is the vengeance
of the LORD, the vengeance of his temple....

His device is the Sword of the Lord, the asteroid.
This broken piece of Satan's planet Rahab is large enough to
wipe out civilization as we know it.

Behold, I am against thee, O destroying
mountain (the binary asteroid), saith the
LORD, which **destroyest all the earth** (a
severe sentence): and I will stretch out mine
hand upon thee, and roll thee down from the
rocks, and will make thee a burnt mountain.

1 It is found sandwiched in the middle of chapter 14.
2 Revelation 14:1,2
3 Revelation 5:9
4 Revelation 14:2,3
5 Revelation 14:4,5
6 I John 5-10
7 Luke 19:40
8 Revelation 14:6-8
9 Revelation 14:9-11
10 Revelation 14:12,13
11 Revelation 14:14-16
12 Revelation 14:17-20
13 Psalm 94:13
14 Revelation 14:11
15 Matthew 13;37-43
16 Revelation 15:2
17 Revelation 15:3,4
18 Revelation 19:20
19 John 14:2
20 Exodus 19:3,4
21 Exodus 19:16-20
22 Revelation 5:9,10
23 Revelation 8:10
24 Revelation 16:6,7
25 Luke 21:25
26 Revelation 14: 8
27 Revelation 16:2
28 Exodus 9:10
29 Exodus 7:14
30 Revelation 16:3
31 Exodus 7:20,21
32 Revelation 16:4-7
33 Revelation 11:7
34 Revelation 12:17
35 Revelation 16:8,9
36 Revelation 16:10,11
37 Exodus 10:22
38 Revelation 16:12
39 Revelation 16:13-16
40 Revelation 13:13,14
41 Revelation 16:17
42 Revelation 16:18,19
43 Ezekiel 10:2
44 Revelation 16:20,21

[45] Revelation 6:12-17
[46] Revelation 8:1-5
[47] Revelation 11:15-19
[48] Revelation 15:1-7
[49] Revelation 16:12
[50] Revelation 16:17-20
[51] Genesis 3:24
[52] Psalms 60:8; 108:9

10

Unraveling the Mystery

ifferent views of Babylon are presented to us by our playwright, the Lord Jesus Christ, in the next section of his first-rate dramatic production.

These are like film clips made with his special zoom lens that can penetrate the mists of time. Something that is actually a few years away can be brought close enough to take a good look at it. The trick is to recognize the particular time that each shot represents.

Revelation 17:14, mentions Christ, the Lord of lords, and King of kings and the called, chosen, and faithful ones "that **are** with him." This shows that **the Rapture has already taken place** and we are looking forward through time to see what is coming after Rapture I.

Jesus wrote the whole play from the vantage point of the Rapture, when it is "at hand.'" It is as if he wrote it today. He began his own words with "I am Alpha and Omega, the beginning and the ending...which is (at the Rapture), and which was (at the First Advent), and which is to come (at the Second Advent), the Almighty."

In his long monologue, he told the Philadelphian Church that has the open door set before it, "Behold, I come quickly: hold that fast which thou hast, that no man take thy crown." He comes quickly at the Rapture.

In the twenty-second chapter, Christ ended his words to us with, "I come quickly: and my reward is with me, to give every man according as his work shall be. I am

Alpha and Omega, the beginning and the end, the first and the last...I am the root and the offspring of David, and the bright and morning star...Surely I come quickly."[2]

Each section following the "Come up hither" in Revelation 4:1 zeros in on some segment of the future following the Rapture. This part is no different, but remembering it here is absolutely crucial to the correct interpretation.

Many think that "MYSTERY, BABYLON THE GREAT, THE MOTHER OF HARLOTS AND ABOMINATIONS OF THE EARTH" of Revelation seventeen is headquartered in Rome, the city of seven hills, and that commercial Babylon is seen in Revelation eighteen after religious Babylon has been burned.

The former seems to make sense because the ninth verse says that there are "seven mountains, on which the woman sitteth." That fits Rome, which sprawls over seven hills. A Roman coin has been found that portrayed those seven hills.

The clincher seems to be Revelation 17:18, which says, "And the woman which thou sawest is that great city, which reigneth over the kings of the earth." That fits Vatican City quite well because the Pope claims to be the sovereign over the church and the world.

Backing up this interpretation is the fact that the iron legs of the image in Nebuchadnezzar's dream represent the Roman Empire. The two legs represent the eastern and western divisions. Even though the feet and toes are made of iron (Rome) and clay (other nations), they still have some of the iron that symbolizes Rome in them. In some way, the feet and toes of the end times proceed from the iron legs and have the stamp of Rome on them.

We are living in the days of the feet. In just a few years, the kings represented by the ten toes will receive their crowns in the world empire as the Tribulation begins.

The view in Revelation eighteen is of literal Babylon on the Euphrates River in Iraq. Saddam Hussein has rebuilt the city, so there can be no doubt of that. After she is destroyed this time no man will ever set foot there.

The commerce that we see being carried on there includes items used in religion. The same harlot religion seen in Revelation seventeen seems to rear its head in eighteen. Her descriptions match, almost word for word. The reason they match is because the harlot religion of Babylon found in Rome is moved to literal Babylon under Satan's guidance at the beginning of the Tribulation. She will probably move to temporary quarters in Babylon **"To build** it an house in the land of Shinar."[3]

There are two men who head up false religion during the Tribulation. Isaiah 9:15 describes them.

> The ancient and honourable, he is the head;
> and the prophet that teacheth lies, he is the
> tail.

The "ancient and honourable" is the Tribulation Pope called the Beast in Revelation 13:4-10 and 19:19. He is the sixth head of the great red dragon. The "tail" is the Israeli False Prophet, who heads up the false religion during the last part of the Shortened Tribulation. He is the seventh and last head of the dragon and will be indwelt by Satan, the tail of the dragon, himself.

Both men will move to Babylon on the Euphrates River in Iraq, where the Tower of Babel was begun in Nimrod's day. They will supervise the building of twin towers for the world empire headquarters and rebuild the Tower of Babel.

"Come hither"

Listen to John carefully to see if the harlot religion actually is based in Rome. His script is in Revelation seventeen.

> AND there came one of the seven angels
> which had the seven vials, and talked with
> me, saying unto me, **Come hither;** I will
> shew unto thee the judgment of the great
> whore that sitteth upon many waters:

"AND" hooks this verse to chapter sixteen, where the seven vials, or bowls of wrath were poured out. One of those angels who has dumped his bowl on Babylon comes to take John somewhere and show him more details concerning the harlot's judgment. We have to figure out where he is taken and what segment of time is in view.

The waters are "peoples, and multitudes, and nations, and tongues."[4] This harlot religion sits upon nations, plural.

John continues giving us clues. We hear him say,

> With whom the kings of the earth **have** (past tense) committed fornication (joined), and the inhabitants of the earth have been made drunk with the wine of her fornication.[5]

The kings have already joined the harlot. This takes us to the Tribulation. Almost the same description is found in Revelation 18:3. It says,

> For all nations have drunk of the wine of the **wrath** of her fornication, and the kings of the earth have committed fornication with her.

In Revelation seventeen, the kings of the earth are already bound in a bundle with this harlot Mystery Religion of Babylon. They are so blinded by her heady wine that they do not realize how wrong this is, but the wrath of God has not yet been poured out. That comes in Revelation eighteen.

Flying to the wilderness

Next, John tells us something that seems to have been overlooked by those who claim the harlot in Revelation seventeen represents Rome. The angel flew John to the wilderness. Rome does not seem like a wilderness, but Babylon is in a desert area. Jeremiah 50:12 says of Babylon,

> Your mother (the religion at the Tower of Babel) shall be sore confounded; she that bare you shall be ashamed: behold, the hindermost (last) of the nations (Babylon III) shall be a **wilderness, a dry land**, and a **desert**.

We got to view a lot of that desert area on television during Operation Desert Storm to liberate Kuwait. It is just such things as Saddam Hussein's attack on Kuwait that cause the kings of the Earth to look more and more to world government to bring peace.

Habakkuk 1:6-10 foretold Iraq's violence upon Kuwait when it said,

> For, lo, I raise up the Chaldeans (Babylonians), that bitter and hasty nation, which shall march through the breadth of the land, to possess the dwelling-places that are not their's. They are terrible and dreadful: their judgment and their dignity shall proceed of themselves. Their horses (military transportation) also are swifter than the leopards, and are more fierce than the evening wolves (they kill maliciously): and their horsemen (military men) shall spread themselves, and their horsemen shall come from far; they shall fly (in airplanes) as the eagle that hasteth to eat (swooping down suddenly on their prey). They shall come all for violence...they shall gather the captivity as the sand. And they shall scoff at the kings, and the princes shall be a scorn unto them: they shall deride every strong hold; for they shall heap dust (their tanks stirred up lots of dust), and take it.

As John continues in chapter seventeen, pay attention to the place he flies to and what he sees the woman do there.

> So he carried me away in the spirit into the wilderness (*eremon*, desert): and I saw a woman sit upon a scarlet coloured beast, full of names of blasphemy, having seven heads and ten horns.[6]

John saw her sit down on the beast in the desert. As he flew, she flew. Therefore, this is probably when the

Beast comes to power over the world empire and moves to Babylon at the beginning of the Tribulation.

In Revelation 13:1, we saw the seven-headed beast come up out of the sea, which symbolizes nations. That beast was like a costume donned by the great red dragon, who energized it. Since this harlot sitteth upon many waters, it is as if she was sitting upon the dragon as it came up out of the sea, or nations. Here, we see the picture clearly. She sits on the dragon, whose heads represent world empires, in the desert.

When John is flown to the wilderness of Babylon, it demonstrates the time when the harlot religion flies there, to the land of Shinar. Zechariah 5:5-11 foretold that day:

> Then the angel...said...see **what is this that goeth forth**. And I said, What is it? And he said, This is an ephah (largest wheat measure, i.e., the largest church[7]) that goeth forth. He said moreover, This is their resemblance through all the earth (the world church). And, behold, there was lifted up a talent of lead: and this is a woman (the harlot religion) that sitteth in the midst of the ephah. And he said, This is wickedness. And he cast it into the midst of the ephah; and he cast the weight of lead upon the mouth thereof (foretelling her doom). Then lifted I up mine eyes, and looked, and, behold, there came out two women (religious groups), and the wind was in their wings; for they had wings like the wings of a stork: and they lifted up the ephah between the earth and the heaven. Then said I to the angel that talked with me, Whither do these bear the ephah? And he said unto me, **To build** it an house in the land of Shinar: and it shall be established, and **set there upon her own base.**

The Tower of Babel was at Shinar, which is Babylon.[8] The city is in modern Iraq. The Mystery Religion of

Babylon began there. It is "her own base" and she truly is the "MOTHER."

At Babel, the Lord confused the languages. At Babylon during the Tribulation, there will be a confusion of languages there because every nation will send ambassadors to the world capitol. The United Nations operates with nine official working languages, English, Chinese, French, Russian, Spanish, and Arabic.

This world church flies to Babylon "To build" the new house. Therefore, she must have some kind of temporary quarters there during construction. The new house will be finished by the time the False Prophet takes over in the middle of the Tribulation. Satan is preparing his own throne and sanctuary for the occupancy of the False Prophet.

In Zechariah, the angel said to "lift up now thine eyes, and see what is this that goeth forth." That is precisely what we are doing in Revelation seventeen. The register marks on both pictures match. The Rapture has already taken place, and we are looking forward to when the world church is moved to Babylon in the desert. Do you remember what Jesus said in Matthew 24:24-26? He warned,

> For there shall arise false Christs, and **false prophets**, and shall shew great signs and wonders; insomuch that, if it were possible, they shall deceive the very elect. Behold, I have told you before. Wherefore if they shall say unto you, Behold, he is **in the desert** (*eremo*); go not forth: behold, he is in the secret chambers; believe it not.

Literal Babylon is in the desert. Rome originated on marshy ground by the Tigris River and very early spread up the Palatine hill. That does not fit this wilderness image.

Positive identification of the scarlet beast that has seven heads and ten horns upon whom the woman sits is found in Revelation 12:3,4,9. It says,

> behold a great red dragon, having seven heads and ten horns, and **seven crowns**

upon his heads. And his tail drew the third part of the stars of heaven, and did cast them to the earth....And the great dragon was cast out, that old serpent, called the Devil, and Satan, which deceiveth the whole world: he was cast out into the earth, and his angels were cast out with him.

The great red dragon is Satan. At the time that is in view in Revelation twelve, the seventh head, the False Prophet, is crowned. This takes place in the middle of the Tribulation, when there are but 1,260 days of the 2,520 left. From that time on, Satan is not allowed in Heaven again. Our picture in chapter seventeen is three and one half years before this, at the beginning of the Tribulation.

The description of this beast that we saw in Revelation 13:1 said that the beast rising up out of the sea has

seven heads and ten horns, and upon his horns **ten crowns**, and upon his heads the name of blasphemy.

The name of blasphemy that has appeared upon all the great red dragon's heads is Pontifex Maximus, the high priest of the Babylonian Mystery religion.

We are looking at the first of the Tribulation, when the woman sits on the dragon in the desert. The seventh head, the False Prophet, is not crowned until the middle of the Tribulation, but the ten horns and the sixth king, the Beast, are crowned as the Tribulation begins.[9] This agrees with Daniel 7:7:

a **fourth beast** (Rome)...devoured and brake in pieces, and stamped the residue with **the feet** of it: and it (the empire of the feet) was **diverse** (different) from all the beasts that were before it; and **it had ten horns** (the beginning of the Tribulation). I considered the horns, and, behold, there came up among them **another** little horn (Mid-Tribu-

lation), before whom there were three of the
first horns plucked up by the roots.

The fourth beast in Daniel was Rome, but when we
get down to the feet, it has changed. It is made up of iron
and clay,[10] Rome plus other nations. The collagen that glues
the pieces of the feet together is the United NATIONS.

I did not intend to capitalize "NATIONS." It just
happened. This is the seventh time this has happened. I was
about to say "the United Nations and the world church." I
think the Lord wants me to leave off "and the world church."
In its final configuration, it comes later, as those left behind
in the first Rapture enter the toe section, the Tribulation.

At the beginning of the Tribulation, the Beast is
crowned head of world government and the ten kings receive
their crowns as sub-regents under the Beast. We do not
know who they will be at the time of the Rapture for they
"have received no kingdom as yet."[11] When "another" beast,
the False Prophet, receives his crown, it is the middle of the
Tribulation. Three of the ten kings are deposed at that time,
but they are replaced because ten oppose Christ at Armageddon.[12]

John continues:

And the woman was arrayed in purple and
scarlet colour, and decked with gold and precious stones and pearls, having a golden cup
in her hand full of abominations and filthiness of her fornication:[13]

This is exactly the same harlot that is seen in Revelation 18:16, which says, "Alas, alas that great city, that
was clothed in fine linen, and purple, and scarlet, and
decked with gold, and precious stones, and pearls!"

Where else have you heard this harlot called a great
city? In Revelation 17:18, which says, "And the woman
which thou sawest is that great city, which reigneth over
the kings of the earth." The terminology is the same. She is
called "that great city" in both chapter seventeen and
eighteen. That suggests that they both are talking about the

same city, the great city built at Babylon to be the world capitol. It will surpass Vatican City by far. It will be the costliest city the world has ever known. All nations will trade in her "fairs."[14]

A cup is mentioned in relation to both the city in chapter seventeen and the one in chapter eighteen. In 17:4, the harlot holds it in her hand, and it is "full of abominations and filthiness of her fornication." Fornication here indicates joining with the world. This she has already done. Her cup is full.

In chapter 18:6, it says, "in the cup which she hath filled fill to her double." This is the same harlot, located in the same place, but the time is 2,300 days[15] later.

Let's listen to John some more and see what other clues turn up. He says,

> And upon her forehead *was* a name written, MYSTERY, BABYLON THE GREAT, THE **MOTHER** OF HARLOTS AND ABOMINATIONS OF THE EARTH.[16]

We are talking about the "MOTHER." Rome is not the mother of false religion. She came along the tracks of time far too late to be the mother.

The Mystery religion of Babylon began at the Tower of Babel with king Nimrod, queen Semiramis, and their son, Tammuz, whom she said was miraculously conceived. Semiramis and Tammuz were worshipped as madonna and child. Idols depicting this pair were used. Semiramis said that Tammuz was killed by a wild boar and came back to life. His birthday was celebrated with evergreen trees on December 25. The spring festival, Easter, was celebrated with eggs. Many of the rites were secret. People had to be initiated into it to learn its mysteries.

Tammuz was called the seed and the deliverer. This Mystery Religion was Satan's counterfeit religion. He wanted to delude with an imitation so that when the true seed of the woman[17] came, mankind would not recognize him.

Babylon was the fountainhead of idolatry. It would make perfect sense to call literal Babylon the mother. It does not make as much sense to call Rome the mother, even though she calls herself the mother church. As a mother, Babylon reaches back much farther.

As John continues, we hear a sad tale. She has killed so many saints that she is said to be drunk with their blood.

> And I saw the woman drunken with the
> blood of the saints, and with the blood of the
> martyrs of Jesus: and when I saw her, I
> wondered with great admiration (wonder).[18]

Revelation eighteen ends with essentially the same thing. It says,

> And in her was found the blood of prophets,
> and of saints, and of all that were slain upon
> the earth.

They are the same woman. In Revelation seventeen, the zoom lens has just picked up an earlier view of the harlot. As soon as she moved to literal Babylon, John saw her sit down there.

Change of scene—the Rapture "is"

As John continues, the angel starts to give him a different view, a closeup. Here, the Rapture has just taken place.

> And the angel said unto me, Wherefore didst
> thou marvel? I will tell thee the mystery of the
> woman, and of the beast that carrieth her,
> which hath the seven heads and ten horns.

In this picture, the Tribulation has not yet begun. It is taken at the time of the Rapture. Revelation 17:12 says that the ten kings "have received no kingdom as yet," and they get their kingdom at the beginning of the Tribulation, because the beast seen coming out of the sea in chapter thirteen has ten crowns on his horns.

As John continues his narration, we hear more about this strange beast, the great red dragon, who is Satan.

The beast (Satan) that thou sawest was (in Judas Iscariot), and is not (in man at the time of the Rapture); and shall ascend out of the bottomless pit (and enter into the False Prophet Mid-Tribulation), and go into perdition: and they that dwell on the earth shall wonder, whose names were not written in the book of life from the foundation of the world, when they behold the beast that was, and is not, and yet is.[19]

Satan was in Judas Iscariot. He is not in man when the Rapture takes place, yet he exists, biding his time. He will enter into the False Prophet in the middle of the Tribulation when his house and throne are ready in Babylon.

In the Scripture that John read, Satan "was (in Judas), and is not (in man at the Rapture), and yet is (he exists)." This corresponds to the same point in time when the Rapture takes place, when Christ says, "I am Alpha and Omega...which is (at the Rapture), and which was (at the First Advent), and which is to come (at the Second Advent), the Almighty" in chapter 1:8.

Seven world empires, and one "is"

Next, John begins to give us some very important information. We must pay close attention now. We have a puzzle to work, and need wisdom and discernment. We are viewing this scene near the time of the Rapture. In fact, it has just happened. The ten kings have "no kingdom as yet"[20] and the saints "are" already with Christ.[21] John says,

And here is the mind which hath wisdom. The seven heads are seven mountains (world empires), on which the woman sitteth.[22]

The Revised Standard Version has, "This calls for a mind with wisdom." That makes the meaning clearer to us. We must look at this section carefully with new eyes. The first thing that comes to mind is that Rome is the seat of a large religious group, and that Rome has seven hills. These things are both true, but the hills are not very high, maybe not even high enough to be called mountains. Also, Vatican City is actually only on one, the Palatine hill. It does not physically sit on all seven hills. However, its influence is felt city wide.

The original settlement of Rome was on the marshy ground by the Tigris and on the Palatine hill around 753 B.C. It expanded, and Servius Tullius (B.C. 578-534) enclosed all seven hills with a wall.

Yet, a better interpretation of the above scripture seems to be that the seven mountains are the same as the seven heads of the beast upon which the woman sits. Both mountains and the heads of the beast are symbols of world empires.

As John continues, we come to a section that has been grossly misunderstood in the past. John says,

> And there are seven kings; five are fallen, and **one is**, *and* the other is not yet come; and when he cometh, he must continue a short space. And the beast that was (Satan), and is not, even he is the eighth, and is of the seven, and goeth into perdition.[23]

For many years, I thought that the kingdom that "is" represented the Roman Empire that was in power when John put the script of this play on his sheepskin, or parchment, in 96 A.D. That looked like the unassailable anchor in this lineup. I was wrong.

Remember, this play is written as if the Rapture is at hand. This section is written when the Church saints "**are**" with Christ, as in 17:14. Therefore, the kingdom that "**is**" has to be the one that is already in power right after the Rapture takes place. The only possibility seems to be the Pope at Rome. Verse eleven says that the "ten kings...have received no kingdom as yet," so the Tribulation has not yet arrived.

At the beginning of the Tribulation, the Beast is crowned. He is the sixth head of the great red dragon and therefore the sixth head of the beast out of the sea. There are ten kings under him that also are crowned at that time. The "other" that has not yet come is the seventh head, the False Prophet, who will be crowned in the middle of the Tribulation.

This identification of the kingdom that "is" solves a problem that bothered me in the past. Since the harlot is the Mystery Religion of Babylon, and that system started with Nimrod, Semiramis, and Tammuz at the Tower of Babel, the first kingdom in this list should be Babel. Only Babel could truly be called the "MOTHER." Yet many list the same empires as found in Halley's Bible Handbook, Egypt, Assyria, Babylon, Persia, Greece, Rome, and Babylon the Harlot.

Now that I know which kingdom "is," I find that Babel turns out to be the first kingdom, as it should be. That makes far better sense, and the whole list is more logical.

Some time after the language was confounded and they stopped building the Tower of Babel (Babylon I), Nebuchadnezzar built Babylon the Great (Babylon II). Daniel was shown what world empires would follow. The golden head of the image in Nebuchadnezzar's dream[24] was Babylon II. The silver breast and arms were Media-Persia. The brass belly and sides were Greece. The legs of iron were Rome, with the feet, part iron and part clay, representing the end times. The ten toes are the Tribulation, when there are ten kings who are co-regents with the Beast and the False Prophet.

Daniel 7:2-8,17 gives us another view of these same world empires. It says,

> And four great beasts came up from the sea (nations), diverse one from another. The first was like a lion (Babylon[25])...a second, like to a bear (Media-Persia[26])...another, like a leopard (Greece[27])...After this...a fourth beast (Rome[28]), dreadful and terrible, and strong exceedingly; and it had great iron teeth: it devoured and brake in pieces, and stamped the residue with **the feet** of it: and it was diverse from all the beasts that were before it; and it had ten horns (kings)....there came up

among them another little horn (the False Prophet), before whom there were three of the first horns plucked up by the roots: and, behold, in this horn were eyes like the eyes of man, and a mouth speaking great things. ...These great beasts...are four kings, which shall arise out of the earth.

Here is the list of world empires.

AT THE TIME OF THE RAPTURE

Five kings are fallen

(1) Babylon I	Tower of Babel	Nimrod
(2) Babylon II		Nebuchadnezzar
(3) Media-Persia		Cyrus
(4) Greece		Alexander the Great
(5) Roman Empire		The Caesars

One king is

(6) Ecclesiastic Rome	The Pope

One king is yet to come

(7) Babylon III	Tower of Babel	False Prophet

The sixth and seventh will read differently a little later on. I believe the Tribulation Pope will be elected Secretary General of the United Nations. At the beginning of the Tribulation, the sixth world empire will be the United Nations, and the sixth king will be the Beast.

Whoever the Beast turns out to be, he will be an older man who has been left behind at the Rapture. Isaiah 9:15 says, "The ancient and honourable, he is the head; and the prophet that teacheth lies, he is the tail" (and the final head).

AT THE BEGINNING OF THE TRIBULATION

(6) Eccl. Rome/UN	Moves to Babylon	The Beast

IN THE MIDDLE OF THE TRIBULATION

(7) Babylon III	Tower of Babel	False Prophet

We have to identify the vantage point from which we are viewing each picture to understand perfectly what is being shown.

Four Jewish years prefigured

The Lord likes to teach us by furnishing us similitudes or examples,[29] and Jeremiah said that "the fourth year of Jehoiakim the son of Josiah king of Judah...was the first year of Nebuchadrezzar king of Babylon."[30]

This suggests that the leader in Israel that will become the False Prophet in the middle of the Tribulation may come to power in Israel four years before the Tribulation Pope is elected head of world government. He will probably come to power in Israel right after the Rapture. The restraining influence of the Holy Spirit will be removed at that time.

If this is so, both end-time leaders could be placed in leadership positions immediately after the Rapture. They could plan together and attend Middle East summit meetings of the world's leaders like the one that took place March 13, 1996. Thirty of the world leaders joined President Clinton at the Red Sea resort Sharm El-Sheikh in Egypt to talk about the peace process and terrorism.

This would give those two beasts enough time to convince the kings of the world that their plan for world peace makes sense, get architectural plans drawn up, and start putting the preliminaries in action during the four Jewish years between the Rapture and the Tribulation.

Temporary quarters could be prepared ahead of time for their immediate occupancy after the seven-year peace covenant is signed in Rome on the Feast of Weeks that begins the Seventieth Week of Daniel, the Tribulation.

The four years, figured by Jewish inclusive reckoning, between the Rapture and the beginning of the Tribulation are revealed in Jesus' parable of the barren fig tree:

> A certain man (the Lord) had a fig tree
> (Israel) planted in his vineyard; and he came
> (at the Rapture) and sought fruit thereon, and
> found none. Then said he unto the dresser of
> his vineyard, Behold, these **three years** (the

year of the Rapture plus two more) I come seeking fruit on this fig tree, and find none: cut it down; why cumbereth it the ground? And he answering said unto him, Lord, let it alone **this year also**, till I shall dig about it, and dung it: And if it bear fruit, well: and if not, then after that thou shalt cut it down (the ax will strike her during the Tribulation).[31]

During these four Jewish years, the temple should be rebuilt in Jerusalem because sacrificing starts at the beginning of the Tribulation.[32] It is possible that sacrificing could begin as soon as the altar is finished. In the days of Ezra, they built "the altar of the God of Israel, to offer burnt-offerings thereon" before the Temple foundations were laid.[33] The False Prophet could sit in the Temple as soon as it is finished in the middle of the Tribulation. The occasion could be the dedication ceremony. However, since John was told to measure the temple of God in Revelation 11:1,2, when the two witnesses start their ministry at the beginning of the Tribulation, it is more likely that the temple will be rebuilt between the Rapture and the beginning of the Tribulation.

The Ten kings
The ten kings are crowned as the Tribulation begins.

And the ten horns which thou sawest are ten kings, which **have received no kingdom as yet**; but receive power as kings one hour with the beast (the Beast of Rome). These have one mind, and shall give their power and strength unto the beast.[34]

The Rapture has taken place, but the ten kings who receive crowns at the beginning of the Tribulation have not gotten them yet. This is evidence of the gap between the Rapture and the beginning of the Tribulation.

There are ten kings but only one kingdom. They are co-regents under the Beast in the single kingdom, the world empire, Babylon III. They receive power (and crowns) one hour with the Beast. This hour is the "hour of temptation (*peirasmou*, trial), which shall come upon all the world, to try them that dwell upon the earth,"[35] the Tribulation. They will receive these crowns as it begins because the "ten crowns" are seen on the horns of the beast out of the sea in Revelation 13:1.

In a momentary digression in the script, Christ throws in a future glimpse of the ten kings at Armageddon. He then reverts to the present, right after the Rapture.

> These **shall** (in the future) make war (Armageddon) with the Lamb (after the Second Advent), and the Lamb **shall** overcome them: for he is Lord of lords, and King of kings: and they that **are** (right now) with him (Church saints) *are* called, and chosen, and faithful.[36]

Those that are already with Christ are the Church saints that have just arrived in Heaven in Rapture I. They **"are"** with Christ in Heaven. Ecclesiastical Rome's Pope **"is"** in power on Earth right after the Rapture. The ten kings have received **no kingdom as yet**. These things are keys that help us understand Revelation seventeen correctly.

The last statement we heard John read in this script that has been given him is important. To be with Christ, we must not only be called, but chosen, and faithful. Take care to assure that you are wearing white and that you remain faithful if you want to escape the hour of trial that is coming upon the Earth. Continuing, John says,

> And he saith unto me, The waters which thou sawest, where the whore sitteth, are peoples, and multitudes, and nations, and tongues.[37]

The beast of Revelation 13:1 came out of the sea, and this harlot religion sits on many waters. Both are associated with each other and with the federated nations when she sits on the dragon at Babylon as the Tribulation begins.

Mid-Tribulation

The next picture we are shown jumps to the middle of the Tribulation. We hear John saying,

> And the ten horns which thou sawest upon (the best MSS have *kai*, **and**) **the beast** (now the seventh head, Satan in the False Prophet), these (all ten plus the beast) **shall** (in the middle of the Tribulation) hate the whore, and shall make her desolate and naked, and shall eat her flesh, and burn her with fire. For God hath put in their hearts to fulfil his will, and to agree, and give their kingdom (the world empire, Babylon III) unto the beast (the False Prophet[38]), until the words of God shall be fulfilled.[39]

The Revised Standard Version has, "And the ten horns that you saw, they **and** the beast will hate the harlot." Both the ten kings and the False Prophet will burn the harlot.

The translators of the RSV had the *Codex Siniaticus*, and other important manuscripts, which those of the King James Version, begun in 1604, did not have. For instance, *Codex Siniaticus* was not discovered until 1844. I do not agree with all they changed, but here, it makes sense.

The attack seems to come at the same time that the False Prophet kills Moses and Elijah. It looks like Satan is determined to wipe out the last vestiges of the Christian element in his world kingdom as soon as possible. This is also when he sets up the idol and commands all to worship it.

In Luke 12:17-21, Jesus told a parable of a foolish rich man. It probably refers to the Beast. The rich man said,

> What shall I do, because I have no room where to bestow my fruits? And he said, This will I do: I will pull down my barns, and build greater; and there will I bestow all my fruits and my goods. And I will say to my soul, Soul, thou hast much goods laid up for many years; take thine ease, eat, drink, and

be merry. But God said unto him, Thou fool, this night thy soul shall be required of thee: then whose shall those things be, which thou hast provided? So is he that layeth up treasure for himself, and is not rich toward God.

If this applies to the Beast, the one who will get those things will be the False Prophet, and this transfer will take place as he comes to power.

The False Prophet will pluck three of the original ten horns up by the roots. This may be a result of a disagreement over the burning of the harlot.

In the Old Testament, Daniel interpreted a dream of Nebuchadnezzar's. The head of gold stood for Babylon. The breast and arms of silver represented Media-Persia. The belly and thighs of brass portrayed Greece. The legs of iron were the Eastern and Western Roman Empire. The feet were part iron (Rome) and part clay (other nations). The toes of the feet of the image were these ten kings.

Maybe Daniel's interpretation will shed some more light on these kings. Daniel 2:40-45 says,

And the fourth kingdom (the Roman Empire) shall be strong as iron: forasmuch as iron breaketh in pieces and subdueth all things... shall it break in pieces and bruise. And whereas thou sawest **the feet and toes**, part of potters' clay, and part of iron, **the kingdom** (world empire) **shall be divided**; but there shall be in it of the strength of the iron...And as the toes of the feet were part of iron, and part of clay, so the kingdom shall be partly strong, and partly broken (brittle). And whereas thou sawest iron mixed with miry clay, they (Romans) shall mingle themselves with the seed of men: but they shall not cleave one to another, even as iron is not mixed with clay. And in the days of these kings shall the God of heaven set up a kingdom, which shall never be destroyed...it

(Christ's kingdom) shall break in pieces and consume all these kingdoms...Forasmuch as thou sawest that the stone (the asteroid, the means Christ will use to break in pieces so his kingdom can be set up) was cut out of the mountain (the planet Rahab) without hands, and that it brake in pieces the iron (Rome), the brass (Greece), the clay (other nations), the silver (Media-Persia), and the gold (Babylon); the great God hath made known to the king what shall come to pass hereafter.

The toes are part of the feet. They represent the ten kings that are given crowns as part of the world empire as the Tribulation begins, but they will probably be kings in their own countries before that time. The feet and toes are both part iron and part clay. Therefore, the national lineup is similar both before and after the Rapture of the Church.

The collagen that glues the divided kingdom of the feet together is world government. This began tentatively in 1920 with the League of Nations and has been carried on officially as the United Nations since October 24, 1945. We are living in the foot section just before it separates into the ten toes that represent the Tribulation. That is now drawing near.

Daniel also saw a vision of this final world empire. It grew out of the old Roman Empire and still has the strength of Rome in its devouring teeth. It has the ten horns.

I saw in the night visions, and behold a fourth beast, dreadful and terrible, and strong exceedingly; and it had great iron teeth: it devoured and brake in pieces, and stamped the residue with **the feet** of it: and it was diverse (different) from all the beasts that were before it; and it had ten horns. I considered the horns, and, behold, there came up among them another little horn (the False Prophet), before whom there were three of the first horns plucked up by the roots: and, behold,

in this horn were eyes like the eyes of man,
and a mouth speaking great things.[40]

The Roman Empire first broke into the Eastern Empire and the Western Empire. Then in 476 A.D. the western part fell. The eastern part toppled in 1453. The power of Rome was carried on by the Popes. We are down to the feet now, when we have separate nations bound together by the United Nations and stamped with the pervading influence of ecclesiastical Rome. When we get down to the toes, the Tribulation will begin.

It looks to me like the Tribulation Pope will be elected Secretary General of the world government, and under him in the world empire will be the ten kings that are ruling when the False Prophet makes his appearance. As they accept the Beast at the beginning of the Tribulation, they accept the False Prophet in the middle of the Tribulation and turn over control to him. According to Daniel 7:24, he will have to subdue three of the ten.

Zechariah 11:8 may also speak of these three:

Three shepherds also I (the Lord) cut off in one month; and my soul lothed them, and their soul also abhorred me.

John finishes reading chapter seventeen:

And the woman which thou sawest is that great city, which reigneth over the kings of the earth.[41]

This great city is the same as "that great city" mentioned in Revelation 18:16, literal Babylon. She is already "in the wilderness" when we first see her. However, Vatican City is the city that is moved to Babylon. It is like the older so-called "Vatican of Babylon" that surrounded the ziggurat.

The crash at the Tower of Babel
Chapter eighteen jumps to a view of Babylon at the end of the 2,300-day Shortened Tribulation. We hear of her doom.

> AND after these things I saw another angel
> come down from heaven, having great pow-
> er; and the earth was lightened with his glory.
> And he cried mightily with a strong voice,
> saying, **Babylon the great is fallen, is
> fallen**, and is become the habitation of dev-
> ils, and the hold of every foul spirit, and a
> cage of every unclean and hateful bird.[42]

The words "Babylon the great is fallen, is fallen" are
register marks that align this section with Revelation 14:8,
which says, "Babylon is fallen, is fallen, that great city." We
are about to get a closer and more detailed look at her down-
fall as the angel promised.

John continues his narration, saying,

> For all nations have drunk of the wine of the
> wrath of her fornication, and the kings of the
> earth have committed fornication (joined)
> with her, and the merchants of the earth are
> waxed rich through the abundance of her deli-
> cacies.[43]

Joining political power and religious power is not
good. The main problem arises because not all politicians are
Christians. The political power ends up corrupting the religion. It happened in Constantine's day, it happened after the
Reformation, and it will culminate in the great harlot Mystery
religion of Babylon III.

Rapture two

As John speaks again, we find another register mark to
show us exactly where this belongs on the track of time.

> And I heard another voice from heaven (as in
> Revelation 4:1) saying, **Come out of her,
> my people**, that ye be not partakers of her
> sins, and that ye receive not of her plagues.
> For her sins have reached unto heaven, and
> God hath remembered her iniquities.[44]

Here is another voice from Heaven saying, "Come." This is Rapture II. Since the voice says, "my people," it is the voice of Christ.

At the time of Rapture I, the harlot religion is housed in Rome, but will soon move to Babylon on the Euphrates. At Rapture II, both the harlot religion and Babylon's destruction are imminent—destined to happen the same day.

At Rapture II, the last trump,[45] mankind will look up and see the Sign of the Son of man, just as Stephen saw the Lord as the rocks began to fall. Matthew 24:28-30 says,

> For wheresoever the carcase (body, i.e., the Body of Christ) is (in Heaven), there will the eagles (Tribulation saints) be gathered together. Immediately after the tribulation of those days shall the sun be darkened, and the moon shall not give her light, and the stars shall fall from heaven, and the powers of the heavens shall be shaken: And then shall appear the **sign of the Son of man** in heaven: and then shall all the tribes of the earth mourn.

The eagles remind us of Psalm 103:2-7, which says,

> Bless the LORD, O my soul, and forget not all his benefits: Who forgiveth all thine iniquities; who healeth all thy diseases; Who redeemeth thy life from destruction; who crowneth thee with lovingkindness and tender mercies; Who satisfieth thy mouth with good things; so that **thy youth is renewed like the eagle's.** The LORD executeth righteousness and judgment for all that are oppressed. He made known his ways unto Moses, his acts unto the children of Israel.

Isaiah 41:1 also speaks of these eagles. It says,

> But they that wait upon the LORD shall renew their strength; **they shall mount up**

with wings as eagles; they shall run, and not be weary; and they shall walk, and not faint.

Rapture I is as the days of Noah, but Rapture II is as the days of Lot, when one shall be taken and the other left. The disciples asked Jesus, "Where Lord? and he said unto them, Wheresoever the body (the Body of Christ) is, thither will the eagles (the Tribulation saints) be gathered together."[46]

Those participating in the first Rapture are one foot of the Body of Christ. The main Body is already in Heaven because those believers have died. The ones taken to Heaven in the second Rapture are the other foot. They complete the birth of the Body of Christ into another world.

Zechariah 9:14-15 also speaks of the day of Rapture II. It is the Feast of Trumpets when the Lord will save Israel from her enemies.

> And **the LORD shall be seen over them**, and his arrow shall go forth as the lightning: and **the Lord GOD shall blow the trumpet,** and shall go with whirlwinds of the south. The LORD of hosts shall defend them; and they shall devour, and subdue with sling stones; and they shall drink, and make a noise as through wine; and they shall be filled like bowls, and as the corners of the altar.

Did you notice that the Lord blows this trumpet? It is a different trumpet blast than the seven trumpet judgments. Those are sounded by "seven angels."[47] At the first Rapture, Christ's voice "was as it were of a trumpet talking with me; which said, Come up hither."[48] I Thessalonians says that he comes "with the trump of God." That is the first Rapture. At the second Rapture, Christ will also call his saints with a trumpet blast.

Some say that the Rapture of the Church will not take place until the last of the seven trumpet judgments sound. They base this belief on I Corinthians 15:51-54, which says,

Behold, I shew you a mystery; We shall not all sleep, but we shall **all** be changed, In a moment, in the twinkling of an eye, **at the last trump**: for the trumpet shall sound, and the dead shall be raised incorruptible, and we shall be changed. For this corruptible must put on incorruption, and this mortal must put on immortality. When this corruptible shall have put on incorruption, and this mortal shall have put on immortality, then shall be brought to pass the saying that is written, **Death is swallowed up in victory**.

This takes place at the end of the Shortened Tribulation, as you can see from Isaiah 25:8. Look for the register marks.

He will swallow up death in victory; and the Lord GOD will wipe away tears from off all faces; and the rebuke of his people shall he take away from off all the earth: for the LORD hath spoken it.

What many people fail to see is that this is not talking about the first Rapture, but the second. It is when "all" the Body of Christ is completed. By that time all that are to be part of the heavenly Body of Christ are changed. The Body is complete. Just as there are different comings of Christ, there are different ranks in the first resurrection. I Corinthians 15:22,23 tells us that

as in Adam all die, even so in Christ shall **all** be made alive. But every man in his own order (*tagmati*, rank): Christ the firstfruits; afterward they that are Christ's at his coming.

Christ comes in the air at Rapture I. He also comes in the air at Rapture II. At the Second Advent, he walks on Earth again for awhile. He will restore the environment, set up the Millennial government, put king David back on his throne, restore the judges, and then return to his heavenly throne. He's King of kings and Lord of lords, and he will be the supreme ruler throughout the Millennium, the Day of the Lord.

At Gethsemane, on the eve of the Crucifixion, Christ prefigured three comings before the Millennial rest. He told Peter, James, and John,

> tarry ye here, and watch. And he went forward a little, and...prayed...And **he cometh** (i.e., Rapture I), and findeth them sleeping, and saith unto Peter, Simon, sleepest thou: couldest not thou watch one hour? **Watch ye and pray, lest ye enter into temptation** (*peirasmon*, trial, i.e., the Tribulation[49]). The spirit truly is ready, but the flesh is weak. And again he went away, and prayed...And when **he returned** (i.e., Rapture II), he found them asleep again...**And he cometh the third time** (i.e., the Second Advent), and saith unto them, Sleep on now, and take your rest (symbol of the Millennial rest[50]).

Jesus said to "watch one hour." One hour of a millennial day is 41.66 years. If the Sign of the End of the Age was the Six-Day War in 1967, when Israel grew leaves and fulfilled the fig tree parable of Matthew 24:32-34, the hour would be up in 2008. (1967 + 41.66 = 2008.66)

David slew Goliath with a sling stone, one out of a possible five (I Samuel 17:40). It pictured Christ, the Son of David, who will slay the army of the giant world confederacy with a sling stone. Will it also be one of a possible five?

As soon as the Tribulation saints are in Heaven, they renew their strength and then participate in the proceedings at the Judgment Seat of Christ. John's next words sound like jury instructions from the judge:

> Reward her even as she rewarded **you**, and double unto her double according to her works: in the cup which she hath filled fill to

her double. How much she hath glorified herself, and lived deliciously, so much torment and sorrow give her: for she saith in her heart, I sit a queen (claims to be the Bride of Christ), and am no widow (not cut off, i.e., left behind), and shall see no sorrow. Therefore shall her plagues come in one day, death, and mourning, and famine; and she shall be utterly burned with fire: for strong *is* the Lord God who **judgeth** her.[51]

As Jerusalem "hath received of the LORD'S hand double for all her sins,"[52] Babylon will receive double.

Jerusalem will also receive double joy in the end, as Job did. Isaiah 60:6,7 says of Israel,

But ye shall be named the Priests of the LORD: men shall call you the Ministers of our God: ye shall eat the riches of the Gentiles, and in their glory shall ye boast yourselves. For your shame ye shall have double; and for confusion they shall rejoice in their portion: therefore in their land they shall possess the double: everlasting joy shall be unto them.

In Jeremiah 16:18,21, the Lord says,

And first (before Israel is restored) I will recompense their iniquity and their sin double; because they have defiled my land, they have filled mine inheritance with the carcases of their detestable and abominable things.... Therefore, behold, I will **this once** cause them to know, **I will cause them to know mine hand and my might**; and they shall know that my name is The LORD.

This one show of his might will be enough. Israel will know that he is the LORD from this day on. The scriptures are true. Jesus said, "For verily I say unto you, Till heaven and earth pass, one jot or one tittle shall in no wise pass from the law, till all be fulfilled."[53]

In Heaven, Jeremiah will have his part in the judgment. We already know his sentiments on the matter. While he was still on Earth, he said, "bring upon them the day of evil, and destroy them with double destruction."[54]

Jeremiah 51: 35-37,49 says,

> The violence done to me and to my flesh be upon Babylon, shall the inhabitant of Zion say; and my blood upon the inhabitants of Chaldea, shall Jerusalem say. Therefore thus saith the LORD: Behold, I will plead thy cause, and take vengeance for thee; and I **will dry up her sea**, and make her springs dry. And Babylon shall become heaps... without an inhabitant....As Babylon hath caused the slain of Israel to fall, so at Babylon shall fall the slain of all the earth (representatives of all nations are there).

Jeremiah 51:11 gives a reason for the destruction:

> the LORD...his device is against Babylon, to destroy it; because it is the vengeance of the LORD, the vengeance of his temple.

The stone is referred to in Zechariah 5:1-4 as "the curse." It will destroy the houses at Babylon built by the two final kings. Zechariah said,

> THEN I turned, and lifted up mine eyes, and looked, and behold a flying roll (*megillah*, rolling thing, i.e., a binary asteroid). And he said unto me, What seest thou? And I answered, I see a flying roll; the length thereof is twenty cubits, and the breadth thereof ten cubits (twice as long as wide). Then said he unto me, This is **the curse** that goeth forth

over the face of the whole earth: for every one that stealeth shall be cut off as on this side according to it (a "mountain" will hit the Mediterranean); and every one that sweareth shall be cut off as on that side (a "star" will hit Babylon) according to it. I will bring it forth, saith the LORD of hosts, and it shall enter into the house of the thief (the False Prophet), and into the house of him that sweareth falsely by my name (the Beast): and it shall remain in the midst of his house, and shall consume it with the timber thereof and the stones thereof.

The kings' lament

As our play proceeds, we hear the kings' grieve for her:

And the kings of the earth (including the ten kings), who have committed fornication and lived deliciously with her, shall bewail her, and lament for her, when they shall see the smoke of her burning. Standing afar off for the fear of her torment, saying, **Alas, alas**, that great city Babylon, that mighty city! for in **one hour** is thy judgment come.[55]

Alas means woe. This aligns with the last two trumpet judgments. Under the sixth, the four angels that were bound in the Euphrates river are loosed to slay one third of the men of the world in "one hour" on one certain day, month, and year. A third of the men are killed by the fire, smoke and brimstone in the first hour after the impact.

Impact at noon

The asteroid strikes at noon. In Amos 8:9,10, the Lord said, "I will cause the sun to go down **at noon**...I will turn your feasts (the Feast of Trumpets, the Biblical *Yom Teruah*, which means **the day of the awakening blast**) into mourning." Job 20:19-29 fills in more details. It says,

Because he (the wicked one) hath oppressed and hath forsaken the poor; because he hath violently taken away an house which he builded not...**When he is about to fill his belly, God shall cast the fury of his wrath upon him, and shall rain it upon him while he is eating...**The increase of his house shall depart, and his goods shall flow away in the day of his wrath. This is the portion of a wicked man from God, and the heritage appointed unto him by God.

The incorrigible

What does it take to get them to repent? Revelation 9:20,21 says,

And the rest of the men which were not killed by these plagues yet repented not of the works of their hand, that they should not worship devils, and idols of gold, and silver, and brass, and stone, and of wood: which neither can see, nor hear, nor walk: Neither repented they of their murders, nor of their sorceries (*pharmakeion*, drugs), nor of their fornication, nor of their thefts.

Merchants weep over her

John continues with the mourning of the merchants that were made rich by her.

And the merchants of the earth shall weep and mourn over her; for no man buyeth their merchandise any more: The merchandise of gold, and silver, and precious stones, and of pearls, and fine linen, and purple, and silk, and scarlet, and all thyine wood, and all manner vessels of ivory, and all manner vessels of most precious wood, and of brass, and iron, and marble, And cinnamon, and odours, and ointments, and frankincense, and wine, and oil, and fine flour, and wheat, and beasts, and sheep, and horses, and chariots, and slaves, and souls of men.[56]

Satan sinned in the first place because of "the multitude of thy merchandise." It caused violence and sin then, as it does now. Addressing Satan as king of Tyrus (which means the rock, i.e., the planet Rahab), the Lord said,

Thou wast perfect in thy ways from the day that thou wast created, till iniquity was found in thee. By the multitude of thy merchandise they have filled the midst of thee with violence, and thou hast sinned: therefore I will cast thee as profane out of the mountain of God: and I will destroy thee, O covering cherub, from the midst of the stones of fire.[57]

No more, no more

As John continues, we hear the sad words concerning Babylon, "no more at all." It is absolutely final. He says,

And the fruits that thy soul lusteth after are departed from thee, and all things which were dainty and goodly are departed from thee, and thou shalt find them no more at all.[58]

There is nothing left of the costliest city the world has ever known, Babylon III, capitol of the world.

John continues,

The merchants of these things, which were made rich by her, shall stand afar off for the fear of her torment, weeping and wailing, And saying, **Alas, alas that great city,** that was clothed in fine linen, and purple, and scarlet, and decked with gold, and precious stones, and pearls! For **in one hour so great riches is come to nought.** And every shipmaster, and all the company in ships, and sailors, and as many as trade by sea, stood afar off, And cried when they saw the smoke of her burning, saying, What *city is* like unto this great city![59]

Nebuchadnezzar's Babylon the Great is the magnificent forerunner, but the final Babylon outstrips in splendor every city that has ever been built. John says,

And they cast dust on their heads, and cried, weeping and wailing, saying, **Alas, alas that great city,** wherein were made rich all that had ships in the sea by reason of her costliness! for **in one hour is she made desolate.** Rejoice over her, *thou* heaven, and ye holy apostles and prophets; for God hath avenged you on her.[60]

This harlot killed the apostles, prophets, and many other saints, but there is a payback. Nahum 1:1-9 explains,

God is jealous, and the LORD revengeth... and is furious; the LORD will take vengeance on his adversaries, and he reserveth wrath for his enemies. The LORD is slow to anger, and great in power, and will not at all acquit the wicked: the LORD hath his way in the whirlwind and in the storm, and the clouds are the dust of his feet. He rebuketh the sea (the Mediterranean), and maketh it dry, and drieth up all the rivers: Bashan languisheth, and Carmel, and the flower of Lebanon languisheth. The mountains quake at him, and the hills melt, and the earth is burned at **his presence,** yea, the world, and all that dwell therein. Who can stand before his indignation? and who can abide in the fierceness of his anger? his fury is poured out like fire, and **the rocks are thrown down by**

him.The LORD is good, a strong hold in **the
day of trouble**; and he knoweth them that
trust in him. But with an overrunning flood
(tsunami) he will make an utter end of the
place thereof, and darkness shall pursue his
enemies. What do ye imagine against the
LORD? he will make an utter end; affliction
shall not rise up the second time.

At his "presence," he will pull out the Tribulation
saints just before the main rock hits. It is the Day of Jacob's
Trouble, but it also is the day of salvation for the Tribulation
saints. They are saved out of the fiery furnace, yet their
clothing will not even smell of smoke.

The planet will be turned upside down, throwing the
seas against the walls. The whole globe will shake, "and
every wall shall fall to the ground."[61] Isaiah 24:1 says,

> BEHOLD, the LORD maketh the earth emp-
> ty, and maketh it waste, and **turneth it up-
> side down**, and scattereth abroad the inhab-
> itants thereof.

The stone cast down
As John continues, we get a graphic picture of Babylon's
destruction by the asteroid. He says,

> And a mighty angel took up a stone like a
> great millstone, and cast *it* into the sea, say-
> ing, Thus with violence shall that great city
> Babylon be thrown down, and shall be found
> no more at all.[62]

The mighty angel is the Angel of the Lord. Isaiah
22:17,18 says,

> Behold, the LORD will carry thee away with
> a mighty captivity, and will surely cover thee.
> **He will surely violently turn and toss
> thee like a ball into a large country.**

This ball belongs to Satan. The Lord will use a whirlwind to turn this asteroid into its final landing pattern. It must hit just right, destroying much of civilization as we know it, but not breaking the planet into pieces. The Lord said he would

> cut off from Babylon the name, and remnant, and son, and nephew, saith the LORD. I will also make it a possession for the bittern, and pools of water: and I will sweep it with the besom (broom) of destruction.[63]

Not only will Babylon be destroyed, Egypt will be swept so hard that no one will even live there for the next forty years. Ezekiel 29:9-14 tells us that

> the land of Egypt shall be desolate and waste; and they shall know that I am the LORD: because he hath said, The river is mine, and I have made it. Behold, therefore I am against thee, and against thy rivers, and I will make the land of Egypt utterly waste and desolate, from the tower of Syene even unto the border of Ethiopia. No foot of man shall pass through it, nor foot of beast shall pass through it, neither shall it be inhabited forty years. And I will make the land of Egypt desolate in the midst of the countries that are desolate, and her cities among the cities that are laid waste shall be desolate forty years, and I will scatter the Egyptians among the nations...At the end of forty years will I gather the Egyptians...And I will bring again the captivity of Egypt, and will cause them to return into the land.

As John continues, it sounds like a dirge.

> And the voice of harpers, and musicians, and of pipers, and trumpeters, shall be heard no

> more at all in thee; and no craftsman, of
> whatsoever craft *he be*, shall be found any
> more in thee; and the sound of a millstone
> shall be heard no more at all in thee; And the
> light of a candle shall shine no more at all in
> thee; and the voice of the bridegroom and of
> the bride shall be heard no more at all in thee:
> for thy merchants were the great men of the
> earth; for **by thy sorceries were all na-
> tions deceived.**[64]

Satan was a deceiver from before the days of Adam
and Eve. Satan has worked very hard to deceive man from
that day to this, and by the end of the Shortened Tribulation,
all nations are deceived. It is a sad story.

As John ends this section of script, his concluding
words sound like her epitaph:

> And in her was found the blood of prophets,
> and of saints, and of all that were slain upon
> the earth.[65]

This mention of blood ties in with the third bowl judgment,
which is poured out at this time. Revelation 16:5,6 says,

> I heard the angel of the waters say, Thou art
> righteous, O Lord, which art (at the Rapture),
> and wast (at the First Advent), and shalt be
> (at the still future Second Advent), because
> thou hast judged thus. For they have shed the
> blood of saints and prophets, and thou hast
> given them blood to drink; for they are wor-
> thy.

Does she get what she deserves? Yes. Justice prevails. Job 19:29 says,

> Be ye afraid of the sword (of the Lord): for
> wrath bringeth the punishments of the sword,
> that ye may know **there is a judgment.**

Psalm 58: 10,11 shows that there is a reward for the righteous and vengeance for the others.

> The righteous shall rejoice when he seeth the vengeance: he shall wash his feet in the blood of the wicked. So that a man shall say, Verily there is a reward for the righteous: verily he is a God that judgeth in the earth.

Jeremiah 51:49 ties the destruction of Babylon to her attack on Israel.

> As Babylon hath caused the slain of Israel to fall, so at Babylon shall fall the slain of all the earth.

All nations will be represented in Babylon. They will all have ambassadors and merchants in this great international city.

Jeremiah 46:10 shows that this happens in the millennial Day of the Lord. Actually, it takes place on the very first twenty-four-hour day of that thousand-year Day of the Lord.

> For this is the day of the Lord GOD of hosts, a day of vengeance, that he may avenge him of his adversaries: and the sword shall devour, and it shall be satiate and made drunk with their blood: for the Lord GOD of hosts hath a sacrifice in the north country by the river Euphrates.

The nations labor only for the fire

> Woe to him that buildeth a town with blood, and establisheth a city by iniquity! Behold, is it not of the LORD of hosts that the peoples shall **labor only for fire**, and the nations shall weary themselves for nothing? (Habakkuk 2:12,13, New Scofield Bible).

Dreams of Babylon as a capital of the world will end in fiery flames. It has been a long time coming.

In the early days, Nimrod tried to build the Tower of Babel. God had to step in and confuse the languages to keep it from being finished before its time had come.

Later, after rebuilding Babylon, Nebuchadnezzar had the idea that he would build another great capital city. There he intended to store products from all the world before they were sent on to Babylon, which would then control the entire international market. It did not materialized at that time.[66]

Under Nebuchadnezzar, Babylon did become the bank of the ancient Orient. He was also able to turn the city into an international center of both commercial and religious activity. He also rebuilt the ziggurat Etamenanki, "House of the foundation of heaven and earth."[67]

Even Alexander the Great intended to rebuild the city as a trading center to link India and Egypt.[68] He wanted to make it his capital city, but died before he could do it.

Satan chose Babylon as his capital long ago. You can see his influence on Nebuchadnezzar, who said, "When the god Marduk, the great Lord, created me, he commanded me solemnly to maintain order in the land, to raise cities, to rebuild the temples. I obeyed, full of fear. I established Babylon, the sublime city...On the threshold of her gates I set huge bulls and footed serpents."[69] The red snake, or the dragon, *sirrush*, represented Marduk (Bel, Baal), i.e.,Satan.

Babylon will become Satan's capital city when he indwells the False Prophet, but it will be destroyed in the midst of terrible destruction on Earth. Isaiah 24:1 says,

> BEHOLD, the LORD maketh the earth empty, and maketh it waste, and **turneth it upside down,** and scattereth abroad the inhabitants thereof....The land shall be utterly emptied...because they have transgressed the laws, changed the ordinance, broken the everlasting covenant. Therefore hath **the curse devoured the earth,** and they that dwell therein are desolate: therefore the inhabitants of the earth are burned, and few men left.

[1] Revelation 1:3
[2] Revelation 1:8;22:12-20
[3] Zechariah 5:11
[4] Revelation 17:15
[5] Revelation 17:2
[6] Revelation 17:3
[7] Matthew 13:24-30,38
[8] Genesis 11:2; Daniel 1:1,2
[9] Revelation 6:1,2
[10] Daniel 2:33
[11] Revelation 17:12
[12] Revelation 17:14
[13] Revelation 17:4
[14] Ezekiel 27:12
[15] Daniel 8:14
[16] Revelation 17:5
[17] Genesis 3:15
[18] Revelation 17:6
[19] Revelation 17:7,8
[20] Revelation 17:11
[21] Revelation 17:14
[22] Revelation 17:9
[23] Revelation 17:10,11
[24] Daniel 2:31-45
[25] Daniel 2:38
[26] Daniel 5:30-31
[27] Daniel 8:20,21
[28] Daniel 9:26
[29] Hosea 12:10
[30] Jeremiah 25:1
[31] Luke 13:6-9
[32] Daniel 8:14
[33] Ezra 3:2,3,8-11
[34] Revelation 17:12,13
[35] Revelation 3:10
[36] Revelation 17:14
[37] Revelation 17:15
[38] Revelation 13;11
[39] Revelation 17:16,17
[40] Daniel 7:7,8
[41] Revelation 17:18
[42] Revelation 18:1,2
[43] Revelation 18:3
[44] Revelation 18:4,5

[45] I Corinthians 15:52
[46] Luke 17:37
[47] Revelation 8:2
[48] Revelation 4:1
[49] Revelation 3:10
[50] Hebrews 4:9
[51] Revelation 18:6-8
[52] Isaiah 40:2
[53] Matthew 5:18
[54] Jeremiah 17:18
[55] Revelation 18:9,10
[56] Revelation 18:11-13
[57] Ezekiel 28:15,16
[58] Revelation 18:14
[59] Revelation 18:15-18
[60] Revelation 18:19,20
[61] Ezekiel 38:20
[62] Revelation 18:21
[63] Isaiah 14:22,23
[64] Revelation 18:22,23
[65] Revelation 18:24
[66] Champdor, Albert. Babylon. (N.Y., G.P. Putnam's Sons, 1958) p. 96
[67] *Ibid*, p. 114, 116
[68] *Ibid*, p. 122
[69] *Ibid*, p. 115

11

*R*eturn of the *K*ing of *k*ings

Revelation 19 and 20

𝔍esus is crowned in Heaven on his birthday, Tishri 1.

Solomon, son of David, wisest of men, is a type of Christ. Since Solomon's mother crowned him on the day of his wedding, it looks like Mary has the honor of placing the golden crown on the the greater Son of David's head. Song of Solomon 3:11 in the New American Bible mentions

> the crown with which his mother has crowned him on the day of his marriage, on the day of the joy of his heart.

Just as our President is first elected and then inaugurated at a later date, Jesus is first crowned in Heaven and then returns to Earth to publicly take over the reigns of government at a later date. As a type, king David was anointed as king some time before he took office.[1]

The King of kings will return to Earth on the following Nisan 1, the first day of the Jewish Regnal year and sacred year, on the same date that their other kings officially took office.

Satan said, "I will be like the most High,"[2] and just as Christ will be honored when he returns on Nisan 1, Satan saw to it that in Babylonia (in Assyria also), the Festival of the New Year at Babylon honored Marduk, which is the same as Bel, i.e., Satan. Bel was associated with founding Babylon. Each king of Babylon had to participate in the New

Year ceremony called *akitu* and "take the hand of the God Bel" before his enthronement was complete.[3] Satan tries to counterfeit things concerning Christ to confuse mankind.

Israel, God's reluctant fig tree, finally sprouts instant fruit on Tishri 1, the day of the great catastrophe. When they blow the trumpet of alarm, the Lord saves tiny Israel from the confederated armies of all nations on Earth. With new eyes to see, the Israeli remnant now understands that Jesus Christ is their true Messiah. They realize that they should bury the dead and cleanse the land for his return in glory. Scurrying to accomplish the task, they hire men to continually work at it.

Seven months

Ezekiel 39:12 establishes the length of the interval between the catastrophe and the return of Christ in glory.

> And **seven months** shall the house of Israel be burying of them, that they may cleanse the land. Yea, all the people of the land shall bury them; and it shall be to them a renown the day that I shall be glorified, saith the Lord GOD.

The day that he will be glorified is the day of his second advent. Matthew 25:31 says, "When the Son of man shall come in his **glory**, and all the holy angels with him, then shall he sit upon the throne of his **glory**."

The seven months during which Israel buries the dead are Tishri, Cheshvan, Kislev, Teveth, Shevat, Adar, and Adar II, because it is a leap year when an extra month is added to keep their calendar aligned with the seasons. The seven months will not work out in a year that is not a leap year. It is obvious that the Lord planned to return in a leap year.

The Lord calculated everything in advance. Isaiah 46:10,11 in the New International Version says,

> I make known the end from the beginning, from ancient times, what is still to come. I

> say: My purpose will stand, and I will do all
> that I please...What I have said, that will I
> bring about; what I have planned, that I will
> do.

The scene in Heaven

When John finished chapter eighteen, he was viewing the
earthly arena. As he begins chapter nineteen, he is looking at
the heavenly scene right after the catastrophe happens on
Earth. We hear him saying,

> AND after these things I heard a great voice
> of much people in heaven, saying, Alleluia;
> Salvation, and glory, and honour, and pow-
> er, unto the Lord our God:

There are now three groups of saints in Heaven, Old
Testament, Church, and Tribulation saints. Included in those
groups are the apostles and prophets. In Revelation 18:20,
they were told, "Rejoice over her (Babylon), thou heaven,
and ye holy apostles and prophets; for God hath avenged
you on her."

It is still Tishri 1, but we see that the judgment on
Babylon is past as John continues his narration;

> For true and righteous *are* his judgments: for
> he hath judged the great whore, which did
> corrupt the earth with her fornication, and
> hath avenged the blood of his servants at her
> hand. And again they said, Alleluia. And her
> smoke rose up for ever and ever.[4]

The main reason that she felt the avenging sword is
because she killed the servants of the Lord. She will not be
inhabited again because she hath striven against the Lord.
Jeremiah 50:13,23-25 says,

> Because of the wrath of the LORD it shall not
> be inhabited, but it shall be wholly desolate:
> every one that goeth by Babylon shall be as-

tonished, and hiss at all her plagues....How is **the hammer of the whole earth** (the binary asteroid) cut asunder (cut into two main pieces) and broken (smaller chunks spew from the break)! how is Babylon become a desolation among the nations! I have laid a snare for thee, and thou art also taken, O Babylon, and thou wast not aware: thou art found, and also caught, because thou hast striven against the Lord. **The LORD hath opened his armoury**, and hath brought forth the weapons of his indignation: for this is the work of the Lord GOD of hosts in the land of the Chaldeans.

Luke 18:7 shows that God avenges the elect who pray day and night to him. It says,

shall not God avenge his own elect, which cry day and night unto him, though he bear long with them. I tell you that he will avenge them speedily.

Even though answers are a long time coming, know that there is a response to prayer. The Lord does not forget. When the answer to these come, things will happen *f a s t*.

As John continues, the saved in Heaven fall down and worship Christ, who is "God that sat on the throne."

And the four and twenty elders and the four beasts fell down and worshipped **God that sat on the throne**, saying, Amen; Alleluia. And a voice came out of the throne, saying, Praise our God, all ye his servants, and ye that fear him, both small and great.[5]

The response to this call to praise our God is instantaneous. Individual voices blend and swell into a great roar, even as mighty thunderings. Joy is everywhere. The ears know it. The eyes know it. The heart knows it. John says,

> And I heard as it were the voice of a great
> multitude, and as the voice of many waters,
> and as the voice of mighty thunderings, say-
> ing, Alleluia (which means praise God): for
> the Lord God omnipotent reigneth (*ebasileu-*
> *sen*, has reigned).[6]

The Coronation is past. Jesus Christ is wearing
many crowns, including the golden one mentioned in Revelation 14:14, when he was ready to harvest the Tribulation
saints.

Marriage Supper of the Lamb in Heaven

The next passage is confusing in the King James translation.
However, important manuscripts like the Codex Sinaiticus
were discovered after the King James Version was completed. The Revised Standard Version reflects a change in tense
in the following. Instead of "is come," the RSV says, "has
come."

The King James Version says,

> Let us be glad and rejoice, and give honour to
> him: for the marriage of the Lamb **is come**,
> and his wife hath made herself ready. And to
> her was granted that she should be arrayed in
> fine linen, clean and white: for the fine linen
> is the righteousness (lit., righteousnesses) of
> saints. And he saith unto me, Write, Blessed
> *are* they which are called unto the marriage
> supper of the Lamb. And he saith unto me,
> These are the true sayings of God.[7]

Because of the KJV wording, it is hard to reconcile
the time of the Marriage of the Lamb. The New Scofield
Reference Bible says that the "The marriage of the Lamb"
above is literally "the marriage supper of the Lamb." The
Lamsa translation has "for the time of the marriage feast of
the Lamb has come."

Green's Interlinear has "For the marriage of the
Lamb **has come**...the fine linen **was** given to her...they

who are called to the supper of the marriage of the Lamb."
The literal Concordant Version has "for the wedding of the
Lambkin came." The RSV has "for the marriage of the
Lamb has come...those who are invited to the marriage
supper of the Lamb."

There is a change in tense. The Lord has reigned.
The marriage has come. The fine linen was given. The Bride
has already become the "wife." What is in view now is the
Marriage Supper of the Lamb. The marriage supper, similar
to a fancy wedding reception, is now ready to take place.

Luke 12:35-37 shows that the wedding took place
before the Tribulation saints (the foolish virgins and Laodiceans) were raptured.

> Let your (the foolish virgins') loins be girded
> about, and your lights burning (i.e., have
> enough oil of the Holy Spirit like the wise
> virgins); And ye yourselves like unto men
> that wait for their lord, when **he will re-
> turn from the wedding**; that when he
> cometh and knocketh (as he knocks on the
> door for the Laodiceans[8]), they may open
> unto him immediately. Blessed are those
> servants, whom the lord when he cometh
> shall find watching: verily I say unto you,
> that he shall gird himself, and make them to
> sit down to meat (the Marriage Supper of the
> Lamb), and will come forth and serve them.

The righteousness of saints is what they receive
when they first believe in Christ. That is imputed righteousness, "the righteousness of God...upon all them that
believe."[9] Afterward the righteousnesses of saints are their
righteous acts.

To be saved, we have to have faith in Christ. To earn
rewards, we must have faith and works. Our works demonstrate that we have faith. Our light must shine brightly to be a
member of the Bride. We must confess our sins to God, as
in I John 1:9, and be forgiven so none of our light becomes
shadow. We are warned not to quench the Holy Spirit.[10]

The Old Testament saints are not the Bride. James 2:23 says that "Abraham believed God, and it was imputed unto him for righteousness: and he was called the Friend of God." John the Baptist referred to himself as "the friend of the bridegroom."[11]

The Bridegroom is Christ. The Bride is the Church. The Old Testament saints are the friends of the Bridegroom. The Tribulation saints are the friends of the Bride. All attend the Marriage Supper of the Lamb.

John continues,

> And I fell at his feet to worship him. And he (the angel) said unto me, See *thou do it* not: I am thy fellowservant, and of thy brethren that have the testimony of Jesus: worship God: for the testimony of Jesus is the spirit of prophecy.[12]

We are not to worship angels, period. That includes God's angels, Satan, and his demon angels. Worship God Almighty, the Lord Jesus Christ. Isaiah 45:21-23 declares,

> Tell ye...who hath declared this from ancient time...have not I the LORD? and there is no God else beside me; a just God and a Saviour; there is none beside me. Look unto me, and be ye saved, all the ends of the earth: for I am God, and there is none else. I have sworn by myself, the word is gone out of my mouth in righteousness, and shall not return, That unto me every knee shall bow, every tongue shall swear.

In Philippians 2:5-11, Paul explained,

> Christ Jesus: Who, being in the form of God, thought it not robbery to be equal with God: But made himself of no reputation, and took upon him the form of a servant, and was made in the likeness of men: And being

found in fashion as a man, he humbled himself, and became obedient unto death, even the death of the cross. Wherefore God also hath highly exalted him, and given him a name which is above every name: That at the name of Jesus every knee should bow, of things in heaven, and things in earth, and things under the earth; And that every tongue should confess that Jesus Christ is Lord, to the glory of God the Father.

The Second Advent

As we hear John continue his narration, Christ has mounted up to return to Earth. The fact that he rides a horse this time suggests war. Donkeys were not used for fighting, but horses were. The first time, Jesus did not come to fight. This time it is different. He is now the great King of kings with the legal right to the Earth and is coming to bring true lasting peace. However, to do that, he must get rid of those who want to go to war against him to try to keep him from being King over the Earth. John says,

And I saw heaven opened, and behold a white horse; and he that sat upon him *was* called Faithful and True, and in righteousness he doth **judge and make war**.[13]

The judgment in view is the Judgment of the Nations. The war is Armageddon, which cannot take place until Christ is on Earth. His return is after the catastrophe. He shall return like rain after the Lord's mowing.

He shall come down like rain upon the mown grass: as showers that water the earth.[14]

Grass represents people. I Peter 1:24 says that "all flesh is as grass." When the catastrophe is over, few will be left after the Lord's mowing.

Matthew 25:31-46 tells us how Jesus will separate the sheep and goats at the Judgment of the Nations:

horses, showing that they are guided by the Holy Spirit. According to Matthew 25:31, "all the holy angels" will be with him too.

Operation Wipe-up is about to begin. In the next verses, listen to what John says:

> And out of his mouth goeth a sharp sword, that with it he should smite the nations: and he shall rule them with a rod of iron (symbol of strength): and he treadeth the winepress of the fierceness and wrath of Almighty God. And he hath on *his* vesture (robes of our high priest) and on his thigh a name written, KING OF KINGS, AND LORD OF LORDS.

This sharp sword goes out of the Lord's mouth. It sounds like his word, as in Ephesians 6:17: "And take the helmet of salvation, and the sword of the Spirit, which is the word of God."

There will be physical changes in the land in Israel when Christ arrives with all his saints following him. Zechariah 14:4-7 tells us of the changes and also of the strange lighting conditions on that day.

> And his feet shall stand in that day upon the mount of Olives, which is before Jerusalem on the east, and the mount of Olives shall cleave in the midst thereof toward the east and toward the west, and there shall be a very great valley; and half of the mountain shall remove toward the north, and half of it toward the south. And ye shall flee to the valley of the mountains; for the valley of the mountains shall reach unto Azal: yea, ye shall flee, like as ye fled from before the earthquake in the days of Uzziah king of Judah: and the LORD my God shall come, **and all the saints with thee**. And it shall come to pass in that day, that the light shall not be clear, nor dark: But it shall be one day which shall

be known to the LORD, not day, nor night:
but it shall come to pass, that at evening time
it shall be light.

The supper of the great God, on Earth

At the Judgment Seat of Christ, there were good rewards handed out in Heaven and bad rewards handed out on
Earth. This duality still prevails; there are two kinds of sup-
pers. As John goes on reading, we find that after the Marriage Supper of the Lamb in Heaven, there is "the supper of
the great God" on Earth. The former is good, the latter bad.
John continues:

> And I saw an angel standing in the sun; and
> he cried with a loud voice, saying to all the
> fowls that fly in the midst of heaven (margin,
> mid-heaven), Come and gather yourselves
> together unto the supper of the great God;
> That ye may eat the flesh of kings, and the
> flesh of captains, and the flesh of mighty
> men, and the flesh of horses, and of them
> that sit on them, and the flesh of all *men*,
> *both* free and bond, both small and great.[19]

The world government has dispatched its entire military might to try to keep Christ from becoming king of the
world. All it takes to end it is the word of God. John says,

> And I saw the beast, and the kings of the
> earth, and their armies, gathered together to
> make war against him that sat on the horse,
> and against his army.[20]

Their hope is in vain. Right away, we hear the out-
come of Armageddon. John declares,

> And the beast was taken, and with him the
> false prophet that wrought miracles before
> him, with which he deceived them that had
> received the mark of the beast, and them that

worshipped his image. These both (*duo*) were cast alive into a lake of fire burning with brimstone. And the remnant were slain with the sword of him that sat upon the horse, which *sword* proceeded out of his mouth: and all the fowls were filled with their flesh.[21]

Actually, all the Lord has to do is withdraw "the breath of life"[22] and the rest will die. He may not choose to do it this way, however. Psalms 149:5-9 says,

Let the saints be joyful in glory: let them sing aloud upon their beds. Let the high praises of God be in their mouth, and a twoedged sword in their hand; To execute vengeance upon the heathen, and punishments upon the people; To bind their kings with chains, and their nobles with fetters of iron; To execute upon them the judgment written: this honour have all his saints.

Satan chained

Satan is still free after the False Prophet is cast into the Lake of Fire. As John continues, we find out what happens to the Devil himself. John's script here is in Revelation twenty.

AND I saw an angel come down from heaven, having the key of the bottomless pit and a great chain in his hand. And he laid hold on the dragon, that old serpent, which is the Devil, and Satan, and bound him a thousand years, And cast him into the bottomless pit, and shut him up, and set a seal upon him, that he should deceive the nations no more, till the thousand years should be fulfilled: and after that he must be loosed a little season.[23]

Satan is not said to be cast into the Lake of Fire until the Millennium is complete. The Beast and False Prophet are cast into the Lake of Fire after Christ returns, but Satan is cast into the Bottomless Pit. There evidently is some difference between the two. The Bottomless Pit seems to be the molten center of the Earth, where all directions are up. The Lake of Fire is molten magma that has surged to the surface through split rock after the asteroid detonated at Babylon.

The first resurrection

Next, we are to be shown a scene at the end of the first resurrection, when all are present, as pictured in I Corinthians 15:51. The elders will be associate judges at the Judgment Seat of Christ.

Jesus told the apostles that they would judge Israel and told the saints that they would judge the world (*kosmos*, world order) and the angels. Matthew 19:28 says that "in the regeneration when the Son of man shall sit in the throne of his glory, ye also shall sit upon twelve thrones, judging the twelve tribes of Israel." First Corinthians 6:2,3, says, "Do ye not know that the saints shall judge the world?...Know ye not that we shall judge angels?" Man may have been created to prove a point to the angels. We will find out for sure in glory.

John continues his narration,

> And I saw thrones, and they (the elders) sat upon them, and judgment was given unto them: and *I saw* the souls of them that were beheaded for the witness of Jesus, and for the word of God, and which had not worshipped the beast, neither his image, neither had received *his* mark upon their foreheads, or in their hands; and they lived and reigned with Christ a thousand years. But the rest of the dead lived not again until the thousand years were finished. This *is* the first resurrection. Blessed and holy *is* he that hath part in the first resurrection: on such the second death (Lake of Fire[24]) hath no power, but they shall be priests of God and of Christ, and shall reign with him a thousand years.[25]

Since Christ is to rule a thousand years, he must be crowned the first day of the millennial Day of the Lord. The Tribulation martyrs are seen alive, so the first resurrection is already complete. Rapture II has taken place. It has to take place on the first day of the Millennium because they live and reign with Christ a thousand years also.

Some say that the Day of the Lord begins when Rapture I takes place. That cannot be for Elijah must come before the Day of the Lord can begin.[26] However, the Millennium does begin the day Rapture II takes place.

The Millennium

During the Millennium, Christ will restore the Kingdom to Israel. Psalm 72:7-19 shows some of what the Lord will do during the thousand years.

> In his days shall the righteous flourish; and abundance of peace...He shall have dominion also from sea to sea, and from the river (Euphrates) unto the ends of the earth....his enemies shall lick the dust...all kings shall fall down before him: all nations shall serve him. For he shall deliver the needy when he crieth, the poor also, and him that hath no helper....His name shall endure for ever: **his name shall be continued as long as the sun**...all nations shall call him blessed. Blessed be the LORD God, the God of Israel, who only doeth wondrous things. And blessed be his glorious name for ever: and let the whole earth be filled with his glory.

An interesting name of the Lord that is seldom mentioned is Yinon because of the King James Translation above. In Fred John Meldau's booklet, "Messiah in Both Testaments" he said that the original Hebrew of Psalm 72:17 (the part in bold face type above) said, "Before the sun was, His name (was) Yinon." He adds that this is the only time this name occurs in Scripture and that "all ancient Jewish commentators agree that it is a name of the Messiah."[27]

Isaiah 65:21-25 tells us more about life on Earth during the thousand-year Day of the Lord:

> And they shall build houses, and inhabit them; and they shall plant vineyards, and eat the fruit of them. They shall not build, and another inhabit; they shall not plant, and another eat: for as the days of a tree are the days of my people, and the elect shall long enjoy the work of their hands. They shall not labour in vain, nor bring forth for trouble; for they are the seed of the blessed of the LORD, and their offspring with them. And it shall come to pass, that before they call, I will answer; and while they are yet speaking, I will hear. The wolf and the lamb shall feed together, and the lion shall eat straw like the bullock: and dust shall be the serpent's meat. They shall not hurt nor destroy in all my holy mountain (i.e., kingdom), saith the LORD.

There are lions on Earth during the Millennium, but "no lion shall be there" in Heaven.[28]

Joel 3:18-20 tells us of more kingdom blessings on this planet.

> in that day...the mountains shall drop down new wine, and the hills shall flow with milk, and all the rivers of Judah shall flow with waters, and a fountain shall come forth of the house of the LORD, and shall water the valley of Shittim. Egypt shall be a desolation, and Edom shall be a desolate wilderness, for the violence against the children of Judah, because they have shed innocent blood in their land. But Judah shall dwell for ever, and Jerusalem from generation to generation. For I will cleanse their blood that I have not cleansed: for the LORD dwelleth in Zion.

The Shittim tree is the acacia that grows in very dry soil, so this western Jordan valley above the Dead Sea is evidently very dry and much in need of these waters.

Amos 9:11-15 also describes millennial conditions:

> In that day will I raise up the tabernacle of David that is fallen, and close up the breaches thereof; and I will raise up his ruins, and I will build it as in the days of old: That they may possess the remnant of Edom, and of all the heathen, which are called by my name, saith the LORD that doeth this. Behold...the plowman shall overtake the reaper, and the treader of grapes him that soweth seed; and the mountains shall drop sweet wine, and all the hills shall melt. And I will bring again the captivity of my people of Israel, and they shall build the waste cities, and inhabit them; and they shall plant vineyards, and drink the wine thereof; they shall also make gardens, and eat the fruit of them. And I will plant them upon their land, and they shall no more be pulled up out of their land.

Zechariah 14:9,10,16,17 shows that if a certain group does not go to Jerusalem to worship Christ and keep the Feast of Tabernacles, they will not get rain.

> And the LORD shall be king over all the earth: **in that day shall there be one LORD, and his name one**. All the land shall be turned as a plain from Geba to Rimmon south of Jerusalem: and it shall be lifted up, and inhabited in her place, from Benjamin's gate unto the place of the first gate, unto the corner gate, and from the tower of Hananeel unto the king's winepresses.... every one that is left of all the nations which came against Jerusalem shall even go up from year to year to worship the King, the LORD

of hosts, and to keep the feast of tabernacles. And it shall be, that whoso will not come up of all the families of the earth unto Jerusalem to worship the King, the LORD of hosts, even upon them shall be no rain.

After the Millennium

And when the thousand years are expired, Satan shall be loosed out of his prison, And shall go out to deceive the nations which are in the four quarters of the earth, Gog and Magog, to gather them together to battle: the number of whom *is* as the sand of the sea. And they went up on the breadth of the earth, and compassed the camp of the saints about, and the beloved city: and fire came down from God out of heaven, and devoured them. And the devil that deceived them was cast into the lake of fire and brimstone, where the beast and the false prophet *are*, and shall be tormented day and night for ever and ever.[29]

After 1,000 years in the heat of the bottomless pit ("hell...the foundations of the earth"[30]), Satan comes out alive. He is tossed into the Lake of Fire "where the beast and the false prophet are." They are still alive after all that time too. The Satanic trinity all end up in the Lake of Fire.

Man is made up of three parts, body, soul, and spirit,[31] but there are only two deaths. The body dies. "The soul that sinneth, it shall die,"[32] but I cannot find any mention of spirits dying, ever.

Satan tries his best to muster another army to defeat Christ. He goes to all nations, as he did in Ezekiel 38, where Gog, the chief prince of Meshech and Tubal in the land of Magog, "and many people with thee,"[33] banded together to annihilate Israel. Just as that army attacked Israel on the first day of the Millennium, this army surrounds Jerusalem after the 1,000 years. As fire came down and stopped the army of

Ezekiel 38, fire will come down and devour this army before a battle can take place. Armageddon is the last battle fought.

In the end, all nations will serve Christ, "For the nation and kingdom that will not serve thee shall perish; yea, those nations shall be utterly wasted."[34]

The Great white throne judgment

> And I saw a great white throne, and him that sat on it, from whose face the earth and the heaven fled away; and there was found no place for them. And I saw the dead, small and great, stand before God; and the books were opened: and another book was opened, which is *the book* of life: and the dead were judged out of those things which were written in the books, according to their works. And the sea gave up the dead which were in it; and death and hell delivered up the dead which were in them: and **they were judged every man according to their works.**[35]

The second death

There seem to be degrees of punishment, according to their works. The Lord concludes this section with the sad news that works will not save. A Hebrew Christian friend once told me that his Doctor was such a good man that he would go to heaven no matter what. I'm sorry, but no amount of good deeds is enough. Only those whose names are written in the book of life are saved. Others go into the Lake of Fire.

Be certain that your name is in the book of life. If you have not done so, pray and ask Jesus to save you. Tell him you believe in him, and he will save you.

> And death and hell were cast into the lake of fire. **This is the second death**. And whosoever was not found written in the book of life was cast into the lake of fire.[36]

1 I Samuel 16:12,13- II Samuel 2:7;5:3
2 Isaiah 14:14
3 Champdor, op. cit., p. 128, 160
4 Revelation 19:2,3
5 Revelation 19:4,5
6 Revelation 19:6
7 Revelation 19:7-9
8 Revelation 3:20
9 Romans 3:22
10 I Thessalonians 5:19
11 John 3:29
12 Revelation 19:10
13 Revelation 19:11
14 Psalm 72:6
15 Isaiah 63:3
16 Revelation 19:12,13
17 Revelation 1:14;2:18
18 Revelation 19:14
19 Revelation 19:17,18
20 Revelation 19:19
21 Revelation 19:20,21
22 Genesis 2:7
23 Revelation 20:2,3
24 Revelation 20:14
25 Revelation 20:4-6
26 Malachi 4:5
27 Meldau, Fred John. *Messiah in Both Testaments* (Denver, The Christian Victory Publishing Co., 1956) p. 90
28 Isaiah 35:9
29 Revelation 20:7-10
30 Isaiah 14:15, LXX
31 I Thessalonians 5:23
32 Ezekiel 18:20
33 Ezekiel 38:6
34 Isaiah 60:12
35 Revelation 20:11-13
36 Revelation 20:14,15

12

New Heaven, Earth, Jerusalem

Revelation 21 and 22

Three things have often been misunderstood, the new heaven, new Earth, and New Jerusalem.

It has been taught that the holy city is a triangle or a cube. However, it is probably a sphere, as we will see later.

The new heaven and new earth have been thought to be total recreations of Heaven and Earth after they have disintegrated sometime after the Millennium has run its course. The new Earth is supposed to have no sea. However, close inspection of Scripture paints a different picture.

The new heaven and new earth are at the beginning of the Millennium, not at some distant undetermined time in the future. Revelation 22:6 says that the Lord sent his angel to show "the things which must shortly be done."

Standing as if with John in Heaven at the time of the Rapture, we are given a view of the churches when the Rapture is at hand. This includes a sketchy backward look at their history. We are also given a brief forward glimpse of the Great White Throne Judgment at the end of the Millennium. Other than that, Revelation zeros in on the time from the Rapture to the setting up of the Lord's kingdom on Earth, the "things which must shortly be done."

I make all things new (fresh)

In Revelation 21:5, Jesus said, "Behold I make all things new." The word *kaina* means new, especially in freshness.

The Lord is talking about renewal, renovation, making the habitat for mankind fresh like the Garden of Eden. Psalm 104:30 says, "Thou...renewest the face of the earth." This restoration is absolutely necessary for all green grass and a third of the trees were burned. The water was poisoned. The Mediterranean became a dead sea.

The Lord "will make her (Israel's) wilderness like Eden, and her desert like the garden of the LORD."[1] "And they shall say, This land that was desolate is become like the garden of Eden."[2]

That the waters of the Mediterranean and Dead Sea in the Millennium are healed is shown by Ezekiel 47:8-10. Water comes "out from under the threshold of the house eastward," forming a river.

> These waters issue out toward the east country, and go down into the desert, and go into the sea: which being brought forth into the sea, **the waters shall be healed.** And it shall come to pass, **that every thing that liveth, which moveth, whithersoever the rivers shall come, shall live: and there shall be a very great multitude of fish, because these waters shall come thither: for they shall be healed; and every thing shall live whither the river cometh. And it shall come to pass, that the fishers shall stand upon it from En-gedi (on the west shore of the Dead Sea) even unto En-eglaim; they shall be a place to spread forth nets; their fish shall be according to their kinds, **as the fish of the great sea** (the Mediterranean), exceeding many.

Think of the renovation as we hear Revelation 21:1:

> AND I saw a new (*kainos*, new in freshness) heaven and a new earth: for the first heaven and the first earth were passed away (*parerchomai*, carried past their prime, neglected); and there was no more sea.

The sea here is symbolic, for the oceans still exist during the Millennium. The Lord "shall have dominion also **from sea to sea**, and from the river (Euphrates) unto the ends of the earth."[3] When Ezekiel describes the borders of Israel during the Millennium, both the **"east sea"** and the **"great sea"** are mentioned.[4]

When the beast came up out of the sea in Revelation 13:1, and the harlot church sat upon "many waters" in Revelation 17:1, that sea was symbolic. It stood for "peoples, and multitudes, and nations, and tongues."[5] They were joined together under the United Nations banner at Babylon.

During the Millennium, there is no "sea" in the sense that there is no United Nations. The world is Christ's kingdom and he will rule from Jerusalem.

This "new heaven" is not talking about God's heaven. Earth and its atmospheric heavens (or "sky," as in the Amplified) are to be renewed as Earth was renovated in Genesis 1:3-25 and after Noah's flood. The sun, moon and stars, which include God's heaven, will not cease to be.

> Thus saith the LORD, which giveth the sun for a light by day, and the ordinances of the moon and of the stars for a light by night...If those ordinances depart from before me... then the seed of Israel also shall cease from being a nation before me for ever.[6]

The Earth will exist forever. Psalm 104:5 asks, "Who laid **the foundations of the earth**, that it should **not be removed forever?**" Abraham was told, "For all the land which thou seest, to thee will I give it, and to thy seed for ever."[7] That land will always be there.

The Earth did not disintegrate during Noah's flood. Its exterior facade was marred. Second Peter 3:5-7 says,

> the heavens were of old, and the earth standing out of the water and in the water: Whereby the world that then was (from Adam to Noah), being overflowed with water, perished (*apoleto*, was destroyed or marred):

> But **the heavens and the earth, which are now,** by the same word are kept in store, **reserved unto fire** against the day of judgment and perdition of ungodly men.

It is clear that Second Peter 3:10-13 is talking about that portion of the atmospheric heavens that shall "pass away."

> But the day of the Lord will come as a thief in the night; in the which the heavens (the atmosphere) shall pass away (*parerchomai*, be carried past, be neglected, i.e., go past their prime) with a great noise, and the elements shall melt with fervent heat, the earth also and the works that are therein shall be burned up....the day of God, wherein **the heavens being on fire shall be dissolved, and the elements shall melt with fervent heat?** Nevertheless we, according to his promise, look for **new heavens and a new earth,** wherein dwelleth righteousness.

The atmosphere that is dissolved by the asteroid impact must be restored right away for the health of the remnant that is still inhabiting Earth. Since "righteousness" will dwell on Earth during the Millennium, the "new heavens and a new earth" appear during the thousand years.

The same word translated "passed away" above is also used in II Corinthians 5:17:

> Therefore if any man be in Christ, he is a new creature: old things are **passed away;** behold, all things are become new.

When believers become "in Christ," they are not annihilated and recreated, but changed. That is what happens to the blast-damaged atmospheric heavens and the fractured and burned Earth. More energy has been released by the impacts than all the atomic bombs ever manufactured on Earth.

The face of the Earth and her atmosphere are changed, renovated, renewed. The air is once again healthy to breathe. The land is fertile. The green grass, herbs, and trees are restored. The water is once again pure. This probably has a lot to do with the longevity of life during the thousand years. At present, our world is seriously polluted.

It only took a few days to renovate the face of this planet in Genesis. It will not take long this time, either. The Lord can say, "Let there be light," and there will be light. He can say "Let the earth bring forth grass, the herb yielding seed, and the fruit tree," and it will be so. He can say, "Let the waters bring forth abundantly," and it will happen.

Before Adam appeared on Earth, a piece of Satan's planet Rahab hit Earth, punching up mountains and forming the Pacific Basin. Then the Lord renovated Earth to make it a fit habitat for Adam. Before Christ, the "last Adam,"[8] appears again on Earth, another piece of Rahab will hit Earth. Both times there has to be renovation, a "new" heavens and a "new" Earth to make Earth a fit habitat for man.

In Isaiah 55:11-13, the Lord says,

> So shall my word be that goeth forth out of my mouth: it shall not return unto me void, but it shall accomplish that which I please, and it shall prosper in the thing whereto I sent it....Instead of the thorn shall come up the fir tree, and instead of the brier shall come up the myrtle tree: and it shall be to the LORD for a name, for an everlasting sign that shall not be cut off.

Isaiah 51:6 says that the heavens will vanish like smoke. This happens on the first day of the Millennium.

> Lift up your eyes to the heavens and look upon the earth beneath: for the heavens shall vanish away **like smoke**, and the earth shall wax old **like a garment** (an overcoat, the outer layer that the eyes can see), and they that dwell therein shall die in like manner.

God's Heaven will not vanish away like smoke, but a lot of Earth's lower atmosphere will be blown into the stratosphere by the impact blasts of the two large sections of the binary asteroid. Part of the atmosphere will be "dissolved."

Psalm 102:25,26 says,

> Of old hast thou laid the foundation of the earth: and the heavens are the work of thy hands. They shall perish, but thou shalt endure: yea, **all of them shall wax old like a garment; as a vesture shalt thou change them,** and they shall be changed.

The Earth waxing old like a garment shows us what will be damaged, the outer coat, or face, of Earth. Only the exterior needs rejuvenating. The foundation is okay.

Joy in earthly Jerusalem

In Isaiah 65:17-20; 66:22,23, the Lord explains that he creates new heavens and a new Earth in a passage that is obviously Millennial for death has not yet been abolished:

> I create **new heavens and a new earth:** and the former shall not be remembered, nor come into mind....behold, I create Jerusalem a rejoicing, and her people a joy. And I will rejoice in Jerusalem, and joy in my people: and the voice of weeping shall be no more heard in her, nor the voice of crying. There shall be no more thence an infant of days, nor an old man that hath not filled his days: for the child shall die an hundred years old; but the sinner being an hundred years old shall be accursed....For as **the new heavens and the new earth, which I will make, shall remain** before me, saith the LORD, so shall your seed and your name remain. And it shall come to pass, that from one new moon to another, and from one sabbath to

another, shall all flesh come to worship before me, saith the LORD. And they shall go forth, and **look upon the carcasses** of the men that have transgressed against me.

Since they look at the dead bodies before they become nothing but a pile of bones, the new Earth is not a different planet, just a renewed one. We still dig up bones of mammoths that died before the Earth was renovated in Genesis. This will be similar to the restoration in Adam's day. This time, the renewed heavens and Earth will remain.

I will **this once** cause them to know, I will cause them to know mine hand and my might; and they shall know that my name is The LORD (Jeremiah 16:21).

No death in heavenly New Jerusalem
As John continues the script of Revelation 21, the subject changes abruptly. Here, it refers to our heavenly home, New Jerusalem coming down closer to the Earth near the beginning of the Millennium. In Revelation 21:2,3, John says,

And I John saw the holy city, new Jerusalem, **coming down from God out of heaven,** prepared as a bride adorned for her husband. And I heard a great voice out of heaven saying, Behold, the tabernacle of God *is* with men, and he will dwell with them, and they shall be his people, and God himself shall be with them, *and be* their God.

Before Jesus ascended at the First Advent, he said,

In my Father's house are many mansions (*mone*, residences, abodes): if it were not so, I would have told you. **I go to prepare a place for you**. And if I go and prepare a place for you, I will come again, and receive you unto myself; that where I am, there ye

may be also. **And whither I go ye know**
(he goes to Saturn), and the way ye know
(we know; we have sent space vehicles out
there to photograph Saturn). (John 14:2-4)

The place he is preparing for us is New Jerusalem.
The holy city is "coming down from God out of heaven." It
is actually descending toward the Earth. Some teachers have
said that it will hang above the Earth like a chandelier. It will
orbit, but that is a good picture, for it will give off light. The
nations "shall walk in the light of it."[9]

The Philadelphian over comers were promised:

Him that overcometh will I make a pillar in
the temple of my God (the temple of the Holy
Spirit, there is no physical temple in New Jerusalem[10]), and he shall go no more out: and I
will write upon him the name of my God,
and the name of the city of my God, *which is*
**new Jerusalem, which cometh down
out of heaven from my God.**

Revelation 21:10 also mentions "the holy Jerusalem,
descending out of heaven from God." We can build
space stations and put them in orbit, but the Lord can create
another world, and move it from one planet to another. That
will certainly demonstrate his power.

John continues in Revelation 21:4,5:

And God shall wipe away all tears from their
eyes; and there shall be no more death, neither sorrow, nor crying, neither shall there be
any more pain: for the former things are
passed away. And he that sat upon the throne
said, Behold, I make all things new (*kaina*,
new in freshness). And he said unto me,
Write: for these words are true and faithful.

In New Jerusalem, orbiting near Earth's race track in
space, there will be no death. On Earth, during the Millenni-

um, life spans will be longer, but there will still be death. "The last enemy that shall be destroyed is death."[11]

The making all things new is the renovation of Earth. The clincher is Matthew 19:28; 25:31. Jesus himself called the time of his kingdom "the regeneration (*palingenesia*, re-creation, making new)."

> Jesus said...ye which have followed me, in **the regeneration** when the Son of man shall sit in the throne of his glory, ye also shall sit upon twelve thrones, judging the twelve tribes of Israel....When the Son of man shall come in his glory, and all the holy angels with him, then shall he sit upon the throne of his glory.

It is done

As Jesus begins to speak, he says, "It is done." At this point all things are fresh and new. It happened right away. In Revelation 21:6, he reminds us that he is the Alpha and Omega just as he did in Revelation 1:8.

> And he said unto me, **It is done**. I am Alpha and Omega, the beginning and the end. I will give unto him that is athirst of the fountain of the water of life freely.

Jesus is the Almighty, the beginning and the end, Lord of the Old Testament and Lord of the New Testament. He offers you the water of life freely.

Water stands for the Holy Spirit. Accept Jesus and you will be filled with his Holy Spirit. Do not put it off. When you sin afterward, confess your sins to God to be filled with the Holy Spirit again. Ephesians 5:18 says, "And be not drunk with wine, wherein is excess; but be filled with the Spirit." We cannot get into Heaven with soiled garments.

The Lord promises in Revelation 21:7,

> He that overcometh shall inherit all things; and I will be his God, and he shall be my son.

The mention of over comers takes us back to when the Rapture is at hand. This section goes with the messages to the seven churches in chapters two and three. It shows that the over comers will be counted as sons of the adoption.

> But when the fulness of the time was come, God sent forth his Son, made of a woman, made under the law, To redeem them that were under the law, that we might receive the adoption of sons (Galatians 4:4,5).

Continuing in Revelation 21:8, the Lord says,

> But the fearful, and unbelieving, and the abominable, and murderers, and whoremongers, and sorcerers, and idolaters, and all liars, shall have their part in the lake which burneth with fire and brimstone: which is the second death.

The alternative is not attractive. We should be over comers. In Revelation 21:9, John says,

> And there came unto me one of the seven angels which had the seven vials full of the seven last plagues, and talked with me, saying, **Come hither**, I will shew thee the bride, the Lamb's wife.

This "Come hither" shows that we are taken back to the point when the Rapture takes place. We are going to get another picture of where we are headed.

We listen with rapt attention as John describes our beautiful new home. In Revelation 21:10,11, he says,

> And he carried me away in the spirit to a great and high mountain (Saturn), and shewed me that great city, the holy Jerusalem, **descending out of heaven from God,** Having the glory of God: and her light *was* like unto

a stone most precious, even like a jasper stone, clear as crystal;

This city is separating from God's heaven and descending Earthward. Until the beginning of the Millennium, it is a secret place. Since there are 24 elders, it may be a 24th satellite, hidden from our view by Saturn's feathery golden clouds and the shadow of the silvery rings that look like wings. There are several scriptures that mention wings:

> HE that dwelleth in the secret place of the most High shall abide under the shadow of the Almighty....He shall cover thee with his feathers...under his wings shalt thou trust.[12]

> yet shall ye be as the wings of a dove covered with silver, and her feathers with yellow gold.[13]

> Keep me as the apple of the eye (a sphere), hide me under the shadow of thy wings.[14]

> in the shadow of thy wings will I make my refuge, until these calamities be overpast.[15]

It sounds like we might hide under the shadow of his rings until the catastrophe is over, then New Jerusalem will come down close to Earth so that the nations on Earth can "bring their glory and honour into it."[16]

New Jerusalem is characterized as perfect and heavenly. There are seven twelves. Seven means perfection and twelve is the heavenly number of administrational perfection. There are twelve gates, twelve angels, twelve names of Israel, twelve names of apostles, twelve foundations, and twelve pearls. In addition, the measurement of the wall is 144 cubits or 72 yards (both multiples of 12). John adds,

> And had a wall great and high, *and* had twelve gates, and at the gates twelve angels, and names written thereon, which are *the names* of the twelve tribes of the children of

Israel: On the east three gates; on the north
three gates; on the south three gates; and on
the west three gates.[17]

Just as there are angels of the Raptured church in
Heaven, there are angels of Israel in Heaven. These are half
of the 24 elders we saw in Revelation 4:4.

Luke 10:36 says of the resurrection from the dead,
"Neither can they die any more: for they are equal unto the
angels; and are the children of God, being the children of the
resurrection." Abraham is there, "for he looked for a city
which hath foundations, whose builder and maker is God."[18]

Three gates on each side is the way the twelve tribes
of Israel camped in a circle around the Tabernacle. Three
tribes camped on the east, three on the north, three on the
south, and three on the west. This too may indicate that New
Jerusalem orbits Saturn now. In Revelation 4:3, there was a
rainbow "round about the throne." Then in the next two
verses, the 24 elders were seen "round about the throne,"
and the sea of glass like unto crystal was seen "before the
throne." It fits the picture.

And the wall of the city had twelve foundations, and in them the names of the twelve
apostles of the Lamb.[19]

Here are the other twelve elders. The twelve apostles
were Israelites who became the foundation of the Church,
which is the temple of the Holy Spirit. Ephesians 2:19-22
tells us of this spiritual temple:

Now therefore ye are no more strangers and
foreigners, but fellowcitizens with the saints,
and of the household of God...built upon the
foundation of the apostles and prophets, Jesus Christ himself being the chief corner
stone; In whom all the building fitly framed
together groweth unto an holy temple in the
Lord: In whom ye also are builded together
for an habitation of God through the Spirit.

As John goes on, he tells us of a city so large it would not fit where Jerusalem, or even Israel, is situated now. New Jerusalem cannot be an earthly city because her size is beyond all earthly city limits. It would cover from approximately the eastern seacoast of the United States to the Mississippi River and from Canada to the Gulf of Mexico.

> And he that talked with me had a golden reed to measure the city, and the gates thereof, and the wall thereof, And the city lieth foursquare, and the length is as large as the breadth: and he measured the city with the reed, twelve thousand furlongs. The length and the breadth and the height of it are equal.[20]

New Jerusalem is represented by a cube just as God's heaven is represented by the cube of the Holy of Holies in the Tabernacle. Both depict spheres, with length, breadth and height equal. The spherical Earth is also represented as having "four corners (*gonias*, corners, quarters)."[21] The four "corners" are actually the four quarters of a sphere.

A furlong is 600 feet, so the diameter of New Jerusalem is 1,363.64 miles. For comparison, our Moon is 2,160 miles in diameter, about a quarter that of the Earth. New Jerusalem is roughly two thirds the size of the Moon.

> And he measured the wall thereof, an hundred *and* forty *and* four cubits, *according to* the measure of a man, that is, of the angel.[22]

The measure of an angel, shows that the man is already equal to the angels in Heaven. It is after the Rapture. A cubit is eighteen inches, so the wall is 72 yards tall.

> And the building of the wall of it was *of* jasper: and the city was pure gold, like unto clear glass (Revelation 21:18).

Gold is a symbol of deity. In I Kings 6:21, "Solomon overlaid the house (temple) within with pure gold." The gold of the Holy of Holies symbolizes both God and Heaven with its golden clouds. The city of New Jerusalem may be real gold, which if pure enough might be transparent, or it could be similar to glass windows reflecting the golden color of Saturn's clouds. Think of how the windows of a house on a hill flash as the sun goes down.

Remember, Psalm 68:13 says, "yet shall ye be **as the wings** of a dove covered with silver, and her feathers with yellow gold." It sounds like New Jerusalem could be orbiting as the crystal rings do around Saturn, which has "clouds shining like gold." Could the resonance (vibration) going out from New Jerusalem cause Cassini's Division in Saturn's ring system? Revelation 21:19,20 continues:

> And the foundations of the wall of the city *were* garnished with all manner of precious stones. The first foundation *was* jasper (purplish); the second, sapphire (blue); the third, a chalcedony (gray, blue and yellow combination); the fourth, an emerald (green); The fifth, sardonyx (pale blue); the sixth, sardius (blood red); the seventh, chrysolyte (purple and green); the eighth, beryl (bluish green); the ninth, a topaz (pale green, blue, or gold); the tenth, a chrysoprasus (mixed blue, green, yellow); the eleventh, a jacinth (red, violet, yellow combination); the twelfth, an amethyst (purple).

The stones and their colors are somewhat uncertain, but it all suggests a rainbow of colors. Where have we heard of a rainbow around Heaven? Right after the Rapture, Revelation 4:3 said that "there was a rainbow round about the throne, in sight like unto an emerald." When Ezekiel saw the throne in Heaven, he said, "As the appearance of the bow that is in the cloud in the day of rain, so was the appearance of the brightness round about. This was the appearance of the likeness of the glory of the LORD."[23] These gemstones and beautiful colors seem to be calculated to remind us of the glory of the Lord that shines around his heavenly throne.

> And the twelve gates *were* twelve pearls;
> every several (respective) gate was of one
> pearl: and the street of the city *was* pure gold,
> as it were transparent glass (Rev. 21:21).

Since Heaven is the Pearl of Great Price, it is not
surprising that these twelve gates are pearls. They are probably used here to help us make the connection between
Heaven and the Pearl of Great Price in Matthew 13:45,46.

> And I saw **no temple** therein: for the Lord
> God Almighty and the Lamb are the temple of
> it (Revelation 21:22).

In Revelation 11:15,19 we saw a temple in Heaven,
but there is none in New Jerusalem. Therefore, there seems
to be two different, but closely associated, localities. There
are two thrones, one of the Father, the other of Christ.

> And the city had no need of the sun, neither
> of the moon, to shine in it: for the glory of
> God did lighten it, and the Lamb *is* the light
> thereof. And **the nations of them which
> are saved shall walk in the light of it**:
> and the kings of the earth do bring their glory
> and honour into it. And the gates of it shall
> not be shut at all by day: for there shall be **no
> night there.** And they shall bring the glory
> and honour of the nations into it. And there
> shall in no wise enter into it any thing that de-
> fileth, neither *whatsoever* worketh abomina-
> tion, or *maketh* a lie: but they which are writ-
> ten in the Lamb's book of life.[24]

On Earth, day and night continue. In New Jerusalem, there is no night because it has its own light. The holy
city seems to orbit Earth. It is smaller than the Moon and has
no dark side.

We are to be priests and kings and rule with Christ.
Travel back and forth between the earthly workplace and the

heavenly home will be easy. Even "the kings of the earth do bring their glory and honour into it."

As John resumes reading Revelation 22:1,2, we hear of water and trees in New Jerusalem.

> AND he shewed me a pure river of **water** of life, clear as crystal, proceeding out of the throne of God and of the Lamb. In the midst of the street of it, and on either side of the river, *was there* the **tree of life**, which bare twelve *manner of* fruits (twelve fruits[25]), *and* yielded her fruit every month: and the leaves of the tree *were* for the healing of the nations.

Here, we find the tree of life that has been missing from the Earth ever since Adam ate of the forbidden fruit.

The leaves of the tree of life must be strong medicine. In earthly Jerusalem, "the inhabitant shall not say, I am sick: the people that dwell therein shall be forgiven their iniquity."[26] The tree is literal, but it also symbolizes Christ, who heals the nations.

Isaiah 33:15-17 shows that water and foliage are there:

> He that walketh righteously...shall dwell on high: his place of defense shall be the munitions of rocks: **bread** shall be given him; his **waters** shall be sure. Thine eyes shall see the king in his beauty: they shall behold the land that is very far off.

This rock on high is where the King of kings and Lord of lords is enthroned.

> And there shall be no more curse: but the throne (one throne) of God and of the Lamb (*tou theou kai tou arniou*, the God and the Lamb) shall be in it; and his servants shall serve him (one person, who is both the God and the Lamb): And they shall see his face

> (one face); and his name (one name) *shall be*
> in their foreheads,[27]

No more curse probably means that no asteroid will hit and cause global destruction.

When Jesus returned to Heaven, he sat down on the right hand of his Father on his Father's throne. Here, we see Jesus on his own throne in New Jerusalem for the purpose of administering his millennial kingdom over Earth.

In those days, the Lord will have one name.

> And the LORD shall be king over all the
> earth: in that day shall there be one LORD,
> and his name one (Zechariah 14:9).

While on Earth setting up his millennial government, Jesus will raise up the tabernacle of David and sit on David's throne. Later, he will return to New Jerusalem as King of kings and put David back on his own throne. Scripture says,

> David my servant shall be king over them;
> and they all shall have one shepherd: they
> shall also walk in my judgments, and observe
> my statutes, and do them. And they shall
> dwell in the land that I have given unto
> Jacob...and **my servant David shall be**
> **their prince for ever.**[28]

> I will set up one shepherd over them, and he
> shall feed them, even my servant David; he
> shall feed them, and he shall be their
> shepherd. And **I the LORD will be their**
> **God, and my servant David a prince**
> **among them;** I the LORD have spoken it.[29]

> **But they shall serve the LORD their**
> **God, and David their king, whom I**
> **will raise up unto them.**[30]

Two thrones in the heavenly places

There is the Father's throne and Jesus Christ's own throne, both in the heavenly places. Revelation 3:21 says,

> To him that overcometh will I grant to sit with me in **my throne**, even as I also overcame, and am set down with my Father in **his throne**.

Before sitting on his own throne, Jesus sits at the right hand of the Father in the heavenly places. Scripture says,

> Christ, when he (the Father) raised him from the dead...set him **at his own right hand in the heavenly places**, Far above all principality, and power, and might, and dominion, and every name that is named, not only in this world (age), but **also in that which is to come**[31] (i.e., he will not stay on Earth during the whole Millennium).

> We have such an high priest, who is set **on the right hand of the throne of the Majesty in the heavens**; A minister of the sanctuary, and, of the true tabernacle, which the Lord pitched, and not man.[32]

> Jesus...for the joy that was set before him endured the cross, despising the shame, and is set down **at the right hand of the throne of God**.[33]

Jesus sits at the right hand of the Father until his enemies are collected in one place and made his footstool.

> THE LORD said unto my (king David's) Lord, Sit thou at my right hand, **until** I make thine enemies thy footstool (Psalm 110:1).

On the first day of the Millennium, Jesus is crowned. After receiving his golden crown and being awarded a dominion, Christ sits on his own throne in New Jerusalem.

Daniel saw him receiving dominion, and glory, and a kingdom. Daniel 7:9-14 says,

> I beheld till the thrones were cast down (placed), and the Ancient of days (the Father) did sit, whose garment was white as snow, and the hair of his head like the pure wool: his throne was like the fiery flame, and his wheels as burning fire. A fiery stream issued and came forth from before him: thousand thousands ministered unto him, and ten thousand times ten thousand stood before him: the judgment was set, and the books were opened. I beheld then because of the voice of the great words which the horn (the Satan indwelt False Prophet) spake: I beheld even till the beast was slain, and his body destroyed, and given to the burning flame. As concerning the rest of the beasts, they had their dominion taken away: yet their lives were prolonged for a season and time. I saw in the night vision, and, behold, one like the Son of man (Christ) came with the clouds of heaven, and came to the Ancient of days, and they brought him near before him. And **there was given him dominion, and glory, and a kingdom**, that all people, nations, and languages, should serve him: his dominion is an everlasting dominion, **which shall not pass away**, and his kingdom that which shall not be destroyed.

We listen as John continues the description of New Jerusalem in Revelation 22:5:

> And there shall be no night there; and they need no candle, neither light of the sun; for

the Lord God giveth them light: and they shall reign for ever and ever.

Our reign with Christ lasts forever. Chances are good that we will replace the fallen angels in his administration.

And he said unto me, These sayings *are* faithful and true: and the Lord God of the holy prophets sent his angel to shew unto his servants the things which must **shortly** be done. Behold, **I come quickly**: blessed *is* he that keepeth the sayings of the prophecy of this book.[34]

"I come quickly" refers to the Rapture. The "things which must shortly be done" are not very far removed from the Rapture. In Revelation 22:8, John says,

And I John saw these things, and heard *them*. And when I had heard and seen, I fell down to worship before the feet of the angel which shewed me these things. Then saith he unto me, See *thou do it* not: for I am thy fellowservant, and of thy brethren the prophets, and of them which keep the sayings of this book: worship God.

This is very clear. We are not to worship angels. We are only to worship God.

And he saith unto me, Seal not the sayings of the prophecy of this book: for the time is at hand. He that is unjust, let him be unjust still: and he which is filthy, let him be filthy still: and he that is righteous, let him be righteous still: and he that is holy, let him be holy still. And, behold, I come quickly; and my reward *is* with me, to give every man according as his work shall be (Revelation 22:10-12).

The time at hand is the Rapture. He is going to come quickly. When it happens, there is no time to prepare for it. You must be ready before that instant arrives. Jesus says,

> I am Alpha and Omega, the beginning and the end, the first and the last. Blessed *are* they that do his commandments, that they may have right to the tree of life, and may enter in through the gates into the city. For without *are* dogs, and sorcerers, and whoremongers, and murderers, and idolaters, and whosoever loveth and maketh a lie.[35]

If we have not understood exactly who he is up to now, he gives us one more chance before he signs off. He is the Almighty, Lord of the Old Testament and Lord of the New Testament. He says,

> I Jesus have sent mine angel to testify unto you these things in the churches. I am the root and the offspring of David, *and* the bright and morning star. And **the Spirit and the bride say, Come.** And let him that heareth say, Come. And let him that is athirst come. And whosoever will, let him take the water of life freely.[36]

As Yahweh, he is the root of David. As Jesus Christ, he is the offspring of David. "God was in Christ, reconciling the world unto himself."[37] He is now on the right hand of the Father on the bright and morning star.

Saturn was a morning star at the time Jesus ascended to Heaven. Not only is it the third heaven, it is third in brightness among the planets, and its steady light is very easy to see.

Saturn will be a morning star if the Rapture takes place on Pentecost, which is a designated harvest time. The beautiful ringed planet Saturn is a morning star five months and an evening star five months. The remainder of the year, it is hidden from our view as it swings around the sun.

For I testify unto every man that heareth the words of the prophecy of this book, If any man shall add unto these things, God shall add unto him the plagues that are written in this book: And if any man shall take away from the words of the book of this prophecy, God shall take away his part out of the book of life, and out of the holy city, and *from* the things which are written in this book.[38]

Nothing can be added or taken away from the script Jesus gave us. This is his final written word to us. The Rapture is at hand. Be ready.

He which testifieth these things saith, Surely **I come quickly. Amen**. Even so, come, Lord Jesus. The grace of our Lord Jesus Christ *be* with you all. Amen.[39]

"Amen," the last word in the Bible, means so be it. If you are wearing white at the time of the Rapture, you will be chosen as part of the Bride of Christ. Confess your sins to God immediately and stay in fellowship, because look what could happen if you are not wearing white at the Rapture.

I tell you, I know you not whence ye are; depart from me, all ye workers of iniquity. There shall be weeping and gnashing of teeth, when ye shall see Abraham, and Isaac, and Jacob, and all the prophets, in the kingdom of God, and you yourselves thrust out.[40]

The lord of that **servant** will come in a day when he looketh not for him, and at an hour when he is not aware, and will cut him in sunder (cut him off), and will appoint him **his portion with the unbelievers**. And that servant, which knew his lord's will, and prepared not himself, neither did according to his will, shall be beaten with many stripes.[41]

Not only is the book of Revelation written as if the Rapture is at hand, the whole Bible is written especially for us upon whom the ends of the ages are come. Both the Age of the Jews and the Age of the Church, and probably the Age of the Gentiles, have extensions that run concurrently during the Tribulation.

> Now all these things happened unto them for ensamples: and they are written for our admonition, upon whom the ends of the world (ages) are come. Wherefore let him that thinketh he standeth take heed lest he fall.[42]

First-century Jerusalem would be a good example for us, if only we had ears to hear and eyes to see. It was destroyed in 70 A.D., 40 years after the Crucifixion, **"because thou knewest not the time of thy visitation."**[43] They should have figured the time out from Daniel 9:24-26. The clues were there. Those who knew their scriptures fled Jerusalem just before she was burned.

We have a parallel in our days. Mankind has had a chance to figure out the time of Christ's next visitation ever since the Sign of the End of the Age, the Six-Day War of 1967, fulfilled the fig tree parable of Matthew 24:32-34. The clues are there. I believe that destruction will strike again in our 2007, after our 40 years of probation end.

Jesus will save us from the terrible things that are coming upon this world if we truly believe in him. We have two chances to escape tragedy. There is a Rapture before the Tribulation, probably on Pentecost Sunday, Sivan 6, 5758 (our May 31, 1998) in the 6,000th year since humans became mortal, and another just before the asteroid hits on the Feast of Trumpets, Tishri 1, 5768 (our September 13, 2007). May the Lord open the eyes of your understanding.

> the path of the just is as the shining light, that shineth more and more unto the perfect day.[44]

1. Isaiah 51:3
2. Ezekiel 37:35
3. Psalm 72:8
4. Ezekiel 47:18,20
5. Revelation 17:15
6. Jeremiah 31:35,36
7. Genesis 13:15
8. I Corinthians 15:45
9. Revelation 21:24
10. Revelation 21:22
11. I Corinthians 15:26
12. Psalm 91:1,4
13. Psalm 68:13
14. Psalm 17:8
15. Psalm 57:1
16. Revelation 21:24
17. Revelation 21:12,13
18. Hebrews 11:10
19. Revelation 21:14
20. Revelation 21:15,16
21. Revelation 7:1
22. Revelation 21:17
23. Ezekiel 1:28
24. Revelation 21:23-27
25. Green's Interlinear
26. Isaiah 33:24
27. Revelation 22:3,4
28. Ezekiel 37:24,25
29. Ezekiel 34:23,24
30. Jeremiah 50:9
31. Ephesians 1:20,21
32. Hebrews 8:1,2
33. Hebrews 12:2
34. Revelation 22:6,7
35. Revelation 22:13-15
36. Revelation 22:16,17
37. II Corinthians 5:19
38. Revelation 22:18,19
39. Revelation 22:20,21
40. Luke 13:27,28
41. Luke 12:46,47
42. I Corinthians 10:11,12
43. Luke 19:44
44. Proverbs 4:18

Selected Bibliography

Agee, M.J.. *Exit: 2007, The Secret of Secrets Revealed*. (8641 Sugar Gum Rd., Riverside, CA: Archer Press, 1991).

_____ *Heaven Found, A Butter and Honey Star*. (Riverside, CA: Archer Press, 1995).

Allen, Jane E. "Comet created a fireball hotter than sun's surface." *The Orange County Register*, Nov. 16, 1994.

Alston, Greg. *The Prophecy Post* Newsletter. (Denver, CO: A Sure Foundation).

The Amplified Bible. (Grand Rapids: Zondervan Publishing House, 1962).

Anderson, Sir Robert. *The Coming Prince*. (Grand Rapids: Kregel Publ., 17th ed., 1969, first published 1895).

Anstey, Martin. *The Romance of Bible Chronology*. (London: Marshall Bros., 1913, Vol. I and II).

Barclay, William. *The New Testament, A New Translation*, Vol. I, *The Gospels and the Acts of the Apostles*. (London: Collins, 1968).

Bedford, Arthur. *The Scripture Chronology*. (London: James and John Knapton, 1730).

The Bible, Revised Standard Version. (N.Y.: American Bible Society, 1952).

Bond, John. *Handy-Book of Rules and Tables for Verifying Dates with the Christian Era*. (New York: Russell & Russell, 1966).

Brenton, Sir Lancelot C.L.. *The Septuagint Version: Greek and English*. (Grand Rapids: Zondervan Publishing House, orig. publ. 1851).

Brown, O.M. *Bible Chronology Vindicated*. (Cleveland: Christian Messenger Publ. Co., 1901).

"Can Machines Think." *Time*, March, 1996, p. 50.

Chafer, L.S. *Systematic Theology*. (Dallas: Dallas Seminary Press, 1947).

Champdor, Albert. *Babylon*. (N.Y., G.P. Putnam's Sons, 1958).

"Comet Hale-Bopp is Coming." *Sky and Telescope*, Nov. 1995, p. 20-23.

Concordant Literal Bible. (Canyon Country, CA: Concordant Publishing Concern, publ. in parts, various dates).

Concordia Cyclopedia. (St. Louis, MO: Concordia Publ. House, 1927).

De Haan, M.R.. *Revelation*. (Grand Rapids: Zondervan

Publishing House, 1946).

Deal, Colin Hoyle. *Armageddon & the 21st Century.* (Rutherford College, N.C.: Colin H. Deal, 1988).

Dickason, C. Fred. *Angels, Elect & Evil.* (Chicago: Moody Press, 1975).

Dyer, Charles H. *The Rise of Babylon.* (Wheaton, IL: Tyndale House Publishers, 1991).

Ehlert, Arnold D. *Syllabus of Bible Chronology.* (La Mirada, CA: unpublished ms. at Bible Institute of Los Angeles, 1946).

"Flights may have found edge of solar system." *The Orange County Registe*r, May 27, 1993, page A10.

Goudoever, *Biblical Calendars.* (Leiden, Netherlands: E.J. Brill, 1959).

Green, Jay. *Interlinear Greek-English New Testament.* (Grand Rapids: Christian Classics, 1972).

_____ *The Interlinear Hebrew/Greek English Bible.* (Wilmington, DE: Assoc. Publ. and Authors, 1976).

Hains, Edmont. *The Seven Churches of Revelation.* (Winona Lake, IN: nd).

Hawkins, Gerald S. *Splendor in the Sky.* (N.Y.: Harper and Brothers, 1961).

Hislop, Alexander. *The Two Babylons*, third ed. (N. Y.: Loizeaux Brothers, 1943.

Holy Bible, The Berkeley Version. (Grand Rapids: Zondervan Publishing House, 1959).

Holy Bible, Confraternity Version. (N.Y.: Catholic Book Publishing Co., 1963).

The Holy Bible, New American Catholic Edition. (N.Y.: Benziger Brothers, Inc., 1952).

Hunt, Dave. *Global Peace and the Rise of Antichrist.* (Eugene. OR: Harvest House Publishers, 1990).

_____ *How Close are We?* (Eugene. OR: Harvest House Publishers, 1993).

_____ *Peace Prosperity and the Coming Holocaust.* (Eugene, OR: Harvest House Publishers, 1983).

Hutchings, Noah W.. *Petra in History and Prophecy.* (Oklahoma City, OK: Hearthstone Publishing Ltd., 1991).

Ironside, H. A. *Lectures on the Book of Revelation.* (Neptune, NJ: Loizeaux Brothers, 1920, 1987).

Jamieson, Robert; Faussett, A.R. and Brown, David. *A Commentary Critical, Experimental, and Practical on the Old and New Testaments.* (Grand Rapids: Wm. B.

Eerdmans Publishing Co., 1945).

Jeffrey, Grant R. *Armageddon: Appointment with Destiny*. (N.Y.: Bantam Books, 1990).

The Jerusalem Bible. (N.Y.: Doubleday, 1990).

Kerrod, Robin. *The Star Guide*. (N.Y.: Prentice Hall, 1993)

Koch, Kurt E. *Demonology Past and Present*. (Grand Rapids, Kregel Publications, 1973).

LaHaye, Tim F.. *Revelation Illustrated and Made Plain*. (Grand Rapids: Zondervan Publishing House, 1981).

Lamsa, George M.. *The Holy Bible*. (Philadelphia: A.J. Holman Co., 1968).

"Lawmaker aims for Earth to avoid the fate of Jupiter." *The Orange County Registe*r, July 22, 1994.

Lewis, David Allen. *Prophecy 2000*. (Green Forest, AR: New Leaf Press, Inc., 1990).

Lindsey, Hal. *The Late Great Planet Earth*. (Grand Rapids, MI: Zondervan Publishing House, 1970, 1977).

_____ *The Rapture: Truth or Consequences*. (N.Y.: Bantam Books, 1983).

Macdonald, Ken and Agnes. *The Second Coming*. (USA: Revivals and Missions, Inc., 1991).

Martin, Ernest L. *Restoring the Original Bible*. (Portland, OR: Associates for Scriptural Knowledge, 1994).

_____ *The Star that Astonished the World*. (Portland, OR: Associates for Scriptural Knowledge, 1996).

Meldau, Fred John. *Messiah in Both Testaments*. (Denver, The Christian Victory Publishing Co., 1956).

Miller, D.A. *Forbidden Knowledge or is it....* (San Juan Capistrano, CA: Joy Publishing, 1991).

The New American Bible. (N.Y.: World Publishing, 1970).

New American Standard Bible. (Nashville: Thomas Nelson, Publishers, 1977).

The New English Bible. (London: Oxford University Press, 1970).

New International Version of The Holy Bible. (Grand Rapids: Zondervan Publishing House, 1973).

New Scofield Reference Bible. (N.Y.: Oxford University Press, 1967).

The New Testament and Wycliffe Bible Commentary. (Chicago: Moody Press, 1971).

Newell, William R. *The Book of The Revelation*. (Chicago: Moody Press, 1935).

Pentecost, Dwight. *Things to Come*. (Grand Rapids: Dunham, 1958).

Power, Matthew. *Anglo-Jewish Calendar*. (London: Sands and Co., 1902).

Price, Randall. *In Search of Temple Treasures*. (Eugene, Oregon: Harvest House Publishers, 1994).

The Restoration of Original Sacred Name Bible. (Buena Park, CA: Missionary Dispensary Bible Research, 1970).

Ripley, Fransis J. *This is the Faith*. (N.Y.: Guild Press, Inc., Publishers, 1960).

Schmid, Randolph E.. "Vapor rivers detected above Earth." *The Orange County Register*, Jan. 22, 1993.

Scofield, C.I.. *Scofield Reference Bible*. (N.Y.: Oxford University Press, 1917).

Seiss, Joseph A.. *The Apocalypse*. (Grand Rapids: Kregel Publications, reprint 1967, orig. publ. 1904).

Sitchin, Zecharia. *The 12th Planet*. (N.Y.: Avon Books, 1976).

Strauss, Lehman. *The Book of Revelation*. (Neptune, N.J.: Loizeaux Brothers, 1964).

Strong, James. *The Exhaustive Concordance of the Bible*. (N.Y.: Abingdon Press, 1894)

Thayer, Joseph Henry. *Greek-English Lexicon of the New Testament*. (Grand Rapids: Associated Publishers and Authors, Inc., n.d.).

Thompson, Frank Charles. *The New Chain-Reference Bible*, 4th ed. (Indianapolis: B.B. Kirkbride Bible Co., Inc., 1964).

Tregelles, Samuel Prideaux, translator, *Gesenius Hebrew-Chaldee Lexicon*. (Grand Rapids: Baker Book House, 1979).

Unger, Merrill F.. *Unger's Bible Dictionary*. (Chicago: Moody Press, 1957).

Walvoord, John F. *The Rapture Question*. (Grand Rapids: Zondervan Publishing House, 1957).

_____ *The Revelation of Jesus Christ*. (Chicago: Moody Press, 1966).

Whiston, William. *The Works of Josephus*. (Philadelphia: David McKay Co., nd).

Young, Robert. *Young's Analytical Concordance*. (Grand Rapids: Associated Publisheers and Authors, Inc., nd).

Zinberg, George. *Jewish Calendar Mystery Dispelled, A Systematic Study of the Jewish and the General Calendar Systems*. N.Y.: Vantage Press, 1963).

Index